Curriculum Development: Issues and Insights

Curriculum Development:
Issues and Insights

Donald E. Orlosky,
University of South Florida

B. Othanel Smith,
University of South Florida

Rand McNally College Publishing Company / Chicago

Rand McNally Education Series
B. Othanel Smith, Advisory Editor

Cartoon credits

Ford Button: pages 2, 28, 148, 194, 222, 246, 268, 318, 342, 368, 392
Joe Buresch: page 60
Bardulf Uueland: pages 80, 170
Bo Brown: page 104
Tony Saltzman: page 122
Reg Hider: page 292
Lowell Hoppes: page 418

78 79 80   10 9 8 7 6 5 4 3 2 1

Library of Congress Catalog Card Number: 76-17180

Preface

The professional specialty, "curriculum developer," only emerged once educators realized that the program of studies in schools was more than a collection of courses. Curriculum includes courses but it also includes issues such as scope, balance, and sequence. Major issues developed when school administrators began examining the comprehensive structure of the school's program. Questions asked were about adapting content to individual differences, linking schools to society, and correlating studies with each other.

Individual educators can create their own niche but the relationship of their niche to the total school program is ignored unless someone looks after coordinating the school's program.

Curriculum directors and advisers to curriculum personnel are most effective when they bring a knowledgeable and experienced perspective to curriculum issues. Curriculum text writers must recognize their audience and ask themselves how to best present topics for information, issues for discussion, and plausible solutions to curricular problems.

In this book we have attempted to meet these objectives by combining our viewpoints with selected readings from curriculum authorities. We believe that readings in each of the major curriculum areas should be provided so the reader can study and use them as a starting point for curriculum analysis.

We have written an orientation to each section that includes background information, explains issues, raises questions, and summarizes the major contributions of each article. These articles, taken from nearly 100 sources, have been reduced to those issues that most thoroughly address the purpose of this book. We have taken considerable liberty with many articles and are indebted to the publishers—their cooperation and granted permissions—to reprint portions or all of the selection articles. Thus, this book is an effort to combine the traditional approach of representing content according to author's views with the "readings approach" that in many instances is merely a collection of articles that lack a unified theme. We hope we have combined the best of both approaches.

This book should be useful to inservice and preservice teachers who want to become more informed about the options and problems in curriculum development. In addition, it whould be useful to undergraduate or beginning graduate students of curriculum development. It is a book that curriculum specialists or people preparing to work as curriculum developers should also find helpful. Curricular problems are not limited to those individuals who are directly responsible for making curriculum decisions. All professionals face increased responsibilities to participate in curricular decisions. Unless professional educators are equipped with information about curricula and the best ways to consider curriculum decisions, they are handicapped in influencing others. This book is intended to help all professionals become more adequate in coping with curriculum problems.

Curriculum is a complex topic and presents curriculum workers with unique decisions. No major formulas for curriculum decisions exist. Values, biases, and priorities vary among those who study and influence the school's curriculum. But in conjunction with all these differences there are clearly distinguishable orientations that enable the reader to benefit from others' work. The chief benefit intended in this book is to make it easier for educators to make informed decisions and predict consequences of those decisions. If this book enables the reader to deal more effectively with curriculum analysis and promotion of effective curricular change, then the book will serve its purpose.

The sections in the book include: (1) curriculum as a field of study, (2) styles of curriculum theorizing, (3) operative concepts and principles, (4) putting the curriculum to work, (5) curriculum change, and (6) evaluation of the curriculum. Each section can "stand alone" but is best understood in the context of the total book. Our sequence seems logical but some will prefer a different organization. Whatever the particular use of this text, curriculum should emerge in such a way that curriculum analysis and development should become a more manageable activity to the student .

D. E. Orlosky
B. O. Smith

Contents

Part III: Operative Concepts and Principles

Figure List

Part **I**

Curriculum as a Field of Study

Schools serve their purposes by combining curricula, personnel, administration and school facilities, and resources into a workable program. Each area contains elements such as methods, materials, and theories. These factors influence the characteristics and provide the basis for school activities. Of all the school components, curriculum is probably the most ambiguous and difficult to define. This is true partly because curriculum reflects a complex society, a society in which there is never perfect agreement on the characteristics of that society. Defining curricula is also complex because of uncertainties about proper schools' role and validity of school practices.

The purpose of this part of the book is to provide information and raise questions about the curriculum as a field of study: how it evolved from its early beginnings in the last century and how it gained prominence as an area of professional endeavor during the first half of the present century.

Chapter **1**

The Nature of Curriculum Study

"After an exhaustive study of your new curriculum which evaluated all available data, using multivariable longitudinal analysis with particular attention to IQ, SES, and academic-cognitive and affective-social factors as they relate to stated goal-orientation, I find that you were doing it better before."

Phi Delta Kappan 56. 3 (November 1974): 179.

Curriculum is the substance of the school program. It is the content pupils are expected to learn. Some consider the primary purpose of the curriculum as the acquisition of cognitive knowledge. Others consider it as a program for helping pupils develop humane and rational qualities; thus, academic content is relegated to a secondary position. There is general agreement that the schools' curriculum consists of the learnings that pupils are expected to acquire, but there is little unanimity regarding the "best" content of the school program. The curriculum can be classified into cognitive skill and affective domains. It can be organized according to grade and age levels. It can be discussed according to required and elective learnings.

The role of schools in society and the purpose of the curriculum have been major, closely related, issues since schools were first established. Society's expectations for its schools and schools' response to society are both reflected in the school curriculum. In a dynamic society with responsive schools, curricular changes are constant concerns, but the cause and effect relationship between societal changes and school programs is never unequivocally clear. The relationship between society and schools is complex because the school and society change at different rates and in different ways and are, in themselves, diverse and complex.

For example, what is society and how are the views of society obtained? Is society's view the opinion expressed in the latest public opinion poll, the voice of elected or appointed officials, or the decisions made by the local school board? Is society the voice heard through newspaper editorials, the views of labor leaders, or the preferences of professional organizations? Is society's voice the legislation that prescribes privileges and constraints to society's activities, or is society more clearly reflected in court rulings that may promote or prevent change? The society as a single entity with a clear and unshakable voice does not exist, but collectively the society adds up to a voice that influences the role of its institutions. The school is one of those institutions.

Who speaks for the schools? Some might argue that school boards speak for them, others may contend that school administrators are the real speakers whose decisions determine school activity. The increasingly strong voice of teacher organizations may be the most powerful and widely based voice of all. Also pupils have raised questions about their rights to receive adequate instruction, the language in which the instruction will be provided, and due process in discipline and student records. Rulings about book censorship, prayer in schools, and desegregation all originated external to the school and made direct impact on the school. Because the Constitution of the United States reserves decisions about the schools to the states, are not the state legislators and the state departments of education the real decision makers? It is apparent that the school as an institution is also a many-faceted enterprise, subject to many of the same interactions that complicate society. The voice of the school is no easier to identify than is the voice of society.

In schooling youth should the school be a subordinate agency to society or should it be an equal or dominant force? When school issues arise how should they be arbitrated? Where does the major weight of persuasion and eventual decision rest? The challenge to match society's demands to school resources is the task of those who arbitrate and make responsible decisions about the schools. In the decision-making process, certain resources are assembled to fulfill school responsibilities. These resources include school buildings, facilities, organizational arrangements, administration, personnel, and the content to be learned. None of these components is easy to characterize because it varies according to local circumstances, the people involved, and other important factors that make each one a study in itself. But the content of the school's program, and the knowledge and behavioral growth of pupils, represents the pay load for which all the other elements have been assembled. This pay load is the curriculum of the school. It is "what" the school sets out to transmit to youth as knowledge, skills, and attitudes. Because of the changing nature of society, and the shifting characteristics of the schools, curriculum does not "hold still" or solidify as well as most objects of study. And yet the curriculum must be studied, monitored, modified, and improved so that schools can meet their ever changing purposes.

Curriculum Movement in Historical Perspective

We can look at schools through different perspectives. If we look at schools according to teachers, we might study teacher preparation programs, teacher performance, teacher characteristics, and so forth. If we study the conditions for schooling, we might look at facilities, materials, working conditions, or other factors that determine the environment in which schooling takes place. But when we choose to look at the curriculum of the schools, we are confronted with a different view of the schools from that when we look at personnel conditions, or any other factor that might be studied. We are then concerned about the program of studies in terms of its content, sequence, and balance. We are concerned about the unique roles assumed by those who direct, evaluate, and alter the curriculum of the schools. We are also confronted with some very difficult problems of defining the curriculum and determining its scope.

To look at curriculum within an appropriate context we can see how curriculum as a field of study has evolved and the task that curriculum workers are expected to accomplish. This historical perspective is provided by Cremin as he traces the development of the field of curriculum as a special area of educational concern. Cremin raises additional questions about the influences on youth that occur in agencies other than the schools. This article provides a basis from which the issues that appear in the remainder of this book emerge.

"Curriculum" in its English usage is a comparatively recent term, dating from the nineteenth century, if one accepts the examples in *The Oxford English Dictionary* as authoritative. The word seems first to have been used to describe formal courses of study in the schools and universities, for example, the high school curriculum or the medical curriculum, and it doubtless served to distinguish between such courses and the particular subjects they comprised, that is, reading or arithmetic or anatomy or physiology. In its very nature the term carries a variety of connotations, such as coherence, sequence, and articulation, for a course of any kind has a beginning, a middle, and an end. But interest in these values long antedates the term itself, going back at least to the time of the Sophists and perhaps even earlier.

Not surprisingly, sustained concern with curriculum emerged in the United States during the early decades of the Progressive Era, when for good reason and bad the schools and colleges found themselves teaching an astonishing variety of subjects to an immensely heterogeneous clientele. Elementary schools had added nature study, drawing, music, manual training, and physical education to the traditional core of reading, writing, arithmetic, history, and geography. High schools were teaching natural sciences, social studies, and a host of trade and vocational subjects alongside the older fare of languages and mathematics. Colleges were offering all manner of literary, scientific, and professional instruction under the twin banners of equal opportunity and public service. Inexorably expansionist about the role and function of schooling, progressives of every persuasion pressed for including their favorite subjects in programs of study; relentlessly rationalistic about the nature and

Lawrence A. Cremin, "Curriculum Making in the United States," *Teachers College Record* 73, 2 (December 1971): 207–20. Reprinted by permission of the author and publisher.

Footnotes have been renumbered consecutively throughout the chapter.

management of institutions, they pressed as vigorously for a rethinking of that program as a whole. The result was the modern curriculum movement, with all its infinite diversity and with all its prodigious influence.

The story begins in earnest with the efforts of William Torrey Harris, superintendent of the St. Louis school system during the 1870s. The leading figure of a post-war generation of school leaders that included Barnas Sears and Albert P. Marble of Massachusetts, James Pyle Wickersham of Pennsylvania, F. Louis Soldan of Missouri, William Henry Ruffner of Virginia, and James M. Greenwood of Kansas, Harris has been portrayed as a staunchly conservative, or at best confusingly "transitional," figure whose Hegelian metaphysics buttressed a half century of antiprogressive thought. Yet in his own time Harris was generally perceived as a reformer, and the difficulty of a proper appraisal may lie less in the character of his contribution than in the categories and definitions we have used to judge it. In the last analysis, though, whether Harris himself was a progressive may be less important than the characteristic solution he and his generation developed for the seemingly intractable problem of universal schooling in an increasingly urban society, namely, the rationalizing of the school system along bureaucratic and industrial lines. For that solution was widely adopted by the most influential segments of the progressive movement, with incalculable significance for the curriculum.[1]

Education, Harris once explained in a brief statement of his pedagogical creed, is a process "by which the individual is elevated into the species," or alternatively, a process by which a self-active being is enabled to become privy to the accumulated wisdom of the race. And it is the task of the curriculum to make that accumulated wisdom economically and systematically available. "The question of the course of study—involving as it does the selection of such branches as shall in the most effective manner develop the substantial activity as well as the formal activity of the child, is the most important question which the educator has before him." And the only defensible course of study is one that "takes up in order the conventionalities of intelligence." Those "conventionalities" include the two great provinces of thought, nature and spirit, and it is the duty of the school to lead the child sequentially through those provinces in as coherent a manner as possible, viz.: *Topics Relating to Nature and Topics Relating to Man.* The instrument of the process would be the textbook, which Harris saw as the pedagogical tool par excellence in a newspaper civilization where public opinion ruled and where the entire community needed access to similar facts and arguments if harmony was to be achieved. The

---

[1] The critique of the traditional historiography on Harris suggested here is based on Martin Dworkin's forthcoming volume in the *Classics in Education* series entitled *William Torrey Harris on Education.* For bureaucratization as a characteristic progressive response to the problems of urban schooling during the last decades of the nineteenth century, see Michael Katz, "The Emergence of Bureaucracy in Urban Education: The Boston Case, 1850–1884," *History of Education Quarterly* 8(1968):155–88, 319–57; David Tyack, "Bureaucracy and the Common School: The Example of Portland, Oregon, 1851–1913," *American Quarterly* 19 (1967): 475–98; and David Conrad Hammack, "The Centralization of New York City's Public School System, 1896: A Social Analysis of a Decision," unpublished master's thesis, Columbia University, 1969.

energizer of the process would be the teacher, who would use the recitation to get the pupil to deliberate over what he had read and to relate it to his own life. And the monitor of the process would be the examination, whereby pupils could be frequently classified and then moved individually through a carefully graded system.[2]

Now, the particulars of Harris' course of study need not concern us for the moment, though it is significant that in comprehensiveness, detail, and theoretical coherence it was unique for its time. What is of special interest is rather the analytical paradigm. There is the learner, self-active and self-willed by virtue of his humanity and thus self-propelled into the educative process. There is the course of study, organized by responsible adults with appropriate concern for priority, sequence, and scope. There are materials of instruction which particularize the course of study. There is the teacher who encourages and mediates the process of instruction. There are the examinations which appraise it. And there is the organizational structure within which it proceeds and within which large numbers of individuals are enabled simultaneously to enjoy its benefits. All the pieces were present for the game of curriculum making that would be played over the next half century; only the particular combinations and the players would change.

Burgeoning Literature

Whatever the adequacy of Harris' solution—and his contemporaries argued endlessly over the details (Should manual training be included? Should history be the organizing core?)—the problems of universal schooling sharpened drastically after the 1880s, with the result that the concern for curriculum became the leitmotif of the progressive movement. There were the recommendations of the immensely influential committees of the National Education Association —the Committee of Ten (on secondary schooling, 1893), the Committee of Fifteen (on elementary schooling, 1895), the Committee on College Entrance Requirements (1899), the Committees on Economy of Time (on elementary schooling, 1915–1919), and the Commission on the Reorganization of Secondary Education (1918)—and there were those of the more specialized committees established by such organizations of scholars and teachers as the American Historical Association, the American Political Science Association, and the National Council of Teachers of Mathematics. There were the innovations within particular schools or school systems aimed at developing or demonstrating a specific approach to curriculum—witness the Gary Plan or the Winnetka Plan or the Montessori Method (the Deweys reported on some of these in *Schools of To-Morrow* [1915], stressing the inextricable ties between social need, educational theory, curriculum content, and pedagogical process). And there were the innumerable formulations of individual theorists, the

[2]William T. Harris, "My Pedagogical Creed," *The School Journal* 54 (1897):813; *Fourteenth Annual Report of the Board of Directors of the St. Louis Public Schools, 1868* (St. Louis: George Knapp, 1869), p. 94. The curriculum itself, taken from William T. Harris, "A Course of Study from Primary School to University," *The Western* 2 (1876):521–38, is reproduced in Carl Lester Byerly. *Contributions of William Torrey Harris to Public School Administration* (Chicago: n.p., 1946).

Deweys, the Bobbitts, the Charterses, the Bonsers, the Bagleys, and the Judds.

Several works have attempted to assess the meaning and influence of these efforts, among them Isaac Kandel's *American Education in the Twentieth Century* (1957), Edward Krug's *The Shaping of the American High School* (1964), and my own book, *The Transformation of the School* (1961). There was, to be sure, an extraordinary richness and diversity about the discussion, including as it did a range of ideas that went from Marietta Johnson's preoccupation with the spontaneous activities of the child to W. W. Charters' argument that the "life activities" of adults should be the sole determinant of curriculum content, from Maria Montessori's stress on youthful independence to William Wirt's emphasis on youthful socialization, from William Heard Kilpatrick's abhorrence of "subject-matter-laid-out-in-advance" to John Dewey's insistence on a multiplicity of carefully conceived curricula, from George S. Counts' urging that the curriculum deliberately criticize the social order to Isaac Kandel's questioning whether it ever really could. But for all its variety, there was an undeniable drift of the argument in the direction of expansion, election, activity, and utility in the curriculum. Indeed, by the 1930s the body of writings on curricular reform was so large and the array of alternatives proposed so broad that there began to emerge a secondary literature cataloguing and evaluating the writings themselves.

Some Central Ideas

Once again, my interest for the moment is not in the substance of the alternatives, as fascinating as that may be, but rather in certain characteristics of the movement as a whole. Two points in particular stand out. In the first place, most of the discussion accepted both the structure and the components of Harris' paradigm, seeking either to multiply the number and range of possible curricula or to alter the content and character of individual standardized curricula. I missed this fact some years ago in an article I wrote on the revolution in American secondary education between 1893 and 1918. Comparing the report of the Committee of Ten with the report of the Commission on the Reorganization of Secondary Education, I pointed to a radical change in the concept of schooling, in the prevailing idea of what could and should be its primary goals and responsibilities. Whereas the earlier report had viewed schooling as a preparation "for the duties of life" via the systematic study of a curriculum enlarged to include the sciences and modern languages, the later report had talked of developing in each individual "the knowledge, interests, habits, and powers whereby he will find his place and use that place to shape both himself and society toward ever nobler ends" and had then set forth seven primary objectives of schooling at all levels, namely, health, command of fundamental processes, worthy home membership, vocation, citizenship, worthy use of leisure, and ethical character. In the contrast, I argued, most assuredly lay a pedagogical revolution.[3]

[3]Lawrence A. Cremin, "The Revolution in American Secondary Education, 1893–1918," *Teachers College Record* 56 (1955):295–308.

No one, of course, would deny the extent of change during the quarter-century separating the two reports: the schools were indeed transformed. But one gains a better sense of the character of the transformation if he goes beyond the summary reports to the individual recommendations of the several subject matter committees involved in the work. Thus if we take the social sciences as an example, we discover that the conference on history, civil government, and political economy held under the auspices of the Committee of Ten during the last days of 1892 celebrated the role of the social studies in broadening and cultivating the mind and then went on to be quite specific about curricular topics (for example, "the Puritan movement of the seventeenth century"), textbooks, and related teaching materials. . . .

With the rapid growth of professional training for educators during the progressive period, the burgeoning literature of curriculum making became the substance of a distinct field of study in which those preparing to lead in the development or coordination of public school curricula could concentrate their academic efforts. The roots of this movement toward professionalization doubtless go all the way back to Harris, whose work was widely studied in schools and departments of education; but the movement itself dates from the second decade of the twentieth century, when Frederick Taylor's concept of scientific management swept not only industry but education as well, leaving in its wake certain characteristic notions of economy and efficiency. Raymond Callahan has documented the profound influence of Taylorism on the general management of schooling; in the field of curriculum development, its influence is manifest in the work of Franklin Bobbitt and W. W. Charters, both of whom tended to analogize from the world of the factory to the world of the school, conceiving of the child as the raw material, the ideal adult as the finished product, the teacher as the worker, the supervisor as the foreman, and the curriculum as the process whereby the raw material was converted into the finished product. To the extent that the characteristics of the raw material, the finished product, and the conversion process could be quantitatively defined, rationally dealt with, and objectively appraised, curriculum making could become a science; to the extent that the workers and the foremen could engage together in the scientific determination and rational pursuit of curriculum objectives, teaching could become an applied science, a form of educational engineering.[4]

Such ideas were central in the reports of the Committees on Economy of Time between 1915 and 1919; and they were central in the widely publicized program of curriculum revision that Jesse Newlon introduced at Denver in 1922, probably the first in which classroom teachers participated significantly in a systemwide effort at reform. Once the Denver pattern caught on, it was

[4]Raymond E. Callahan, *Education and the Cult of Efficiency* (Chicago: University of Chicago Press, 1962), Franklin Bobbitt, "Some General Principles of Management Applied to the Problems of City-School Systems," *Twelfth Yearbook of the National Society for the Study of Education,* Part I (Chicago: University of Chicago Press, 1913); and *The Curriculum* (Boston: Houghton Mifflin Company, 1918); W. W. Charters, *Curriculum Construction* (New York: Macmillan, 1923); Mary Louise Seguel. *The Curriculum Field: Its Formative Years* (New York: Teachers College Press, 1966); and Arno A. Bellack, "History of Curriculum Thought and Practice," *Review of Educational Research* 39 (1969):283–92.

obvious that specialists other than the superintendent would be needed to manage the process, and it was for the purpose of training such specialists that the curriculum field was created. Beginning initially as a subfield of educational administration in some universities, of elementary education in others, and of secondary education in still others, the study of curriculum gradually came into its own, achieving academic independence with the organization of the Society for Curriculum Study in 1932 and establishment of a full-fledged department of curriculum and teaching at Columbia's Teachers College six years later.

Professionalization served many purposes, not the least of which was preparation of knowledgeable practitioners to assume an emergent role within school systems committed to curricular innovation. What it also did, willynilly, was to demarcate the analysis and development of the curriculum as the special preserve of a definable group of specialists working within the schools and trained within the education faculty of the university. The consequences of this staking out were prodigious with respect to who would "make" curricula from that time forward and to the assumptions under which curriculum making would proceed.

Definition of Education

Let us return for a moment to Harris' definition of education as a process "by which the individual is elevated into the species," or alternatively, by which a self-active human being is enabled to become privy to the accumulated wisdom of the race. Now, Harris was incisive enough to recognize that the process is by no means confined to the school, and indeed he discussed at many points in his writing the respective domains and responsibilities of the family, the state, the church, civil society (whose most important educative function is "organization of the industry of man in the form of division of labor"), and the school. On some occasions, Harris' effort was to establish a sequence among the agencies: thus the discussion in the *Psychologic Foundations of Education* (1898), in which, using the metaphor of widening concentric circles, Harris indicated a sequence of familial education, schooling, the education of one's special vocation, the education of political participation, and the education of religion (which transcends all others). On other occasions his effort was rather to establish a principle of interaction among the agencies: thus the discussions of moral education in his early reports as superintendent of schools in St. Louis, in which he attempted to relate the school's efforts to those of families and churches; and thus too the discussion in "Education in the United States" (1893), in which the textbook is seen as the vehicle par excellence for "preparation of a people for a newspaper civilization—an age wherein public opinion rules." Yet discussions of this sort were almost always formalistic in Harris' writings, and the fact is that he rarely extended them sufficiently to indicate what a curriculum of instruction in all the chief educative institutions might look like or how the curriculum of the school might reflect an awareness of other curricula. The result is that when Harris considered the course of study, he occupied himself almost exclusively with schooling, acknowledging other domains only in his insistence that the teaching of trades be a concern primarily of civil society and the teaching of religion a concern primarily of the church.[5]

This pattern of acknowledging other domains of education and then proceeding to ignore them became characteristic during the Progressive Era. To take but two examples, Dewey began his analysis in *Democracy and Education* (1916) with a discussion of the distinction between the broad educational process inherent in the very idea of social life and "a more formal kind of education—that of direct tuition or schooling"; but he proceeded to confine his attention to schooling, the initial discussion apparently intended not to introduce a consideration of the educative process in its entirety but to ensure that the subsequent treatment of schooling would be seen as essentially continuous with the larger educative process of living. Similarly, Franklin Bobbitt distinguished in *The Curriculum* (1918) between two quite different definitions of curriculum: (1) the entire range of experiences, both directed and undirected, concerned in unfolding the abilities of the individual and (2) the series of consciously directed training experiences that the schools use for completing and perfecting the unfoldment. "Our profession uses the term usually in the latter sense," Bobbitt explained.

> But as education is coming more and more to be seen as a thing of experiences, and as the work- and play-experiences of the general community life are being more and more utilized, the line of demarcation between directed and undirected training experience is rapidly disappearing. Education must be concerned with both, even though it does not direct both.

Yet the "profession" to which Bobbitt alluded was a profession of schoolmen, and it is not surprising that, like Dewey, he too went on to deal almost entirely with the problems of schooling. By the end of World War I the drift was unmistakable, with the curriculum being most commonly conceived over the quarter-century that followed as a sequence of planned experiences taking place entirely in or under the auspices of the school.[6]

What if we were to go back to Harris' definition of education and consider the curriculum as the accumulated wisdom of the race, to be made available to individuals through a variety of institutions in a variety of modes? And what if we were to conceive of education as the effort to define that wisdom in the large and then assist individuals in the business of sharing it more comprehensively, more economically, more self-consciously, and more critically. Several perspectives would immediately change. In the first place, we would be forced to contend with the question of how what is taught and learned in one institution relates to what is taught and learned in another.

In the second place, we would be forced to a conception of a radically individualized educative process. Dewey once described the child and the

---

[5]William T. Harris, *Psychologic Foundations of Education* (New York: D. Appleton and Company, 1898); *Seventeenth Annual Report of the Board of Directors of the St. Louis Public Schools, 1871* (St. Louis: Plate, Olshausen & Co., 1872); and William T. Harris, "Education in the United States," Nathaniel Southgate Shaler, ed. *The United States of America* (New York: D. Appleton and Company, 1894).

[6]Franklin Bobbitt, *The Curriculum* (Boston: Houghton Mifflin, 1918).

curriculum as two limits which define a single process. "Just as two points define a straight line, so the present standpoint of the child and the facts and truths of the studies define instruction. It is continuous reconstruction, moving from the child's present experience out into that represented by the organized bodies of truth we call studies." But as Dewey pointed out again and again in his writings, the child is always a particular child with a particular experience, not some abstraction in the curriculum maker's mind. And that child from the moment of his birth is in continuing interaction with many curricula in many educative institutions, or, if one prefers, with an extended curriculum taught and learned (and mistaught and mislearned) in a variety of situations. The various segments of the process are as often conflicting as they are complementary, as often random as they are sequential, and as often confusing as they are meaningful. And the very nature of a free and complicated society precludes our ever wholly ordering or rationalizing them—or, I would argue, wanting to. But they can at least be viewed in their full range and complexity whenever we contemplate instruction. And to do so would be to move us in several directions. It would press us to prescribe modes and sequences of instruction for particular individuals rather than for age groups or other equally artificial categories—thus the promise of the Cronbach-Snow paradigm of aptitude-treatment interaction. It would focus our concern on the results of instruction in those particular individuals and not merely on the design of the substance presented. And it would dramatize the necessity for developing far more effective means of self-appraisal, one critical mark of maturity in a pluralistic educational situation being a growing ability to diagnose and prescribe for oneself (such self-appraisal, incidentally, would supplement rather than supplant societal examination of individuals and groups for purposes of selection or certification). None of these points, of course, would deny the need to hold some larger conception of a desirable curriculum (or curricula) constantly in mind; but that larger conception can never take the place of an equally necessary understanding of the diverse processes by which individuals come to share the knowledge, values, skills, and sensibilities embodied in such a curriculum.[7]

In the third place, we would be forced to acknowledge the diversity of curricula being defined and taught at any given time by a variety of groups, more or less professional in character, and the need to call such groups to a measure of public responsibility. The staff of the *Book of Knowledge* has a curriculum; the staff of the Children's Television Workshop has a curriculum; the staff of the Boy Scouts of America has a curriculum; and the staff of the *New York Review of Books* has a curriculum. So too do the advertising agencies that serve the American Tobacco Company and the American Cancer Society;

[7]John Dewey, *The Child and the Curriculum* (Chicago: The University of Chicago Press, 1902). The Cronbach-Snow paradigm is the basis of a series of experiments on instruction at the USOE Research Center at Stanford University. The "classic" article is Lee J. Cronbach, "The Two Disciplines of Scientific Psychology," *The American Psychologist* 12 (1957):671–84. The recent research is summarized in Lee J. Cronbach and Richard E. Snow, *Final Report: Individual Differences in Learning Ability as a Function of Instructional Variables* (Stanford: Stanford University, 1969); and Glenn H. Bracht, "Experimental Factors Related to Aptitude-Treatment Interactions," *Review of Educational Research* 40 (1970):627–45.

so too do the public relations counsels that serve the Democratic and the Republican parties.

Finally, we would be forced to recognize that in a pluralistic society marked by a pluralistic education, it becomes a matter of the most urgent public concern to look at all these curricula in their various interrelations and to raise insistent questions of definition, scope, and priority. Philosophers since Plato have told us that education is more than a succession of units, courses, and programs, however excellent, and that serious considerations of curriculum must call into play the most fundamental questions of value, belief, and loyalty. Philosophers today seem to have turned away from such questions, thinking, perhaps, that their historic responsibility to ask them carries a corresponding obligation to come up with timeless answers. I for one would hope they return to the charge, for if they do not others will, only less thoughtfully, less systematically, and less responsibly.

Curriculum and Instruction: One Thing or Two?

Cremin's descriptions of the development of curriculum and the nature of curriculum as a field of study present the background of numerous attempts to put the curriculum into operation. These attempts often aim at determining the goals of education and the means of attaining them. The phrase "Curriculum and Instruction" is often deployed to describe goals and means. These two are closely related and some would argue that they are the same. The similarity of the two is predicated on the assumption that the "real" curriculum is found in the activities of pupils which is closely tied to instruction. Others suggest that a distinction between curriculum and instruction provides for a logical delineation between the intentions and the practices of the schools. A discussion of these distinctions is provided by Popham and Baker. They relate curricular decisions to instructional methods by specifying procedures for establishing the curriculum of the schools and the development of instructional goals. Their discussion captures the thrust of the movement to convert school goals into pupil objectives that enable teachers to verify the attainment of their teaching purposes.

Educators at every level, from classroom teachers to school superintendents, are concerned with "the curriculum." Countless hours are spent discussing curriculum questions. There are probably more school district curriculum committees in America than schools; and enough curriculum guides exist in school district offices to supply school paper drives for the next several decades. Despite all this curricular planning activity, does the educator know just what

W. James Popham and Eva L. Baker, *Establishing Instructional Goals* (Englewood Cliffs, N.J.: Prentice-Hall, 1970), pp. 81–100. Copyright © by Prentice-Hall. Reprinted by permission of the publisher.

"the curriculum" is? Who are the "curriculum workers"? What do they do?

A simple, and very clear, explanation of curricular planning is: an educator who is involved with curricular questions is exclusively concerned with determining the *objectives* of the educational system. There are basically two kinds of decisions that the educator must make. First, he must decide what the objectives (that is, the *ends*) of the instructional system should be, and second, he must decide on the procedures (that is, the *means*) for accomplishing those objectives. When he is engaged in the selection of objectives for the particular segment of instruction with which he is concerned, whether an academic year or a single class period, he is engaged in *curriculum* decision making. When he is concerned with the selection or evaluation of the instructional schemes by which those goals are to be accomplished, he is engaged in *instructional* decision making. Thus, *the distinction between curriculum and instruction is essentially a distinction between ends and means.*

This distinction is a particularly critical one because quite different approaches should be used in making curricular and instructional decisions. Instructional questions usually are amenable to empirical solutions, curricular questions generally are not. Without exception, the determination of what an educational goal should be is a value-based process. . . .

Once educational goals have been selected, it is possible to test *empirically* the efficacy of alternative procedures for achieving those goals.

Given a particular goal, . . . the teacher can gather empirical evidence regarding the merits of alternative instructional schemes which he might use to attain that goal. One procedure can be pitted against another, and the teacher can—through a process that is essentially free of value preferences—collect evidence regarding which procedure best brings about the intended change in the learners. . . .

With this distinction between ends and means in mind, we can turn to an examination of a scheme designed to improve the quality of the educational ends to be selected. It may occur to you that the really important selections have already been made by educators in the past, so that there is little sense in even pursuing this question. After all, curriculum guides have been written in every large school district and most of the smaller ones as well. In spite of these guides, however, there is much curricular decision making to be done. Most current curriculum guides contain instructional objectives that are so general that they allow the teacher considerable latitude in the specification of objectives for particular teaching situations. . . .

Of all the schemes available for selecting objectives, the most widely accepted is the one developed a number of years ago by Professor Ralph Tyler.[8] This system for making curricular decisions, often referred to as the "Tyler Rationale," offers an approach to the selection of objectives that is designed to make the educator more systematic and circumspect in the selection. Schematically, the Tyler Rationale can be depicted as follows.

According to this scheme, the curriculum maker looks to three sources—student, society, and subject—from which he derives general, tentative objec-

---

[8]Ralph W. Tyler, *Basic Principles of Curriculum and Instruction* (Chicago: The University of Chicago Press, 1950).

Figure 1-1. Tyler's curricular rationale.

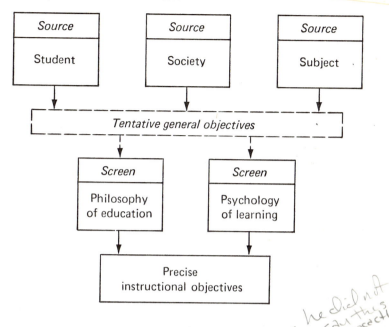

he did not say this exactly

INVOLVES AN EXAMPLE

tives. He then screens these tentative goals by means of his philosophy of education and a psychology of learning. Next, he states the objectives that survive this screening in precise terms of measurable learner behaviors. These precise objectives serve as the ends for which the teacher designs effective instructional means. . . .

By studying the learners themselves, particularly their needs and interests, the curriculum maker may discover worthwhile objectives that might otherwise not have occurred to him. If he can gather information about the current status of the learners and compare that status with some conception of an acceptable norm, then he can generally refer to any difference between the two as a need. An investigation of elementary school youngsters in a particular community may reveal dietary deficiencies and a need with respect to physical condition. Such a need might suggest an objective in health education. Similarly, by studying the current status of students with respect to how much they know about municipal government, the curriculum maker might discover needs that could be met by certain objectives in social science courses. . . .

A second area of useful information regarding the learner can be secured by studying his interests. The general notion supporting the usefulness of this source is that the student learns best those things in which he is vitally involved. Such involvement occurs most easily when the student is permitted to study the things in which he is interested. Hence, by selecting instructional objectives consonant with learner interests, the schools can promote more efficient learning. For example, if the curriculum makers discover that a group of youngsters of junior high school age are particularly interested in space exploration, they might generate a number of objectives to match this interest. In the process of studying outer space, the students may learn all sorts of related skills—and learn them to last for a long time—because they are truly interested in achieving the objectives. . . .

Study the Society

(handwritten: INVOLVES FIELD RESEARCH)

A second source of possible objectives can be found in an examination of contemporary life outside the school. In general, the reason for studying the nature of the present society is to be able to determine more accurately the kinds of competencies needed by today's citizens. With this knowledge, educational objectives can be established which are designed to produce these competencies. Of course, arguments exist for and against the use of the current status of society as a source of objectives. However, since the society does support the very existence of our school system, it seems only reasonable to consider educational objectives based on a societal analysis.

Because of the complexity of any modern society, it is necessary to develop manageable categories for study. Tyler suggests as one alternative the following set of classifications. . . .

Society can be studied in terms of:

Health
Family
Recreation
Vocation
Religion
Civic affairs

Study the Subject

A final source of objectives in the Tyler Rationale is based on the suggestions of subject specialists. This source of objectives is most commonly used in typical schools and colleges. Until relatively recent times the subject specialist was legitimately criticized on the grounds that his suggestions for educational objectives were too technical, too specialized, and inappropriate for the majority of students. Too often the subject specialist tended to suggest objectives that were more suitable for the training of subject specialists than for the average citizen. This situation has now been altered, and in recent years prominent experts have given much attention to the identification of goals that all learners should achieve. Curriculum recommendations of prominent individuals or groups, such as the National Council of English Teachers, contain a wealth of suggestions for possible objectives.

We have briefly examined the three data sources in Tyler's curriculum scheme. Consideration of each can lead to the identification of possible objectives.

At this point in the use of the rationale the curriculum maker should have a collection of general objectives, quite probably more than can be reasonably

"Realistic"

attained in the instructional time available. Too many educators make the serious mistake of "covering" too much territory. Surely they can assert that they have "covered" much material, but it is usually the case that this coverage results in little, if any, important modifications in the behavior of learners. The next step in the Tyler scheme is to rank the tentative objectives in some rough sort of hierarchy so that those which are unimportant or impossible to achieve can be discarded. This ranking is accomplished through the use of two screens.

Turning first to the screen of philosophy of education, it should be pointed out that what Tyler had in mind was no elaborate educational philosophy, replete with metaphysical postulates.

Rather, by philosophy of education he simply meant the set of values one holds regarding what should be taught in the schools. All of us undoubtedly have some primitive notions of what the goals of the schools ought to be. In the use of the philosophical screen the educator brings these values to bear on the tentative objectives and deletes any that are inconsistent with those values. . . .

After using the philosophical screen, the curriculum maker should roughly order his objectives according to those which must be achieved if time permits, and those which need not be achieved. The psychology of learning screen can then be applied. A primary purpose of this screen is to distinguish between those objectives which are feasible from those which are apt to take a very long time or are nearly impossible to attain at the age level contemplated. For instance, evidence shows that it is incredibly difficult to bring about any profound personality modifications in human beings much past the first five or six years of life. Objectives, however laudable, that attempt to do so in one high school semester should undoubtedly be discarded. Educators know much less than they wish they knew regarding what kinds of objectives are teachable at given age levels. As evidence regarding this question accumulates, the psychology of learning screen will become more efficient in filtering out unteachable goals.

The order in which the two screens should be used is arbitrary. One could employ the psychology screen first and the philosophy screen second. . . . Regardless of the order, as long as the curriculum maker considers all five components of the rationale, he should in the end have a screened set of objectives stated in terms of measurable learner behaviors. It is this set of objectives that guides the selection of instructional and evaluation schemes.

The Need for a New Approach

The systematic procedures outlined by Popham and Baker are deceptively convincing in their straightforward simplicity. In recent times the Tyler Rationale has served as a basis for much of the curriculum development undertaken by schools. But the illusion that if we follow these procedures all is well in the curriculum field is challenged by Joseph Schwab. In the following selection he addresses the gap between the logic of curriculum theory and the realities of school operations.

Schwab questions the notion that curriculum development can proceed from tightly woven theories and be implemented in the schools. Possibly the usual ways of theorizing may not apply to the field of curriculum. For example, one must ask if the ways of knowing about mathematics are different from the ways of knowing about the social sciences. One must ask if the questions to be answered in the physical sciences are like the questions that are asked by philosophers. By analyzing these concerns one must ask questions about how curriculum is studied and the answers curriculum study is intended to provide. Because possibly we have relied on previous techniques in other fields to understand curriculum we may need to use entirely new approaches.

It is worthwhile to distinguish between such questions as, "What are the causes of economic depressions?" and "What are the most important learnings for youth" and "How do you determine the mechanical advantage of an inclined plane?" Are these questions that require the same or different techniques for their answer? Are these questions whose answers must be reported in different form and with different degrees of precision? Do these questions have no common orientation and require distinctly different procedures for their answers? Can one be answered by opinion, another by experimentation, another by measurement? And how can we determine the appropriate procedures to use to arrive at the appropriate solution?

Most fields of study go through a period of infancy when the appropriate procedures and techniques are formulated. It is likely that the field of curriculum is in its infancy and that drastically different approaches to curriculum study must be devised. The analysis by Schwab questions the state of curriculum study and offers suggestions about how to alter and rejuvenate it.

☐

I have three points. The first: that the field of curriculum is moribund, unable by its present methods and principles to continue its work and desperately in search of new and more effective principles and methods.

The second point: the curriculum field has reached this unhappy state by inveterate and unexamined reliance on theory in an area where theory is partly inappropriate in the first place and where the theories extant, even where appropriate, are inadequate to the tasks which the curriculum field sets them. There are honorable exceptions to this rule, but too few (and too little honored) to alter the state of affairs.

The third point, which constitutes my thesis: there will be a renaissance of the field of curriculum, a renewed capacity to contribute to the quality of American education, only if the bulk of curriculum energies are diverted from the theoretic to the practical, to the quasipractical, and to the eclectic. By "eclectic" I mean the arts by which unsystematic, uneasy, but usable focus on

Joseph J. Schwab, "The Practical: A Language for Curriculum," *School Review* 78 (1969): 1–23. Reprinted by permission of the author and publisher.

a body of problems is effected among diverse theories, each relevant to the problems in a different way. By the "practical" I do *not* mean the curbstone practicality of the mediocre administrator and the person on the street for whom the practical means the easily achieved, familiar goals which can be reached by familiar means. I refer, rather, to a complex discipline, relatively unfamiliar to the academic and differing radically from the disciplines of the theoretic. It is the discipline concerned with choice and action, in contrast with the theoretic, which is concerned with knowledge. Its methods lead to defensible decisions, where the methods of the theoretic lead to warranted conclusions, and differ radically from the methods and competencies entailed in the theoretic. I shall sketch some of the defining aspects of practical discipline at the appropriate time.

A Crisis of Principle

The frustrated state of the field of curriculum is not an idiopathology and not a condition which warrants guilt or shame on the part of its practitioners. All fields of systematic intellectual activity are liable to such crises. They are so because any intellectual discipline must begin its endeavors with untested principles. In its beginnings, its subject matter is relatively unknown, its problems unsolved, indeed, unidentified. It does not know what questions to ask, what other knowledge to rest upon, what data to seek, or what to make of them once they are elicited. It requires a preliminary and necessarily untested guide to its inquiries. It finds this guide by borrowing, by invention, or by analogy, in the shape of a hazardous commitment to the character of its problems or its subject matter and a commitment to untried canons of evidence and rules of inquiry. What follows these commitments is years of their application, pursuit of the mode of inquiry demanded by the principles to which the field has committed itself. To the majority of practitioners of any field, these years of inquiry appear only as pursuit of knowledge of its subject matter or solution of its problems. They take the guiding principles of the inquiry as givens. These years of inquiry, however, are something more than pursuit of knowledge or solution of problems. They are also tests, reflexive and pragmatic, of the principles which guide the inquiries. They determine whether, in fact, the data demanded by the principles can be elicited and whether, if elicited, they can be made to constitute knowledge adequate to the complexity of the subject matter, or solutions which, in fact, do solve the problems with which the inquiry began.

In the nature of the case, these reflexive tests of the principles of inquiry are, more often than not, partially or wholly negative, for, after all, the commitment to these principles was made before there was well-tested fruit of inquiry by which to guide the commitment. The inadequacies of principles begin to show, in the case of theoretical inquiries, by failures of the subject matter to respond to the questions put to it, by incoherencies and contradictions in data and in conclusions which cannot be resolved, or by clear disparities between the knowledge yielded by the inquiries and the behaviors of the subject matter which the knowledge purports to represent. In the case of practical inquiries, inadequacies begin to show by incapacity to arrive at solutions to the problems, by inability to realize the solutions proposed, by mutual frustrations and cancelings out as solutions are put into effect.

Although these exhaustions and failures of principles may go unnoted by practitioners in the field, at least at the conscious level, what may not be represented in consciousness is nevertheless evidenced by behavior and appears in the literature and the activities of the field as signs of the onset of a crisis of principle. These signs consist of a large increase in the frequency of published papers and colloquia marked by a *flight from the subject of the field*. There are usually six signs of this flight or directions in which the flight occurs.

Signs of Crisis

The first and most impotant, though often least conspicuous, sign is a flight of the field itself, a translocation of its problems and solving them from the nominal practitioners of the field to other men.

A second flight is a flight upward, from discourse about the subject of the field to discourse about the discourse of the field, from *use* of principles and methods to *talk* about them, from grounded conclusions to the construction of models, from theory to metatheory and from metatheory to metametatheory.

A third flight is downward, an attempt by practitioners to return to the subject matter in a state of innocence, shorn not only of current principles but of all principles, in an effort to take a new, pristine, and unmediated look at the subject matter.

A fourth flight is to the sidelines, to the role of observer, commentator, historian, and critic of the contributions of others to the field.

A fifth sign consists of marked perseveration, a repetition of old and familiar knowledge in new languages which add little or nothing to the old meanings as embodied in the older and familiar language, or repetition of old and familiar formulations by way of criticisms or minor additions and modifications.

The sixth is a marked increase in eristic, contentious, and ad hominem debate.

I hasten to remark that these signs of crisis are not all or equally reprehensible. There is little excuse for the increase in contentiousness nor much value in the flight to the sidelines or in perseveration; but the others, in one way or another, can contribute to resolution of the crisis. The flight of the field itself is one of the more fruitful ways by which analogical principles are disclosed, modified, and adapted to the field in crisis. The flight upward, to models and metatheory, if done responsibly, which means with a steady eye on the actual problems and conditions of the field for which the models are ostensibly constructed, becomes, in fact, the proposal and test of possible new principles for the field. The flight backward, to a state of innocence, is at least an effort to break the grip of old habits of thought and thus leave space for needed new ones, though it is clear that in the matter of inquiry, as elsewhere, virginity, once lost, cannot be regained.

In the present context, however, the virtue or vice of these various flights is beside the point. We are concerned with them as signs of collapse of principles in a field, and it is my contention, based on a study not yet complete, that most of these signs may now be seen in the field of curriculum. I shall only suggest, not cite, my evidence.

The Case of Curriculum

With respect to flight of the field itself, there can be little doubt. Of the five substantial high school science curricula, four of them—PSSC, BSCS, Chems, and CBA—were instituted and managed by subject matter specialists; the contribution of educators was small, and that of curriculum specialists near vanishing point. Only Harvard Project Physics, at this writing not yet available, appears to be an exception. . . .

On the second flight—upward—I need hardly comment. The models, the metatheory, and the metametatheory are all over the place. Many of them, moreover, are irresponsible—concerned less with the barriers to continued productivity in the field of curriculum than with exploitation of the exotic and the fashionable among forms and models of theory and metatheory: systems theory, symbolic logic, language analysis.

The flight downward, the attempt at return to a pristine, unmediated look at the subject matter, is, for some reason, a missing symptom in the case of curriculum. There are returns—to the classroom, if not to other levels or aspects of curriculum—with a measure of effort to avoid preconceptions (e.g., Smith, Bellack, and studies of communication nets and lines), but the frequency of such studies has not markedly increased.

The fourth flight—to the sidelines—is again a marked symptom of the field of curriculum. Histories, anthologies, commentaries, criticisms, and proposals of curricula multiply.

Perseveration is also marked. I recoil from counting the persons and books whose lives are made possible by continuing restatement of the Tyler Rationale, of the character and case for behavioral objectives, of the virtues and vices of John Dewey.

The rise in frequency and intensity of the eristic and ad hominem is also marked. Thus one author climaxes a series of petulances by the remark that what he takes to be his own forte "has always been rare—and shows up in proper perspective the happy breed of educational reformer who can concoct a brand new, rabble-rousing theory of educational reform while waiting for the water to fill the bathtub."

There is little doubt, in short, that the field of curriculum is in a crisis of principle.

A crisis of principle arises, as I have suggested, when principles are exhausted—when the questions they permit have all been asked and answered —or when the efforts at inquiry instigated by the principles have at last exhibited their inadequacy to the subject matter and the problems which they were designed to attack. My second point is that the latter holds in the case of curriculum: the curriculum movement has been inveterately theoretic, and its theoretic bent has let it down. A brief conspectus of instances will suggest the extent of this theoretic bent and what is meant by "theoretic."

Characteristics of Theory

Consider first the early, allegedly Herbartian efforts (recently revived by Bruner). These efforts took the view that ideas were formed by children out of received notions and experiences of things, and that these ideas functioned thereafter as discriminators and organizers of what was later learned. Given this view, the aim of curriculum was to discriminate the right ideas (by way of analysis of extant bodies of knowledge), determine the order in which they could be learned by children as they developed, and thereafter present these ideas at the right times with clarity, associations, organization, and application. A theory of mind and knowledge thus solves by one mighty coup the problem of what to teach, when, and how; and what is fatally theoretic here is not the presence of a theory of mind and a theory of knowledge, though their presence is part of the story, but the dispatch, the sweeping appearance of success, the vast simplicity which grounds this purported solution to the problem of curriculum.

Consider, now, some of the numerous efforts to ground curriculum in derived objectives. One effort seeks the ground of its objectives in social need and finds its social needs in just those facts about its culture which are sought and found under the aegis of a single conception of culture. Another grounds its objectives in the social needs identified by a single theory of history and of political evolution.

A third group of searches for objectives are grounded in theories of personality. The persuasive coherence and plausibility of Freudianism persuaded its followers to aim to supply children with adequate channels of sublimation of surplus libido, appropriate objects and occasions for aggressions, a properly undemanding ego ideal, and an intelligent minimum of taboos. Interpersonal theories direct their adherents to aim for development of abilities to relate to peers, "infeers," and "supeers," in relations nurturant and receiving, adaptive, vying, approving, and disapproving. Theories of actualization instruct their adherents to determine the salient potentialities of each child and to see individually to the development of each.

Three features of these typical efforts at curriculum making are significant here, each of which has its own lesson to teach us. First, each is grounded in a theory as such. . . . Second, each is grounded in a theory from the social or behavioral sciences: psychology, psychiatry, politics, sociology, history. . . . Third, they are theories concerning *different* subject matters. One curriculum effort is grounded in concern for the individual, another in concern for groups, others in concern for cultures, communities, societies, minds, or the extant bodies of knowledge.[9]

---

[9]It should be clear by now that "theory" as used in this paper does *not* refer only to grand schemes such as the general theory of relativity, kinetic-molecular theory, the Bohr atom, the Freudian construction of a tripartite psyche. The attempt to give an account of human maturation by the discrimination of definite states (e.g., oral, anal, genital), an effort to aggregate human competencies into a small number of primary mental abilities—these, too, are theoretic. So also are efforts to discriminate a few large classes of persons and to attribute to them defining behaviors: e.g., the socially mobile, the culturally deprived, the creative.

Need for an Eclectic The significance of this third feature is patent to the point of embarrassment: no curriculum grounded in but one of these subjects can possibly be adequate, defensible. A curriculum based on theory about individual personality which thrusts society, its demands, and its structure far into the background or ignores them entirely can be nothing but incomplete and doctrinaire; for the individuals in question are in fact members of a society and must meet its demands to some minimum degree since their existence and prosperity as individuals depend on the functioning of their society. In the same way, a curriculum grounded only in a view of social need or social change must be equally doctrinaire and incomplete, for societies do not exist only for their own sakes but for the prosperity of their members as individuals as well. In the same way, learners are not only minds or knowers but bundles of affects, individuals, personalities, earners of livings. They are not only group interactors but possessors of private lives.

The Place of the Practical

I turn now from the fact that the theories which ground curriculum plans pertain to different subsubjects of a common field, to the second of the three features which characterize our typical instances of curriculum planning—the fact that the ground of each plan is a theory, a theory as such.

The significance of the existence of theory as such at the base of curricular planning consists of what it is that theory does not and cannot encompass. All theories, even the best of them in the simplest sciences, necessarily neglect some aspects and facets of the facts of the case. A theory covers and formulates the *regularities* among the things and events it subsumes. It abstracts a general or ideal case. It leaves behind the nonuniformities, the particularities, which characterize each concrete instance of the facts subsumed. . . .

Yet curriculum is brought to bear not on ideal or abstract representatives but on the real thing, on the concrete case in all its completeness and with all its differences from all other concrete cases on which the theoretic abstraction is silent. The materials of a concrete curriculum will not consist merely of portions of "science," of "literature," of "process." On the contrary, their constituents will be particular assertions about selected matters couched in a particular vocabulary, syntax, and rhetoric. They will be particular novels, short stories, or lyric poems, each, for better or for worse, with its own flavor. . . .

These ineluctable characteristics of theory and the consequent ineluctable disparities between real things and their representation in theory constitute one argument for my thesis, that a large bulk of curriculum energies must be diverted from the theoretic, not only to the eclectic but to the practical and the quasi-practical. . . .

Theories from Social Sciences

The significance of the third feature of our typical instances of curriculum work—that their theories are mainly theories from the social and behavioral sciences—will carry us to the remainder of the argument for the practical.

Nearly all theories in all the behavioral sciences are marked by the coexistence of competing theories. All the social and behavioral sciences are marked by "schools," each distinguished by a different choice of principle of inquiry, each of which selects from the intimidating complexities of the subject matter the small fraction of the whole with which it can deal.

The theories which arise from inquiries so directed are, then, radically incomplete, each of them incomplete to the extent that competing theories take hold of different aspects of the subject of inquiry and treat it in a different way. Further, there is perennial invention of new principles which bring to light new facets of the subject matter, new relations among the facets and new ways of treating them. In short, there is every reason to suppose that any one of the extant theories of behavior is a pale and incomplete representation of actual behavior. There is similar reason to suppose that if all the diversities of fact, the different aspects of behavior treated in each theory, were somehow to be brought within the bounds of a single theory, that theory would still fall short of comprehending the whole of human behavior—in two respects. In the first place, it would not comprehend what there may be of human behavior which we do not see by virtue of the restricted light by which we examine behavior. In the second place, such a single theory will necessarily interpret its data in the light of its one set of principles, assigning to these data only one set of significances and establishing among them only one set of relations. It will remain the case, then, that a diversity of theories may tell us more than a single one, even though the "factual" scope of the many and the one are the same.

It follows, then, that such theories are not, and will not be, adequate by themselves to tell us what to do with human beings or how to do it. What they variously suggest and the contrary guidances they afford to choice and action must be mediated and combined by eclectic arts and must be massively supplemented, as well as mediated, by knowledge of some other kind derived from another source.

Some areas of choice and action with respect to human behavior have long since learned this lesson. Government is made possible by a lore of politics derived from immediate experience of the vicissitudes and tangles of legislating and administering. Institution of economic guidances and controls owes as much to unmediated experience of the marketplace as it does to formulas and theories.

It is this recourse to accumulated lore, to experience of actions and their consequences, to action and reaction at the level of the concrete case, which constitutes the heart of the practical. It is high time that curriculum do likewise.

The Practical Arts

The arts of the practical are onerous and complex; hence only a sampling must suffice to indicate the character of this discipline and the changes in educational investigation which would ensue on adoption of the discipline. . . .

The practical arts begin with the requirement that existing institutions and existing practices be preserved and altered piecemeal, not dismantled and replaced. It is further necessary that changes be so planned and so articulated with what remains unchanged that the functioning of the whole remain coherent and unimpaired.

This is well seen in the case of the law. Statutes are repealed or largely rewritten only as a last resort, since to do so creates confusion and diremption between old judgments under the law and judgments to come, confusion which must lead either to weakening of law through disrepute or a painful and costly process of repairing the effects of past judgments so as to bring them into conformity with the new. . . .

The same requirements would hold for a practical program of improvement of education. It, too, would effect its changes in small progressions, in coherence with what remains unchanged, and this would require that we know *what is and has been going on in American schools.*

At present, we do not know. My own incomplete investigations convince me that we have not the faintest reliable knowledge of how literature is taught in the high schools, or what actually goes on in science classrooms. There are a dozen different ways in which the novel can be read. Which ones are used by whom, with whom, and to what effect? What selections from the large accumulation of biological knowledge are made and taught in this school system and that, to what classes and kinds of children, to what effect? . . .

What is wanted is a totally new and extensive pattern of *empirical* study of classroom action and reaction; a study, not as a basis for theoretical concerns about the nature of the teaching or learning process, but as a basis for beginning to know what we are doing, what we are not doing, and to what effect —what changes are needed, which needed changes can be instituted. . . .

A second facet of the practical: its actions are undertaken with respect to identified frictions and failures in the machine and inadequacies evidenced in felt shortcomings of its products. . . .

These concerns of the practical for frictions and failures of the curricular machine would, again, call for a new and extensive pattern of inquiry. The practical requires curriculum study to seek its problems where its problems lie —in the behaviors, misbehaviors, and nonbehaviors of its students as they begin to evince the effects of the training they did and did not get. This means continuing assessment of students as they leave primary grades for the secondary school, leave secondary school for jobs and colleges. It means sensitive and sophisticated assessment by way of impressions, insights, and reactions of the community which sends its children to the school; employers of students, new echelons of teachers of students; the wives, husbands, and cronies of ex-students; the people with whom ex-students work; the people who work under them. Curriculum study will look into the questions of what games ex-students play; what, if anything, they do about politics and crime in the streets; what they read, if they do; what they watch on television and what they make of what they watch, again, if anything. . . .

A third facet of the practical I shall call the anticipatory generation of alternatives. Intimate knowledge of the existing state of affairs, early identification of problem situations, and effective formulation of problems are necessary to effective practical decision but not sufficient. It requires also that there be available to practical deliberation the greatest possible number and fresh diversity of alternative solutions to the problem. The reason for this requirement, in one aspect, is obvious enough: the best choice among poor and shopworn alternatives will still be a poor solution to the problem. Another aspect is less obvious. The problems which arise in an institutional structure which has enjoyed good practical management will be novel problems, arising from changes in the times and circumstances and from the consequences of previous solutions to previous problems. Such problems, with their strong tincture of novelty, cannot be solved by familiar solutions. . . .

As the last sampling of the practical, consider its method. It falls under neither of the popular platitudes: it is neither deductive nor inductive. It is deliberative.

The problem of selecting an appropriate man for an important post is a case in point. It is not a problem of selecting a representative of the appropriate personality type who exhibits the competencies officially required for the job. The person we hire is more than a type and a bundle of competencies. He is a multitude of probable behaviors which escape the net of personality theories and cognitive scales. He is endowed with prejudices, mannerisms, habits, tics, and relatives. And all of these manifold particulars will affect his work and the work of those who work for him. It is deliberation which operates in such cases to select the appropriate person.

Commitment to Deliberation

Deliberation is complex and arduous. It treats both ends and means and must treat them as mutually determining one another. It must try to identify, with respect to both, what facts may be relevant. It must try to ascertain the relevant facts in the concrete case. It must try to identify the desiderata in the case. It must generate alternative solutions. It must make every effort to trace the branching pathways of consequences which may flow from each alternative and affect desiderata. It must then weigh alternatives and their costs and consequences against one another and choose, not the right alternative, for there *is* no such thing, but the best one.

I shall mention only one of the new kinds of activity which would ensue on commitment to deliberation. It will require the formation of a new public and new means of communication among its constituent members. Deliberation requires consideration of the widest possible variety of alternatives if it is to be most effective. Each alternative must be viewed in the widest variety of lights. . . .

Concretely, this means the establishment of new journals, and education of educators so that they can write for them and read them.

Needless to say, such journals are not alone sufficient. They stand as only one concrete model of the kind of forum which is required. Similar forums, operating viva voce and in the midst of curriculum operation and curriculum change, are required: of the teachers, supervisors, and administrators of a school; of the supervisors and administrators of a school system; of representatives of teachers, supervisors, and curriculum makers in subject areas and across subject areas; of the same representatives and specialists in curriculum, psychology, sociology, administration, and the subject matter fields.[10]

The education of educators to participate in this deliberative process will be neither easy nor quickly achieved. The education of the present generation of specialist researchers to speak to the schools and to one another will doubtless be hardest of all, and on this hardest problem I have no suggestion to make. But we could begin within two years to initiate the preparation of teachers, supervisors, curriculum makers, and graduate students of education in the uses and arts of deliberation—and we should. . . .

By means of such journals and such an education, the educational research establishment might at last find a means for channeling its discoveries into sustained improvement of the schools instead of into a procession of ephemeral bandwagons.

Summary

The two major questions raised and answered in this chapter are "What is curriculum?" and "What do curriculum workers do?" The first question was asked directly, the second was not. But anyone who either intends to work as a curriculum developer, or to interact with those who do, should clearly understand these two questions. The answers may vary in emphasis from one person to another, but all respondents must generally agree before curriculum development can proceed.

Before turning to the remainder of this text, the reader should answer these two questions and discuss his or her answer with others. Discussion with others should enable one to determine the degree of compatibility among answers. The question of "What do curriculum workers do?" should be answered directly by contrasting the activities of the curriculum worker with activities of others such as teachers and administrators.

---

[10]It will be clear from these remarks that the conception of curricular method proposed here is immanent in the Tyler Rationale. This rationale calls for a diversity of talents and insists on the practical and eclectic treatment of a variety of factors. Its effectiveness in practice is vitiated by two circumstances. Its focus on "objectives," with their massive ambiguity and equivocation, provides far too little of the concrete matter required for deliberation and leads only to delusive consensus. Second, those who use it are not trained for the deliberative procedures it requires.

Chapter **2**

Frame Factors in the Curriculum

Instructor 84. 8 (April 1975) 136

"Your project's theoretical underpinnings and conceptual framework are intellectually sound and innovative, but your implementational strategies lack focus and reality orientation. Or as we used to say when I was a kid—it's a good idea, but it won't work."

1. Frame Factors and Instruction
2. School Control
3. Knowledge Explosion
4. Censorship
5. An Overview of Factors
6. Summary

Through curriculum theorizing one can speculate about the curriculum and the appropriate work of the schools. However, in making decisions about the implementation of the school curriculum one must consider practical and realistic constraints. These practical matters include factors that limit the potential of the schools and those that "drive" or charge the school with certain responsibilities. Both of these must be taken into account. They provide the framework that helps clarify what the schools can and cannot do. Because they frame the territory in which the schools function they are referred to here as "frame factors."

These frame factors can be broadly classified under five headings:

1. What the schools "must" do.
2. What the schools are "not allowed" to do.
3. What the schools "know enough" to do.
4. What the school resources "make it possible" for the schools to do.
5. What the schools "cannot control."

What the Schools Must Do

The public has certain expectations for the school, expressed in state curriculum requirements, accrediting criteria, standardized tests, and local school policy. When the schools fail to provide adequate education in an area such as reading or computational skills, objections are raised and pressure exerted by state boards of education, the legislature, or local agencies. The schools' obligations may vary from state to state and community to community but no school is exempt from these influences.

What the Schools Are Not Allowed to Do

Some subjects and activities are controversial. In certain communities and at certain times the schools are denied the right to offer instruction in areas that are taboo. For example, during the Hitler regime in Germany, teaching the German language was disallowed in many schools in the United States. Community mores sometimes censor the schools' curriculum or the materials used in the schools. Book banning or protests against sex education are examples of limits communities impose on the schools. Sometimes communities object to the schools assuming more responsibility than the parents wish them to have.

Recently, many schools have emphasized affective learnings, particularly values. Some communities are challenging the right of the schools to take over this role. They object that the values of the home may be different from those of the schools and that parents' rights should not be superseded by the schools. By a Supreme Court ruling schools are not allowed to require prayer. The schools do not have carte blanche when it comes to deciding the content of the schools' program.

What the Schools Know Enough to Do

Schools are limited by two factors: the size of the existing knowledge base and the ability to provide effective instruction. The schools may be asked to eradicate illiteracy but unless there is sufficient knowledge to do so schools will not accomplish this task for all pupils. The teaching profession, as all professions, is limited by its own ignorance. In teaching, these limits encompass several directions. One dimension is the cognitive learning expected and the dependable knowledge known. Pedagogical knowledge is needed to know the proper sequence and best explanatory language to use with different pupils to effectively bring about learning. Knowledge is needed about how to motivate pupils to learn and inspire them to work independently. Current knowledge is not adequate to overcome all hurdles faced by teachers. Our knowledge serves us but also limits what we can do.

What the School Resources Make Possible

Schools are imperfect institutions that operate with limited budgets, crowded classrooms, inadequate materials, and sparse learning facilities. All these factors limit the schools' teaching potential.

On the other hand, the available resources also determine what content the schools will include. A school with extensive laboratory equipment, a high percentage of motivated students, and an adequate faculty may offer advanced physics and four years of several foreign languages, while a poorly financed small school that lacks a qualified physics or language teacher may offer only general science and a beginning foreign language.

Quite apart from the virtues or disadvantages attributed to advanced work, the school is driven or limited in its choices by these factors. Every school faces the task of establishing a curriculum that capitalizes on the available resources. In some cases these resources open up superior potential and in other instances the resources create narrow limits. In every school the program is framed by its resources and the ingenuity with which those resources are used.

What the Schools Cannot Control

The schools are often asked to assume responsibility for more than they can deliver. The good intentions of the schools to render a useful service wherever needed can burden the schools with impossible tasks. Schools are asked to offset the drawbacks of impoverished homes, social disintegration, and highway wreckage. This is an expression of the American people's faith in the capacity of the schools. However, this may also indicate the abdication of the adult population from its own responsibilities. The public often asks the school to assume more than it has the capacity to accomplish. The schools cannot be mandated to accomplish the impossible anymore than legislators can repeal the law of gravity. There are responsibilities that fall within the purview of agencies and institutions external to the schools. The characteristics of these external factors may limit or enhance the work of the schools.

Frame Factors and Instruction

A discussion of frame factors in the teaching process is the topic of a publication by Ulf P. Lundgren. Frame factors are described according to their constraints that the teacher faces when trying to optimize instruction. In the first reading of this chapter excerpts from Lundgren's work are presented to give an orientation to frame factors and to illustrate how their analysis provides another way of looking at school decisions and school curriculum.

Our thesis is that if we are to understand, study, analyze, or change the teaching process, it is necessary to see it as a process occurring within limits; that it is to some extent governed or steered by the frames the curriculum establishes in its goals and content, by the organizational frame established by a group of pupils in the class—we call it the steering group—and by the time

Ulf P. Lundgren, *Frame Factors and the Teaching Process* (Stockholm: Almquist and Wissell, 1972), pp. 12–14, 40–44. Reprinted by permission of the author and publisher.

Footnotes have been renumbered consecutively throughout the chapter.

frame (time available for instruction).

Our theoretical model is simple and is developed from Dahllöf (1967a, 1970c, 1971a, c, d; Dahllöf, Lundgren, & Siöö, 1971). We show its three components in a paradigm:

Figure 2-1. A paradigm of the general approach and the outlines of a model.

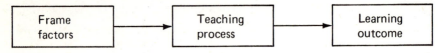

This paradigm expresses in a general way the relations which probably have guided most educational planners.

How does this model differ from other models or theories on these relations?

The first component is the concept of frame factors. There are three:

a) Factors given in the curriculum—goals and content.
b) Time available for instruction.
c) The composition of the class according to the time different pupils need to reach a certain goal.

The first type of factors has to do with the relations various curriculum theories are intended to explain. Existing models and theories on curriculum are often based on another point of view than the one we have. Since, for the most part, the teaching process is a steered process of communication between different individuals, it seems natural to build a curriculum theory around this communication process, around its content and form. In order to steer this process, earlier researchers have concentrated on influencing the person who is regarded as steering the process—the teacher. The implied assumption has to some extent been that the teacher's behavior is more or less independent of the total situation of which he is a part. The theories starting from this assumption, and created for the purpose of steering the teaching process, have been directed toward discovering what it is that forms or shapes the end product. In this way a great deal of curriculum theory has tried to apply various learning theories or theories of cognitive processes in an educational context.

Another approach to the relationship between curriculum and teaching process has been to concentrate on the philosophy underlying the choice of goals and content and the form these two components have been given.

The model we present is not an alternative to these two approaches, but must be regarded as a third approach for describing the relationship between curriculum and teaching process. At the same time this third standpoint offers a possibility of integrating the earlier approaches and is an attempt to build a more comprehensive model. We see the composition of the class and the time available as the main frames for the teaching process. Together with other limiting factors, such as the goals, the content, and the way the content is organized, they limit the ways of forming the teaching process. If the interrelations between these factors can be determined in connection with the actual teaching, the theories based on learning and cognitive processes can be used in a pedagogical model. Different theories can then be compared with each other and with various types of curricula, making it possible to point to different solutions as to the time needed for instruction and different organizational solutions.

There is at present no educational theory in existence on how time limits the teaching process in relation to goals, content, and the composition of the class. There is a line of research on the relations between the composition of the class and the outcome of the teaching process. There are relatively many studies on the effects of various organizational measures on the achievement of pupils and on changes in their attitudes. These studies are, however, simple empirical studies without any clearly expressed theories as to why various organizational solutions lead to varying effects.

So far, I have attempted to point out the pedagogical thinking represented by our model. The relationship between frames and process means that we see the process as not only steered by the frames but also limited by them. The outcome of the teaching process is limited by the interrelations of the frame factors. But within these limits, different ways of steering the process may be carried out. It is only by mapping these limits that the various methods of steering the process become meaningful. The question of forming goals and content can then be realistically judged according to the available resources.

The next question is: How to comprehend the various frame factors? In the earlier studies (Dahllöf 1967 a, 1971 a, c, d; Dahllöf, Lundgren, & Siöö, 1971), the frame factors have been defined as organizational measures (figure 2–2).

We shall here study the frame factors from the teachers' point of view. From this aspect the curriculum will be included as a frame factor. It is of course a moot point, whether the goals and content of the teaching should be seen as frame factors. But if we define frame factors as factors which limit the variation of the teaching process, the curriculum will, from the teachers' point of view, function as a frame factor. In relation to our general and specific models, we have to distinguish between curriculum frames and organizational frames.

We shall use three types of frame factors in our specific model that builds on the assumption that the teaching is traditional classroom instruction. By traditional classroom instruction we mean "front of the class teaching," where the teacher verbally or with the aid of various simple teaching aids and materials teaches the whole class at the same time.

The first factor is the objectives of the teaching. This factor is a variable in so far as it can vary in exactitude. We see a possibility of variation from generally expressed to clearly stated goals of behavior. We shall concentrate on the specific objectives for the subject. The second factor is the sequence of content units, within which the various educational goals can be reached. Even this factor may vary from clearly stated sequences to one carried out according to the teachers' wishes. The third factor is the groups into which the pupils fall with regard to the time needed by different pupils to master the units. We may speak of these three factors as variables, first when we set them against

Figure 2-2. Paradigm of the relations between frame factors, curriculum, teaching process, and learning outcome (from Dähllof, Lundgren, & Siöö, 1971, p. 102).

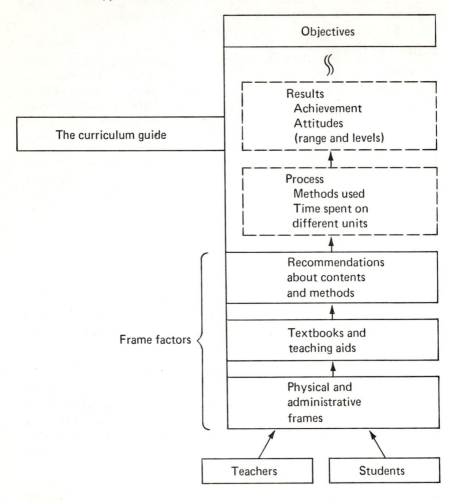

external criteria, and second when considering them in relation to the internal criteria the teacher has and his way of experiencing these factors. We see the total time in three ways. First, it may be sufficient to satisfy the relations between the frame factors. Second, it may be longer than what is needed in order to reach the intended outcomes. Third, it may be insufficient to satisfy these three types of frame factors. In that event, the teacher must make various decisions. Since the total time cannot be prolonged, the teacher must place a priority on certain goals or pupils or both.

These decisions are dependent on the curriculum and the organizational measures (ability grouping and size of class) and on the teachers' perception of them, as well as on his conception of his duty as a teacher toward the classes he is teaching.

School Control

The concept of frame factors can be extended to the entire curriculum of the schools. Roald F. Campbell has written about the control of the schools. He comments on the American tradition of local control and other influential factors that interact with local decisions. The examples he uses not only reveal changes in school conditions but also illustrate the permanence of the factors that still affect our schools. The factors listed in this passage are elements that influence curricular decisions and school actions. Oftentimes these factors are subtle or culturally ingrained forces that may be stronger influences than some efforts to change or maintain the schools' program of studies. After studying the selection you should be able to identify examples of the frame factors alluded to by Campbell.

There are in the United States some 30,000 school districts, and in these districts there are about 100,000 elementary schools and 30,000 high schools. For each district there is a board of education and one or more teachers. In at least half of the districts there is also a superintendent of schools, and for many of the larger districts a number of other school administrators. But who really controls these schools? The citizens? The boards? The administrators? The teachers?

I am using the word *control* to mean more than legal control; *influence* might be a better term. My purpose is to suggest how decisions about American schools get made. I would first like to indicate briefly the kinds of controls, or influences, that appear to affect American schools, then note how the larger society attempts to shape the school, and, in turn, suggest how the school mediates such influences.

Kinds of Controls

The controls or influences that affect schools may be grouped into three major categories. First, there is the legal structure. Despite the fact that the Constitution does not mention education, the federal government, chiefly through the Congress and the courts, has always exerted some influence on the schools. Every state constitution deals with schools specifically, in each state there is also a body of statutory law regarding education; and each state legislature is, in a sense, the big school board. There is some justification in the contention

Roald F. Campbell, "The Control of American Schools," *Elementary School Journal* 65 (December 1964): 120–29. Reprinted with permission of the University of Chicago Press and the author.

that there are fifty school systems in this country. In nearly every state, however, the actual operation of schools has been delegated to local school districts. There are other structural refinements, but this is the essential picture.

What of the actors within this structure? For the sake of simplicity, let us mention only those in the local school district. There is first the board of education, usually elected by the people of the district. In legal terms, the board is the administrative body for the district, but the board operates under many constraints, including state law and local tradition. Moreover, most boards employ an administrative officer, most commonly called a superintendent, and he tends to influence the board as well as do its bidding. But school cannot be kept without teachers, and teachers individually and collectively determine in large part what the school is and what it does.

These official actors—board members, administrators, and teachers—important as they are, do not perform in a social vacuum. Thus we must say a word about the social matrix within which the school operates. At the local or school district level this leads us to such considerations as the power structure of the community.

Some of these groups such as parent-teacher associations and the League of Women Voters are usually disposed to support school programs, while others such as taxpayers associations and militant civil rights groups often feel that school programs go too far or not far enough.

But special interest groups are seldom a local phenomenon only. The position of the interest group on a particular school program—whether expressed by chambers of commerce, farm bureaus, the John Birch Society, or the local education association—is often an expression espoused by the national organization, which has expended great effort to keep the locals in line. In the social matrix as in the legal structure, schools are not controlled locally; they are a part of the larger society.

Even this sketchy treatment of schools suggests that controls are numerous, that they are formal and informal, legal and extra-legal, covert and overt. While some controls reside within the school organization, others appear to reside outside the organization. For the school is a subsystem of a larger social system, a relationship not always clearly perceived and one to which we now turn.

Society and the School

The controls that the larger society exerts over the schools appear to fall into three major categories. These may be identified as the constraints imposed by the traditions and values of society, the economic resources made available by society for the schools, and the governmental structures established by society through which schools must operate.

Traditions and Values Two traditions or values appear to be particularly relevant here. The first might be called a faith in education and the second a strong tradition of localism. Faith in education, or perhaps more specifically in schooling, has long been characteristic of the American people.

This faith in education was probably born of our independence, our lack of an elite class, our decades of experience with an expanding frontier, our abundance of resources, and our conviction that one person is as good as another. Egalitarianism became a dominant value in our national development, and the school was seen as one way of giving expression to that value. . . .

The belief in the efficacy of education as a way of meeting our social and economic problems still persists. When we have unemployment, we tend to establish retraining programs. When we fall behind in space technology, we get congressional provisions for augmenting science and mathematics instruction. When juvenile delinquency increases, we look to the schools for remedial measures. This great faith in education may at times retard instead of advance the solution of our problems. Too much reliance on the school may mean too little reliance on the family, the courts, and the other agencies of our society. . . .

The people of America also have a long tradition of localism. This, too, is probably a product of our settlement and our long frontier experience. We believed firmly that the federal government should have limited powers and that other powers should be reserved to the states or to the people. The phrase "to the people" was not an idle one. There was a disposition to rely on government for no more than was necessary and to expect the people as individual citizens to do the rest. . . .

The American tradition of localism, so appropriate in our early history, has been identified with private enterprise, chiefly by the business groups of our society. Anyone who does not subscribe to such a view is almost seen as a subversive. But the frontier society is gone, and in its place we have an urban, industrial society which poses many problems that are not local in nature. Most of our major problems such as poverty, unemployment, civil rights, mass transportation, communication, world peace, and educational opportunity require local, state, national, and even worldwide effort if they are to be solved. It is this shift in the nature of our problems that is behind the growth of federalism.

Recognition of this fact is essential if the educational problems of the nation are to be solved. Many localities cannot provide educational opportunity for the children, the youth, and the adults of their communities; they must have state assistance. In turn, some states cannot or will not provide adequate educational opportunity for the people within their boundaries; the only alternative is federal assistance. Our tradition of localism provides the basis for resisting these solutions, but gradually that tradition is being modified. . . .

Economic Resources Schools require economic support. While money expended is not a perfect measure of the quality of an educational program, it is probably the best single index of quality. Expenditure levels vary greatly among school districts. The differences are due in part to the uneven distribution of economic resources. One district may have many pupils to be placed in school and may depend for its assessed valuation entirely on low- and medium-priced residences. A second district may have few pupils and enjoy an assessed valuation made up in major part by a large industrial complex. The alternatives that confront these two districts are very different. . . .

But the economy is called upon to support services other than schools. Municipal government, police and fire protection, roads, sewers, water, and other services must also be provided. Often the school bond issue must compete with the bond issue of the sanitary district. Salary increases for teachers may be caught up in the issue of salary increases for firemen and policemen. In new suburban communities, particularly, many of these demands are concurrent. In these cases, it is not only a question of the level of economic resources, but of the allocation of these resources; and decisions on allocation will have direct import for the schools.

In the long run, level of education and economic resources are interdependent. Education becomes the chief vehicle for creating human capital, which in turn affects the total economy. A skilled labor force is as necessary to a healthy economy as natural resources are. . . .

The integrated nature of the economy represents another reason for providing economic resources for the schools on more than a local basis. State aid and particularly federal aid can help spread the benefits of the economy over the nation so that the educational level of the entire nation can make its best contribution to the economy. This concept is not fully accepted by all groups in American society, but continued movement toward acceptance appears likely.

In the meantime, economic resources available from local sources, from existing state sources, and from existing federal sources will continue to affect the nature and level of the school program which any school district can mount.

Governmental Structure   Governmental arrangements in this country are numerous and overlapping. A single small school district may overlap eight or ten other units of government. These units may include one or more villages, a fire district, a water district, a sanitary district, a recreation district, a toll road, and other special purpose governments. For a citizen to participate responsibly in such an environment is almost impossible. Perhaps multiplicity of government has contributed to the indifference many people exhibit toward government.

The school district itself is an example of special government. When the government of the school district must be conducted within numerous overlapping jurisdictions, complications ensue for the school as well as for the citizen. . . . In any case, many special governments and frequent overlapping jurisdictions often affect school district operation.

But governmental structure affects schools even more directly. Some structures are relatively open to the expression of local aspirations for education. In such structures, the board of education and the people can exercise some control over the local school. Other structures are relatively closed, and neither the board of education nor the people of the local district can exercise much of an option regarding education. In the closed situations most decisions are made at the county or the state level. This condition tends to pull all educational programs to the mean, lifting the bottom programs and reducing the top programs. Thus, the level of government at which educational decisions are made affects the nature of the school program.

The School and Society

It is clear that the larger society creates the school, imposes its values upon the school, decides what resources the school may use, and prescribes the way the school is to be governed. But the school or school district has ways of resisting or mediating these controls. The bureaucratic nature of organizations, the professionalism of teachers, and the leadership of the administrator represent these countervailing forces.

Organizational Characteristics   Schools, like other bureaucracies, have a hierarchical authority structure. Authority proceeds from the board of education to the superintendent, to the principal, to the teacher. While many people lament these hierarchical arrangements, no adequate alternative has yet been evolved. There are, however, wide differences in how the hierarchical structure is employed.

In some school situations, almost complete reliance is placed on the flow of authority. Thus, the board directs the superintendent, the superintendent directs the principal, and the principal directs the teacher. While the formal structure permits and accepts this state of affairs, complete reliance on such an arrangement may produce a number of dysfunctions. For instance, giving and taking orders may prevent the development and consideration of ideas, organization members may devise informal means of "beating the system," and potentially able contributors may develop indifference toward the organization.

In some school systems, the authority dimension is mediated by recognition of the competence of staff members. While authority flows down, influence flows both ways. Teachers make suggestions to principals, principals to superintendents, and superintendents to school boards. Communication is down, up, and across. These organizations have an open climate. Such a climate may contribute to greater productivity in the organization and to greater satisfaction on the part of organization members, both of which can be important influences on schools.

Organizations have built-in protections against the larger society. Personal detachment, reliance on rules and regulations, and hierarchical structure all provide protection against the larger world. In a school, for instance, a case can usually be made against granting a request to a particular parent on the grounds that similar requests could not be granted to other parents; in other words, parents must be treated in a universalistic not in a particularistic manner.

For the parent to go to the superintendent takes effort. In the meantime, the principal may alert the superintendent to the impending visit of the parent and make a case against the granting of the request. When the parent finally gets to see the superintendent, he may encounter the same arguments he did with the principal; need to keep the matter in a universalistic context, prohibition by the policies of the board of education, and, as a final resort, an appointment with the board of education. . . .

Professionalism   Still another influence on the school is what may be called professionalism. The teacher who would be a professional finds he must cope with a growing body of knowledge in one or more content areas as well as with increasing knowledge about the teaching and learning process. . . . School systems are recognizing the growing importance of inservice education programs for teachers.

Professionalism has a way of resisting intervention from the larger society. For instance, some school districts have withstood pressure from lay citizens to adopt an all-out phonics approach in the teaching of reading. In the process, the teachers and the administrators in the school system marshalled evidence from members of their professional groups across the nation to support their current practice. Citizens were told that this was a professional matter, that the evidence was fairly clear, and that only the professionals should make such a decision. . . .

The increased professionalism of teachers has another kind of relevance for the school district. There is a growing conflict between professional and hierarchical control of schools. Obviously, the administrator cannot become expert in every content area of the curriculum. Thus, in some ways, he is not prepared to make decisions about many matters that are central to the school program. The board of education, composed of laypersons, is even less well prepared to decide what and how to teach. If only teachers have the expertise required for some decisions, board members and administrators are obligated to find some way of modifying hierarchical control so as to use the expertise of the professional.

Leadership of Administrators   The school can also resist the larger society through the leadership of the administrator. Some administrators do little more than maintain an organization. Others affect some changes in the goals, programs, and procedures of an organization. The latter activity represents leadership. While changes in goals, programs, or procedures may be expressed within the organization, their legitimation must reside in the world surrounding the organization. Thus, the administrator who would lead is required to stimulate his staff as well as to convince his public. . . .

By way of summary, may I note that the larger society tries to shape the school by imposing its traditions and values, by controlling the resources made available to the school, and through the governmental arrangements established for the school. The school does not simply accept these impositions; countervailing forces are marshalled to mediate the impingements of the larger world. These forces include the bureaucratic nature of the school, the growing professionalism of teachers, and the leadership of the administrators. In this interaction between society and the school, bureaucracy gives the school some protection from immediate access by every subpublic in the larger world, professionalism marshals an expertise not possessed by the larger world, but administrative leadership is required to help the larger world reconceive its expectations for the school. It is this interaction which gives us h̶o̶p̶ school will not only mirror society but help to improve it.

Knowledge Explosion

One of the significant factors in curriculum planning is selecting appropriate content from the vast body of knowledge that exists. Criteria for this selection are not easy to formulate. In the next selection Ralph W. Tyler has dealt with the issue of increased knowledge and limited capacity of the schools to provide everything asked of them. In this instance, the knowledge explosion brings pressure on the schools to do more and the realities of their capacity reduces the amount of responsibility the schools can accept. The tug-of-war between heavy demand from the knowledge arena and limited capacity of the schools is presented as factors that also frame curriculum development.

☐

We speak of the knowledge explosion because of the exponential rate at which new facts are being discovered in the sciences. Scientific information is doubling every 10 to 15 years so that its mere storage is a very serious problem. Great libraries are crowded beyond belief, and electronic methods for locating articles, books, and papers are being experimented with in an effort to keep all this new knowledge available for the public's use. . . .

This obviously has implications for the school curriculum. Are our high school courses up-to-date or do they represent science and scholarship which has been outmoded? Can we cover all we need to cover? Textbooks cannot be expanded indefinitely. Learning takes time. For young people to gain an understanding of ideas, of principles, and of facts, requires an active effort on their part in expressing these ideas, principles, and facts in their own words, in using them to explain phenomena, and to guide actions. . . .

Knowledge can be used in several ways. Some knowledge helps in developing understanding so that we now can explain things that we could not explain before. Some is useful for guiding action, such as knowledge of technology that tells how to do things. Some knowledge is useful in developing our feelings so that we are aided in getting new satisfactions and meanings out of various kinds of esthetic experiences. All of these uses of knowledge require active participation on the part of the learner. When more material is presented to students than they have time to treat in this way, they attempt to memorize it by rote and to parrot back statements from their textbooks. This is not the

Ralph W. Tyler, "The Knowledge Explosion: Implications for Secondary Education," *The Educational Forum* 29, 7 (January 1965):145–53. Reprinted by permission of Kappa Delta Pi, An Honor Society of Education, owners of the copyright.

Tyler acknowledges the three domains of learning

kind of learning required for knowledge to be a part of their thinking, feeling, and acting.

Not only are the numbers of facts increasing at a rapid rate, but new discoveries change the meanings and implications of many of the facts which were previously known. Hence, memorizing huge numbers of facts today will not provide adequate understanding for tomorrow. . . .

School Learnings

What can the high schools do when knowledge is expanding so rapidly? I should like to suggest six approaches or steps which can be taken to aid in solving this difficult problem. A first step is to concentrate the major efforts of the high school on important tasks which it can do best. This is not new. High schools have been giving some attention to this since the end of World War II, seeking to identify educational tasks so as to emphasize those particularly appropriate for the school in contrast to those that are best carried on by other educative agencies. . . .

Second, what is to be learned necessitates well-organized experiences over time. The basic concepts and modes of inquiry in science, English, history, or mathematics cannot usually be picked up in a few hours here and a few hours there. Such learning must be carefully organized over time, so the student is building a structure systematically in order to reach a relatively high level of understanding.

Third, the school is particularly needed to provide learning opportunities in cases in which the essential factors are not obvious to the observer and the principles, concepts, and meanings must be specially brought to the attention of the learner. Thus, the scientific concepts and principles which explain the growth and development of plants are not obvious to the observer of plants or even to an uneducated farmhand. The school can more effectively provide for this learning than can the job.

Fourth, it is particularly appropriate for the school to provide learning experiences that cannot be provided directly in the ordinary activities of daily life. Geography and history are excellent illustrations of fields where daily life experience alone is not likely to provide sufficient insight into historic matters and affairs relating to places far removed.

Fifth, a kind of learning particularly appropriate for the school is that which requires more "purified" experience than is commonly available in life outside the school. Students may learn something of art, music, literature, or human relations from the examples commonly found in the community, but when these fall short of the best, the students have no chance to set high standards for themselves.

Finally, another kind of learning particularly appropriate to the school is that in which reexamination and interpretation of experience are essential. Our basic ethical values are commonly involved in the daily experiences of youth. Questions of justice, fairness, goodness arise again and again on the playground, in the market place, and elsewhere. It is not likely, however, that mere contact with these ideas will be enough to help youth develop for themselves values that are clearly understood and effectively utilized. . . .

These six kinds of learning which are peculiarly appropriate to the school ought to be strongly emphasized in the school program in contrast to other learnings which can be provided by other agencies. This selection will reduce the educational tasks of the school somewhat, but the fields remaining are vast and growing rapidly, so that this step alone is not enough to solve the problem.

Updating Curriculum

A second step is to see that the curriculum in each field is periodically, if not continuously, updated as to its objectives, its content and emphasis, and its learning experiences. . . .

What is required in order to do an adequate job in updating a curriculum is to bring together scholars, scientists, teachers, experts in learning, administrators, and other persons familiar with school conditions who will work on the several major parts of the task. They will seek to clarify the kinds of contribution that each field can make to the education of young people that will help them to understand the world and their own lives, to act effectively, and to get more meaning and satisfaction from their experiences. In the light of the proposed objectives, relevant content is then selected, learning experiences and materials are designed and then tried out. Revisions are made as a result of the tryouts. This is a long-term effort, but nothing less will do.

Lifelong Learning

A third step in dealing with the rapid explosion of knowledge is to emphasize throughout the curriculum the concept of education as a process of continued life-long learning. It is not possible for us to master in three years, twelve years, sixteen years, or in any specific time, all that we need to learn. Hence, the secondary school should help students develop the interests, abilities, and habits required for carrying on lifelong learning. . . .

Furthermore, the school can help students acquire the habit of seeking new knowledge and understanding. For habits to be formed, the students need consistent and continuing practice in study and inquiry. Each high school course will provide opportunities for investigation and study rather than a series of recitations from the textbook. In science, for example, questions are being raised, and students are going to the laboratory, to books, and to the field for information on which to formulate and test ideas. To take another illustration, the course in literature becomes a quest for meanings and satisfactions in books. In all courses, stressing the process of study and the use of inquiry in the daily lives of students helps them to become life-long learners.

Organize Material

A fourth step which helps to make significant education possible, in spite of the great mass of material accumulating in each field, is to select and organize the content in a way that can be understood by the student and used by him effectively. Knowledge is not a vast collection of isolated items. . . . Because of the structure developed by the scholars in each subject it is possible to organize learning experiences for more efficient learning. Hence, although knowledge may double in ten or fifteen years it is not actually true that the requirements for understanding double in that period.

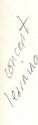

The curriculum work of the Physical Science Study Group is a good illustration of the economy of learning with an organized body of knowledge. This high school physics course utilizes only a relatively small number of concepts, such as energy, time, and motion. Actually only thirty-four concepts are stressed, and around these concepts the whole high school physics course is built. If the youngster understands these basic notions, and the facts related to them, he is able to explain most physical phenomena with which he has experience. . . .

Implicit in the <u>structure of every subject</u> are the kinds of questions it seeks to answer, and the kinds of methods it uses in carrying on its inquiry. These are matters which the student should understand and that will help him to find his way about in the great mass of current knowledge. To summarize, content can be organized for teaching and learning so as to aid the student in understanding its structure. In every course, the student should be able to answer the following:

1. What kinds of questions does this subject seek to answer?
2. What kinds of methods does it use to study these questions?
3. What concepts are basic in this subject to give order and meaning to its specific data?
4. What generalizations are being obtained and what are illustrations of the specific items to which these generalizations apply?
5. How can this subject be used in my daily life?

If he can answer these five questions, we have helped to organize the subject for learning. It is amazing how much can be understood, remembered, and used by the students when materials are selected and dealt with in this way.

Better Sequences

A fifth step for dealing with the knowledge explosion is to work out better sequences of learning in the several fields. We do not have yet good sequences of learning in all subjects. . . . When a comprehensive sequence is developed, the students can attain a much higher level of competence than when sequential treatment is neglected and each course starts at the beginning.

Conditions of Learning

Finally, a sixth step is to give much more careful attention to efficient learning. Although there are many specific factors about learning which are not precisely understood, research and experience have provided knowledge of several

this is different to the process-led curriculum, which concerns itself with what the teacher does in terms of principles of procedure.

conditions which influence the effectiveness of learning. If these conditions were more adequately met, the efficiency of education could be markedly increased.

I mean such well understood conditions for learning as that the learner must carry on the behavior he is to learn. In the final analysis, it is not what the teacher does, but what the learner does, which determines learning. If the learner is to acquire a skill, he must perform the operations involved in the skill until it has become part of his continuing repertoire of behavior. . . . Furthermore, learning not only requires the learner to carry on the behavior he is to learn, but he must also find it rewarding. Unless he obtains satisfaction from the behavior, it will not become a continuing part of his repertoire of behavior.

These two basic conditions for learning provide the primary guides to devising educational programs. Whatever the forms of teaching and learning used, they must enable the student to carry on the behavior he is to learn, and they must enable him to obtain satisfaction from carrying on the behavior successfully. Keeping these two conditions in mind helps greatly in planning what is to be done, but there are several other conditions required for learning to be effective which can be used in planning. One of these is the motivation of the student. Since he learns what he is thinking, feeling, or doing, learning is not possible except as the learner is involved in it. This must be considered in planning the educational program. What present motivations can be built on? What new motivations can be developed which will involve the students more deeply in the program?

A fourth condition is that the student finds his previous ways of reacting unsatisfactory so that he is stimulated to try new ways. As long as he does not recognize that earlier modes of behavior in this field are inappropriate, he will keep on doing what he has been doing before and will not really learn anything new.

A fifth condition is for the student to have some guidance in trying to carry on the new behavior he is to learn. If he simply tries new behavior by trial and error, learning is very slow and he is often discouraged and gives up. . . .

A sixth condition is for the student to have appropriate materials to work on. If he is to learn to solve problems, he has to have problems to be solved; if he is to gain skills, he must have tasks which give him the opportunity to practice these skills; if he is to develop attitudes, he must have opportunities to see the phenomena in a new perspective and to be able to respond to the situation with new feeling tones. . . .

A seventh condition is obviously a corollary of the sixth. The student must have *time* to carry on the behavior, to keep practicing it. Often educational programs assume that if time is provided for the presentation of material, adequate time has been allocated for learning. Actually, the time the student spends in practicing the behavior to be learned is the most critical in determining whether he really learns. . . .

These seven are not all the conditions which are known to have a marked influence on the effectiveness of learning, but they are among the most important ones.

Censorship

The news media regularly report on book bannings, censorship, and other restrictions that frame the schools' curriculum. The curriculum worker must be realistic about and sensitive to the public's feelings about "controversial" areas. Entire publications have been devoted to this topic and only a brief reminder of the importance of this concern is provided here. Because textbooks are such vital components in operating schools, it is appropriate to present an article that focuses primarily on textbook issues. Censorship and public reaction, however, are not limited to textbooks. Controversy can and has emerged in most every area of the schools ranging from hair styles to the school song. This selection on censorship by Clifford A. Hardy organizes and lists some of the major factors in curriculum controversies.

Legislation recently passed by the Tennessee Senate would prevent textbooks from presenting as scientific fact the various theories concerning man's origin. This legislation would stipulate that the Book of Genesis' explanation, as well as Darwin's and other theories of man's origin, be presented as theories rather than as scientific fact. The action is similar in nature to a recent California ruling whereby textbooks are being modified by the insertion of conditional statements concerning evolution.[1]

While these events and others that will doubtless follow in their wake may seem harmless enough to many, perhaps evoking only amusing memories of the Scopes trial and little else, there are implications of a serious nature that perhaps should be considered. Since these changes have been brought about generally by forces external to the scientific and academic communities at a time when the specter of censorship in the form of intimidation of newsmen, news sources, and network television is on the rise, perhaps we should give pause to consider the ever-present problem of censorship and the school curriculum.

There have been numerous and powerful advocates of censorship in every age. While the advocates operate in different ways, there are recurring patterns that tend to emerge. In this regard, Sloan has suggested that:

> Today's censors still exhibit one or more of the four traditional characteristics of the censor: they espouse *secrecy,* attempt to *edit* that with which they disagree, and/or make themselves judges for what is morally or politically acceptable for society.[2]

Clifford A. Hardy, "Censorship and the Curriculum," *Educational Leadership* 31 (October 1973): 10–13. Reprinted by permission of the publisher.

[1]Laurel N. Tanner and Daniel Tanner, "Charles Darwin Needs Clarence Darrow," *Educational Leadership* 30, 6 (March 1973):579.

[2]George W. Sloan, "Censorship in Historical Perspective," *Top of the News* 22 (April 1966):271.

Textbook Selection

Perhaps in no other area have all of these characteristics been expressed more than in the area of textbook selection in the social studies. The persistent efforts of a handful of persons can often result in the banning of a particular text or in its alteration or modification. In this regard, Nelson and Roberts have provided a detailed and interesting case study illustrating how the character of a textbook can be transformed through alteration. The brief example to follow, drawn from their study of a Texas State Textbook Committee hearing, represents the kind of subtle alteration that along with several other changes resulted in the substantial modification of a geography text adopted by that state.

Original Version: "Because it needs to trade, and because it needs military help, the United States needs the friendship of countries throughout the world. But to keep its friends, a country must help them, too."

Changed to: "The United States trades with countries in all parts of the world. We are also providing military help to many nations. In addition, the United States aids many countries in other ways."[3]

While instances of censorship can be treated as isolated cases, the pressure of textbook censorship is not a welcome event when one considers the time and money spent on emphasizing the inquiry approach to social studies during the past decade. Unfortunately, the adoption of sterile, safe textbooks may create a climate of self-imposed censorship that can run counter to the values of the inquiry method as well as inhibit in various other ways the teaching of social studies by the process approach.

While English teachers have traditionally borne the brunt of book-banning attempts, there seems to be little "rhyme or reason" to this type of censorship. Apparently nearly every book of consequence, including such classics as *Gone with the Wind, Huckleberry Finn, 1984, To Kill a Mockingbird,* and *The Grapes of Wrath,* has fallen victim to the censor at one time or another. The conclusion that few books have indeed escaped the would-be censors' wrath seems to be highlighted by the fact that:

In the files of the National Council of Teachers of English are reports of efforts to ban *Robin Hood,* because he advocates sharing the wealth and is therefore Communistic; *The Scarlet Letter,* because it deals with adultery; *The King and I,* because it mentions a concubine; a short account of the life of Plato, because he advocated something like free love; the *Odyssey,* because this book from the ninth century B.C. is "non-Christian."[4]

While this kind of censorship has often affected the school library in a general way, it can also be felt in quite specific ways, as in the case of the recent banning of the best-seller *Body Language* by a New York school board. Concerned with nonverbal communication and used in an elective "communi-

---

[3]J. Nelson and G. Roberts, *The Censors and the Schools* (Boston: Little, Brown, 1963), p. 130.

[4]H. Norris, "Should We Censor What Adolescents Read?" *The PTA Magazine* 50 (March 1965):11.

cations" course, the book was banned by a review committee following the complaint of a local citizen. In addition to the banning of *Body Language,* the school principal was apparently "instructed by the committee to draft a policy assigning textbook selection and curriculum solely to board members."[5]

Influence on Science

While the effect of censorship in the area of humanities should be evident, its effect on the science curriculum has perhaps been less noteworthy. However, with the advent of the kind of action mentioned at the beginning of this article concerning the treatment of evolution in science textbooks, several factors should be kept in mind. The first and perhaps most important would question the effect that this kind of censorship might have upon the science curriculum in general and student learning in particular.

Few educators need to be reminded of the fact that since 1956 the National Science Foundation has contributed vast sums to support major curriculum projects primarily in science and mathematics. This is, of course, in addition to the large amounts contributed by private organizations and the U.S. Office of Education toward the goal of improving course content in the sciences. The outgrowth of this work and expenditure has resulted in the development of the PSSC physics, the CHEM Study chemistry, and the BSCS biology materials, in addition to various other projects with similar aims, objectives, and methods. As a by-product, many of the objectives, methods, and unifying ideas from these courses have been incorporated into several of the so-called traditional textbook approaches in science.

It should be kept in mind that each of the curriculum projects mentioned has been centered around certain unifying or organizing themes. For instance, one of the principal organizing themes for the BSCS biology materials is the concept of evolution. As such, evolution plays a central role in organizing, unifying, and clarifying the content of modern biology.[6] At this point, the question must come into play as to whether or not it is sound learning practice to begin isolating the organizing element of modern biology, namely evolution, in order to present it as a discrete isolated theory, and in order to place it in competition, so to speak, with other discrete isolated theories.

While this approach may be applauded by some, the fact that it might represent a serious step backward toward the discreteness of the subject-centered curriculum should at least be given consideration. An interesting action in this regard can be seen in a recent decision by the Texas State Board of Education to remove two BSCS biology textbooks from the state-approved list, in addition to the requiring of all textbooks treating evolution to insert a preface to the effect that "evolution is presented not as a fact, but as a theory."[7]

Finally, it should be remembered that whether a censorship action is local

---

[5]"N.Y. School Board Bans Body Language," *Library Journal* 98 (April 15, 1973):1332.

[6]J. Marshall and Ernest Burkman, *Current Trends in Science Education* (New York: Center for Applied Research in Education, 1966), p. 39.

[7]Tanner and Tanner, "Charles Darwin Needs Clarence Darrow."

in nature, as in a recent Connecticut case where an entire chapter was removed from the local high school physiology text,[8] or whether an action is statewide in nature, students in other parts of the country may well be affected. It appears to be the case that the textbook industry is too often vulnerable both directly and indirectly to censorship efforts.

An Overview of Factors

The final selection in this chapter on frame factors is from an article on curriculum policy making. In this article by Michael Kirst and Decker Walker the influence and impact of a wide variety of agencies are presented. As you read the selection you should look for specific instances of agencies that either limit the schools or influence them to adapt their curriculum to these agencies. If you will prepare a written list of influences and consequences described in this selection, then you can compare your list with those of others. This can lead to a productive discussion and increased awareness of the frame factors operating in policy making for our schools.

Major Influences on Curriculum Policy

At this point we would like to turn our attention to the structure and process of political influence in the making of local school district curriculum policy. By influence we mean the ability to get others to act, think, or feel as one intends (Banfield, 1961). A school superintendent who persuades his board to install the "new math" is exercising political influence on a curriculum issue. A related concept is what Gergen (Bauer & Gergen, 1968) called points of leverage—individuals or institutions that have the capacity to effect a substantial influence on the curriculum output of a school system. An individual or group that has leverage is one that can make a big difference in the outcome of conflicts over curriculum policy. Our focus here is on the content of curriculum policy rather than the priority curriculum receives in budget allocations. Our perspective is that of the local school system and our focus is on the decisions of what to teach to children.

A mapping of the leverage points for curriculum policy making in local schools would be exceedingly complex. It would involve three levels of government, and numerous private organizations including foundations, accrediting associations, national testing agencies, textbook-software companies, and interest groups (such as the NAACP or the John Birch Society). Moreover, there

[8]"Physiology Text Mutilated: Depicts Sexual Reproduction," *Library Journal* 98 (April 15, 1973):1331.

Michael W. Kirst and Decker F. Walker, "An Analysis of Curriculum Policy-Making," *Review of Educational Research* 41, 5 (1971):479–509. Copyright 1971, American Educational Research Association.

would be a configuration of leverage points within a particular local school system including teachers, department heads, the assistant superintendent for instruction, the superintendent, and the school board. Cutting across all levels of government would be the pervasive influence of various celebrities, commentors, interest groups, and the journalists who use the mass media to disseminate their views on curriculum. It would be very useful if we were able to quantify the amount of influence of each of these groups or individuals and show input-output interactions for just one school system. Unfortunately, this is considerably beyond the state of the art, and we must settle for a less precise discussion.

We distinguish three ways in which national or regional agencies affect state and local curriculum policy making: by establishing minimum standards, by generating curricular alternatives, and by demanding curriculum change. We treat these three types of effect on policy making separately, even though some groups affect policy making in more than one of these ways.

Groups That Establish Minimum Curriculum Standards   From the vantage point of a local public school system, flexibility in determining curriculum content is constrained greatly by several outside groups. The political culture of this country has emphasized "local control" and played down the role of the national government. The curriculum area has been singled out as one where a uniform national standard and substance should be avoided. Federal aid to education was stalled for years, in large part because of a fear that the federal dollar would lead to a uniform national curriculum (Sundquist, 1969). Visitors from abroad, however, are usually surprised by the coast-to-coast similarity of the curriculum in American public schools. In effect, we have granted political influence over curriculum to national *nongovernment* agencies that demand a minimum national curriculum standard below which few public schools dare to fall.

A good example of this is the leverage on curriculum that private accrediting associations display. State governments also accredit but it is the private regional accrediting organizations that really concern the local school officials. These accrediting agencies define specific curriculum standards and criteria required for their stamp of approval.

The political influence of the accrediting agency is based on the faith other people have in the accreditation. Since loss of accreditation is dreaded by every school person, these accrediting agencies can bring almost irresistible pressure on the curriculum offerings of a local school. The accrediting agencies often are a force for supporting the traditional curriculum and resisting radical changes (Koerner, 1968). In effect, accrediting agencies make value judgments about what should be taught while their credo stresses professional judgments.

Testing agencies in the United States are also largely in private hands and exert a "standardizing" influence on curriculum. Educational Testing Service, for instance, has an income of about $20,000,000 a year from its tests. Over 1,000,000 students take the College Boards and 700 institutions require it. Consequently, local schools do not have a choice as to whether or not they offer the dozen subjects covered by the achievement exams of the College Boards. These tests do not entirely determine the detailed content of the curriculum but they do limit what teachers can spend their time doing. Moreover, national standardized reading or math tests given in the prehigh school grades may determine a great deal of the specific content of the reading or math curriculum. Local schools want to look good on these nationally normed tests.

While the testing agencies and their panels of expert advisers largely determine the content of the standard tests used in elementary and junior high schools, in high schools the tests tend to be dictated largely by the colleges and universities. The tests follow guidelines presented by colleges as part of their entrance requirements. For those students who take a college preparatory course, the high school curriculum is determined almost entirely by college entrance requirements. And the prestige accorded to the subjects required for entrance by colleges undoubtedly influences many non-college-bound students (probably via their parents) to take these courses. The tyranny of college entrance requirements over the secondary school curriculum has been a persistent complaint of high schools. In the late thirties the Progressive Education Association sponsored a study, called the Eight Year Study (Aikin, 1942), of the secondary school curriculum in which they asked for and received permission to waive entrance requirements for the students in the experimental schools. Students from these schools were not required to have so many units of English, history, etc. in order to be admitted to college; only a recommendation from their principal was needed. An evaluation of the performance of these students in college showed them to be equal to students in similar schools in every respect and superior in many (Chamberlin, 1942). The design of this study has been criticized (see Travers & Wallen, 1963, pp. 472–493), but no one has attempted to replicate it, and entrance requirements remain.

State departments of education and state boards of education have also had a traditional role in setting and enforcing minimum curriculum standards. This role has varied enormously depending on whether the political culture of the state supported what Elazar (1965) called a centrist or localist policy. In New England, the local schools enjoy an autonomy from state controls that goes back to the hatred of the English royal governor, while some southern states often mandate textbooks and courses of instruction. Most states do not mandate the school curriculum to any great extent. A 1966 survey (Conant, 1967) revealed that the great majority of states mandated courses in the dangers of alcohol and narcotics, only half required work in U. S. history and physical education, and less than half (ranging from 46 percent to 2 percent of the states) required instruction in other specific subjects.

It is often the newer subject areas (vocational education, driver training) that have used state law to gain a secure place in the curriculum. These subjects were introduced into the curriculum after 1920, amid great controversy, whereas mathematics and English never had to use political power to justify their existence in the school curriculum. Consequently, the "standard" subjects are less frequently mandated by state law.

Associations of teachers and special subjects can be very influential at the state level and use their power base for preserving state curriculum requirements. Vocational education, physical education, and home economics teachers use their NEA state affiliate to ensure that their specialities are stressed in the local schools. They are also supported by the manufacturers of sports equipment and home appliances. The driver education teachers are a new state lobby, but so effective that almost all states mandate driver education.

Ironically, teachers of academic subjects are usually poorly organized and not united at the state level. Nobody consults them and their minimal influence is indicated by the national trend to require less professional training for teaching licenses in physics, math, or history than for home economics or industrial arts (Conant, 1967).

Alternative Generators   Operating in the political environment of the local school are several organizations and individuals who provide alternatives with respect to curriculum. The range and nature of the curriculum alternatives proposed by these organizations is restricted by the minimum standards and requirements discussed in the prior section.

Most curriculum decisions are made at the local level; outside agencies can only provide alternatives to choose from. School boards, superintendents, directors of curriculum, principals, department chairpersons, and teachers must take the final steps in deciding what to teach. As we have seen, state officials and the state legislature usually prescribe certain rather broad limits. The power of local officials to select is also bounded, however, perhaps more severely than by state laws, by the decision alternatives available to them. If, ten years ago, a school had wanted to teach a history of America that gave the black man a place in it, the teachers would have had to write the textbooks themselves. Some schools attempt such things, but most do not. Teachers do not feel able to do the job, and the board has little money for released time or research assistants. So, until recently, most schools could not opt for an integrated history even if they were so inclined. It is only now becoming possible for schools to teach a reasonably balanced account of the wresting of this continent from its aboriginal inhabitants. Until 1960 it was not possible for a school to teach modern physics unless it was blessed with a truly out-standing teacher.

The bald fact is that most teaching in our schools is and must be from a textbook or other curriculum package. We do not trust teachers to write their own materials, we do not give them the time or money, and we insist on standardization. So long as this is true, the suppliers of teaching materials will have a potentially powerful effect on the curriculum.

Who supplies decision alternatives to local schools? Until ten years ago the unequivocal answer to this question would have been "textbook publishers." But a lot has happened in the interim. Textbook publishing has become part of an enlarged education industry which produces all sorts of printed, electronic, and mechanical devices for classroom use. Also, the federal government, private foundations, and various nonprofit organizations of scholars, teachers, and laypersons have taken a more active role in producing curriculum materials. Nevertheless, the textbook is undoubtedly still the most widely used piece of educational technology and textbook publishers are still powerful influences on the curriculum. It was estimated in Texas that 75 percent of a child's classroom time and 90 percent of his homework time is spent using textbooks (Governor's Committee on Public Education, 1969).

Thus the publisher's control of the content of the textbook is virtual control over the curriculum.

But the power of the textbook publishers is a brittle sort of power that cannot stand up against serious opposition from any large segment of the population. Some publishers still put the unit on evolution in the center of the biology textbook so that the books destined for southern and western schools can readily be bound without those pages. Sections on "Negro history" were once added in the same way. Publishers cannot (or will not, which amounts to the same thing) stand against the demands of their customers. Nor can publishers spend millions of dollars developing materials for one course in the way the National Science Foundation has supported projects in the sciences and mathematics. Apparently, in spite of their potential power, publishers have not been able to operate as independent agents. Instead, they reflect the conflicting desires of their customers, i.e., the local schools and in some areas the state authorities.

Research is also needed on the relative efficacy in determining what is actually taught in classrooms of textbooks and various other factors such as teachers' guides, courses of study, and the teachers' own views. Most studies of the curriculum assume that what appears in the textbook or course of study is what is taught. But a few observational studies of science teaching (Gallagher, 1967; Smith, 1969; Kaiser, 1969) seem to show that teachers do not simply reflect the views of the curriculum writers.

Where there is state adoption, the state department of education seems to exercise considerable leverage. In Texas the State Commissioner nominates members to serve on the State Textbook Committee and must approve books recommended by the committee. Texas State Department specialists draw up the detailed criteria for the publishers' bids including the topics to be covered. The selected books are distributed at state expense to every schoolroom, but the same textbook must stay in service for six years. Districts who want to "stay on top of things" must do so at their own expense (Governor's Committee, 1969).

The U.S. government has become a very powerful influence on the curriculum in the past ten years. Because of the fragmented federal budgeting of monies for curriculum development it is not possible to determine exactly how much the government, mainly through the National Science Foundation and the Office of Education, has spent on curriculum development over the past ten years. This figure is very large, however, and dwarfs all previous curriculum development efforts by states, regions, localities, and private enterprise.

No one can forsee the path federal curriculum policy will take in even the next few years. Agencies of the federal government jumped from virtually no influence to a place of preeminence at one stroke when the National Defense Education Act was signed into law. President Nixon proposed the creation of a National Institute of Education. He also inaugurated a "right to read" campaign to encourage emphasis on reading in elementary and junior high schools. "Sesame Street," a nationally televised preschool program, has been produced under the auspices of the U.S. Office of Education. Until now, the federal government's influence has been a conservative one, educationally speaking; but the government's role has been an important one, and when the right circumstances arise we have every reason to believe that federal agencies will seize the initiative in curriculum matters.

Another set of powerful agents in curriculum making are the foundations. Over the past ten years they have generally seen their role as one of supplementing and balancing the efforts of the federal government. When the federal government was financing only projects in mathematics, science, and foreign languages, the foundations were financing projects in the arts and social sciences. The foundations have also been bolder in funding efforts in nonstandard courses including psychology, economics, and photography, among many others. All that is known of the policies of the foundations that have supported curriculum development over the past decade—chiefly the Ford, Rockefeller, Carnegie, and Kettering foundations—are their declarations. We have not been able to locate a single study or evaluation of the foundations' effects on curriculum.

Although the two major sources of funds for curriculum planning in this country are relatively new and therefore not fully dependable, there are steadier, if less copious, sources. Professional associations of scientists, engineers, and business and professional people have supported curriculum development efforts related to their professional interests. They will no doubt continue to do so as long as they can be convinced of the need for new curricula in their special field. Local school districts provide a modest amount of money for updating their schools' curriculum. We have no dependable estimates of the amount of money spent by individual school districts on curriculum but the figure must surely be quite small for individual districts. Occasionally regional or statewide curriculum development projects have been funded well enough and long enough to permit thorough substantial efforts. The state of New York through its Board of Regents has been outstanding in this respect. And, of course, private businesses (chiefly textbook publishers in the past, but increasingly amalgams of publishing and electronic firms) spend nobody knows how much for curriculum development. Curriculum development will likely be forced to rely chiefly on these traditional sources of money in the next decade, since the pressing problems of foreign involvement and noneducational domestic issues such as race relations, the environment, and poverty will leave at best a moderate priority for educational concerns unrelated to such issues.

But sources of money are not the only factors influencing the alternatives placed before the local decision maker. Sources of ideas and expertise are also crucial. The major source of ideas for curriculum change has always been the college or university. The last twenty years have seen an intensified reliance on college and university professors in the form of national curriculum commissions and university-based projects. In most cases the participation of professors has been as subject matter experts, e.g., scientists, mathematicians, or historians. But a few psychologists have been employed to advise projects on methods. Education faculty have not been heavily involved in projects.

University professors do not, of course, constitute anything like a unitary block of opinion on curriculum questions. In fact, they have been a major source of much needed diversity in the once seemingly stagnant curriculum of the American school.

If university faculty do not represent any organized body of opinion, their professional associations sometimes do, and when they do they can be extremely influential. The role of the American Association for the Advancement of Science and the American Institute for Biological Sciences in getting evolution into biology books over the strong objections of fundamentalist Christians (Grobman, 1969; Black, 1967), shows that these associations can be influential when they are united and determined. The American Mathematical Society sponsored the School Mathematics Study Group (SMSG) until the Sputnik-induced National Defense Education Act authorized the National Science Foundation to finance SMSG as an independent enterprise. As Turner (1964) described its activities, the American Council of Learned Societies was extremely influential in recent revisions of social studies curricula.

In addition to universities and professional associations, private firms harbor vital curriculum expertise. Publishers use their sales organizations to ferret out the likes and dislikes of the schoolpersons who buy their books and they "edit" the books with one eye on this information (Black, 1967). Strangely enough, this network of salespeople is the only reasonably dependable comprehensive mechanism for compiling the preferences and prejudices of local schools on curriculum matters. This part of the curriculum policymaking process badly needs careful study.

Twenty years ago the contributions of private firms to curriculum decisions were restricted to textbooks. But not anymore. IBM has bought SRA, Xerox has bought American Educational Publications, GE and Time have formed General Learning, RCA has bought Random House, and CBS has bought Holt, Rinehart and Winston. These firms can produce curriculum alternatives in the form of text materials, programmed sequences, films, software and hardware for use in computer-assisted instruction, and similar devices which have potentially powerful effects on the school curriculum, and which few other agencies have the resources or expertise to produce.

Finally, we cannot conclude this discussion of groups that generate curricular alternatives without considering professional educators themselves. Teachers, former teachers, supervisors, and administrators write textbooks and devise curriculum materials. Their ideas, published in professional journals and school district publications, constitute a constantly renewing pool of alternatives from which they and their colleagues can draw in making curriculum decisions. Frequently, however, teachers' contributions are specific practices rather than general principles. But teachers often produce the teachers' guides and courses of study that embody the details of district curriculum policy. Furthermore, teachers served on the staffs of the major curriculum development projects which have powerfully affected the public school curriculum in recent years.

Groups Demanding Curriculum Change   Most of the groups generating curricular alternatives are also important sources of demands for curriculum change. Foundations are concerned mainly with inducing certain kinds of changes in schools. They supply money to finance individuals willing to generate alternatives that show promise of encouraging these changes. The U.S. Office of Education has in recent years taken a more active stance in dispensing funds for research, development, demonstration, and dissemination. They stated that "the goal of these efforts is to generate alternatives to current educational practices that schools may adopt in whole or part as they see fit [U. S. Office of Education, 1969, p. i]." But they seem more and more to see their role as one of producing change, rather than simply making change possible. Some organizations demand curriculum changes but do not concern themselves with creating additional options. Rather, such groups support one of a number of existing competing alternatives. An example of this sort of organization is the Council for Basic Education (CBE). The CBE has lobbied consistently for greater emphasis on the fundamental intellectual disciplines.

Most large national organizations, e.g., the Chamber of Commerce, the National Association of Manufacturers, the John Birch Society, and the AFL-CIO, have attempted at one time or another to influence curriculum policy on particular nationwide issues. In fact, such a variety of powerful national interest groups can enter the arena on any given disputed question that it is probably desirable to think of two separate policy making processes—normal policy making and crisis policy making. . . .

In summary, when a school district faces the problem of putting together a course they have only three basic choices. The whole problem can be left to individual teachers; groups of teachers can make the plans and devise teaching materials for the whole school; or materials can be purchased. American public schools increasingly favor the last approach. Therefore the sources of these materials are, and will probably remain, important determinants of the curriculum. The sources we have identified are the projects financed by the federal government and private foundations, college and university faculties, professional associations, private businesses, and organizations of laypersons. But the fact of the matter is that any group with sufficient talent and resources can prepare curriculum materials and possibly start a trend that will sweep these other sources either aside or along.

Summary

This chapter on frame factors provides an overview of some of the forces that affect the schools' curriculum. The factors that are most influential vary according to time and place. In a community that holds strong traditions, such as favoring a given foreign language or a strong commitment to a fundamentalist religion, the factors that dominate curriculum decisions may be quite different from a community less influenced by tradition. As a culminating activity on frame factors you should select a curricular change that you might wish to advocate and then list the frame factors that bear upon your recommendation. Discuss your views with others and see how they respond to your analyses of the proposed change and the factors that may impede or enhance your proposal.

Styles of Curriculum Theorizing

Curriculum development has been a controversial subject throughout the history of schooling. This fact is not difficult to understand when it is realized that what is taught in the school shapes, in some manner, by hypothesis at least, not only the individual but society. Naturally, there will be disagreement about the content and method when we believe these values are at stake. Furthermore, the belief that personal relations generated in the schools and the classroom affect the student no less than the content has gained much support in recent years. This development has extended the range of curriculum issues. All these controversies and issues have encouraged the growth of differing points of view about what curriculum is and should be. Part II presents some of the major approaches to curriculum development and ways of theorizing about it.

Everyone remembers the story of the blind men and the elephant. One man felt its legs and said the elephant was a tree. Another felt its tail and called the elephant a rope. And after feeling its side, one said the elephant was a wall. Just as the blind men perceived the elephant differently so do we conceive objects differently. What we think about an object, either concrete or abstract, depends on the mental content we bring to it and how we perceive it. A blind man who knows nothing about ropes but is acquainted with gasoline hoses is likely to think he has felt a hose.

The influence of perspective on our thinking can be illustrated in several ways. It is well-known that the events of history can be approached from more than one angle. Consider the Protestant Revolution. We can interpret the revolt geographically. Using this approach, we can point out that the persons who led the revolt were in northern Europe and geographically were on the periphery of church control. The revolt leaders were far from Rome making communication difficult. This gave them as well as their followers a sense of religious independence.

We can also look at the same set of events from an economic standpoint. In this case, we would point out how the church in Rome economically drained the inhabitants of northern Europe. Their discontent with the church was rooted in what they perceived to be oppressive economic measures.

The Protestant Revolution can also be interpreted as a case of the great hero view of history; that the economic and geographic conditions had persisted for some time and would probably have persisted indefinitely had it not been for the appearance of a great character—Martin Luther. There are many other perspectives from which the Protestant revolt could be approached and interpreted and so it is with any historical event. What we think about past events, or the way we evaluate them, depends on our point of view. What has just been said about historical events will apply also to psychological, sociological, biological, and physical phenomena.

The belief that the human mind can approach any object or event from a universal perspective that includes and unifies all points of view is false. In the absence of a universal perspective, we search for ways to harmonize our various outlooks and enrich our interpretation and understanding of the phenomena we work with by viewing them from as many perspectives as possible. The organization of our knowledge of any object or event for the purpose of understanding and controlling it, and our behavior toward it, is what is here meant by the expression "style of theorizing."

Curriculum development entails such questions as these: What objectives of instruction are to be selected and how shall they be formulated? What content of instruction is to be identified and in what sequence is it to be arranged? Now, when we bring our concepts, our sense of what is worthwhile, and our modes of thinking to bear upon such questions as these and attempt to answer them, we are engaging in curriculum theorizing. Such thinking can be about the schools' program of formal instruction or about all the school factors that affect the students, formally or informally, depending upon how one perceives the curriculum.

Efforts to theorize about the school program in the broad sense have been declining in the last three or four decades. A notable effort to consider the curriculum in the broadest perspective was that of Caswell and Campbell in their conception of the curriculum as all the experiences pupils have while under the schools' direction. More recent curriculum theorizing has been less comprehensive.

For example, rebuilding school subjects to conform to the structure of the disciplines was confined to the schools' formal program of instruction. The recent reorganization of elementary school mathematics exemplifies an even more limited approach. It was based on the notion that this elementary subject should emphasize the understanding of mathematics as a discipline. This meant that the program should reflect the structure of mathematics and emphasize the basic concepts of mathematics such as set and number.

Some curriculum theorizing would reduce the curriculum to sets of tasks analyzed into elements for learning. Others would be less concerned with learning tasks than with the social and personal development of the student. Between these two extremes are at least two other modes of thinking about the curriculum, making four styles of curriculum theorizing: humanistic, discipline, analytic, and futuristic. While none of these styles is homogeneous, the components that comprise any one of them are similar enough to be grouped under a common title. The humanistic style, as will be seen, involves several ways to think about a curriculum for the individual's self-realization and welfare. Similarly, the discipline style embraces several conceptions of structure. And so it is with the other styles of curriculum theorizing.

Chapter **3**
The Humanistic Style

"This paper. 'Identity Crisis' with the poor grade—are you sure it's mine?"

Today's Education 63 (September–October 1974) 8.

Process-led Curriculum

1. Psychosocial Humanism
2. Classical Humanism
3. Scientific Humanism
4. Humanism: Critique of Its Three Faces
5. Can You Put It All Together?

Currently much is being said and written about humanistic education. The term "humanism" often captures the mind and leads the individual to accept ideas and to follow courses of action with little understanding. For this reason it is important to point out some of the brands of humanism that have prevailed historically and are now influencing our thoughts about the curriculum.

In general it can be said that humanism is any set of beliefs in which a person's well-being is paramount. It has had a long and varied career in our intellectual life, taking on different forms from time to time but always focusing on the well-being of the individual. Among its many forms the following are current in educational circles: psychosocial humanism, classical or traditional humanism, scientific humanism.

Psychosocial Humanism

Psychosocial humanism is the view that emphasizes the self as an achievement rather than a given. The realization of self, while never finished, is a supreme condition of well-being. It entails openness to, and trust in, experience and is to be achieved through freedom, self-expression, and creativity in both school and life affairs. Socially this notion of humanism emphasizes the extension of such ideals as love and kindness, which historically prevailed in face-to-face relationships, to complex social associations and ultimately to all human beings.

Classical or Traditional Humanism

A belief in a classical form of education, is usually expressed as a study of the humanities, as opposed to vocational education. This form of humanism is often referred to as traditional or classical humanism.

Scientific Humanism

Scientific humanism is the belief that the well-being of mankind can be served by extending our knowledge about people and nature and using it to improve social, moral, and material life.

Each of these views considers the welfare of mankind to be a primary concern. They differ in the way in which a person's well-being is defined, achieved, and safe-guarded. Consequently they have differing conceptions not only of the curriculum but also of the role of the teacher and of how the school should be organized and operated.

The roots of psychosocial and classical humanism are to be found in Greco-Roman society. Cicero is as good a spokesman as any for that period. He used the term "Humanitas" to mean the feelings and dispositions that should characterize society. From this general view emerged two meanings: first, the humane feelings that human beings should exhibit toward one another and the conduct toward others that is compatible with those feelings; and second, the cultivation of the mind through the study of language, literature, philosophy, and history. These two strands of humanism have assumed different forms from time to time. Presently the first of these meanings is uppermost in the minds of many educational theorists and practitioners. It has gained new interpretation and support from humanistic and clinical psychology and from existential philosophy. The second meaning dominated curriculum thought and the school program during the nineteenth century only to give way in considerable measure to scientific humanism in the twentieth century.

Psychosocial Humanism

The objectives of this type of humanism focus on the continuous growth of the self in specified directions. The self is to become ever more adequate, open, positive, and creative. To promote such growth the person must have an accurate self-view, accept it, and identify with others. These objectives require no specific knowledge from the subjects of instruction for their realization, but they do require knowledge appropriate to the individual's needs as he perceives them. In addition, their realization depends upon appropriate school conditions and teachers whose personalities enable them to accept their students as persons and to relate to them positively.

The school conditions essential to self-growth are set forth in the 1962 yearbook of the Association for Supervision and Curriculum Development. In this yearbook, four authorities—Earl C. Kelley, Carl R. Rogers, Abraham H. Maslow, and Arthur W. Combs—propose the basic concepts and principles of the psychosocial theory of humanistic schooling. The yearbook committee developed the educational implications of these concepts and principles. Its work is one of the best accounts of the curricular implications of this form of humanism. While the following excerpt gives only a brief part of the committee's deliberations, it presents some of the basic points of this form of humanistic schooling.

☐

For the self to be freed for growth, it must be accepted as it is currently structured. The atmosphere of acceptance can be created under the guidance of an accepting teacher. As students are accepted by the teacher as persons of dignity and worth, the individual moves toward acceptance of self, which is requisite to acceptance of others. And as peers accept each other, growth is further facilitated.

To accept a student, the teacher must accept his values and standards as a part of him, i.e., the teacher must be willing for him to hold these values. It does *not* mean that the teacher accepts the student's values and standards as his own. Combs, Kelly, and Rogers state that an individual is free to change his values only when he is free to hold them. When he is free to hold them he is not forced to defend them. When he feels that his values are *not* condemned or categorized as "bad," he can then allow them to be explored (explored, not judged) by himself and by others. Out of exploration can come change and the development of new values based upon facts and upon new ways of seeing or perceiving. This is the free atmosphere in which perceptions and behavior patterns are changed.

The Adequate Classroom Atmosphere Is Permissive

Permissiveness is often taken to mean freedom to create physical chaos, to upset or destroy property and the decorum of the classroom. Permissiveness, as used here, means the freedom to have ideas, beliefs, values—permission to be oneself and to pursue interests and curiosity in search for meaning in life. A recent advertisement sponsored by a large corporation which manufactures electronic equipment states that "for scientists to be creative and productive they must be free to follow their curiosity." It seems reasonable that children will be most productive when they are similarly allowed to follow their curiosity. This means teaching becomes an individual matter in which the curiosity of the student is considered in deciding what the subject matter will be. The teacher is a facilitating person who assists the immature person to find effective ways of getting the information he needs to satisfy his curiosity about the world in which he lives.

The adequate classroom, then, must be a facilitating environment. It is an

Association for Supervision and Curriculum Development, *Perceiving, Behaving, Becoming: A New Focus for Education*, Yearbook 1962 (Washington, D.C.: Association for Supervision and Curriculum Development, 1962), pp. 95–97, 130–33. Reprinted by permission of the publisher.

Footnotes have been renumbered consecutively throughout the chapter.

environment in which the student finds himself accepted with warmth and friendliness and in which he is helped through planned experiences to satisfy his need to know about himself and his world. It is a safe fortress from which he may venture into unknown and hitherto dangerous (to him) areas. It is an environment in which vigorous and healthy growth toward adequacy can be achieved.

Providing Accurate, Realistic Information

The adequate personality requires accurate, realistic information about himself and the world. He needs dependable data, correct facts, sure knowledge, and a broad perspective on which to base his behavior. Without such information he is not able to act efficiently, to make wise choices, to judge accurately, or to predict the results of his action. Indeed, information true to reality and not distorted by personal fears and anxieties is the only basis on which an individual can make a sensible adjustment. One cannot move from what he is not; one can only move effectively from the facts. Effective behavior can begin only from reality.

If, therefore, schools are to produce more adequate personalities, it is necessary to provide ways to help children face facts about themselves. This cannot be a mere telling operation. A child becomes informed about himself first as he has opportunities to interact with his environment. As young children react to one and all the stimuli which a rich school environment can provide—water play, squishy clay, finger paints, new sounds and melodies, ladders to climb, things to touch, smell and view—they are defining not only "what is out there" but "what I sense and feel and know." As children become older and more sophisticated, learning continues with opportunities to explore more deeply the satisfactions of music and art, dance, sports, tools, and models.

A child may learn further about who he is as he reacts to the experiences of others as if they were his own. Vicarious learning, important in its meaning for the individual, occurs as boys and girls become personally involved with books and the many other media—television, recordings, films, and pictures —which portray people and events in other places and at other times. Interaction with peers; the opportunity to be with friends; time to talk through experiences; extend indirect learnings about self. While such learning must be highly personal for each individual, the social setting of the school and the give and take of living with others are important if a child is to learn to group his experiences, to know that in these ways he is like others, in these ways he is his own unique self.

Much of what a child knows and feels about himself is learned through the reflected appraisals of others, a kind of mirror image. Such appraisal, however, must be honest; no sugar-coating, no false praise, no attempt to disguise the facts. The child who is secure in the knowledge that his teacher does trust him and is on his side can accept and build constructively upon the truth about his achievements and his needs, his strengths and weaknesses. Children deserve the truth. To know the truth is the only sure way they can touch bottom, assess where they are and know the progress they have made and have still to accomplish. This kind of confrontation with reality needs to pervade all aspects of the school situations.

Free Access to Information

As the adequate personality requires accurate and realistic information, so, too, does it require full and complete information. Indeed, there is no information a well-adjusted person ought not have about himself. Gaps in knowledge of self, like false information, can hinder acceptance. This raises a series of interesting questions about many school and student personnel practices. For example, for what purposes are test scores noted and facts filed in cumulative records? And for whose benefit? Is the information which is passed on to the next teacher, to the receiving school or to the prospective employer available also to the student? How can the facts, the school records, be shared with individuals who are the subjects of such extensive record keeping? Might not more of them be used to help children and young people in self-discovery?

Since acceptance and understanding of self are based upon complete and accurate knowledge, the school is responsible for making available to the individual all of the facts he needs to acquire that knowledge. But what facts does he need and how should they be provided? These are two questions to which the school must give thoughful consideration if the free access to the information it provides is to be something other than irresponsible telling.

Information Which Is Wanted

First, it seems to us, information which is made available to an individual at any level should be information which he wants. Wanting to know implies a need and a purpose for facts which have personal meanings. It may be a need which is expressed directly, as when a student seeks vocational counseling or help in choosing a particular program of study or the college to attend. All needs for information, however, are not expressed so directly or sought so openly as may be the case in vocational or college counseling. They may be conveyed only indirectly.

The child who sets too high standards for his performance or who plans in terms of unattainable goals may profit from help in understanding where he is at present in terms of strengths and weaknesses and what intermediate steps must be taken before he can achieve his goal. The boy or girl who depreciates his own ability, whose performance does not measure up to his capacity to learn, who is so often labeled the "underachiever," may need the evidence and the reassurance of new information about himself, information which says "he can." The desire for knowledge of self may be read in many facets of behavior —overdependence, fear of new learning activities, noncontribution, retreat from testing situations, fabrication, compensation, cheating, or the various defensive mechanisms. Each may indicate to the discerning teacher that this child needs help in self-appraisal. Whatever information is available or can be obtained from school or community resources should be provided.

Any information, including achievement and intelligence test ratings, which contributes to the accuracy of his view of self should be available to the student. Withholding records of performance, test results, inventories, or other data which can be made available means withholding information important to decision making.

This in not to imply that the school should distribute test scores and the like on a wholesale basis. We too often give students information about themselves that they do not either want or need. Indiscriminate distribution of facts about either ability or achievement may represent a threat to some children and serve only to block self-exploration and discovery. Schools need to make a clear distinction between free access and forced learning. Records need to be open, but the individual's freedom to use or not use those records must also be respected.

Classical Humanism

Classical humanism has a long history, its modern form stemming from the Renaissance. It emphasizes humanistic subjects and by thorough study of language it strives to discipline the mind in philosophy, logic, history, and literature. These studies contain knowledge that society has accumulated about itself. They are at once, it is claimed, the source of wisdom and the instruments through which reason is disciplined and passions and feelings are tamed. These studies dominated the curriculum in the last century. Scientific studies received only minor attention. As the sciences developed, proved their worth not only in industry but also in the professions and agriculture, the humanities began to take a secondary place in the curriculum. Today the tables have been turned. Scientific studies are now under attack while the humanities are being urged in the interest of promoting self-control, morality, and human decency.

This reversal of status can be attributed to social and intellectual factors. Science achievements in space, in explorations of matter, and in communication, not to mention advancements in biology, psychology, and medicine, have caused widespread apprehension about our society becoming so materialistic that it would lose its humane qualities. The increasing violent crime rate and the rapid change in the folkways have raised fears of social disintegration. Youth have broken with tradition in fundamental ways: many have lost their roots and appear to be adrift and searching for their identity. We must add to these the incessant pounding of the public mind by the media with one sensationalism after another and the likelihood of some terminal event, e.g., atomic destruction, new ice age. These create an acute fear for some impending catastrophe from which there is little hope to escape. These social and psychological conditions have extended the criticism of science that is seen as the root of the trouble and have raised anew the content of the curriculum issue: the humanities versus the sciences.

However, some of the humanities have retained their dominant position in the curriculum. Both history and literature are among the required subjects. And while no Greek and little Latin is studied in school today, modern language enjoys a large enrollment. Philosophy and logic, even at the college level, have been declining for at least a century. History and literature perhaps are studied with less rigor. Literature has become less and less classical. Today one is as likely to find students studying current works as the classics.

The teaching profession is becoming more concerned with moral and value education largely because of the breakdown of traditional values and moral principles coupled with the rising rate of individual and public misconduct. This development has led to an awakening interest in humanities. This is evident from the fact that some of those who are identified with psychosocial humanism have begun to call for a return to some of the traditional humanistic knowledge supplemented by contemporary sources.

Classical or traditional humanism identifies proper education with discipline of the reason attained by mastery of the great works that preserve society's insights and wisdom. The next passage states this view of the curriculum without equivocation. It is taken from a published paper that resulted from a research project at Kenyon College. The question addressed is: What constitutes political education in a free society? The part included here is concerned with only one aspect of the question while the paper in its entirety treats the importance of critical thinking and other elements of a curriculum in social education.

But in a free society, it is precisely literature, history, ideas, and ethical discussion which must be given the highest place in the educational schedule; for a free society places men and women and their dignity, their problems, their freedom, and their salvation in the place of highest importance in its scale of values. This in not all. The free society also draws a sharp line (or *should* draw a sharp line) between that which may be manipulated and conditioned and controlled—i.e., subhuman nature—and that which may only be educated, persuaded, and informed—i.e., human beings. Can there be any question that the very heart and soul of education in a free society must be the humanities and their satellite subjects, history, politics, geography?

When our citizens fail to learn at school the complex challenges of freedom, when they fail to acquire an inkling of the tragic probabilities just under the surface of their temporary comfortableness, there need be no surprise if they behave like scared children when the awful realities of life break in upon their pitiful dreamworld. It is possible to run away from reality for a time but not forever. The correct education for free people (and it is also the kindest education) is that which compels them to be realists from the outset, which makes them learn through their own experience and vicariously through the experience of others the qualities that enable people to be free.

Work and Models

How is education to fulfill this heavy responsibility? First and last, the answer is through hard work. Hard work is the unremitting demand made by life, especially by the free life. Yet hard work alone is not enough; it must be

Raymond English. "Political Education: The Urgent Problem," *Teachers College Record* 62, 6 (March 1961): 489–90. Reprinted by permission of the author and publisher.

directed to the right things, and the central thing at which the free person must
work is his own character. One cannot, however, work at one's own character
without guidance and models, which it is the business of the humanities and
social sciences to provide. It is not indoctrination to insist that children and
young people read those great works of creative or historical imagination in
which human beings are shown in situations of stress and temptation. In the
bad old days, children had to struggle with Livy, Virgil, Caesar, Cicero,
Xenophon, Homer, Thucydides, a bit of Plutarch, and the New Testament. If
they were lucky, they could relax with Macaulay, Burke, Milton, Johnson, and
Shakespeare. Nowadays, these are, in the exact sense of the phrase, closed
books.

Yet without the classics of western civilization it is almost impossible (except for the born saint or hero) to understand, let alone try to imitate, the
moral qualities on which our free societies were founded. Chivalry, fortitude,
temperance, self-sacrifice, love, faith, and hope are not learned instinctively;
nor is the ability to recognize and combat their opposites—lust, anger, greed,
cowardice, and the other deadly sins. The old fashioned liberal education in
the classics cannot now be restored, but there is surely a place for the intensive
study of works which would fill the mind with noble imaginings out of which
a realistic view of life and its problems could be formed freely by the individual
student. One can think of a whole list of works not beyond the capacity of a
wide range of able eleven to thirteen-year olds: *Huckleberry Finn, Captains
Courageous, The Jungle Books, Ivanhoe,* Tennyson's "Death of Arthur,"
"Lotus Eaters," and "The Last Fight of the Revenge," *Julius Caesar, Andro-
cles and the Lion, Pilgrim's Progress, Peter Simple, Henry Esmond, Great
Expectations,* St. Luke's Gospel. From fourteen to eighteen, a magnificent
vista opens: Shakespeare's plays, Boswell, *Paradise Lost,* Browning, Yeats,
Hopkins, Lovelace, The Odyssey, *The Brothers Karamazov, War and Peace,
Pickwick, Gulliver, The Apology,* parts of Thucydides, The Book of Job, *Can-
dide, Moby Dick, The Scarlet Letter, Don Quixote,* Plutarch, *Saint Joan,* and
dozens more.

After decades of spoon feeding alternated with absurd forcings of contemporary "psychological" novels upon our young people, these suggestions may
horrify the orthodox educationist. So much the worse for orthodox education.
It is wrong, and it is ruining not only the aesthetic taste but the ethical faculties
of our leadership. Unless the time is already too late, education must recover
the consciousness of its primary duty in a free society: to hand on the multiple
values of western civilization, the values which made possible the development
of the free, law-guided, constitutional states which are our proper pride.

Scientific Humanism

As noted above, some individuals claim that science is materialistic, that it
is concerned primarily with the physical and subhuman world, and that its
values are those that pertain to the work of the scientists as such rather than
to humanity. But defenders of science have believed that science is itself

humanistic. A hundred years ago when scientific subjects were being urged as significant curriculum content, Thomas Huxley advanced the notion that the sciences were not antihumanistic, as the opposition maintained, but on the contrary were closely identified with society's best interests. Furthermore, he did not see any conflict between the traditional humanities and the sciences. In his view each should be recognized as an essential ingredient in any justifiable program of education. This same view has been maintained by some of the leading humanistic and philosophical thinkers of this century. Among these is John Dewey who set forth the thesis that science is not opposed to literature, philosophy, or history but instead is actually complementary to these disciplines. In *Democracy and Education* he says:

John Dewey
Scientific humanist
a Classical humanist

☐

 . . . There exists an educational tradition which opposes science to literature and history in the curriculum. The quarrel between the representatives of the two interests is easily explicable historically. Literature and language and a literary philosophy were entrenched in all higher institutions of learning before experimental science came into being. The latter had naturally to win its way. No fortified and protected interest readily surrenders any monopoly it may possess. But the assumption, from whichever side, that language and literary products are exclusively humanistic in quality, and that science is purely physical in import, is a false notion which tends to cripple the educational use of both studies. Human life does not occur in a vacuum, nor is nature a mere stage setting for the enactment of its drama. Human life is bound up in the processes of nature; career, for success or defeat, depend upon the way in which nature enters them. Man's power of deliberate control of his own affairs depends upon ability to direct natural energies to use: an ability which is in turn dependent upon insight into nature's processes. Whatever natural science may be for the specialist, for educational purposes it is knowledge of the conditions of human action. To be aware of the medium in which social intercourse goes on, and of the means and obstacles to its progressive development is to be in command of a knowledge which is thoroughly humanistic in quality. One who is ignorant of the history of science is ignorant of the struggles by which society has passed from routine and caprice, from superstitious subjection to nature, from efforts to use it magically, to intellectual self-possession. That science may be taught as a set of formal and technical exercises is only too true. This happens whenever information about the world is made an end in itself. The failure of such instruction to procure culture is not, however, evidence of the antithesis of natural knowledge to humanistic concern, but evidence of a wrong educational attitude.
 Dislike to employ scientific knowledge as it functions in people's occupations is itself a survival of an aristocratic culture. The notion that "applied"

knowledge is somehow less worthy than "pure" knowledge, was natural to a society in which all useful work was performed by slaves and serfs, and in which industry was controlled by the models set by custom rather than by intelligence. Science, or the highest knowing, was then identified with pure theorizing, apart from all application in the uses of life; and knowledge relating to useful arts suffered the stigma attaching to the classes who engaged in them. The idea of science thus generated persisted after science had itself adopted the appliances of the arts, using them for the production of knowledge, and after the rise of democracy. Taking theory just as theory, however, that which concerns humanity is of more significance for society than that which concerns a merely physical world. In adopting the criterion of knowledge laid down by a literary culture, aloof from the practical needs of many, the educational advocates of scientific education put themselves at a strategic disadvantage. So far as they adopt the idea of science appropriate to its experimental method and to the movements of a democratic and industrial society, they have no difficulty in showing that natural science is more humanistic than an alleged humanism which bases its educational schemes upon the specialized interests of a leisure class.

For, as we have already stated, humanistic studies when set in opposition to study of nature are hampered. They tend to reduce themselves to exclusively literary and linguistic studies, which in turn tend to shrink to "the classics," to languages no longer spoken. For modern languages may evidently be put to use, and hence fall under the ban. It would be hard to find anything in history more ironical than the educational practices which have identified the "humanities" exclusively with a knowledge of Greek and Latin. Greek and Roman art and institutions made such important contributions to our civilization that there should always be the amplest opportunities for making their acquaintance. But to regard them as *par excellence* the humane studies involves a deliberate neglect of the possibilities of the subject matter which is accessible in education to the masses and tends to cultivate a narrow snobbery: that of a learned class whose insignia are the accidents of exclusive opportunity. Knowledge is humanistic in quality not because it is *about* human products in the past, but because of what it *does* in liberating human intelligence and human sympathy. Any subject matter which accomplishes this result is humane, and any subject matter which does not accomplish it is not even educational.

Humanism: Critique of Its Three Faces

The different emphases in humanistic education are the subject of the following selection by William Bridges. He considers the three humanistic orientations toward schooling presented in the preceding pages, and presents one of the most constructive and strong critiques of these orientations.

The humanistic protests are indeed valid, but now is the time to explore what we humanists would do if we had a really free hand.

This exploration is complicated by the apparent multiplicity of images presented by the conglomeration of ideas and techniques called "humanistic education." In part, this multiplicity may be the product of careless thinking, and it is certainly due partly to the inherent individual-centeredness of contemporary humanism. But it is also, and to an extent not widely enough appreciated, due to the several different angles from which one may be viewing the subject. For humanistic education presents distinctly different pictures of itself to one who is concerned with the classroom milieu and to another whose concern is with the learner as a whole person; and both of these observers will see something different from the person who approaches humanistic education from the perspective of subject matter. It is only on the basis of an understanding of these different perspectives that we can save ourselves from the kind of confusion that results when "humanistic" becomes simply an honorific term.

Let me begin by summarizing these perspectives quickly.

Classroom milieu. Here the emphasis falls on giving the learner the freedom to learn what he needs to know, and to do that in his own way. This concern leads to a focus on "unstructured" situations: open classrooms, flexible time schedules, free choice of subject. The teacher's role in this learning pattern is that of a facilitator or resource person rather than a teacher in the conventional sense of the word.[1] *= Student-centred learning*

The learner as a person Here the main concern is for ways in which the traditional cognitive approach to learning (acquiring information about things) can be reintegrated with the other ways in which a person apprehends his situation. These ways include his feelings about what he learns, his intuitive reactions to it, the ways in which it fits into his purposes in life. As "unstructuredness" is central to the first perspective on humanistic education, here we find terms like "affective" or "psychological" or "confluent" education dominating the discussion.[2] *Is this cognitive development?*

William Bridges, "The Three Faces of Humanistic Education," *Liberal Education* 59 (October 1973): 325–35. Reprinted by permission of publisher.

[1]Most writing on educational reform these days has some emphasis on destructuring the classroom. Two books that focus on that process are Carl R. Rogers, *Freedom To Learn* (Columbus, Ohio: Charles Merrill, 1969) and Herbert Kohl, *The Open Classroom* (New York: Random House, 1970).

[2]The theoretical aspects of this perspective are explored in Richard M. Jones, *Fantasy and Feeling in Education* (New York: Harper & Row, 1968), while more practical material is presented in George I. Brown, *Human Teaching for Human Learning* (New York: Viking, 1971) and Harold C. Lyon, *Learning to Feel, Feeling to Learn* (Columbus, Ohio: Charles Merrill, 1971).

The subject matter.   As the needs of the total person are taken into account, it becomes clear that the traditional subject matters are simply bodies of information with varying degrees of significance for the person's situation. If history or literature or political science were to be defined by the learner's journey rather than by the map of the area, then it would look quite different.[3]

Let us look at these perspectives, in some detail, one at a time.

Carl Rogers' *Freedom to Learn* is an effective presentation of the argument for unstructured learning situations. Rogers begins by pointing out that significant, as opposed to rote, learning starts with the learner's need to know, and that this need is part of *his* awareness, not the teacher's. It leads to a kind of self-sustained activity in which the payoff is the learner's satisfaction, rather than the external system of rewards and punishments that characterize the grading system and the system of credits and degrees.

It is undeniable that for most of us the significant learning has taken place in this way. We have all uncovered new interests in the process of living or new skills that our situations call upon us to master. That natural process by which we learned what we wanted to know is a model for this aspect of humanistic education. Anyone who is concerned with this aspect will try to organize a classroom or a school as a setting for this kind of self-motivated activity, and he will regard traditional forms of teaching and classroom procedure as intrusive and inhibiting.

Like any view from a single perspective, this one is limited and (if that fact is not acknowledged) limiting. For one thing, it presumes the learner's grasp of his own needs-to-know, when in fact a great many students in our classrooms not only do not wish to be there but are quite alienated from themselves and from ready access to their own needs. Many of these students, when placed in an open classroom and surrounded by free time and no demands, become frightened. It is true enough that in that situation they might at least learn that they don't know what they want and that freedom frightens them. But behind that statement lies a seldom-stated but ever-present condescension toward—and sometimes a rejection of—those sorry creatures who "need structure." (Such people occupy, I believe, one of the lower levels of the humanistic inferno.) Their hang-up excuses the teacher from further concern about them: "It's *their* responsibility," he says, turning away. "I told them at the beginning of the course that I wasn't going to do it for them."[4]

---

[3]There is not yet any comprehensive survey of this dimension of humanistic education comparable to what has been written about the other two. Rather there are some suggestive, if often sketchy, writings about humanistically re-oriented content in particular disciplines. See, for example, David Holbrook, *English for Maturity* (New York: Cambridge University Press, 1967), Staughton Lynd's chapter on history in Theodore Roszak's *The Dissenting Academy* (New York: Random House, 1968), the material coming out of the Earth Science Education Program (Boulder, Colorado, and the selections on sociology in John F. Glass and John R. Staude, eds., *Humanistic Society* (Pacific Palisades, California: Goodyear Publishing Co., 1972).

[4]For a more extended critique of this misuse of the idea of freedom in the classroom, see my article, "Thoughts on Humanistic Education, or Is Teaching a Dirty Word?" in the Spring 1973 issue of. *The Journal of Humanistic Psychology.*

Much of the difficulty with the conduct of an unstructured classroom or course comes from an incomplete embodiment of the model on which it is based. In that model, you or I discovered what we needed to know and then went out and found the resources to help us learn. Those resources usually turn out to have been highly structured: a book, a lecture, a film on the subject, or a lesson from an expert. From my own experience in the past couple of years —I wanted to learn how to construct a compost pile and I bought a book on the subject; I wanted to know how to prune an apple tree and I asked a friend to show me; I wanted to learn to make pottery and I enrolled in a course on the subject. In each of these cases, the learning experience itself was highly structured: *it was the context of choice that was unstructured.* ~Aims are unstructured~

If we are going to adapt this significant learning model to institutional education, we must be clear that it is within the institution (rather than within the particular classroom) that freedom from structure is needed, so that people can gain access to whatever resources their needs demand. These resources, once again, will tend to be structured—though they will most certainly not consist mainly of "courses" on traditional subjects. They will consist of resources in a broader sense, a matter that we shall discuss later in the context of subject matter.

This important distinction between structured resources and unstructured situations, however, leaves unanswered, the difficulty posed by the presence of large numbers of students who do not yet know what they need or want to learn. Our institutions desperately need better ways of helping these people to explore themselves. This need is not at all the same as the widely provided opportunity to explore new and potentially relevant subject matters. For it is less an unfamiliarity with the approaches to knowledge than a real estrangement from their own needs and longings that leaves these students unable to make the basic connections with the learning process that personally significant learning demands.

The solution of this problem goes far beyond ordinary curricular answers, like introductory courses (no matter how "relevant") and general education requirements. It also goes beyond what is usually meant by "advising," but that is not to say that it goes beyond the resources of those who ordinarily do the advising. What such people need is the kind of training which is now being given to lay counselors—a training which does not aim to rescue people from mental illness but which deepens the person's skill in helping another person to listen to himself more sensitively. The kind of institution that could grow out of this dual commitment to help the person discover his own deepest needs-to-know and then to provide him with ready access to a wide variety of resources—this is a subject that goes far beyond the scope of the present discussion. Here our concern is with the general issue of structure and of its place in the institution and the learning situations that it provides.

~the learner as a person~ In turning from the first to the second perspective on humanistic education, to the concern for the learner as a whole person, we find again an important truth that can be very limiting if it is misapprehended. This truth concerns the debilitating effects of ingesting large quantities of information which have little connection with any presently experienced need to know. As we know from our own experience and from a flood of writings, most children learn very early that feelings, fantasies, wild but fascinating ideas, personal interests, and even sensory data are regarded as distractions from the main business of *learning* things. Through the years, the average student learns to trim back the perimeter of his awareness when he is in the classroom, so that he can deal successfully (that is, impersonally) with what he is given to learn.

Insofar as affective or confluent education refers to a sensitivity within the teacher to the noncognitive aspects of the learner's situation, as well as to some courage and skill in dealing with them, no one can argue. And equally important is the teacher's function as a model of integrated feeling and thinking, a model of authentic personal presence. But the affective dimension of humanistic education customarily means more—and, ironically, less—than these things. To many people this aspect of humanistic education is synonymous with the "exercises" that have been developed from Gestalt therapy, sensitivity training, psychosynthesis and the other strategies within the human potential movement.

These exercises tend to fall into four purpose-related categories, although teachers often use them without particular purposes in mind. First, there are exercises designed to facilitate interpersonal communication and to break down the isolation that characterizes the early stages of any class. Second, there are awareness- or sensitivity-training techniques, which are often felt to have their own justification, although they are also sometimes used as preliminaries or corollaries to something else. Third, there are therapeutically-oriented techniques developed by the various schools of therapy, self-exploration and conflict resolution. These exercises also are sometimes used for their own sake, but they are particularly used in clarifying or enhancing the intra- and interpersonal processes that are likely to occur in a learning situation. Finally, there are techniques of all sorts that are used to build a situation in fact or fantasy that corresponds to something that is being studied in more abstract form—techniques for making real conceptual or symbolic material.

There are times in any classroom when each of these tactics is appropriate and valuable. Traditionally-trained teachers almost always underestimate the importance of letting students locate themselves within the interpersonal matrix of a class, as well as the importance of bringing up to awareness the personal and interpersonal aspects of the learning process when they threaten to disrupt it. And, being those people who coped best with the informational and impersonal biases of the educational system, most teachers underestimate the students' needs to make noncognitive connections with what they are learning.

These things are so important, and in many circles so unacknowledged, that it is tempting to say nothing more for fear that any further comment will be taken as a qualification of these statements. But there *are* additional things to say, and even at the risk of giving comfort to the enemy, they must be said.

One of them is that the need for these exercises must emerge from the situation itself, not from the students' or the teacher's desire to do something groovy this morning. And it is sensitivity and creativity rather than a bag of tricks that enables the teacher to meet such a need squarely. To present an exciting exercise from last weekend's wonderful workshop (or a recent article) on humanistic education is a mechanical tactic that is almost sure to violate the nature of the actual situation and surely violates the whole notion of humanistic education.

Another thing that must be said about such techniques is that they are relatively unnecessary when people are engaged in learning what they really want and need to know. In such cases, the whole person (his feelings and purposes as well as his thought) is already present.[5]

Ironically, a good many teachers who trade heavily on these kinds of exercises are also the ones who profess to run "unstructured" classes and to avoid the traditional "authoritarian" teaching style. The irony is that such exercises violate the concept of unstructuredness and require a strong position of authority from the teacher. Asking people to pair up for a blind walk is, after all, just as prescriptive as asking them to read chapter thirteen for tomorrow.[6] In addition, these exercises make the student dependent on the leader for the positive experience that they provide. Tony Athos, of the Harvard Business School, has put the problem well by saying that he feels that he has failed a student if, several years after graduation, the student tells him warmly what great experiences his class provided and how nothing since then has been so meaningful. Most of us are delighted with such reports, but as Athos points out, it means that the student has not been able to internalize the ways of discovering deeply meaningful experiences in his own life.

In many ways, much that is done in the name of affective learning methods perpetuates the affective-cognitive split just as surely as pedantic information mongering does. Part of the difficulty comes from the situation noted earlier, wherein the classroom takes on the task that really belongs to the institution. The same students who do not know what they want to learn are the ones who suffer from the cognitive-affective dissociation. If they can discover deep and genuine interests within their lives, they can enter learning situations as whole persons who relatively seldom need special ways of engaging the noncognitive aspects of their awareness.

More often to the point than techniques for affective teaching are techniques for letting the student express and record the noncognitive relations to the material that he discovers in himself. Examinations are useless for this purpose, and formal papers have serious drawbacks. What is needed are better vehicles for recording the process in which a subject discloses the world within

[5]Humanistic educators and group leaders often overlook this fact and launch enthusiastically into some cunning tactic to combat non-existent disinterest. Perhaps you have gone to "An Evening with X," one of those chances to hear a leading Humanist tell you what is on his mind these days. You have come for just that—to hear what he is thinking—and he starts you off with warm-ups to meet one another and try to get you *really present.* Then, remembering to be unstructured, he asks you what you want to hear (Hell, you came to hear *him,* right?) and says pious things about how no one can really teach anyone anything. Pretty soon, the man you came to hear is playing the neutral role of facilitator in a lot of audience interaction.

[6]The identification of humanistic teaching with the role of facilitator and the avoidance of traditional and formal teaching strategies comes from a failure to see that humanistic education really draws on two traditions. The one comes from Rogerian traditions in psychology, traditions that emphasize nondirective help. The other comes from the much older spiritual disciplines in which the master prescribes tasks for the novices, tasks which nudge or draw or trap the novice's mind into some new way of seeing things. For a discussion of the two traditions, see my aforementioned article, "Thoughts on Humanistic Education."

and around him, as well as what it is more generally and impersonally said to "mean."

Journals are an increasingly common vehicle for conveying this kind of personal learning, although many teachers do not spend enough time helping the student to learn how a journal can be used, with the result that too many mundane diaries and coy confessionals are handed in. In addition to some form of journal, many students profit from being able to express their learnings in nonverbal form. This question of the most appropriate kinds of student work is a whole subject in itself, and so I must leave it here with only the statement that a very important part of the humanistic endeavor in education is developing new ways to record the interface between the learner and the subject.

That brings us to the third aspect of humanistic education, that view of the topic gained from the perspective of subject matter. To begin with, there is a beguiling argument in humanistic circles that the problem of subject matter really doesn't exist, because subject matter itself is all part of the *maya* of a decrepit system. The point of education (so runs this argument) is deepened sensitivity, heightened awareness and enhanced self-expressiveness. If that is the case, then whatever we are purporting to teach is only a vehicle toward those goals. But then, one discovers, history and biology and economics are mighty cumbersome vehicles compared to some kind of quasi-therapeutic group experience.

Something like this reasoning has led an increasing number of teachers to abandon any but the most tenuous connections with the subject matter that they are supposedly teaching. To some of its critics, not too surprisingly, humanistic education refers to classes that focus on nothing but on their own process, just as to other critics it refers to classes which are totally unstructured or ones composed of blind walks, fantasy trips, nonverbal communication exercises, and Gestalt work with an empty chair.

Some kind of group experience designed to promote self-exploration is, as I have already said, the only way of dealing with certain problems presented by today's students. But while it is a matter of the greatest importance to develop ways of providing such group experience readily, it is also important to articulate the relation of that experience to the rest of the student's education. It supplements the other kind of learning, rather than replacing it; and the person who is already clear about what he wants to learn will rightly be frustrated if he discovers that what purported to be piano lessons or a class in financial management turns out to be simply a group experience.

From this perspective, humanistic education presumes a transformation of subject matter rather than its abandonment. There are a number of ways in which the humanistic outlook serves to cast traditional disciplines and fields of study in a new light—each of which may be more or less significant for a given educational venture.

To begin with, humanistic psychology has developed a distinctive image of the person, one that emphasizes his choicefulness, his creativity, and his drive toward actualization. Many of the disciplines have been evolved from a human image that is far more mechanical and deterministic. The difference that a new image of the person can play in human affairs is evident in many of the contemporary reform movements, which are carried forward by individuals who refuse (in spite of social theory and common assumption) to act powerless. Acting as free agents, they have found their faith in their own power to be a self-fulfilling prophecy. One of the issues raised by their careers is what part the social and behavioral sciences may be playing in perpetuating the *status quo* by perpetuating a world view in which the person is an object in all his relations—in which the experience of being a subject is lacking. Beginnings are being made here, but we still have far too little idea of what political science or economics or sociology would be if it were recast in a humanistic mold.

The subject matter would also be changed significantly if teachers recovered a more vital and generous sense of the ways in which we can *know*. Too often this question is reduced to "the question of knowledge" (a thing, not a process), and learning becomes simply the methods by which we collect and arrange information. In these terms, a given field of study is a patterned collection of information.

To see how all of this would change in response to a new approach, one should read a book like Gordon's *The Metaphorical Way of Learning and Knowing*.[7] There, various fields of study including the natural sciences are presented as they would meet the learner if he approached them not from the detached perspective of the uninvolved observer (who, Heisenberg told us decades ago, *is* involved) but from the inside, as it were. Tracing out unsuspected relations through the techniques of analogy and "compressed conflict," and seeing the situation anew by identifying with some element in it, provides the learner with a radically different avenue toward knowledge. To accept the idea that one can come to a state of solid knowledge by imagining what a benzene molecule or the electoral college "feels like" may be a difficult thing, but it is too important an idea to dismiss lightly.

And finally, there is the basic transformation that occurs whenever the learner's needs and the learning process are allowed to define the subject matter. History, in such a view, might be seen as the ever-changing relations of a person to *his* past, instead of as "the important events and forces of *the* past." The person's exploration of this relation with the past will quickly move beyond any of the customary perimeters of a history course—boundaries which are both too broad and too narrow to be useful to the person who has found a significant path of his own to follow. Such a person will find much that a course includes irrelevant to his purpose, while he also finds himself having to move out more widely into areas further afield: the social forces at work in his own community, the national events in some key period in the past, analogous event patterns in a bygone civilization, and the chronology of his own family history.

It may be objected here that I am talking about a *project,* not a course in history, and that such a project could be undertaken within the framework of an intelligently constructed course. To some extent that would be possible, but I am also suggesting that the whole *idea of a course* ought to be questioned.

---

[7]William J. Gordon, *The Metaphorical Way of Learning and Knowing* (Cambridge, Mass.: Synectics Education System, 1973). This book is an outgrowth of Gordon's earlier book, *Synectics.* Inquiries on synectics should be made to Synectics Education System, 1212 Brattle Street, Cambridge, Mass. 02138.

Nowhere else has the mechanization of our culture so imbedded itself in the educational process as in this idea of standardized packages (duly marked as to academic "weight") of processed content. As far as I know, nothing ever conceived by a person's mind naturally takes up three fifty-minute sessions weekly for fifteen weeks. Some things are best dealt with in a thirty-minute lesson every day for a week; other things need to be said or shown only once; still others need an intensive period of concentrated time, a weekend or a week, with no other distractions; and still other things take nearly all of a person's time for several years. The idea of a *course* makes the package take precedence over the substance, distorting the latter, and making it difficult to imagine what a really comprehensive array of educational resources might include.

The very least that can be said is that when the person's need is allowed to shape the substance, then any subject matter is transformed. Literature ceases to be a special branch of history ("The Jacobean writers were reacting against the earlier optimism of. . . .") and justifies itself as a deep, rich experience in its own right in the present. It is one of the great traditional avenues toward the disclosure and clarification of a person's relation to his world. Other branches of the humanities do likewise.

The ways in which each of the traditional disciplines would look to the traveler instead of the cartographer must be suggested by people who know those disciplines intimately. My generalizations are too likely to sound naive, so I shall stop making them. But I do want to repeat that the idea that the familiar disciplines are meaningless bits of the past is in no way a premise of humanistic education.

Where does all this leave an actual teacher in this land and this moment of time? In most cases, it leaves him in a bad way, for it leaves him trying to do in his classroom what the institution as a whole ought to be doing. It forces him to be a resource clearinghouse for those whose aims are clear and a setting for self-exploration for those whose aims are undefined. It forces him to convert whatever he has to offer to both groups into course units of a predetermined weight and length.

Yet these matters that we have been discussing may clarify that teacher's situation as well, and may remove some of the false dilemmas that complicate it unnecessarily. They may do so by distinguishing between structures that should be abandoned because they are a substitute for personal choice and those that should be developed because they serve a goal-related purpose. They may do so by distinguishing between the ends and the means of affective education and by exploring the relation of subject matter to personally significant learning. And finally, they may do so by showing that behind the multiple faces of this entity is something solid and coherent.

Can You Put It All Together?

The story presented in the Part II opening can be translated into education language. The elephant is humanism and you have seen three different parts. Can you put these parts together so that you have a unified conception of the humanistic approach to curriculum development?

Suppose we begin by considering the question of what kind of human being is projected in each of the three conceptions of humanism—psychosocial, scientific, and traditional. Does each approach aim at the same kind of human being? If they do, try to state the essential characteristics of the humanistic person.

Now consider the question of how this humanistic person is developed. Is there a content so essential to the person's development that it must be required? How does Bridges answer the question? How does the psychosocial humanist answer it? What is Dewey's answer? What part of the psychosocial answer, if any, would be rejected by Bridges? By Dewey? What part of the answer by the traditional humanist would be rejected by these authorities? By the psychosocial advocates? You should be able to formulate a synthesis of these views of humanism if you consider carefully the foregoing questions.

Chapter **4**

The Discipline Style

"Wars, population explosion, pollution, and they still haven't figured out how many angels can dance on the head of a pin."

Phi Delta Kappan 56. 3 (November 1974): 196.

Content-led Curriculum.

1. Improvement of the Disciplines
2. Justification of the Disciplines
3. Bruner's Concept of Structure
4. An Assessment of the Discipline Approach
5. Summary

Discipline style is perhaps the oldest way to think about the curriculum. For ages the curriculum, at least above the elementary level, has consisted of such elements as geometry, literature, and languages. Today one finds a multiplicity of subjects, especially at the high school and college levels.

Improvement of the Disciplines

The first attempt to improve the curriculum in this century involved researching the usefulness of the content of history, arithmetic, spelling, grammar, and geography. As a result of this research, infrequently used content was replaced by more useful knowledge. For example, words seldom used were eliminated from spelling books and such measurement information as the dimension of a cord of wood, feet in a fathom, and units of troy weight were removed from arithmetic texts. The most commonly used dates, personages, and events were emphasized in history texts. Less useful geographical information was replaced by more useful facts and concepts.

Despite these changes, most of which occurred from 1900 through 1930, criticisms of the subject curriculum increased. People alleged that the subjects were not suited to instruction because they were logically organized while learning was psychological and proceeded by a different order. People believed the studies were abstract and unrelated to the concrete realities of daily activities and to the interests of students. Also, people felt that the studies fragmented knowledge, dividing it into compartments so that neither students nor teachers could see the interrelated character of knowledge. A number of alternative curriculum patterns were proposed and tried out. Among these were the activity curriculum (with slight modification now called the open curriculum), based primarily on child interest and the doctrine that one activity leads to another and that the justification of the ongoing series of activities is that education is its own end. Another alternative was the core curriculum, based, at least in one of its forms, on the notion that students should understand the social functions by which societies maintain and advance themselves.

While these alternatives affected some schools and left a residue of ideas and practices, the subject curriculum, especially at the junior and senior high school levels, continued to dominate the school program. In the early 1950s the subject curriculum shifted emphases and gained new support. This new orientation, first suggested by Max Bebberman, was in mathematics. Bebberman introduced the fundamental concepts of mathematics at both the secondary and the elementary level based on the theory that students would not only understand mathematics as a discipline but would become more interested because the subject would challenge their intelligence and save them from the monotony of meaningless exercises.

In the late 1950s came the great scare: the Russians' success in space! Immediately schools were blamed for inferiority in space research and technology. It was claimed that the schools had practiced soft pedagogy, pampered children, and flouted the subject curriculum. Partly to rectify these alleged abuses and partly to inject a new content into the subject curriculum the academic community—scientists, mathematicians, psychologists, and others—began a movement to reconstruct the "basic" subjects that now were called the "disciplines."

During the 1960s, with financial support from the National Science Foundation and a number of private foundations, representatives from the universities revamped curricula—physics, chemistry, biology, mathematics, and social studies. Teaching the basic concepts, the structure, and the modes of thought of the disciplines were emphasized.

During these years the teaching profession was concerned with such questions as What is a discipline? What are concepts and how does one tell which ones are basic? What is meant by the "structure of the disciplines"? Is inductive teaching more effective than didactic instruction? These questions persist because they have not been unequivocally answered. The first three are curriculum questions. The nature of the disciplines, their structure, and justification as curriculum components will be treated in the following pages. Concepts will be considered in a later chapter.

These questions were raised at a conference at Woods Hole, Massachusetts; a "report" of which was issued as *The Process of Education* by Jerome Bruner. Following the Woods Hole Conference a large number of papers on the structure of the disciplines were published. These papers did little to clarify the meaning of either "discipline" or "structure."

According to one definition, a discipline is a body of knowledge selected and organized for instruction. In this sense, "discipline" is synonymous with "subject," "study," or "course" as these are understood in school par-lance. According to another definition discipline is a branch of knowledge. Discipline is also used to mean training to develop the mental and moral character. Then, too, there is punitive discipline, and also we sometimes speak of the discipline of self-control. All of these uses of the term, except the first two, can be ruled out for it is clear from the discourse on the disciplines that the reference is either to a branch of knowledge or to a body of knowledge selected and organized for instruction.

Neither of these two definitions, however, expand our understanding. What do they mean? Consider physics. Is it a branch of knowledge? If so, what about mechanics, optics, thermodynamics, electricity? These are branches of physics. If we grant that physics is a branch of knowledge and hence a discipline, what shall we say about a branch of physics? Is a branch of a discipline to be counted as a discipline? Let us mention some newcom-ers. Is library science a branch of knowledge? Education? Journalism? Are they to be counted among the disciplines?

If the criterion of a discipline is "knowledge selected and organized for instruction," how are instructional modules and units to be classified? Are they disciplines? Is a course in beginning physics to be counted as a discipline on a par with a course in elementary school social studies?

Finally, what justification can be given for a curriculum made up of disci-plines however defined?

Justification of the Disciplines   *Knowledge & Understanding?*

The previously cited are considered by Philip H. Phenix in the following passage. This is one of the most insightful justifications for a discipline curriculum to be found in the literature.

☐

I.

My thesis, briefly, is that *all* curriculum content should be drawn from the disciplines, or, to put it another way, that *only* knowledge contained in the disciplines is appropriate to the curriculum.

Exposition of this position requires first that we consider what is meant by a "discipline." The word "discipline" is derived from the Latin word *dis-cipulus,* which means a disciple, that is, originally, one who receives instruc-tion from another. *Discipulus* in turn stems from the verb *discere,* to learn. Etymologically, then, a discipline may be construed as knowledge the special property of which is its appropriateness for teaching and its availability for learning. A discipline is knowledge organized for instruction.

Phillip H. Phenix, "The Uses of the Disciplines as Curriculum Content," *The Educational Forum* (March 1962):273–80. Reprinted by permission of the publisher.

Footnotes have been renumbered consecutively throughout the chapter.

Basic to my theme is this affirmation: the distinguishing mark of any discipline is that the knowledge which comprises it is instructive—that it is peculiarly suited for teaching and learning. Implicit in this assertion is the recognition that there are kinds of knowledge which are not found within a discipline. Such nondisciplined knowledge is unsuitable for teaching and learning. It is not instructive. Given this understanding of what a discipline is, it follows at once that all teaching should be disciplined, that it is undesirable to have any instruction in matters which fall beyond the disciplines. This means that psychological needs, social problems, and any of a variety of patterns of material based on other than discipline content are not appropriate to the determination of what is taught—though obviously such nondisciplinary considerations *are* essential to decision about the *distribution* of discipline knowledge within the curriculum as a whole.

I hardly need to remind you that the position here taken is quite at odds with the one taken by many people both in the field of education and in the several disciplines. The common assumption of these people is that the disciplines are in the realm of pure knowledge—of specialized professional scholarship and research—and that the ordinary education is quite a different sort of enterprise. The disciplines have a life of their own, it is held, and knowledge in them is not directly available for the purposes of instruction, but to be suitable for education must be translated and transformed so as to become useful and meaningful to ordinary learners. Thus, the argument goes, for the curriculum we should draw upon life situations, problems, projects, and the like, for the primary *content* of instruction, using the knowledge supplied by the disciplines as auxiliary material to be employed as required by the basic instructional process. The person is supposed to learn primarily from experience as it comes naturally and not as it is artificially conceptualized and organized in the academic fields.

Correspondingly, under this customary view, there are two disparate realms of method: there are methods of professional scholarship and research, and there are quite different methods of instruction. There is a specialized logic of the disciplines and there is a largely unrelated psycho-logic of teaching and learning. From this division arises the well-known bifurcation between the academic scholars and the professional educators. The former pride themselves on their erudition and despise or neglect pedagogy, while the latter busily pursue the problems of teaching and learning, often with little understanding or concern for the standards of rigorous scholarship.

This common dualism is destructive both to scholarship and to education. It presupposes a concept of the academic disciplines which has no relation to the instructiveness of the knowledge contained therein and a concept of teaching and learning disconnected from the essential structure of the products of disciplined inquiry. We need to recover the essential meaning of a discipline as a body of instructive knowledge. So understood, the disciplines will be seen as the clue to good teaching and learning, and instructiveness will be seen as the mark of a good discipline. Furthermore, scholars will learn once more to measure their success by their ability to teach, and teachers will again be judged by the depth of their understanding, and the academics and the educationists will dwell together in peace, if indeed any such distinction will any longer be required!

It is wrong to suppose that the more profound scholarly inquiry is the further removed it is from suitability for teaching purposes. On the contrary, profundity is in proportion to illuminative quality. The esoteric knowledge that is often described as profound is more aptly termed obscure. The characteristic feature of disciplined intelligence is that difficulties and confusions are overcome and understanding of the subject is thereby facilitated. In short, the test for quality in knowledge is its communicability. Knowledge which is hard to teach is for that reason inferior. Knowledge which readily enlightens the learner's understanding is superior.

Now what is it that makes knowledge instructive? How does undisciplined differ from disciplined understanding? There are three fundamental features, all of which contribute to the availability of knowledge for instruction and thus provide measures for degree and quality of discipline. These three are (1) analytic simplification, (2) synthetic coordination, and (3) dynamism. Let us consider each criterion in turn.

II

First, analytic simplification. The primal essential for effective teaching is simplification. All intelligibility rests upon a radical reduction in the multiplicity of impressions which impinge upon the senses and the imagination. The infant begins life with the booming, buzzing confusion of which James spoke, and his learning consists in the growing ability to sort and select, that is, to simplify. The lower animals have built-in simplers in the instinctive mechanisms. Human beings have a much more interesting and powerful apparatus of simplification, through intelligence. The index of intelligence is of course, the power of symbolization. Symbols—pereeminently but not exclusively those of language—are means of marking out useful and memorable features of experience for special notice. All significant words are such markers. Thus, the word "hand" designates a *kind* of object to which an indefinite member of particular objects (hands) correspond. The point for emphasis is that a symbol —for example, a word—allows human beings drastically to reduce the complexity of their experience by subsuming an indefinite wealth of particulars under a single concept.

The secret of human learning is in generalization, that is, in transcending the multifariousness of raw experience. All thinking requires conceptualization. Concepts are classes of particulars. They are selections from the inchoate mass of impressions of certain features of things which enable them to be treated as a class rather than one by one. Thought proceeds by a process of rigorous selection, emphasis, and suppression of data. A person is intelligent to the degree that he actively discriminates in his entertainment of stimuli. In our pursuit of the full, rich life we may forget that the key to felicity and wisdom lies as much or more in our power of excluding as in receiving impressions. Our humanness rests upon a wise asceticism, not upon indiscriminate hospitality to every message impinging upon us from the world about us.

This simplification of experience through the use of symbols may be called analytic. The sorting out of classes of things is the process of analysis. It proceeds by the discrimination of similarities and differences, whereby entities may be divided and arranged in orderly fashion. Analysis is possible only because the human mind is able to *abstract,* that is, to discern properties, qualities, or forms of things. Every concept is an abstraction—a drawing out of certain features of a class of things for purposes of generalization and grouping. The function of abstraction is to simplify—to reduce the complexity of unanalyzed experience by selecting certain shared properties of kinds of things and neglecting their other features. *removing irrelevant information*

It is commonly assumed that abstract thinking is difficult and complicated. This assumption betrays a misunderstanding of what abstraction is. Analytic abstraction is a way of thinking which aims at ease of comprehension and reduction of complexity. For this reason all learning—all growth in understanding—takes place through the use of simplifying concepts. It is the key to effectiveness of instruction. *Can learners learn concepts without instruction?*

All of this bears directly on the question of the place of the disciplines in teaching and learning. A discipline is essentially nothing more than an extension of ordinary conceptualization. It is a conceptual system whose office is to gather a large group of cognitive elements into a common framework of ideas. That is, its goal is the simplification of understanding. This is the function of the techniques, models, and theories which are characteristic of any discipline. They economize thought by showing how diverse and apparently disparate elements of experience can be subsumed under common interpretive and explanatory schemes.

Thus, contrary to the popular assumption, knowledge does not become more and more complicated as one goes deeper into a discipline. If it is a real discipline and not merely a field for the display of erudition, the further one goes in it the more pervasive are the simplicities which analysis reveals. For example, how grand and liberating is the simplicity afforded by the atomic theory of matter as one seeks to comprehend the endless complexity of the world of material substances! Again, how much simpler Copernicus made the understanding of the apparent motions of the stars and planets, and how much easier Darwin made the comprehension of the varieties of living things!

The test of a good discipline is whether or not it simplifies understanding. When a field of study only adds new burdens and multiplies complexities, it is not properly called a discipline. Likewise, when a real discipline in certain directions begins to spawn concepts and theories which on balance are a burden and hindrance to insight, in those areas it degenerates into undisciplined thinking.

One of the greatest barriers to progress in learning is the failure to catch the vision of simplicity which the disciplines promise. When students (and their teachers) consider the movement from elementary to advanced stages in a subject as requiring the taking on of more and more burdens of knowledge, of ever-increasing complexity, just as physically one becomes with exercise capable of carrying increasingly heavy loads, it is little wonder that they so often resist instruction and postpone learning as long as possible. If, on the other hand, it can be made clear that, like Christian in Bunyan's allegory, the academic pilgrimage aims at release from the burdens of merely accumulated experience and leads to intellectual salvation through the insightful and revelatory concepts and theories contained in the traditions of the disciplines, how eager students become to learn and how ready to exchange their hampering ignorance for liberating understanding!

III

Let us now turn, more briefly, to the second feature of a discipline which makes knowledge in it instructive, namely, synthetic coordination. A discipline is a conceptual structure whose function is not only to simplify understanding but also to reveal significant patterns and relationships. Analysis is not an end in itself; it is the basis of synthesis. By synthesis is meant the construction of new wholes, the coordination of elements into significant coherent structures. Disciplined thinking is *organized* thinking. Differences and distinctions are recognized within an ordered framework which permits synoptic vision.

Such synthetic coordination is not opposed in tendency to analytic simplifications; both are aspects of a common process of intelligible ordering. The perception of meaningful differences is possible only against some common measure. Thus, the notion of parts within an ordered whole involves both the differentiation which is presupposed by the idea of parts and the unity which is implied by the idea of a whole. A discipline is a synthetic structure of concepts made possible by the discrimination of similarities through analysis. It is a hierarchy of ideas ordered as a unity in difference.

It is only in this sense that disciplined knowledge can be called complex. The simplifications of abstraction make possible the construction of cognitive complexes—i.e., the weaving together of ideas into coherent wholes. Concepts are no longer entertained in isolation, but are seen in their interconnections and relationships.

What occurs in disciplined thinking is a reconstruction of experience. The brute multiplicity of primordial experience is simplified by conceptual abstraction, and these abstractions are then synthesized into more and more comprehensive patterns of coordination. In this way naive experience is transformed from a meaningless hodgepodge of impressions into a relatively meaningful pattern of understanding.

Herein lies the great pedagogical virtue of a discipline. Whatever is taught within a discipline framework draws strength and interest from its membership within a family of ideas. Each new idea is illuminated by ideas previously acquired. A discipline is a community of concepts. Just as human beings cannot thrive in isolation, but require the support of other persons in mutual association, so do isolated ideas wither and die, while ideas comprehended within the unity of a discipline tend to remain vivid and powerful within the understanding.

IV

The third quality of knowledge in a discipline I have called its dynamisim. By this is meant the power of leading on to further understanding. A discipline is a *living* body of knowledge, containing within itself a principle of growth. Its concepts do not merely simplify and coordinate; they also invite further analysis and synthesis. A discipline contains a *lure to discovery*. Its ideas excite

A discipline displays analytic, synthetic e dynamic qualities
or, the characteristics of a discipline are analytics, synthesis and
dynamism

88 Styles of Curriculum Theorizing

the imagination to further exploration. Its concepts suggest new constructs which provide larger generalizations and reconstituted modes of coordination.

James B. Conant has pointed to this dynamism as a distinguishing feature of scientific knowledge. Science is an enterprise in which fruitfulness is the mark of a good conceptual scheme. Theories which merely coordinate and organize a given body of data but do not stimulate further experimentation and inquiry are scientifically unimportant. This principle may also be taken as definitive for any discipline. Instructiveness is proportionate to fruitfulness. Knowledge which only organizes the data of experience but does not excite further questions and inquiries is relatively undisciplined knowledge. Disciplined ideas not only constitute families of concepts, but these families beget progeny. They have generative power. This is why they are instructive. They lead on and out: they educate. Instruction here does not mean a teacher-led pedagogy

There is, of course, no sharp dividing line between disciplined and nondisciplined knowledge. There are on the one extreme isolated bits of information which are not within any organized discipline, and on the other extreme there are precisely articulated theoretical structures which are readily recognized as disciplined according to the meaning developed above. In between are bodies of knowledge which have all degrees of discipline. Perhaps it would be well also to speak of weak disciplines and strong disciplines, the difference being in the degree to which their contents satisfy the three criteria for instructiveness earlier stated. Thus, mathematics, with powerful analytic tools and the dynamic for endless fruitful elaborations, by the present criteiria would appear to be a stronger discipline than most present-day political science, which (from my limited knowledge of it) seems to have relatively few unifying concepts and theoretical schemes permitting wide synthesis and creative expansion. Again, I would rate comparative linguistics which seems to possess a powerful and productive set of concepts as a stronger discipline than esthetics, which still operates largely in terms of individual subjective judgments about particular objects, one by one.

A distinction may also be useful between a discipline and an area of study. Not all areas of study are disciplines, since not all of them display analytic, synthetic, and dynamic qualities. Thus, it seems to me that "education" is an area of study rather than a discipline. Within this area disciplined learning is possible. For example, I think a good case can be made for a discipline of curriculum, or of educational psychology, or of educational philosophy—though I would not wish to rate these disciplines as to strength. Similarly, "business" and "social studies" appear to be areas of study rather than disciplines. Not everyone that cries "discipline, discipline" shall enter the kingdom of learning, but only those who can show analytic simplification, synthetic coordination, and dynamism in their knowledge schemes.

My theme has been that the curriculum should consist entirely of knowledge which comes from the disciplines, for the reason that the disciplines reveal knowledge in its teachable forms. We should not try to teach anything which has not been found actually instructive through the labors of hosts of dedicated inquirers. Education should be conceived as a *guided recapitulation of the processes of inquiry which gave rise to the fruitful bodies of organized knowledge comprising the established disciplines.*

In this brief analysis there has been no time to consider the problem of levels. I do not intend to suggest that the whole conceptual apparatus of a discipline should be brought to bear on teaching at every level of education. There are elementary and advanced stages of disciplined inquiry. The great simplicities, the comprehensive syntheses, and the powerful dynamisms usually belong to the more advanced stages. Nevertheless, from the very earliest years on up, it is only discipline knowledge which should be taught in the curriculum. Every discipline has in it beginning concepts and more developed concepts, all of which belong to the discipline authentically and properly. There is no place in the curriculum for ideas which are regarded as suitable for teaching because of the supposed nature, needs, and interests of the learner, but which do not belong within the regular structure of the disciplines, for the disciplines are in their essential nature bodies of knowledge organized for the most effective instruction.

This view asserts the identity of the psycho-logic of teaching and learning with the logic of the disciplines, contrary to many of the current theories of the teaching-learning process. Or, it might be more generally acceptable among educators to say that the view measures the logic (and the authenticity) of a discipline by its instructiveness.

Bruner's Concept of Structure

Perhaps the most intriguing notion to come out of the Woods Hole Conference was that of the structure of a discipline. The teaching profession had been exhorted for decades prior to the conference to avoid teaching isolated concepts and facts. Yet the questions of what these were related to and how they were to be related were seldom carefully considered. Two typical answers were that facts and concepts should be related to generalizations and that they should be used in problem solving. The notion that *structures* could be identified in subjects of instruction and that facts as well as concepts were related within these *structures* appeared to give a fundamental and practical answer. At the same time the notion of structure, it was claimed, offered other benefits. It gave more assurance of transfer, enhanced comprehension of a subject, and facilitated recall. Little wonder that the interests of curriculum specialists and teachers were engaged to a marked degree by this intriguing concept. The following passage presents what Bruner meant by structure and how he justified its pedagogical use.

☐

A word is needed at this point to explain in fuller detail what is meant by the *structure* of a subject, for we shall have occasion to return to this idea often in later pages. Three simple examples—from biology, from mathematics, and from the learning of language—help to make the idea clearer. Take first a set of observations on an inchworm crossing a sheet of graph paper mounted on

Jerome Bruner, *The Process of Education* (Cambridge: Harvard University Press, 1960), pp. 6–8, 23–26. Reprinted by permission of the author and publisher.

a board. The board is horizontal; the animal moves in a straight line. We tilt the board so that the inclined plane or upward grade is 30°. We observe that the animal does not go straight up, but travels at an angle of 45° from the line of maximum climb. We now tilt the board to 60°. At what angle does the animal travel with respect to the line of maximum climb? Now, say, he travels along a line 75° off the straight-up line. From these two measures, we may infer that inchworms "prefer" to travel uphill, if uphill they must go, along an incline of 15°. We have discovered a tropism, as it is called, indeed a geotropism. It is not an isolated fact. We can go on to show that among simple organisms, such phenomena—regulation of locomotion according to a fixed or built-in standard—are the rule. There is a preferred level of illumination toward which lower organisms orient, a preferred level of salinity, of temperature, and so on. Once a student grasps this basic relation between external stimulation and locomotor action, he is well on his way toward being able to handle a good deal of seemingly new but, in fact, highly related information. The swarming of locusts where temperature determines the swarm density in which locusts are forced to travel, the species maintenance of insects at different altitudes on the side of a mountain where cross-breeding is prevented by the tendency of each species to travel in its preferred oxygen zone, and many other phenomena in biology can be understood in the light of tropisms. Grasping the structure of a subject is understanding it in a way that permits many other things to be related to it meaningfully. To learn structure, in short, is to learn how things are related.

Much more briefly, to take an example from mathematics, algebra is a way of arranging knowns and unknowns in equations so that the unknowns are made knowable. The three fundamentals involved in working with these equations are commutation, distribution, and association. Once a student grasps the ideas embodied by these three fundamentals, he is in a position to recognize wherein "new" equations to be solved are not new at all, but variants on a familiar theme. Whether the student knows the formal names of these operations is less important for transfer than whether he is able to use them.

The often unconscious nature of learning structures is perhaps best illustrated in learning one's native language. Having grasped the subtle structure of a sentence, the child very rapidly learns to generate many other sentences based on this model though different in content from the original sentence learned. And having mastered the rules for transforming sentences without altering their meaning—"The dog bit the man" and "The man was bitten by the dog"—the child is able to vary his sentences much more widely. Yet, while young children are able to *use* the structural rules of English, they are certainly not able to say what the rules are.

Inherent in the preceding discussions are at least four general claims that can be made for teaching the fundamental structure of a subject, claims in need of detailed study.

The first is that understanding fundamentals makes a subject more comprehensible. This is true not only in physics and mathematics, where we have principally illustrated the point, but equally in the social studies and literature. Once one has grasped the fundamental idea that a nation must trade in order to live, then such a presumably special phenomenon as the Triangular Trade of the American colonies becomes altogether simpler to understand as something more than commerce in molasses, sugar cane, rum, and slaves in an atmosphere of violation of British trade regulations. The high school student reading *Moby Dick* can only understand more deeply if he can be led to understand that Melville's novel is, among other things, a study of the theme of evil and the plight of those pursuing this "killing whale." And if the student is led further to understand that there are a relatively limited number of human plights about which novels are written, he understands literature the better for it.

The second point relates to human memory. Perhaps the most basic thing that can be said about human memory, after a century of intensive research, is that unless detail is placed into a structured pattern, it is rapidly forgotten. Detailed material is conserved in memory by the use of simplified ways of representing it. These simplified representations have what may be called a "regenerative" character. A good example of this regenerative property of long-term memory can be found in science. A scientist does not try to remember the distances traversed by falling bodies in different gravitational fields over different periods of time. What he carries in memory instead is a formula that permits him with varying degrees of accuracy to regenerate the details on which the more easily remembered formula is based. So he commits to memory the formula $s = 1/2\ gt^2$ and not a handbook of distances, times, and gravitational constants. Similarly, one does not remember exactly what Marlowe, the commentator in *Lord Jim,* said about the chief protagonist's plight, but, rather, simply that he was the dispassionate onlooker, the man who tried to understand without judging what had led Lord Jim into the straits in which he found himself. We remember a formula, a vivid detail that carries the meaning of an event, an average that stands for a range of events, a caricature or picture that preserves an essence—all of them techniques of condensation and representation. What learning general or fundamental principles does is to ensure that memory loss will not mean total loss, that what remains will permit us to reconstruct the details when needed. A good theory is the vehicle not only for understanding a phenomenon now but also for remembering it tomorrow.

Third, an understanding of fundamental principles and ideas, as noted earlier, appears to be the main road to adequate "transfer of training." To understand something as a specific instance of a more general case—which is what understanding a more fundamental principle or structure means—is to have learned not only a specific thing but also a model for understanding other things like it that one may encounter. If a student could grasp in its most human sense the weariness of Europe at the close of the Hundred Years' War and how it created the conditions for a workable but not ideologically absolute Treaty of Westphalia, he might be better able to think about the ideological struggle of East and West—though the parallel is anything but exact. A carefully wrought understanding should also permit him to recognize the limits of the generalization as well. The idea of "principles" and "concepts" as a basis for transfer is hardly new. It is much in need of more research of a specific kind that would provide detailed knowledge of how best to proceed in the teaching of different subjects in different grades.

The fourth claim for emphasis on structure and principles in teaching is that by constantly reexamining material taught in elementary and secondary schools for its fundamental character, one is able to narrow the gap between "advanced" knowledge and "elementary" knowledge. Part of the difficulty now found in the progression from primary school through high school to college is that material learned earlier is either out of date or misleading by virtue of its lagging too far behind developments in a field. This gap can be reduced by the kind of emphasis set forth in the preceding discussion.

The notion of structure, like many other pedagogical ideas, turned out to be less potent than its followers had promised. This can be attributed to two things: first, the concept was not adequately defined; and second, it failed to provide an answer to the question of how to overcome the separation of the disciplines from each other and from everyday problems of life.

The concept was not explored by followers of the notion of structure but instead was defined ostensively. It is not easy to construct the meaning of a complex concept such as "structure" from characteristics exhibited in a few illustrations. One does not know from this sort of definition whether or not the structure is conceived of as logico-deductive or anything more than simply the use of concepts and principles to interpret observations and events.

An Assessment of the Discipline Approach

The theory of the disciplines as an approach to curriculum development was criticized not only because its basic concepts were not clearly defined but also because the theory failed to take into account several questions that curriculum specialists had long considered significant. Among these were: How do the disciplines relate to each other? How do the disciplines, or the content comprising them, relate to the affairs of life? In this final reading, Arno Bellack speaks to these questions from a rich background as a curriculum specialist and research scholar.

☐

Contemporary efforts to redefine the role of knowledge in the curriculum place emphasis on the *logical* order inherent in knowledge itself and on the structure of concepts and principles of inquiry that characterize the various fields of learning. Whereas formerly factual and descriptive content were stressed, now the emphasis is on basic concepts and methods scholars use as intellectual tools to analyze and order their data.

Arno Bellack, "What Knowledge Is of Most Worth?" *The High School Journal* 48 (1965): 318–32. Reprinted by permission of the publisher.

Several claims are made for teaching the fundamental structures of the disciplines, two of which are of central importance and worth considering here. The first is that understanding of fundamental ideas is the main road to adequate transfer of training. Professor Bruner, who is largely responsible for introducing the concept of structure into educational discourse, observes that

> Knowledge is a model we construct to give meaning and structure to regularities in experience. The organizing ideas of any body of knowledge are inventions for rendering experience economical and connected. We invent concepts such as force in physics, the bond in chemistry, motives in psychology, style in literature as means to the end of comprehension. . . . The power of great organizing concepts is in large part that they permit us to understand and sometimes to predict or change the world in which we live. But their power lies also in the fact that ideas provide instruments for experience.

Therefore, he contends "the structure of knowledge—its connectedness and its derivations that make one idea follow another—is the proper emphasis in education."[1]

The second important claim for emphasis on structure is that by constantly reexamining material taught in the schools for its fundamental patterns of organization, the schools will be able to narrow the gap between "advanced" knowledge and "elementary" knowledge. Since scholars at the forefront of their disciplines are able to make the greatest contribution to the substantive reorganization of their fields, current curriculum projects place great emphasis on the participation of university researchers in continuing revision of the program of studies. Scholars in the various disciplines and their professional organizations have in recent years made proposals for revamping the curriculum in elementary and secondary schools—first in mathematics, physics, chemistry, and biology; then in English; and recently and belatedly in economics, geography, anthropology, and history.

The focus of attention in each of these projects is an individual discipline. Little or no attention is given to the relationships of the individual fields to each other or to the program of studies within which they must find their place. National committees in the fields of chemistry, physics, and biology have proceeded independently of each other. The projects in economics, geography, and anthropology are unrelated to one another or to the other social sciences. Only in mathematics has there been a disposition to view the field as a whole, but this is a reflection of developments within the discipline of mathematics at the highest levels of scholarship.

The situation developing in the elementary and secondary schools thus begins to reflect, at least to some degree, the state of affairs in the universities with respect to the development and organization of knowledge, which Professor John Randall has described in this way:

> As reflected in the microcosm of the modern university, the world of knowledge has today become radically plural. It is a world of many different knowledges, pursued in varied ways to diverse ends. These many inquiries are normally carried on with little thought for their relation to each other. The student of John Donne's poetry,

---

[1] Jerome S. Bruner, *On Knowing* (Cambridge: Harvard University Press, 1960), p. 120.

the student of the structure of the atom—each gives little enough attention to what the others are doing, and none at all to any total picture of anything. Each has his own goals, his own methods, his own language for talking about what he is doing and what he has discovered. Each seems happiest when left to his own devices, glad indeed if he can keep others from treading on his toes. Each is convinced that what he himself is doing is worthwhile. But none has too much respect for the others, though he is willing enough to tolerate them. They have all little understanding of each other's pursuits—what they are trying to do, how they are doing it, and what they really mean when they talk about it.[2]

I emphasize this pluralism in the academic world not to deplore it, but to call attention to the problem that it presents for those who are concerned with the organization of the entire curriculum. For the curriculum builder is concerned not only with the structures of the individual disciplines, but also with the structure of the instructional program within which the fields of knowledge find their place. The problem can be very simply stated, if not easily solved: What general structure of the curriculum can be developed so that autonomy of the parts does not result in anarchy in the program as a whole? This is one of two questions I propose to discuss briefly.

The second question grows out of the proposal that students be introduced to the ways of thinking associated with the various disciplines in such fashion that they in fact become physicists, chemists, or economists. Professor Bruner puts it this way:

> What a scientist does at his desk or in his laboratory, what a literary critic does in reading a poem, are of the same order as what anybody else does when he is engaged in like activities—if he is to achieve understanding. The difference is in degree, not in kind. The schoolboy learning physics is a physicist.[3]

I take it this does not mean that the goal of general education is to train all students as specialists in mathematics, geography, history, or whatever other subjects they might study. Rather, the goal is to make available to students the intellectual and aesthetic resources of their culture in such a way that they become guides for intelligent action and help students create meaning and order out of the world in which they find themselves. . . .

How is this widely accepted objective to be realized? Is the ability to relate what is learned in school to the world of human affairs to come as an inevitable by-product of the study of the disciplines, or must teachers give explicit attention to helping students see the relevance of such study for their own lives as individuals, citizens, and workers? This is the second issue I propose to discuss briefly.

Knowledge and the Structure of the Curriculum

When we look beyond the structures of the disciplines and ask about the structure of the curriculum within which the various fields of study take their

[2] John H. Randall, Jr., "The World to be Unified," in Lewis Leary, ed., *The Unity of Knowledge* (Garden City, N.Y.: Doubleday and Company, 1955), p. 63.

[3] Jerome S. Bruner, *The Process of Education* (Cambridge: Harvard University Press, 1960), p. 14.

place, we face a problem of the greatest complexity. What knowledge from the vast array of intellectual resources shall the schools teach? The accumulated and ever-growing knowledge in all fields has reached such proportions that comprehensive grasp of the total range of knowledge is out of the question for any one individual. The question raised by Spencer a hundred years ago, "What knowledge is of most worth?" is even more relevant today than it was in his time. Given the limited time and capacity of the school, what shall the schools teach to secure results that can be generalized beyond the immediate situations in which the learning takes place?

According to long and honorable tradition, knowledge is grouped for pedagogical purposes in four major categories—the natural sciences, the social sciences, mathematics, and the humanities (the latter an omnibus term that includes art, literature, philosophy, and music). These broad groupings of organized disciplines are generally recognized as basic cultural interests of our society which constitute both the resources and the obligations of the schools. Each major field represents distinctive methods and conceptual schemes in which the world and people are viewed from quite different vantage points. Instruction in these areas has as its primary goal equipping students with key concepts and methods that inform and sustain intelligent choice in human affairs.

Although the four major areas of knowledge are generally recognized as important components of the curriculum, they are not currently used as the context or framework for curriculum building. Instead, as we have already noted, recent curriculum projects have focused attention on individual disciplines without concern for their relationships to allied fields. Thus the economists, the geographers, and the anthropologists have proceeded independently of each other, as have the biologists, chemists, and physicists. To be sure, economists suggest ways in which economic ideas can be taught in history; and anthropologists show how some of their generalizations can be woven into courses in geography. This is all to the good; it even seems to suggest that integration of a limited variety might be appropriate for teaching purposes. But scant attention is given to building a curriculum design within which the individual fields might find their place.

It is my contention that this approach has certain inherent shortcomings and that we would do well to shift the context for curriculum planning from the individual disciplines, as is now the vogue, to the broad groupings of knowledge represented by the natural sciences, the social sciences, mathematics, and the humanities. Let us briefly consider some of the problems involved in curriculum building in the social sciences to show why this proposed shift is desirable and necessary.

The social sciences—economics, social psychology, political science, sociology, anthropology, geography, and history—are all seeking explanations of the same phenomenon, people's social life. This common goal is what makes it reasonable to group them together as the *social* sciences. All of them have grown out of our attempts to interpret, understand, and control the social environment. But each field formulates its own questions about this subject matter and develops its own system of concepts to guide its research. The economist is preoccupied with the concept of scarcity, the political scientist with the concepts of power and authority, the anthropologist with the notion of culture, and the sociologist with social functions and social systems. Each science is thus abstract, dealing with only certain facets of actual social relationships and institutions—facets that do not permit of physical separation, but only of analytical separation.

A person's social life as it is actually lived is therefore far more complex than the limited image of it reflected in the concepts and generalizations of any one of the social disciplines. It follows then, as Professor Kingsley Davis has suggested, that "in so far as the prediction of actual events is concerned, the various social sciences are mutually interdependent, because only by combining their various points of view can anything approaching a complete anticipation of future occurrences be achieved."[4] Policies that are proposed and actions that are taken to deal with problems in social affairs are not of necessity interdisciplinary, for concrete social reality is not mirrored in the findings of any one discipline.

Now this is a matter of central importance to those whose job it is to plan and organize the social studies curriculum. To focus exclusive attention on certain aspects of the social world as seen through the eyes of one or two of the social sciences is to give students a myopic vision of man's social behavior and his institutions. To shape children's conceptions of the social world through exclusive emphasis on the language of the economist, for example, to the exclusion of the language of the sociologist, political scientist, anthropologist, and historian is to determine that they shall interpret human affairs principally in terms that the economist uses to view reality—in terms of supply, demand, scarcity, production, and consumption.

Students must be helped to see the limitations as well as the uses of a single discipline in interpreting events as they actually occur. And for anything approaching a comprehensive view of man's functioning in society, the specialized perspectives of all the social sciences are needed. Curriculum builders in the social studies have the enormously difficult job of providing a place in their programs for all the social sciences, each of which contributes its distinctive perspective on human institutions and human behavior.

It is clear that such a program can be developed only on the basis of collaboration among the various social sciences. Such collaboration does not presuppose a "unified social science" as the basis for planning the elementary and secondary school curriculum. Quite the opposite is the case. For the social disciplines today are characterized by a plurality of methods and conceptual schemes developed by social scientists to deal with problems within their individual spheres. Instead of a unity of method or a single universe of discourse, we find a vast confederation of separate areas of study. Modes of thinking and analysis differ from field to field, and even from problem to problem within the same field. In time, a Bacon of the sciences that bear on the social and cultural behavior of people may emerge, but that time is not yet.

At the same time, in spite of increasing specialization and internal differentiation, there are interconnections among the social sciences that curriculum planning for the schools should take into account. For example, the various social sciences borrow rather handily from each other when it comes to both

[4]*Human Society* (New York: The Macmillan Company, 1948), p. 8.

concepts and methods. Historians make use of concepts from all the other social sciences. Political scientists interested in political socialization get their methods from behavioral scientists and seem in many respects more closely related to sociologists and social psychologists than to fellow political scientists. Certain anthropologists have utilized the Freudian view of human development in analyzing patterns of various cultures. Geographers make extensive use of the perspectives of history and concepts developed by all the behavioral sciences.

Furthermore, we find not only interchange of concepts and methods but growing collaboration among specialists. For example, studies of the nature and function of "authority" are now undertaken jointly by political scientists and sociologists; and there have been recent studies conducted by economists in collaboration with anthropologists to determine whether certain economic theories hold for different types of economic systems. The convergence of social scientists upon the same problems has given rise to what Professor Robert Merton calls "interdisciplines" such as social biology, political sociology, and sociological history.

The picture that emerges from this cursory review of the current state of affairs in the social sciences is one of great diversity. Given this mosaic of disciplines and interdisciplines, each characterized by multiple conceptual schemes and methods, the curriculum builder is faced with the problem of developing structures for teaching that relate the social sciences to each other in meaningful ways and avoid undue fragmentation of knowledge.

What has been said about the social sciences applies in principle to the natural sciences, mathematics, and the humanities. The significant point is that there is a need for a broader context for curriculum planning than the separate disciplines, and the broad fields of knowledge furnish a useful framework for this purpose. I am not calling for indiscriminate scrambling of superficial knowledge. Indeed, at this point we would do well to suspend judgment as to when in the school program teaching should be organized around the individual disciplines, and when around the broad groupings of the disciplines. In all likelihood, different patterns of organization will be found to be appropriate for different levels of the school program. Dewey's notion of the "progressive organization of knowledge," long ignored by most of his interpreters, might serve as a guiding hypothesis in planning the sequence of the program through the elementary and secondary school years.

In sum, scholars in the natural sciences, the social sciences, mathematics, and the humanities should now be invited to join in the search for new structures for teaching—structures that respect the integrity of the individual fields and at the same time help these fields find their place in a pattern of studies that provides a substantial measure of coherence and relatedness for the program as a whole.

But there is not only the question of relationship among disciplines that deal with similar problems or phenomena, but also the question of the relationships among the broad areas of knowledge—the sciences and mathematics on the one hand, and the humanities on the other. The growing separation and lack of effective communication between the arts and sciences have been widely noted and greatly deplored. C. P. Snow's analysis of this situation in terms of the two cultures of the literary intellectuals and the scientists is well-known to all of us. That this state of affairs should somehow be remedied is the theme of many earnest discussions. The upshot of the discussion is usually that there is one way out of all this: it is, as Snow suggests, by rethinking our education.

But how shall the school go about bridging the gulf between the literary and aesthetic and the scientific studies? It seems reasonable to inquire first of all if human knowledge in its many dimensions forms a recognized unity within which the fields of inquiry and creativity fall neatly into place. Is there a sense in which all knowledge is one, with the arts and the sciences having a place in a unity of fundamental principles or basic methods of inquiry?

The progressives, taking their cue from Dewey, found for themselves such a unity in the "scientific method" (or the "method of intelligence," as it was frequently labeled) that was assumed to characterize all types of rational, intelligent activity in academic pursuits and in artistic and practical affairs as well. The problem-solving method came to be viewed as the basic ingredient in programs of general education.

But by no means is there agreement among scientists that there is a single all-encompassing set of procedures, even in the natural sciences, as assumed by those who talk about *the* scientific method. There seems to be little warrant for assuming that there is one overarching method sufficiently flexible and inclusive to deal with problems in the various scientific fields, to say nothing of the arts, crafts, and applied areas. Indeed, as we have already noted, the intellectual world today is characterized by a plurality of methods and conceptual schemes developed by the disciplines to deal with problems within their individual spheres. Analysis of the various disciplines reveals a wide range of organizations and intellectual methods associated with them. Instead of a unity of method or a single universe of discourse, we are confronted with a vast confederation of separate areas of study. Modes of analysis differ from field to field, and even from problem to problem within the same field.

The heterogeneous character of the intellectual resources that are a part of the culture is a fact of major significance for the curriculum builder. We would do well frankly to recognize this and make a place in our programs for the variety of logical orders that characterize the fields of knowledge on which we draw in building the curriculum.

But what then of the relationships among the various fields of creativity and inquiry? Is it perhaps possible, in spite of the variety of logical orders characteristic of knowledge in its various branches, to identify the principal kinds of cognitive operations or modes of thinking that characterize a person's intellectual activities?

A proposal to facilitate students' insight into relationships among the various fields of knowledge by introducing them to the "principal modes of intellectual activity" comes from Professor Peterson of Oxford University. In making suggestions for the reform of secondary education in Britain, Peterson urges educators to stop thinking of general education in terms of "general knowledge":

It is not a sign that a man lacks general education if he does not know the date of The Treaty of Utrecht, the latitude of Singapore, the formula for nitro-glycerine or the author of the Four Quartets. It does denote a lack of general education if he cares nothing for any of the arts, confuses a moral judgment with an aesthetic judgment, interprets the actions of Asian political leaders in terms of nineteenth century English parliamentarianism or believes that the existence of God has been scientifically disproved.[5]

Peterson urges therefore that the British secondary schools devise programs of general education not in terms of wide general knowledge, but in terms of development in the main modes of intellectual activity, of which he identifies four: the logical (or the analytic), the empirical, the moral, the aesthetic. These different modes of thought are associated with different uses of language. For example, the empirical mode has to do with statements about the world based on our experience of it. The analytic mode has to do with statements that do not describe the world of fact, but rather tell us how the meaning of symbols are related to one another logically. (A definition is a special case of analytic sentences.) The moral and the aesthetic modes are concerned with statements of preferences, evaluations, and judgments of the good and the evil, the beautiful and the ugly, the desirable and the undesirable.

Any one discipline gives opportunity for the development of more than one mode of thought, and each mode can be developed through more than one of the disciplines. For example, literature can contribute to the development of both moral and aesthetic judgment. Mathematics and philosophy both contribute to the development of the analytic mode. History has probably the widest range of any discipline, for the historian employs all four modes in constructing his comprehensive interpretation of what happened in the past.

If students are to gain understanding of the similarities and differences among the fields of knowledge, the different modes of mental activity must be made explicit to them:

> They must have time and guidance in which to see that what is a proof in the Mathematics they pursue on Tuesday is not the same kind of thing as a proof in History, which follows on Wednesday; that the truth of George Eliot or Joseph Conrad is not the same thing as the truths of Mendel or Max Plank; and yet that there are similarities as well as differences.[6]

Peterson accordingly suggests that in addition to giving attention to these varying modes of thought in the subject fields, the secondary program include a special course in which these ways of thinking are the object of study. One important aspect of such teaching has to do with ways in which these modes of thought are verified. Verification is particularly significant in that it is the guide to meaning of the various types of thought. For exmple, empirical statements are verified by tests conducted in terms of experience, whereas moral statements are verified by reference to criteria or principles of judgment. On the other hand, analytic statements depend for their truth on an agreed upon set of rules, and follow logically from accepted definitions.

[5]Arthur Bestor, *Educational Wastelands.* (Urbana, University of Illinois Press, 1953), p. 15.
[6]Bestor, *Educational Wastelands,* p. 18.

Thus far I have suggested that in structuring the curriculum with due regard for the relationships among the fields of knowledge we view knowledge from two complementary perspectives. In the first, emphasis is on the conceptual schemes and methods of inquiry associated with the broad fields of knowledge, the natural sciences, the social sciences, mathematics, and the humanities. In the second, attention is focused on modes of thought—the analytic, the empirical, the aesthetic, and the moral—that transcend the boundaries of the individual fields. These two views thus represent mutually reinforcing conceptions of knowledge that serve well as the basis for curriculum planning.

Professor Toulmin has coined two terms that might be helpful in clarifying the relationships between these two views of knowledge. He distinguishes between "participant's language" and "onlooker's language."[7] Participant's language is the language used by members of a professional group or discipline as they carry on their work in their specialized field. Hence we talk today about the language of science, the language of psychology, the language of mathematics, and even the language of education. In the context of our discussion, participant's language has to do with the language systems that are the distinguishing characteristics of the various disciplined areas of study such as the sciences, mathematics, and the humanities.

Now if we want to examine or talk about the language we use in any one of these fields, we must use another level of discourse. We must, in Toulmin's terms, use onlooker's language. For example, it was suggested that students need help in understanding that a proof in mathematics is not the same as a proof in science or that the "truth" of a scientist is not the same as the "truth" of the poet or novelist. To make these comparisons and contrasts we need a language system that enables us to look at these various areas of study from the outside, as it were. The principal modes of thought—the analytic, the empirical, the moral, and the aesthetic—furnish us with language tools that are useful for this purpose. Hence their importance in teaching.

In view of the significance of knowledge in our lives today, it seems reasonable to suggest that knowledge itself should become an object of study in the schools. At what points in their educational career students are able to carry on such study with understanding is an empirical question, certainly not answerable in the abstract. High schools might experiment with courses similar to the one suggested by Mr. Peterson for British schools. Already there are available in Britain excellent teaching materials prepared specifically for the kind of teaching here envisaged.[8]

Relationships of Knowledge to Human Affairs

That the schools ought to provide students with the means for intelligent action is not a new or controversial idea. When, however, it comes to deciding

[7] S. Toulmin, *Philosophy of Science* (London, Hutchinson University Library, 1953), p. 13.

[8] See, for example, the following: E. R. Emmet, *The Use of Reason* (London, Longmans, Green and Company, Ltd., 1960); John Wilson, *Language and the Pursuit of Truth* (London, Cambridge University Press, 1958); and R. W. Young, *Lines of Thought* (London, Oxford University Press, 1958).

what to teach and how to teach to accomplish this goal, we find marked differences of opinion.

Is it sufficient in general education, for example, to have students learn how to think like physicists, historians, or economists? I think not. For the economist *as* economist (to mention just one field) is in no position to prescribe courses of action regarding the host of public policy issues we face, and questions of public policy and decision loom large in general education. To be sure, economics does provide us with a body of theory that is essential in examining the probable consequences of alternative economic policies, and a good many of these analytical tools ought to become part of the intellectual equipment of all students. Economists are able to tell us what the probable consequences will be if the supply of money is increased, or if the interest rates are lowered; but they cannot *as* economists tell us whether we ought to take either of these two courses of action. Decisions regarding these alternative courses of action involve technical economic analysis and weighing of values.

It is therefore clear that both values of economic theory are involved in deciding courses of action in economic affairs, and both must find their place in social studies teaching. Here the different modes of thought come prominently into play. Technical economic analysis involves the empirical mode of thinking (that is, it is concerned with matters of fact and theory), while considering alternative values involves the moral mode (that is, it is concerned with criteria of what is desirable and undesirable). The teacher's job is to help students learn to make these necessary distinctions, so that they recognize when questions of fact and analysis are under consideration and when questions of value are at stake.[9] This would of course hold as well for instruction in fields of study other than economics.

Thus far we have been talking about problems associated with a single field. But problems in the world of human affairs do not come neatly labeled "historical," "economic," or "political." They come as decisions to be made and force us to call upon all we know and make us wish we knew more. It was concern for broad cultural and moral questions that go beyond the boundaries of any one discipline that led the progressives to urge that students have the opportunity to deal with them in all their complexity. They proposed a new curriculum, one centered on the problems of youth and broad social issues and drawing upon the academic disciplines as they become relevant to the problems under study. This idea became the hallmark of progressivism in curriculum building. It gained wide acceptance among educators and found expression in many influential statements of policy and opinion during the 1920s, 30s, and 40s. Attempted applications of this viewpoint were made in courses labeled core, common learnings, and the like.

Difficulties in this approach soon became apparent, not the least of which was the students' lack of firsthand acquaintance with the disciplines that were the source of the concepts and ideas essential to structuring problems under study. Without adequate understanding of the various fields of knowledge, students had no way of knowing which fields were relevant to problems of

[9]See *Economic Education in the Schools*, Report of the National Task Force on Economic Education (New York: Committee for Economic Development, 1961).

concern to them. Indeed, without knowledge of the organized fields it was difficult for them to ask the kinds of questions about their problems that the various disciplines could help them answer.

Giving students an opportunity to grapple with broad social and cultural problems was basically a promising innovation. But at the same time one is forced to recognize that problem solving on such a broad base cannot be pursued successfully without growing understanding of the fields of knowledge on which the problem solver must draw.

Recognizing then the value in systematic study of the fields of knowledge and the importance of developing competence in dealing with problems and issues that are broader than those of any one field, the question arises of why opportunities for both types of activities should not be included in the program of all students. One might envision a general education program that would include basic instruction in the major fields defined earlier in this paper (the natural sciences, the social sciences, mathematics, and the humanities), together with a coordinating seminar in which students deal with problems "in the round" and in which special effort is made to show the intimate relationships between the fields of study as concepts from those fields are brought to bear on these problems. Such a seminar would also furnish excellent opportunities to help students become aware of the different modes of thought and various types of language usage involved in dealing with problematic situations and the necessity for making clear distinctions among them.

Summary

"Discipline" can mean so many things to so many individuals that many of us feel quite contented to use it, for we give it our own meaning. But "discipline" in curriculum development must have a clear and generally agreed upon definition. Unless this is the case, we do not know what other people talk about when they speak of the disciplines. For this reason you may wish to examine with some care how the term is used in the various selections presented in this chapter. Is the use of the term limited to what might be called the basic subjects or does it apply to all subjects in the curriculum including all the various vocational subjects, arts.

Another equally captivating expression is "structure of the disciplines." Again if the term is to be used for any educational benefit, we should be able to understand what other persons mean when they use it. For this reason you may wish again to consider whether or not the meaning of the term as set forth by Bruner is one which is generally understood and used by teachers and curriculum workers.

Finally, consider the question of whether or not the points made by Bellack are valid. Do the various disciplines, however defined, actually neglect their relationship to life activities? Is the interrelationship of the disciplines neglected if one follows a strict interpretation of a discipline curriculum?

Finally we should return to the article by Phenix and face the question of whether or not in reality the curriculum maker and the teacher must rely entirely on the disciplines for the subject matter they teach. If they do not, then where does the additional information to be included in the curriculum come from?

Chapter **5**

Technology: The Analytic Style

Today's Education 63, 3 (Sept./Oct. 1974):66.

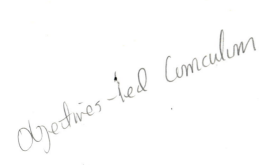
Objectives-led Curriculum

1. Roots of the Analytic Method
2. Systems Analysis and Analytic Style
3. Types and Techniques of Analysis
4. Summary

Suppose we had identified all the tasks and jobs for which preparation should be provided in school. Suppose also that we had determined what one would need to know and do in order to perform these tasks and do the jobs. Arranging these tasks and jobs in appropriate courses; organizing the knowledge and skill for each task or job into a hierarchy; and determining what one needs to know for mastery of each knowledge or skill item produces a complete curriculum. The analytic approach to curriculum development comprises these three steps.

Roots of the Analytic Method

This way of theorizing about the curriculum was as prominent in the early part of this century as it is today, although its current form is more rigorous than its earlier one.

When the analytic approach was first introduced it was closely associated with the development of vocational curriculums. It was used, among other things, to develop programs for training various types of office workers. One investigation applied the techniques of analysis to determine the activities of teachers and thus what they should learn in preparing to teach. It is interesting to note also that the procedure was used to determine what should be taught to develop good citizenship.

In general, the procedure consists of certain steps. First, identify the office worker, teacher, or citizen to be considered as an exemplar. Second, observe their activities and how they are performed. Third, order these performances in such a way as to facilitate learning them. And finally, identify and organize all materials essential to performance training.

This approach to curriculum development has been criticized for several reasons. Some claimed that the approach tended to atomize the knowledge and skills involved in the performance of a task or job, thereby creating mechanical sequences of learning and instruction. Some alleged that the procedure provides no means for discriminating among the different activities as to their importance in the performance of a task or job. A person engages in many activities as a citizen, but which of these characterize him as an exemplar and which are unessential?

The same question can apply to the analysis of the activities of a teacher. Would erasing the board or putting crayons away at the end of the day be as important as the kinds of questions the teacher asks?

It was claimed that the analytic procedure provided no way to answer this question except perhaps to appeal to the criterion of frequency of occurrence. Then, too, the theory was criticized on the grounds that it was static. Because occupations are in a constant state of change, it was said that the analytic approach would simply prepare individuals in knowledge and skills that would be outdated almost by the time they were learned. Although these objections have something to be said for them, they were not considered severe enough to justify abandoning the analytic mode of theorizing.

Recently this mode has gained new followers and a new emphasis. This is primarily because it proved to be successful in training military personnel, using simulation in many cases to enable the learner to work at the performance of tasks and jobs in ways most nearly like the situations in which he would later be involved. It also gained new emphasis from the technique of programmed instruction which relies heavily upon a form of analysis usually called topic analysis. In order to program instruction on a topic such as western expansion in American history it is necessary to break up the topic into its constituent parts in order to guide the learner step-by-step from the most elementary bit of information to complex components and finally to the complete concept of the topic.

The analytic style is basic to educational technology because it lends itself to exact formulation and rigorous procedures. It is compatible with the view that objectives should be stated in precise behavioral terms, that teaching proceeds most efficiently when what is to be learned is arranged hierarchically, that students should be taught what they do not know and not what they know already, and that the goal of instruction is mastery.

Systems Analysis and Analytic Style

Analytic theory fits readily into the theory of systems analysis. This analysis is a way of looking at a set of events in relation to the quality, quantity, and rate of output. Events can be described by variables which have fixed relationships to each other. A ball rolling down an inclined plane can be described by reference to such mutually exclusive variables as time, mass, and distance. But in a teaching-learning system the description involves variables which interact with each other and whose relationships are not fixed. The end result is that a job gets done or intended outcomes occur. Now the analytic mode is just as compatible with this heuristic sort of system as it is with the descriptive type such as the ball on the inclined plane. It can take into account ordering of events so as to facilitate the functional interaction of individuals with other objects of the system. Clegg describes the basic features of a systems approach to curriculum and instruction in the following quotation:

□

In a systems or management approach, planning begins with the analysis of the overall situation and its needs and some ranking of these needs according to priorities. (To "prioritize" is the current federalese word!) Next, specific objectives are defined, often in behavioral or performance terms to help make them more precise and measurable for evaluation purposes.

Curriculum content of the program is carefully selected to meet the particular objectives specified. Learning processes, teaching strategies, content materials, and field or laboratory experiences are defined and described in detail. These are carefully sequenced to be sure that the prerequisite learnings and skills have been acquired. Frequently, alternative choices of strategies and activities may be identified provided that they meet the original objectives.

Evaluation or program assessment in a systems approach is closely tied to program objectives. It is critical to know to what extent each of the objectives has been accomplished, and often at what cost. When program objectives are specified in behavioral or performance terms, it is much easier to spell out some concrete, observable measure of accomplishment that can be used in the evaluation process. Often these measures are quantifiable so that assessment data can be treated statistically or presented graphically to show the degree of accomplishment of each objective. Such techniques can then be related to overall program review and cost-effectiveness analysis. If a decision is made to continue the program, then data from the evaluation process are fed back into the system to adjust either the program or the goals or both. Thus the cycle shown in Figure 5–1 is completed and begun anew.

Types and Techniques of Analysis

The analytic style of theorizing is an incomplete curriculum theory because it begs the fundamental question: How does one determine the jobs to be trained for, the tasks to be performed, or the topics to be analyzed? In order to answer these questions one must resort to some procedure other than

Ambrose A. Clegg Jr., "The Teacher as a Manager of the Curriculum," *Educational Leadership* 30 (January 1973):308. Reprinted by permission of the publisher.

Footnotes have been renumbered consecutively throughout the chapter.

Figure 5-1. The PPBS cycle.

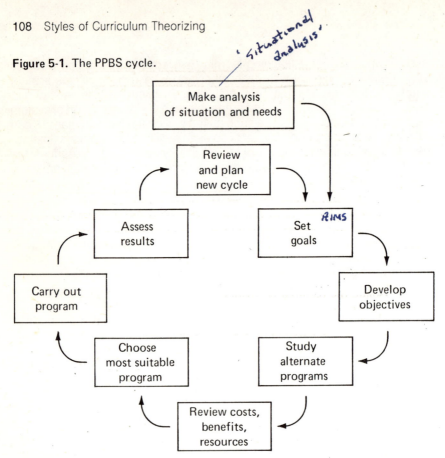

'Situational analysis'

Ambrose A. Clegg Jr., "The Teacher as a Manager of the Curriculum," *Educational Leadership* 30 (January 1973): 308.

analysis. The jobs for which one is to be trained in a given community, state, or region can be identified by assessing the occupational needs. Furthermore, much assessment can be kept up-to-date so that the schools prepare students for jobs that are likely to be available.

But when one turns to the question of what topics to teach in school or which skills to develop the answer is not so easy to come by. Then we face the perennial question: What knowledge is of most worth? This question is dealt with to some extent in this part of the book and it will be treated again in later chapters. However, we are now interested in a further exploration of the analytic style of curriculum theorizing and for that purpose we shall turn to an authority who has clearly set forth the theory.

One of the very first steps in developing an educational or training program is to analyze the nature of the actual task involved. Some tasks, of course, are

I. K. Davies, *Competency Based Learning: Management, Technology, and Design* (New York: McGraw-Hill, 1973):36–51. Copyright © 1973 McGraw-Hill Book Co. (UK) Ltd. Reproduced by permission.

purely academic or intellectual in nature, others are primarily concerned with physical skills. However, regardless of the nature of the task, it is necessary to determine both the ingredients and the characteristics of the topic or job that the student has to learn. It is only when these precise characteristics are known that the training need can be established, and the learning objectives written. For this reason, great care must be exercised in carrying out the task analysis, for the ensuing document forms the basis of the learning prescription.

In some ways, the term 'task analysis' is an unfortunate one. It suggests that what is primarily involved is the breaking down of the task into its constituent parts. This, however, only describes part of the process, for it is also necessary to consider how these constituent parts are related and organized. Task analysis, therefore, is concerned with both analysis and synthesis. Its ultimate aims are to:

1. Describe the task which the student has to learn.
2. Isolate the required behaviors.
3. Identify the conditions under which the behaviors occur.
4. Determine a criterion of acceptable performance.

Without a proper task analysis, it is not possible to justify what you intend to teach, nor is it possible to decide on an optimal teaching strategy.

Types of Task Analysis

Three different types of task analysis are readily recognizable, each fulfilling entirely different needs:

1. *Topic analysis.* This involves a detailed analysis of intellectual tasks such as Ohm's law, latitude and longitude, solving simultaneous equations, and considering the character of Brutus in Shakespeare's *Julius Caesar.*
2. *Job analysis.* This involves a detailed analysis of tasks involving physical or psychomotor skills. The technique concentrates on *what* is done when the task is carried out. Job analysis would involve such tasks as renewing the contact points in a car, setting up a lathe, fitting film in a camera.
3. *Skills analysis.* This involves the further analysis of psychomotor tasks, but this time concentrating on *how* the job is accomplished. Skills analysis will need to be carried out, in addition to job analysis, when either the whole task or part of the task involves complex, intricate and subtle hand-eye coordinations. For instance, a full skills analysis would be necessary for such jobs as glassblowing and panel-beating; whereas renewing the contact points in a car would include a skills analysis, for instance, for that part of the job that involves using a feeler gauge.

There has been a tendency among many teachers and trainers to imagine that task analysis is only applicable to tasks involving psychomotor skills; furthermore, skills analysis and job analysis have often been regarded as competing rather than complementary techniques. Indeed, in the past, certain industrial organizations went so wholeheartedly for skills analysis that they created the impression that all training should be based upon it. This was a time wasting and costly error of judgment. An essential component of the teacher's and trainer's role is to recognize the circumstances in which one strategy of analysis is likely to be more efficient than another.

Sources of Information for Task Analysis In carrying out a task analysis, whether it involves topic, job, or skills analysis, a number of sources of relevant information must be tapped, so as to ensure that a complete picture has been obtained. Obviously, the most important source of information must always be the 'master'; in other words, the person who can do the job at the required level of mastery. He must always be selected with great care, and steps must be taken to ensure that he is, indeed, proficient at the level which all students will be expected to attain. If the master's level of proficiency is too high, then the task analysis will set needlessly high levels of performance, with all the resultant dangers of overtraining. If the master's level of proficiency is set too low, the resulting task analysis will be invalid, with a consequent danger of undertraining.

Once the master's behavior has been analyzed, his performance must be checked for accuracy and completeness. It is also important to check the analysis under other operating environments and conditions, for these can sometimes affect the way that the task is accomplished. Other sources of information are indicated in Figure 5-2 (see Davies, 1965). Teachers and instructors must be consulted, course materials and examination papers studied, students who are either learning or have just finished learning the task interviewed, and the person who initially sparked off the project questioned. All kinds of procedures can be used in consulting these sources, but the most common ones include observation, interviews, questionnaires, work diaries, film, closed circuit television, job checklists, and activity analysis. A detailed description of these techniques will be found in Gagné (1963).

Figure 5-2. Main sources of information for a task analysis.

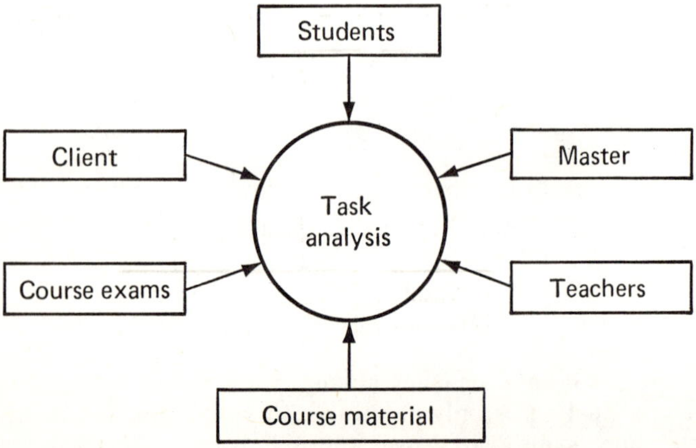

Components of a Task Analysis

A task analysis is really an audit and inventory. In it, knowledge, skill, and attitudes are identified and isolated, with a view to ultimately synthesizing them into a hierarchial organization relevant to the writing of a learning prescription (see Gilbert, 1962). In carrying out such an analysis, the analyst or teacher must consider not only the physical components of the subject (use of tools, references, job aids), but also the mental components (procedures, decisions, abstractions).

The task analysis must isolate all those overt acts which characterize either the subject material or job mastery. One way of doing this is to think of a topic or job as a hierarchical organization of levels or components, each of which describe the job in successively greater detail. At the highest level is the topic or job itself. This consists of a number of duties; each duty contains a number of tasks, and each task consists of a number of task elements. Such an organization is schematically illustrated in Figure 5–3. In topic analysis and job analysis, the task element is the smallest meaningful unit; in skills analysis, the task element is further broken down into 'acts.' An act is very similar to a therblig in time and motion study, and consists of a basic movement that must be repeated if it is interrupted. Four acts or therbligs occur most frequently; reaching for an object, grasping it, moving it, and positioning it.

Let us take an example. In making a job analysis of a psychomotor skill, the job could be that of an engine mechanic. His job is made up of a number of duties, including tuning the carburetor, adjusting the tappets, changing the oil, and cleaning the spark plugs. Each of these duties is made up of a number of separate tasks, all closely related to each other in sequence. For example, the

Figure 5-3. The hierarchy of behavioral levels in a task analysis.

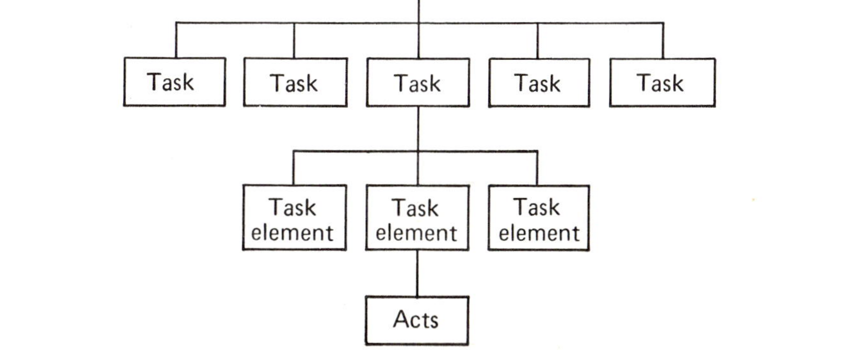

duty of changing the engine oil includes the tasks of jacking up the car, placing an oil container underneath the sump, taking out the sump drain plug, allowing the oil to drain away. Finally, each task includes a number of task elements. Jacking up the car, for instance, involves acquiring the right kind of jack, positioning it underneath the jacking-up points, and manipulating the jack so that it raises the car to the required level.

Even in more specifically cognitive or intellectual skills, a similar classification can be employed. The job or topic of solving mathematical problems by using logarithm tables, could include the duty of multiplying two numbers together. This duty would consist of the following tasks: finding the characteristics and mantissa of the two numbers, adding the logarithms together, antilogging the sum, fixing the decimal point, and connecting the answer to the appropriate number of significant figures. Finally, the task elements involved in finding the mantissa, for example, would consist of locating the first two significant figures of each number in the lefthand column of the logarithm tables, locating the third figure of each number in the appropriate middle columns headed 0–9, and locating the fourth figure in the add column headed 1–9 on the righthand side of the page.

Writing a Topic Analysis

Although there are a number of different ways of making a topic analysis (see Evans, Glaser, and Homme, 1962; Glaser, 1963; Mechner, 1965), few of them are structurally detailed enough as to make them practicable for our purpose. One of the most useful methods of topic analysis is based on the well-known matrix technique of program writing (Thomas, Davies, Openshaw, and Bird, 1963). . . .

In order to make a topic analysis, the teacher—who in this case is the master —will need to collect together all the relevant subject material and ensure that it is technically accurate and up-to-date. It would be old fashioned, for instance, to cite the use of fishplates between lengths of railway line as a precaution against the effects of expansion. Science and technology have now become popular, and scientific facts and applications, which were previously the preserve of the enlightened, are now everyday knowledge. This means that the teacher can no longer rely on the standard textbooks and reference books, but must look elsewhere for the latest findings and applications. Many teachers may well feel that this step is unnecessary because of their level of scholarship or their considerable teaching experience, but no step highlights deficiencies in knowledge more than topic analysis.

Once the subject material has been collected, the next step is to refine and limit the topic that the student is required to learn, and to ensure that it is as self-contained as possible. For instance, the topic of the theory of conservation of energy, involves duties such as Ohm's law and Joule's law. Often these topics and duties will be laid down in the syllabus, or prescribed in some other way, but usually in only the vaguest of terms. In any case, syllabuses are only an indication of content, and do not attempt to prescribe the order in which topics should be taught. Many teachers fall into the trap of slavishly following the order given in a syllabus to the detriment of their student's learning. One of the most important duties of the teacher is to reconcile the dictates of the syllabus, on the one hand, with the educational and learning needs of their students on the other.

Identifying Task Elements or Rules   Once the duty has been carefully delimited, it must be broken down into its *smallest* constituent parts. These, as we have seen, are called task elements, but in topic analysis they are more usually referred to as 'rules.' The identification of rules is probably the most skilled part of the whole process of topic analysis, and it demands that the teacher or analyst is—in every sense of the term—a subject matter expert. Although the teacher-analyst will be aided in his task by his experience, there is a considerable risk that the rules that he identifies will be too wide. It is also essential to ensure that the rules are carefully written and sequenced. Although the task of rule writing will be initially somewhat lengthy and laborious, experience and practice soon speed up the process.

In order to identify the rules, the teacher-analyst should ask himself five critical questions:

1. What does he expect the student to *do* to demonstrate that he has learned the topic?
2. What questions does he expect the student to answer?
3. What tasks, procedures, and techniques does he expect him to perform, and at what level does he expect them to be executed?
4. What discriminations does he expect the student to make, and in what terms does he expect these discriminations to be made?
5. What total changes in behaviour does he expect, and in what form does he expect to observe and measure them?

Such a definition of what the student is intended to *do* as a result of the planned learning experience, can best be referred to as the anticipated or *criterion* behavior.

Writing the Rule-Set   Writing rules is a way of life, a habit soon acquired by practice. In essence, a rule is a statement of generality, a definition, a fact, or an item of information. For instance, each of the following statements constitutes a rule:

1. Metals expand when heated.
2. A sonnet has fourteen lines.
3. A contract is an agreement enforceable by law.
4. Latitude is angular distance north and south of the Equator.

Each rule should be complete in itself, a complete fact or idea. They form the raw materials or building blocks, which—related and interrelated together— will make up first the duty and then the topic.

Rules should be written in such a way that:

1. They contain only *one* fact or idea.
2. They are written at the same level of generality as all preceding rules.
3. They take the form of simple, declarative (kernel) sentences.
4. They avoid negative forms, qualifications, and conjunctions.
5. They possess only *one* active verb.
6. They are critical and essential to the task.

Generally speaking, they will rarely contain more than a dozen words; indeed, the shorter and simpler the rule, the better it will be.

It must be borne in mind that the objective is not to write as many rules as possible, but only to write those that are intellectually necessary to the task. Every step must be taken to avoid the common mistake of attempting to teach too much in too short a time. Accordingly, the rules must be carefully sifted; each fact should be considered in relation to the task, and material outside the chosen parameters should be rejected. In this way, rules can be gradually revised and refined until only the absolutely essential ones remain.

Arranging the Rules into a Logical Sequence   As the rules are written, of course, they will be arranged into some type of natural sequence. Steps must now be taken to ensure that this sequence is a completely logical one from the point of view of the subject material. Each rule should lead naturally to the next, so that—in effect—they set up and completely describe the duty. This sequence is likely to be based upon the teacher's own subject expertise, upon his teaching experience, upon intuition, and upon his own learning experience.

The following, traditional rules of sequence will often prove helpful in arranging the rules:

1. Proceed from the known to the unknown.
2. Proceed from the simple to the complex.
3. Proceed from the concrete to the abstract.
4. Proceed from observation to reasoning.
5. Proceed from a whole view to a more detailed view to a whole view.

In accomplishing this, it will often be found useful to so write and arrange the rules that they appear to complement each other. A word, topic, or concept introduced in one rule, is built-on or expanded upon in the next. In this way, the rules are chained or dovetailed together, and new teaching points are not suddenly, but gradually, introduced into the sequence. . . .

Writing a Job Analysis

In a topic analysis, the teacher or instructor is the master, but in a job analysis the master[1] is the tradesman doing the job at the required level of mastery.

[1]In work study and work measurement, the term 'experienced worker standard' (EWS) is usually employed to refer to the master. EWS is equivalent to the 100 performance of the British Standard Scale.

For this reason, a job analysis takes place at the workplace, not in the library or study. The task analyst observes what the tradesman does, how he does it, what he does it with, what he does it to, and, finally, why he does it. This enables the characteristics of the job to be identified and isolated, so that meaningful predictions can be made about the training requirements of the task.

Every job is but a small part of a much larger system, and, furthermore, is affected by that larger system. Thus, the first step in carrying out a job analysis is to describe, analyze, and review the relevant operational system within which the job is performed. In this analysis, every effort must be made to study the management system in so far as it affects the job, both from the point of view of the task itself and from the point of view of the interpersonal relationships that are involved. Work, in other words, is viewed within the framework of a sociotechnical system (see Trist *et al.,* 1963), and in this way it is possible to ask what *combination* of technology, initial worker characteristics, and organizational structures are most likely to result in an effective and efficient work organization. Such an approach ensures that the job is not viewed in isolation, and that solutions other than training are explored.

After having carried out this general systems analysis, the analyst will have defined the major parameters of the job. Once these have been determined, he is ready to begin making his analysis of an actual job within the system. The first step is to identify and isolate a particular task, and to interview the tradesman so as to determine the objectives that he wishes to realize. It is important that the job should then be done at the usual workplace, and, during this run-through, the analyst should make no attempt to make any record. The aim of this initial phase is to gain an overview of the task, which can serve as a conceptual framework for the actual analysis. Questions involving the working strategy can then be discussed, and particular difficulties highlighted.

Identification of Cues or Signals   In analyzing any job, the identification of cues that signal a required course of action is particularly important. The cue may be a light, a needle on a dial, the pitch of gear whine, the smell of hot and inadequate lubricant supply. On the other hand, the cue may be a partially complete table, a particular mathematical symbol, or even a rebuke from the supervisor. However, while there can be an endless list of cues, they can be broadly classified into one of four types—depending upon the type of information that they carry.

The following types of cues are readily recognizable:

1. *Cues which carry two state or go-no-go information.* Here the cue is a simple one, and is presented in an unambiguous form, e.g., the warning lights on a dashboard of a car, a particular temperature, a flat car tire.
2. *Cues which carry digital information.* Here the cue is *one* of a discrete number of states, e.g., the position of a gear lever, tabular information, a predetermined film rinsing time.
3. *Cues which carry continuous or scalor information.* Here the cue constantly signals any theoretically infinite number of states, e.g., an instrument reading, a micrometer reading.

4. *Cues which carry vector information.* Here the cues have both magnitude and direction, e.g., an ammeter with charge and discharge positions, a turn and slip indicator, metal shaping.

In some jobs, only one type of cue may be involved; in others, all types of cues are present, e.g., in the cockpit of a VC 10 aircraft. Each cue, with information as to its type, must be recognized and entered on the task analysis record sheet, since it may well determine the course of action that is taken by the master.

Identifying Task Elements   Once the cues have been recognized, it is a fairly straightforward matter to identify the resulting behavior. This is best done by asking, 'What does the master *do*'? And then get the master to carry out the job at a speed dictated by the analyst. As each of the task elements is performed, a short description of it should be entered on the analysis sheet— together with an occasional note on any special difficulties, tips or hints, or operating standards. . . .

Just as particular care has to be taken in writing the rules for a topic analysis, so the task elements of a job analysis must be precisely recorded. Task elements, as we have seen, form the basic raw material of the job. They should be written in such a way that:

1. They contain only *one* action or movement.
2. They are written at the same level of generality as all the preceding task elements.
3. They take the form of a simple, declarative (kernel) sentence.
4. They avoid negatives, qualifications, and conjunctions.
5. They possess only *one* active verb.
6. They are critical and essential to the task.

The cardinal principle in writing task elements is that they should be expressed in such specific detail that a student, who knows only the names, location, and identity of the components, can perform the task—but without the speed and accuracy of the master.

Classification of Task Elements   In order to determine the actual conceptual nature of the work involved, each task element should be categorized. Such a classification scheme has been devised by Davies and Thomas (1967), and used successfully on a large-scale task analysis of a complete RAF trade. In this scheme, each task element is graded on a five-point scale, the details of which are shown in Figure 5–4.

It will be seen that from the taxonomy of task levels that:

1. *Level 5 is defined as a signal task.* Task elements that are categorized as level 5 involve simple actions that are carried out in response to a cue or prompt. In every case, there will be clear indication that an action is required, and there will also be immediate feedback as to whether the action has been successfully accomplished.

Figure 5–4. A taxonomy of task elements or levels for use in a job analysis.

Level	Definition	Description	Example
5	A signal task element	A simple action—the need for the action is obvious and there is immediate feedback as to success of action.	Switching on lights at nightfall.
4	A procedural task element	An action forming part of a routine or subroutine. The actions have to be carried out in a fixed order.	The changing of a wheel on a motor car would follow a prescribed pattern.
3	A simple discriminatory task element	An action in which essential differences or similarities have to be recognized; the discriminations will be simple and straightforward.	The reconnection of ignition leads to spark plugs.
2	A complex discriminatory task element	An action, similar to 3, involving finer and/or multiple discriminations.	The same example as in 3, but where the lengths and curvature of the leads cannot be used as cues for discrimination. The firing order would have to be determined and reference made to the distributor.
1	A diagnostic or problem-solving task element	An action concerned with the detection, isolation, identification, or correction of faults.	The use of an electronic test set on a faulty vehicle and subsequent interpretation of results would include the type of task element.

2. *Level 4 is defined as a procedural task.* Task elements that are categorized as level 4 form part of a series of associated elements, which have to be carried out in a fixed sequence as a routine or subroutine. Most routine servicing and functional checks are procedural in character. While there may be some latitude in the sequencing of subroutines, once a particular subroutine has started, the order of the task elements is fixed and predetermined. It is true, of course, that the first task element in a procedure could be classified as level 5, but the convention is to categorize every task element in the routine or subroutine as level 4.

3. *Levels 3 and 2 are defined as discriminatory tasks.* Both these levels involve the recognition of essential differences or revealing contrasts. In

some cases, the discriminations are easily made but are, nevertheless, critical (level 3); in other cases, the discriminations are more difficult and subtle, and can involve multiple discriminations of a fine order (level 2).

4. *Level 1 is defined as a diagnostic or problem-solving task.* Task elements that are categorized as level 1 involve diagnostic or problem-solving strategies and cover three related activities:
   (a) The detection of faults from observable symptoms.
   (b) The isolation and identification of the sources of the fault.
   (c) The correction of faults. . . .

Checking the Job Analysis When the analysis of a particular job has been completed, the analyst should check it out. This should be done first with the tradesman himself, in case certain task elements have been omitted, and then with the tradesman's supervisor, so as to ensure that the actions and standards are acceptable. Once the job analysis is agreed, it should be repeated under as wide a range of operating conditions and environments as possible. This, in fact, is a very rapid procedure, since the analyst simply watches the job being done, compares the actions with those on his analysis sheet, and records any deviations.

In this way, differences in carrying out a job can be isolated and identified. These must then be critically studied so as to determine whether they are due to:

1. Operating under different working conditions.
2. Variations in the nature of the task itself.
3. Differences in skill levels or attitudes to the job.
4. Employing more or less effective methods of working.
5. Simple variations in style.

The analysis sheets can then be amended or annotated accordingly, and the differences agreed.

Writing a Skills Analysis

Skills analysis is clearly distinguishable from topic and job analysis, in the sense that it is concerned with *how* a job is done, in addition to *what* is done. In other words, skills analysis builds on the basis laid down by job analysis and adds to it an analysis of the knowledge and skills used by an experienced, as distinct from an inexperienced, worker. Every job has a 'knowing' and a 'doing' side, and the important thing is to identify these two aspects of the task. . . . Job analysis and skills analysis are not mutually exclusive in character; skills analysis is supplementary to job analysis.

Initially, the late Dr. A. H. Seymour called the technique of skills analyses 'process analysis,' although in America the term 'analytical method' (AM) is still preferred. The Department of Employment and Productivity *Glossary of Training Terms* (1967) defines skills analysis as: 'The identification and recording of the psycho-physiological characteristics of skilled performance and the determination of the effector,[2] receptor[3] and decision-making functions involved.' In other words, skills analysis is concerned with studying both the overt and the covert manifestations of skill, and—in so doing—has redeemed the tendency to concentrate only on the observable manifestations of a worker's behavior. It is, therefore, a depth analysis of skilled performance, and its application has dramatically reduced training time and costs by at least 50 percent (Ramsden, 1966). The excellent book by W. D. Seymour (1968) is particularly recommended as a simple, but authoritative guide to the technique.

The Objectives of Skills Analysis   Skill has been defined by Mace (1950) as 'an ability to produce consistently an intended effect with accuracy, speed, and economy of action.' In order to gain an adequate view of such behavior, it is necessary to consider:

1. What actions does the experienced worker perform at each stage of the task?
2. What information does he obtain via his five senses at each of these stages?
3. How does he use this information to determine and control those bodily movements that are necessary to skilled performance?

The answers to these three questions supply the raw material of skills analysis. By using this information, it is argued, it is possible to bring unskilled personnel up to the master's or experienced worker's standard (EWS) of quality and output in the shortest possible time, since one can concentrate on the critical interactions between manual, sensory, and mental work processes.

Analyzing the Skill   Crossman and Seymour (1957) have developed a comprehensive method of analyzing perceptual activities. Each activity, they argue, is first, planned, then, initiated, next, controlled, then, terminated, and, finally, checked. These five phases extend to effector, receptor, and mental (decision-making) processes, and enable the tradesman to organize the information coming to his senses more effectively. In this way, the acquisition of such a temporary sequence allows him to make decisions more effectively and quickly, and so become more efficient and skilled at the job. Analyzing a skill necessitates the recognition and isolation of these successive stages in the perceptual processes, and the identification of the relative importance of each to each of the senses in particular jobs. For instance, an experienced typist will spend less time than a trainee visually checking that she is using the right finger, since she will know by the feel and rhythm that she is making the correct movements.

---

[2]Effector processes involve those senses which are concerned with actual motor movements, e.g., fingers, hands, legs, muscles, etc.

[3]Receptor processes involve those senses which are concerned with incoming sensations, e.g., sight, touch, hearing, taste, and smell.

Some jobs, like assembly work, are mainly concerned with manual skills, but a large proportion of industrial work involves jobs in which knowledge is as important, or more important, as the manual skills involved. This knowledge will include information about the factory and workplace, information about the job itself and the processes involved, as well as quality information about fault finding and fault diagnosis. In order to obtain this information about the knowledge requirements of the job, it is necessary to talk to the master at considerable length, and try to get him to say why he carries out particular actions and how he knows when the actions are necessary. All this involves striking up a close personal relationship, so as to obtain and record the shop-floor job lore in the skills analysis. Merely watching a workman doing the job will reveal little of the complex decision-making processes involved.

The first step in carrying out the skills analysis is to identify and record every detail of every act or body movement that the master makes in doing the job. This will include such details as which parts of the body are involved and over what distances, as well as identifying which senses are used in order to accomplish each of the actions. Each piece of information must be seen within the five-stage activity framework of planning, initiating, controlling, terminating, and checking; and particular care should be taken to identify and isolate the cues which begin and terminate each cycle or subroutine. . . .

Circumstances Calling for a Skills Analysis It has been pointed out by Wellens (1968) that there is a tendency to consider that 'all training of operators and other manual workers should, without exception, be based on skills analysis. This is quite wrong.' In the majority of work situations, a job analysis is sufficient, particularly when it is remembered that making a full skills analysis may involve many months of highly skilled work. The real difficulty lies in deciding when a skills analysis may be profitably carried out.

Generally speaking, the following circumstances, while not exhaustive, may be used as indicators of situations calling for skills analysis:

1. Tasks that call for operations involving complex, subtle hand, finger, and/or eye coordinations.
2. Tasks that call for unusual movements, postures, or rhythms not found in everyday life, e.g., movements concerned with the hand-operated safety guards on power presses.
3. Tasks that call for abnormal use of the senses, e.g., inspection of hand-sewing needles requires highly developed discrimination in the senses of touch.
4. Tasks that call for a great deal of covert information processing and decision making which might be overlooked in a conventional job analysis. On some occasions, a complete skills analysis of the task may be necessary. Whenever possible, however, skills analysis should be confined to those subroutines where the special circumstances listed above are found to occur. In this way, the expense and time involved in making a skills analysis can be reserved for those occasions when benefits are likely

to be greatest. It is interesting to note, in this regard, that many so-called skills analyses are often no more than job analyses set down in the skills analysis format. Only in particular critical areas does the analysis become a skills analysis in the *real* sense of the term.

Summary

The analytic approach to curriculum development has proved to be useful in vocational programs and in other parts of the curriculum where hierarchical learning is involved. As noted earlier, it has been strongly criticized for being atomistic, static, and rigid to the point of allowing the student little choice about what and how he will learn. But in parts of the school program where the end product is determined and the order of learning is relatively fixed, these objections have less weight than in areas such as literature and social studies where the learning outcomes are more varied and more open to pupil choice. At any rate, this approach is of long standing, dating back to the beginning of the century, and the arguments in its defense are not to be taken lightly.

Chapter **6**

The Futuristic Style

Instructor, 84, 6 (February 1975):154.

"Educational time machines must be on the horizon. That's a kindergarten class from the future on a field trip into the past."

That the world, no less than our own society, is different today from what it was at the beginning of this century cannot be doubted. To what are we coming is the question. Will the future be like the present, or will it be so different as to constitute a new age?

Social Transition: In What Direction?

Prophets of both hope and doom are among us. Part of the intellectual community suffers from anxieties over an impending world disaster. If the world is not destroyed by an atomic holocaust, it most likely will be by inadvertent yet, overproduction of energy. The ozone layer may be eroded and our lives lost by the sweep of deadly rays. Daily we pollute the air, water, and earth, thereby destroying the source of our sustenance. Some deadly form of life may be produced in laboratories and accidently, or by design, released upon society. And if we escape all these, we shall surely be doomed because the world's population growth will outstrip our capacity to produce the materials to sustain us.

Another part of the intellectual community is optimistic. They see no reason to fear the future, for it will be better than the past. These prophets of hope believe that the world will have adequate sources of energy, metals, food, and the technical ability to meet safely the needs of the world's people. The real problems, in their view, are political and institutional rather than scarce resources.

123

If we are in a period of social transition, as some authorities claim, the question the curriculum worker faces is: What does it mean for education? Should the schools develop programs of instruction to enable individuals to cope with the problems of the transition? If so, what does such a program entail? Should the school program prepare individuals for the future society that will issue from the transition? If so, how do we construct an educational program for life in a world that nobody knows?

If indeed the world is entering a new age, much of what is done through the schools will depend on the attitude of the people no less than the leaders. We are told by no less an authority than Alfred North Whitehead that great social transitions induce either hope or despair. It all depends on the social position one occupies, the breadth and depth of evidence, and the weight given to the dumb forces that partly shape the course of history.

Two Contrasting Pictures of the Future

The futuristic style of curriculum theorizing will likely be based on either hope or despair. Each attitude is rooted in its own set of beliefs, assumptions, and forecasts. In the present world situation it is well to stand back and consider the two major perspectives that now color our thinking.

Neo-Malthusian Beliefs and Conclusions	Post-Industrial (and Super-Industrial) Perspective
Basic Model	
1. Fixed Pie: We have a fairly good idea of what the world can provide. Therefore it can be thought of as a "fixed pie." Since there is only so much pie, it should be distributed more evenly. Otherwise the rich will grow richer and the poor will grow poorer. We should not irresponsibly use up or destroy the common patrimony of man, thus denying it to our grandchildren.	*1. Growing Pie:* No one knows exactly what the earth holds or can produce—or what new uses may be made of its resources. Thus the situation can be likened to a "growing pie." The more one produces, the more one can produce (within limits). Increases in productivity or affluence anywhere often create conditions that lead to similar conditions everywhere.
More Technology and More Capital	
2. Diminishing Returns: New technology and additional capital investment, necessary to extract marginal	*2. Absolutely Necessary:* New technology and capital investment are necessary not only to increase pro-

"Two Characteristic Current Views on Technology and Economic Growth." Adopted by *The Futurist* from a Hudson Institute Document. Reprinted from *The Futurist,* vol. 9, no. 6 (December 1975): 335–38, by permission of World Future Society.

Footnotes have been renumbered consecutively throughout the chapter.

resources, will vastly increase pollution—probably to lethal levels—and markedly accelerate the approaching exhaustion of resources. In any case, we shall have to cope increasingly with diminishing marginal returns and utilities—increasingly facing situations in which the effort required for the returns gained increases dramatically.

duction to desirable levels, but to help protect and improve the environment, to keep resource costs down, and to provide an economic surplus to solve our problems and to meet crises. If we are reasonably prudent and flexible, we will not have to contend with any really serious shortages in the medium run and will do even better in the long run. (However, we must be on the alert for far-fetched and unlikely but potentially catastrophic events that may result from misunderstood innovations or inappropriate growth.)

Management and Decision Making

3. Likely Failure: The rapidity of change, the growing complexity of problems, and the increase of conflicting interests will all make it surprisingly difficult to manage resources effectively, control pollution, and resolve conflicts. We must have some sort of slowdown of change, a simplification of issues, and centralized region/wide (or worldwide) decision making—even if revolutionary or other drastic actions are required to get them.

3. Probable Success: The systematic internalization of relevant external costs and the normal use of the price and other market mechanisms can deal with most issues. Some low but practical degree of public regulation and international cooperation can deal with most or all of the rest. With some possible exceptions, the level of management required is not remarkably high, particularly if the system learns from experience. (Good management can, of course, increase the speed and accuracy of reaction and reduce the pain.)

Resources

4. Rapid Depletion: Man is rapidly depleting the earth's food, energy, and mineral resources. He is even running out of space for getting rid of pollution products. Many key resources will soon be seriously depleted. While most of these problems will not arise in catastrophic form until early in the next century, environmental pollution and increasing shortages of food, materials, and other resources are not only becoming critical problems now

4. Adequacy: Leaving aside for the moment some very specialized and/or far-fetched issues, it would be possible to support, more or less satisfactorily (at least by likely middle-class standards) world populations of 20 or 30 billion at levels of $20,000 or $30,000 per capita for centuries. We could do this with current and near current technology; given likely technological progress we should do much better. Further, technological progress and

but are clearly precursors of more disastrous events in the medium- and long-term future.

large economic surpluses make it likely that we can deal with specialized and/or far-fetched issues if they arise.

Current Growth

5. Uncontrolled Exponential and/or Cancerous: The gross world product now is doubling every fourteen years and world population every thirty-three years. Even if the current level of population and production could be sustained indefinitely, current exponential growth in both will accelerate dramatically the approaching exhaustion of resources and of our ability to cope with pollution; indeed, unless stopped soon by drastic programs, today's exponential growth will lead inevitably to an early and catastrophic collision with resource limitations or pollution constraints.

5. Eventually a Transition to Stability: While such long-run projections are inherently uncertain, one can make a plausible case for world population stabilizing in the twenty-first century at about 15 billion, gross world product (GWP) at about $300 trillion, and GWP per capita at about $20,000 per year. These figures could go up or down by factors of perhaps two, three, and four, respectively. That is, population should be between seven and thirty billion, GWP between $50 and $1,000 trillion, and GWP per capita between $5,000 and $60,000.

Resources
Innovation and Discovery

6. A Trap: New discoveries of resources, new technologies, and new projects may postpone the immediate need for drastic actions, but not for long. Such postponement will make the eventual collapse more severe and possibly come even earlier. Prudence demands immediate restraint and cutbacks. There must be a basic change in values and objectives; the time for short-run palliation is past.

6. Huge Improvements: New resources, technology, and economic growth often produce new problems and crises but they can still be used to solve problems, improve efficiency, and upgrade the quality of life. Even more important, they increase the toughness and flexibility of the economy and society, thus giving us insurance against bad luck or incompetency.

Income Gaps and Poverty

7. Gaps Increase: Dangerous gaps in income (both domestic and international) are widening rapidly. A worldwide "class war" or a series of desperate political crises is imminent. The likelihood of these tragedies occuring is heightened by increasing growth in the rich nations, particu-

7. Poverty Decreases: The next century will likely see worldwide abolition of most absolute poverty. However, some arithmetical gaps will probably increase until the middle or end of the century. Both the rich and the poor will get richer, but some people will continue to be much

larly when they selfishly consume—or even squander—the resources obtained at bargain prices from the poor nations.

richer than others. Gaps between rich and poor will make it easier to accelerate economic development for the poor.

Industrial Development

8. A Disaster: Further industrialization of the third world would be disastrous, and further growth of the developed world even worse. Therefore, the rich should halt their industrial growth and share their present wealth with the poor. The poor nations should not sell their increasingly valuable resources so cheaply or so rapidly.

8. Must Continue: Industrialization of the third world will (and should) continue. The rich nations will not deprive themselves in order to share with the poor. And the poor will not be strong enough in the foreseeable future to seize much of the wealth of the rich by force. The poor nations cannot benefit greatly from resources left in the ground.

Quality of Life

9. Growth vs. Quality of Life: Continued growth of the world's population and economy means further deterioration of the environment, overcrowding, suburban sprawl, and a society suitable for automobiles, trucks, and planes but not for human beings. We must change our priorities. In particular, market demand is not the same as need; GNP is not wealth; high technology is not the same as the good life; automation and appliances do not necessarily increase human happiness.

9. Eventually Everyone Will Have A High Quality of Life: If one does not adequately internalize appropriate external costs, growth can cause much unnecessary destruction of important values. Once there is adequate internalizing of appropriate external costs (by the criteria of most members of society), the complaints may still be very shrill and visible but largely inappropriate or very specialized.

Long Range Outlook

10. The Current Emergency Is Total: Unless revolutionary changes are soon made, the twenty-first century will see the greatest catastrophe since the black death. Large-scale damage is a plague to the environment and to the ecology of many areas. Billions will die of hunger, pollution, and/or wars over shrinking resources. Other billions will have to be held down by harsh authoritarian governments. Indeed it may be better to have some

10. Things Are Going Reasonably Well: The twenty-first century is likely to see a post-industrial economy in which most of the more desperate and seemingly eternal problems of human poverty will have been solved or greatly alleviated. Most misery will derive from the anxieties and ambiguities of wealth and luxury, not from physical suffering due to scarcities. While many tragic mistakes and much suffering will mark the

die today than to have many die in the future. The crisis is grave and some draconian measures may be justified now to alleviate the extent and intensity of the future collapse.

transition to a materially abundant life for almost everyone, the ultimate prospect is breathtakingly superior to the poverty and scarcity that have been man's lot through history. The postindustrial society and culture which will eventually accompany the postindustrial economy should be close to a humanistic utopia by most historic standards.

A Futurist Looks at The School And Curriculum

If the teaching profession accepts the beliefs of either the prophet of doom or the prophet of hope, fundamental modifications in the structure of the educational system as well as in the curriculum will probably be made. Harold G. Shane, in the following selection, discusses what these modifications might be. Shane has set forth succinctly some of the modifications in schooling implicit in the futurist orientation to education.

Essentially what is proposed in this selection is that the graded system of schooling be abandoned in the interest of developing a more flexible system. This would allow and encourage more choices by the learner, participation of school youth in adult civic and vocational responsibilities, and the opportunity for the individual to enter school at any point during his life and to exit when his need for further learning has been satisfied. In addition, there is a call for a subject matter that emphasizes, among other things, a humanistic orientation and an understanding of possible futures and of the problems they will confront.

It should be pointed out that the futuristic style of curriculum theorizing like other styles has a history. In this connection, it is perhaps worthwhile to point out that some fifty years ago Harold Rugg advanced the view that the curriculum, at least in the social sciences, should be based on what he called the "frontier thinkers approach." According to Rugg, studies should be made of what the leading thinkers in various fields think the persistent problems and issues of the future will be. From the same sources one was also to learn the opinions about the knowledge that would be required to deal with these problems and issues. From the findings of such a study the curriculum maker would be able to design a curriculum to prepare the youth to deal with the world to come. Today there is new knowledge about people and their environment and new techniques for exploring the probable futures. The work of Harold Rugg had a profound influence upon the social studies curriculum and it will not be surprising were a similar influence to be felt from the research and curriculum thinking identified with the futurist movement.

The following selection begins with the problem of restructuring education and then moves into a discussion of the choice of subject matter for future decades.

◻

Perhaps a simple statement, accompanied by uncomplicated models, is the best means of capturing the educational significance of life-long opportunities for learning and of depicting the idea of a seamless continuum. Let us begin with education for the youngest.

Early Childhood Education   Although a seamless curriculum has no conventional segments, such as "preschool" or "middle school," such familiar terms are used here to facilitate communication and to convey more readily an understanding of the learner's progress through a continuum.

The outset of life-long learning opportunities would begin with the child's first direct contacts with the educational community somewhere near the date of his second birthday. Let us call this the *nonschool preschool* experience. This early introduction to the school would include obtaining data from physical and mental examinations, compiling background information, and so on. The nonschool preschool interval also would provide a beginning for computerized cumulative record forms for what might become a nationwide student data bank, although only if confidentiality can be guaranteed.

Depending on his maturity, direct instructional contact with a school program would begin near a child's third birthday. At this point he would, for half-days, enter a *minischool* group of six or eight other three-year olds. This cluster of experiences quite probably would be directed by a paraprofessional who, in turn, was supervised (along with six or eight other paraprofessionals) by a teacher-consultant with full credentials and experience. Work in the minischool would be educational rather than custodial, carried forward on a "developmental" basis—one deliberately designed to provide socialization and rich cognitive input. This input is gaining greater importance as it becomes recognized that meaningful experiences may very well be the raw material of what is subsequently measured as intelligence. This does not, however, imply a need to provide early "academic" experience in, say, reading or mathematics.

When he is approximately four in the seamless curriculum a child would find himself transposed[1] to the *preprimary component* of the curriculum. He would move from the minischool when deemed ready, not at a set calendar date. Administratively, the change would be analogous to the processes involved when mid-semester transfer pupils appear in a new classroom because their parents have moved to a different school district. Furthermore, the preprimary period proposed here is not the same as most contemporary four- and five-year old kindergartens. It would be more of an *educational* "ready-room" than a *custodial* "romper-room;" a learning center with methodical input rather than a custodial center merely featuring supervised care and entertainment in a safe, plastic environmental bubble.

Harold G. Shane, *The Educational Significance of the Future* (Bloomington, Ind.: Phi Delta Kappa Educational Foundation, 1973), pp. 68–91. Reprinted by permission of the publisher.

[1]The term "transposed" is used in lieu of "promoted." Presumably one cannot be promoted in an unbroken or seamless curriculum through which he moves without the artificial promotions that now take him from one grade to another.

During the variable interval that a child spent in the preprimary continuum, empathizing teachers would create an interesting, challenging climate, and help each student to reach an optimum point of development before his transition into the program designed for him during the primary years. The fast learning and mature, perhaps two or three youngsters out of a total of fifty, might move from the primary continuum into the primary school in as little time as one year, and as early as at age five, to work with children of six or seven. Conversely, some boys and girls (among them the physically handicapped, the disadvantaged, culturally deprived, or slow maturing) might need to invest their time in three or even four make-ready years and postpone any extensive work with six- or seven-year olds until they were eight and occasionally even nine.

During the primary years, which are conceived to be an integral part of a continuum beginning in early childhood, most children would be from six to nine years of age. But the groups in which they work would *not* be based on chronological age. Instead they would be ephemeral groupings built around emergent projects involving inquiry, exploratory, expressive, and cognitive ventures in which a varied mix of ages would be found—just as such children now work or play in informal, neighborhood groups.

The Flow of Learning During the Middle School Years   In the seamless curriculum, the pupil would move without interruption, from the primary continuum to the middle school continuum. The transposition would occur at whatever time during an unbroken school year that it became apparent (in the professional judgment of the faculty) that a young learner was ready to function in a predominantly nine- to twelve-year age range rather than in a predominantly six- to nine-year age cluster or pod. In some instances, where children in the middle school years and primary years are housed in the same building, the child's translation or transposition to older working groups would be virtually undiscernible. In other instances, depending on the physical plant, a change from one building to another would be involved, but it should occur with a minimum of fuss or fanfare.

The governing principles suggested for the primary continuum would tend to prevail in the middle school continuum. In this span of approximately three years, the learner would spend from as little as two years to as many as five. (See Figure 6–1.) The concepts of double promotion or "skipping" would totally disappear, however. So would the retardation practice of "flunking." In a personalized continuum, one would move at his own speed without reference to group norms.[2] In the process, over a period of time, the age range of children in the primary and middle school phases of the continuum would and should extend so that eventually the elementary age range would be not from six to twelve years as at present, but would extend from five- to fifteen-

---

[2]The concept of "group norms" based on evaluation instruments would disappear. They would be replaced by "personalized norms;" i.e., quantified data on samplings of personal progress data for large groups of individuals sharing certain characteristics as to health, sex, intelligence, and so forth. This does not mean that standards would be abolished but the criteria would be different. That is, two persons of widely different abilities and performance levels might be equally successful if each performed at his full capacity.

Figure 6-1. Model of the seamless curriculum: an emerging school structure for the 1980s.

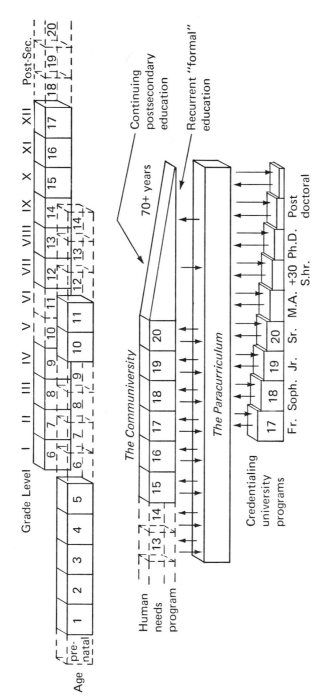

Note: Organizational divisions by ages are

2 Nonschool preschool   10-13 Upper and lower middle school
3 Minischool   14-20+ Secondary-community college continuum
4-5 Preprimary continuum   15-70+ University and postsecondary continuum
6-9 Primary continuum

Numbers in each cube refer to the learner's approximate age.

year oldness—exclusive of programs for early childhood groups ranging from age two or three to ages five and six. It should be understood, however, that an increase in the age range would not proportionately increase the range in ability. The continuum approach would actually tend to decrease the four-to-eight-year range in performance found in, say, a present-day fourth grade group.[3] Over a period of years in the continuum school, ability-referenced rather than chronologically-referenced groups would emerge.

New Secondary School Concepts: The Paracurriculum   Although the more highly structured content of many secondary schools would require some adjustments, the idea of uninterrupted progress could and should carry over to and continue in the high school phase. This would involve careful guidance of the individual learner, abandonment of many rigid contemporary requirements for admission, for exit, and for reentry and require considerable reeducation on the part of those teachers who are predominantly subject and semester minded. Improving educational technologies, the development of more sophisticated programmed materials, and the increased use of differentiated staffing seem likely to ease many problems in the gradual transition to a continuum at the early and middle adolescent levels.

The most formidable impediment to changes in the secondary school program is likely to be found in the minds of some teachers, parents, and administrators. Even those who quickly accept the merit of the seven points on subject matter are likely to need considerable convincing and reeducation with respect to cross-disciplinary approaches to subject matter, the flexible "teaching partnership" concept, and teaching to develop desired attitudes and values in addition to subject matter content *per se.*

One of the most interesting but little discussed and least explored developments implicit in the continuum is the concept of the paracurriculum and its implications for major modifications in the compulsory education laws presently found in many states in the union. The *paracurriculum concept recognizes that schooling provides only a part of the experiential input that adds up to the learner's education.* Indeed, in many instances the nonschool learnings of children and youth may be by far the most extensive (and sometimes the most valuable) components or factors in helping him to cope with, to manipulate, and to control his environment.

Before continuing further, the term "paracurriculum" should be defined more explicitly. The word refers to the body of out-of-school experiences that help to strengthen the intellectual ability, general background, and coping powers of the child or youth. To whatever extent possible, secondary and postsecondary education institutions should deliberately plan to make greater and more deliberate use of the paracurriculum. As shown by the model in Figure 6–2, the paracurriculum—the world of nonschool experiences for

---

[3]It must be borne in mind that grade groupings often subsumes and conceals enormous ability differences in today's schools. The last year in which I taught grade four, spring achievement test profiles for the group ranged from Paul, with a second grade, eighth month score, to Sally who made 8.5! Obviously, continuum-type progress would help to alleviate such unit classroom discrepancies.

Figure 6-2. Model of an educational continuum: the curricular-paracurricular relationship in their secondary and postsecondary phases.

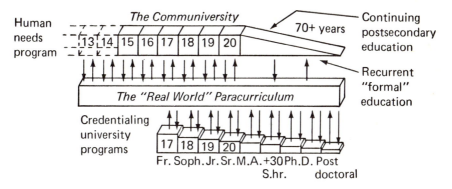

which the school is participatory planner and for which it serves as a broker —parallels the curriculum as the name obviously suggests. As is illustrated by the model, the paracurriculum involves world-of-work experiences, sometimes without but usually with pay, which temporarily or permanently replace in-school activities.

As conceived here, the paracurriculum concept might be implemented as follows:

1. At age fifteen, perhaps even as early as age thirteen in rare instances, a student for whom it is judged appropriate could engage in a useful vocational activity without attending school.

2. His later move from the world of the school to the "real world," as implied in the model, would be arranged or "brokered" by the school. This process would involve teachers' professional judgments, indepth counseling, parental understanding, consent, support, and cooperation, and close working relationships with employers who are socially minded and willing to offer their enterprises as alternatives to conventional schooling without exploiting fourteen- to sixteen-year old worker-learners.

3. The paracurriculum would eliminate "push-outs" and dropouts. One simply does not drop out of an educational continuum; he moves at a 90 degree angle (see model) into planned paracurricular learnings and continues his education in what, hopefully, will be an experience of increased educational significance.

4. An integral part of the paracurriculum is the privilege of infinite, methodically planned life-long exit and reentry privileges carefully coordinated through enlightened guidance practices. (See arrows in Figure 6–1). The planned reentry is an indispensable ingredient. Lacking this ingredient, an early leaving age reopens the Pandora's box of child labor and exploitation of the disadvantaged.

5. The continuum of schooling and the paracurriculum are portrayed as being almost as intimately related as Siamese twins, and both deeply involve the strong and enlightened effort of the educational community. By age fourteen, after approximately a decade of guided, personalized progress, the early adolescent would be helped to move from curriculum to paracurriculum *and vice versa* without problems and without any clinging stigma. Furthermore, with graded structures abandoned, there would no longer be an eighth grade group or a sophomore class from which to withdraw. Age ranges, greatly increased by the flexible and often ephemeral and functional approaches to grouping, would also make exit and reentry inconspicuous and matter-of-fact as in graduate study where persons in their early twenties may rub shoulders with students twice their age.

6. As envisioned here, the paracurricular concept is not a limited innovation applicable at the early adolescent level. Rather, it is part of the total warp and woof of life-long education. It is applicable even in early childhood in the form of simple community service contributions (e.g., keeping a park or playground clean) and in the learner's later maturity when, perhaps at sixty, he returns from the paracurricular to the curricular realm with the hope of making his retirement more meaningful or a postretirement job more feasible through his further education.

Despite the novel organizational configuration of the paracurricular concept, it is made up of components that have already been discussed and sometimes introduced on the U.S. educational scene under such labels as "socially useful work," "continuing education," or "paid internships." If and as the idea of a seamless, life-long, year-round educational continuum gains acceptance, the paracurricular concept might well become a viable and important concomitant source—a kind of launching pad—for many alternative approaches to learning in our educational futures. It clearly reflects the idea that we do not need alternatives *to* schools, so much as we need more imaginative alternatives *within* the established educational community.

Postsecondary Education   Our résumé of possible changes in the infrastructure of U.S. education, as inferred from futures research, now is described with reference to the final phase of the continuum: the postsecondary phase, including, of course, the university but also embracing forms of noncollegiate postsecondary learning resources.

As shown in Figure 6–2, a reproduction of Figure 6–1, the postsecondary student might either be a person who had completed four years of secondary (curricular) education or someone who had been continuing his education in world-of-work (paracurricular) activities. In either case, he would not be deprived of access to, or of the opportunity to complete, whatever components of education that brought him personal satisfaction or increased the likelihood of vocational success.

Also notice in Figure 6–2 that "secondary" and "postsecondary" education are depicted as an uninterrupted continuum. They are paralleled by the life-long paracurriculum and intimately interlinked by infinite exit and reentry privileges, which ensure that no one at any age is deprived of postsecondary educational opportunites from which he believes he can profit.

As noted in the enlarged model, a distinction is made in the proposed infrastructure of the continuum between secondary/postsecondary education and credentialed university or professional education. Presumably, for the foreseeable future, the culture will maintain levels of study leading to advanced certificates or degrees and continue to rely on certification or similar credentials in an effort to ensure that persons are qualified—insofar as laboratories, examinations, classrooms, clinics, and supervised experiences can qualify them —to enter a given professional or service field.[4]

The section representing postsecondary education is also intended to portray a growing recognition in the future of the need for persons of forty, sixty, or older to be able to participate either steadily or periodically in many forms of what was known as adult education, continuing education, or "night school" in past decades. The main differences in provisions for life-long postsecondary education as depicted here reside in:

1. *Imaginative and relevant changes in the curricular and paracurricular offerings at the postsecondary level including not only new, pertinent community college or communiversity programs, but also changes in the secondary program.* In keeping with the "seamless continuum" concept, for the purposes of mature learners,[5] *all* educational resources should be open to them on a noncredit basis, with the prerogative of taking examinations if they decide later to seek credit for advanced study in the credentialing channel at the bottom of the model. (Cf. Figure 6–2)

2. *Gradual but fundamental changes in certain contemporary practices in the liberal arts college and in its image.* In effect, the present-day four-year arts and science component of the university would *become* the communiversity, but with appreciably expanded purpose, scope, and noncredit enrollment. While retaining much of their traditional content and general education function, arts and science offerings, much content would be expanded or modified to meet the needs of more learners of all ages and would "find room in the folds of their academic robes" for every viable form of postsecondary learning to which learners aspired.

It should be clearly understood that the liberal arts would neither be abandoned nor diluted. However, as in Britain's Open University program, no one would be denied access to higher education if he were seriously motivated to

---

[4]Opinions of policy researchers regarding the nature and extent of the preparation of teacher's aides, paramedics, technicians, and the like are varied. Considerable opposition exists to extensive formal preparation lest, by such preparation, various paraprofessionals become specialized to the point that, say, as teacher's aides, they price themselves out of the market by becoming more skilled than need be for services in schools with differentiated staffing.

[5]Some British institutions have a "mature student" category which not only permits but encourages eclectic as well as prescribed studies; a category that might be explored more fully in the U.S.

do work either with or without academic credit. The proposal suggests new emphasis on, and recognition for, teaching and service activities of the faculty in addition to the present reward system for research and scholarship.

3. *A flexible viewpoint regarding grouping for learning as well as for creating a psychological climate for learners of a much wider age range.* Teachers at the secondary and communiversity levels as well as in the university need to become adjusted to working with qualified learners of virtually all ages as the multiple exit and reentry concept penetrates educational practice. A precedent—as noted earlier—may be found in university graduate study where, in a given class or seminar, persons in their early twenties may rub shoulders with individuals thirty years their seniors.

4. *Ways must be explored to permit mature learners to return as "come- backs" or "drop-ins," a reversal of the present dropout phenomenon.* This involves cooperative, enlightened policy planning by industry, govern- ment, and education. Job security, imaginative financial provisions, and changes in employment and retirement policies are a few of the elements that seem certain to be involved in life-long learning opportunities.

The modified organizational infrastructure that has been briefly described above is not capable of existing—nor is it even possible to create—without certain substantial changes in the deployment of teachers in all fields of en- deavor. What are the new needs and possibilities in teachers' roles that seem to be congruent with the research and thinking in the realm of futures studies?

Staff Deployment Among alternative educational futures is the possibility that the current concept of team teaching needs to be extended or at least appreciably modified to develop even more versatile and flexible "teaching partnerships," especially if an educational continuum is introduced on a wid- ening scale. The teaching partnership concept is depicted in Figure 6–3.

Although the model illustrates a teaching partnership as it might appear in the primary or middle school phases of a seamless educational continuum, the basic ideas are applicable even in a departmental structure at the university level. This approach to staff deployment involves:

1. The basic idea of differentiated staffing with a "senior partner," with certificated teachers (numbers 1–4), with paraprofessionals (P) serving as teacher aides, and with residents (R) who are fully qualified teachers either in their first or second year or more mature teachers returning, after some years of absence, to ready themselves for participation in new instructional roles.[6]

[6]The residency concept would be especially important during the next decade since some universities are not now preparing teachers to work either in teams or in differentiated teaching partnerships. The residency should serve to provide the necessary apprenticeship or added preparation that often is needed. At the college and university level, teaching partnerships conceivably could be established to include not only the various academic ranks but mature graduate students in residencies as well. There also should be a role for permanent college and university personnel who have, say, an M.A. plus thirty to sixty hours but who have not completed a doctorate and do not intend to. Their special emphasis would be instruction, and let us note that the Ph.D. and Ed.D. dissertation experience (as now constituted) contribute little or nothing to skillful *classroom* performance.

Figure 6-3. Model of the teaching partnership and its associated support systems.

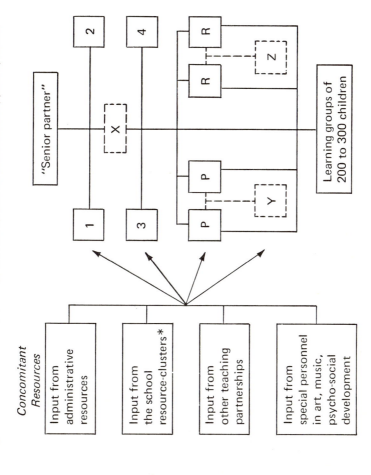

Characteristics

1. Flexible teaching partnerships
2. A seamless curriculum continuum
3. Variable and shared professional responsibilities
4. Shared contacts with several learning groups
5. Personalized instruction
6. Twelve-month "overstaffing"
7. Principal "teams"
8. Individually variable school year
9. Increased use of paraprofessionals (P) and residents (R)
10. Academic balance among partners
11. "Open school" concept
12. "Fail-safe" guidance

Concomitant Resources

Input from administrative resources

Input from the school resource-clusters*

Input from other teaching partnerships

Input from special personnel in art, music, psycho-social development

"Senior partner"

Learning groups of 200 to 300 children

*Resource-cluster components might include: (1) a guidance center, (2) computer facilities, (3) materials development staff, (4) instructional systems-technology cadre, (5) biochemeducationists, (6) Human Relations Center, (7) S-R (Self-Realization) Center, (8) Evaluation-assessment and Performance Analysis Center.

2. Since the "continuum school" presumably would operate on a twelve-month year, it would employ more teachers, aides, and residents than actually are on duty at a given time. This point is depicted by the "X," "Y," and "Z" enclosed by broken lines. The "X," for instance, symbolizes a teacher who does not have a classroom duty assignment during a given time interval. He may be absent but working on a curriculum or materials preparation assignment, engaging in professional study or research, or taking some vacation or leave time. With appropriate modifications, the same generalizations apply to teacher's aide "Y" and to resident "R."

3. As suggested by Figure 6–3, the "teaching partnership approach" influences staff deployment on a wider basis than the flexible teaching cluster, *per se.* In other words, a modified approach is needed to the assignment of other personnel. The lefthand column, "Concomitant Resources," suggests staffing strategies such as administrative resources in the form of principal teams. Instead of working on a one-principal-to-one-building basis, a team of, say, four persons could serve as special leadership consultants in four buildings, plan as a cooperative group, and spend their time as professional judgment dictated. All four might be in one building for a week, for example, or be engaged in any number of individual variations of time investment. An analagous approach could be employed at the communiversity and university when as interdepartmental and interdisciplinary programs continue to develop as "area studies."

4. Various characteristics of the teaching partnership are listed to the right of the model. They serve as a summary of various qualities of the seamless curriculum mentioned earlier and that have a bearing on the differentiated staffing in the partnership.

Like an ancient Gaelic or Greek triskelion, the seamless curriculum has three branches. We have discussed possible developments in the infrastructure and changes in staff deployment. Now what do policies research specialists have to say about changes in the content of instruction during the coming decade?

Subject Matter for 1975–1985

Instructional Perceptions of Futurists As one might logically infer, futures research personnel were deeply interested in educating children and youth to develop the ability (1) to recognize and to select wisely among alternative futures, (2) to develop skills—including "process" skills—needed to implement their pursuit of desirable futures, and (3) to devise motivating experiences that would prompt young learners to become as realistic as possible, both in their views and in their efforts to work for a more viable society both in the United States and internationally.

These three aims, presumably, would permeate or at least influence the selection and design of subject matter for a seamless, personalized curriculum and paracurriculum. At the same time, educational futurists felt that it was the prerogative of professional educationists to determine policies. As a result, they expressed relatively few highly specific ideas regarding the scope, sequence, timing, and pacing of what was taught. To put it concisely, most policy decision personnel advocated reforms in conventional education without prescribing many precise new practices.

In general, however, there was agreement on the broad aims to be sought through instruction, warm acceptance of the need for schooling to develop moral and emotional strengths, to improve physical well-being, and to nurture cognitive power. As might have been expected among a scholarly group (a large majority of the survey participants had at least one earned doctorate), there was great respect for an education to ensure mastery over whatever skills an individual could achieve mastery. But there was also widespread recognition of the point that many different ceilings-of-academic-achievement for individual human beings should be recognized in both the curriculum and in the paracurriculum. As a consequence, according to futurists, schooling in the United States needs to reverse its present stubborn and obsolete practice of overemphasizing the fancied socioeconomic and social status advantages to be gained by entering vocations associated with professional, managerial, ownership, or executive-type roles. Conversely, not enough stress is being placed on the dignity and importance of all kinds of labor with hands as well as minds or on the many kinds of technical jobs open to persons without a college degree.

The typical futures research person emerged as an "idealist" in the sense of seeking curriculum content for better alternative futures and as a "realist" in the sense that he saw a continued need to maintain certain long-established academic goals, firm rather than harsh intellectual discipline, fair but not unreasonable or harshly demanding standards for individual accomplishment, and the need for mastery of substantive content on the part of those whose contributions to society would thereby be increased.

Emerging Characteristics of Curricular Content Designed for the Future
Rather than radical changes in the nature of what was taught, futures researchers felt that major changes were required in what was emphasized in a seamless curriculum. . . . Let us look at plausible new content and emphases based on inferences drawn from interview data but not focused on specific content in a given subject.

First, and perhaps foremost, stress would be placed upon regaining, in enlightened form, the social discipline that gave western man and perhaps most of society a sense of direction before the present value crisis. That crisis, with its relativism and permissive qualities, interferred with the steady whirl of the culturally imposed "inner gyroscope" that provided a course for the individual to follow—or at least to refer to—earlier in the present century. This effort should not be interpreted to imply a retreat to old, outmoded values, but an *advance* toward new values and lifestyles that are needed on our threatened planet.

Second, through education, an assault would be made on the strongly cemented redoubts of materialism; most specifically on the culture's misplaced confidence in materialism—in "consumer stuff"—as the most important goal of life. As David Riesman once noted, the morale of even a meritocracy can be " . . . undermined because its scientific and rationalist temper has no religious basis and the system no transcendent aims, no goal beyond its own further advance." Policy decision specialists would appear to agree that material goods in themselves leave the deeper longings of the human spirit or psyche unsatisfied and can surround us with more and more ecological threats unless —through education—we direct attention to changing our "thing-centered" values and heretofore unchecked appetite for consumer goods. As one West Coast policies specialist (quoting Oscar Wilde) put it, we need to stop turning out millions of youth "who know the price of everything and the value of nothing."

Third, the dangers and problems of the naive use of technology (as powerfully presented by Barry Commoner when he portrays problems in our ecosphere) would provide appreciable content.[7] The attitudes uniformly expressed during the survey not only supported the importance of technology in bettering man's lot in most parts of the world, but also reflected the overwhelming need, through the prudent use of technology, to ease the problems of unthinking use of *La Technique,* as Jacques Ellul called it. At all age levels, as has repeatedly been noted, the need to rethink the use made of technology could be injected into the curriculum.

Fourth, and closely related to point three above, the curriculum should begin to respond more adequately to the threat of damage to the biosphere; damage that could be profound and irreversible in a decade or two. Already, some futurists feel, the present flush of prosperity and even affluence in industrially developed nations is only a mask for pending global catastrophe. While few if any are as pessimistic as Paul Ehrlich, or as harsh as William and Paul Paddock in *Famine 1975,* all probably would agree that:

> Since the environmental crisis is the result of the social mismanagement of the world's resources, then it can be resolved and man can survive in a humane condition when the social organization of man is brought into harmony with the ecosphere.[8]

Patently, education would have an important role here when and if major social decisions are reached with respect to national policy—and in any case there is a great deal of groundwork to be begun in the schools during the interval 1974–1980!

Fifth, . . . most futurists apparently would like to see the schools face up to the fact that in the United States there is no really satisfactory coping doctrine

---

[7]It must be recognized that the new curricular emphases presented would assume many and different forms with children of varied age levels. With younger learners, a way of ecologically sound living would be based mostly on example and simple precept. In the university phase of the curriculum continuum, however, one might, for example, in a school of architecture or engineering find that *how* to build an airport or a thousand foot building is carefully linked to the study of *whether,* and if so *where,* construction occurs to avoid further damage to the biosphere. Here is an example, too, of cross-disciplinary study that is emerging in heretofore "unrelated" fields such as architecture and biology or biochemistry.

[8]Barry Commoner, *The Closing Circle* (New York: Alfred A. Knopf, 1971), p. 299.

for a major and almost totally ignored dilemma of democracy: Most Americans are unwilling to settle for a merely egalitarian society. Instead, they view "democracy" as a social order in which they are free to gamble on attaining "equality" with the top 10 percent, not as a means of attaining equity for all. Many of the concepts of the Founding Fathers have so far managed to survive because of political ingenuity, compromise, and the ability of the social establishment heretofore to accommodate a great deal of upward mobility. But education in the next decade may need to emphasize concepts of greater equity in democracy and discard the dream that everyone can rise above his father's status in life. This has implication not only for guidance counselors but for all teachers who are still selling the Horatio Alger myth.

At the risk of hearing cries of heresy, it seems essential that we reverse some of our long ingrained ideas and vigorously emphasize that "success" does not necessarily reside in the nineteenth-century dictum that the able child should rise above his father's station in life. With social conditions and social attitudes changing (and with chemists, engineers, psychologists, lawyers, teachers, anthropologists, *et al.* unemployed or underemployed), there appears to be new and great merit in school climates—and in mass media—that would encourage some cobblers' sons to remain cobblers' sons, lest we end up unshod a few years hence.

Sixth, education needs to continue to sensitize the learner to the problems and to the neo-Malthusian dangers in unrestricted breeding. Futurists vary as to dates at which the problem might become catastrophic, but there is almost universal agreement that education for population control is imperative. One gloomy estimate by the Scandinavian scientist, Ehrensvaerd, is that beginning in 2050 the world population will shrink from over ten billion to three billion. The latter figure represents all the people that the diminished resources of the world can sustain in 2070 if present rates of consumption and increases in consumption are projected. He concludes that over seven billion people might die off (2020 to 2050 A.D.) in the process of stabilizing population at the 1970 figure of three billion.

Seventh, and last, a number of futures researchers doubtless would urge new educational input to assist learners to cope with the potential power of mass media in shaping opinions and attitudes. Also, the post-elementary curriculum would be shaped by the study of possible dangers in mind control by other means (e.g., chemical and electrical stimuli) in addition to television, radio, or publications.

Controversial New Dimensions in Content and in Instruction: 1975–1985   If the data cited by futurists—and their accompanying recommendations—are taken seriously, we are likely to find that the processes of curriculum change related to the content or instruction are packed with dynamite. Let me explore a few of the implicit and explicit changes that the future may very well demand.

1. *Presenting the concept of the "true-costing" of consumer goods.* We do not repay the biosphere at present for what our consumer goods *really* cost. Consider a subcompact automobile selling for, say, $2,500 F.O.B. De-

troit. If the cost of *reclaiming* the metal from the chassis and body, the lead from the battery, the copper and aluminum from cooling system, air conditioner, and motor are added, if the buyer is charged for final demolition that will eliminate wasteful and unsightly auto graveyards—in short, if every effort is made to restore the land from which the automobile (or refrigerator or electric washer) was wrenched, the cost of capital consumer goods probably would double. But we would be postponing the evil of the day when large areas of the planet will have been stripped naked as the moon. The crucial new curriculum issue is pretty obvious. Shall we begin to face up to the educational implications of diminishing resources?

2. *Interpreting to youth the growing need to reverse our "growth-is-good" doxology in favor of the need for "dynamic contraction."* Thus far, aside from suspending judgment on the SST and the Alaskan oil pipelines, there is little evidence the people in the United States are willing even to *suspend* their attacks on the biosphere—let alone begin to do with less of its riches. The ineluctable truth is that sooner or later, we will need to contemplate instructing young learners as to the importance of *dynamic contraction,* a carefully planned withdrawal from our policy of fueling the economy with more of everything each year.

It simply doesn't make sense, for instance, to talk of producing twelve to fifteen million internal combustion cars in 1980 or in 1985 while our Environmental Protection Agency contemplates gas rationing in California a year or two hence because of smog-breeding exhaust emissions, and when gasoline itself has been in short supply.

Dynamic contraction, a recent concept in economics, concerns itself with such questions as how an overextended airline can reduce its size and be healthier through a loss of mechanized avoirdupois. Or how a transition from a one-or-two car per family economy can be changed to a one-or-no-car per family pattern while public transportation is making a comeback. The dynamics of such contractions suggest decidedly different content in the schools.

3. *Excellence versus growth* is another new input for educators to consider. This is an extension of point two. How shall we wean the young from what Toffler called our throw-away society and begin to restore respect for craftsmanship as distinct from *kitsch* and from mere convenience? How will we begin to teach respect for more durable things?

4. *Developing a sense of fulfillment based on satisfaction rather than possession.* Really such satisfaction often resides in one's creative achievements with hand or mind. How can the curriculum and instruction, broadly conceived, make these satisfactions more widespread? Perhaps Rebecca West gave as good a clue as any when she wrote:

> . . . a nation should be . . . a shelter where all talents are generously recognized, all forgivable oddities forgiven, all viciousness quietly frustrated, and those who lack talent honored for equivalent contributions of graciousness.

5. Yet another challenge is to create, at least in part through schooling, *a recycling society*. In the 1970s we reutilize in some form about a third of our bottles, cans, garbage, and dilapidated consumer goods. Our target should first be 90 percent and then as close to 99 percent as we can come. From early childhood, educational experiences in years ahead will need to redevelop the nineteenth-century spirit echoed in the 1920s by Calvin Coolidge when he said, "Use it up, wear it out, and make it do."

6. *We need to help the young to understand the potential richness of a service-oriented society.* Already, either as producers or consumers of educational services, one-third of the United States goes to school. There are other ways in which a service-and-people centered (rather than thing-centered) culture can be furthered. Better nursing, more paramedical care, better maintained parks and beaches, improved care for young mothers, for the very young, for the aged—all of these require human hands, human minds, and *agapé,* the Greek term connoting love of one's fellows. Human experience is full of the satisfaction of service. Our task, through education, is to enhance recognition for its importance and to restructure an award system that respects service more adequately without downgrading skill and talent.

7. *Refining the merits of simple communal living* today to match the virtues of pioneer life in a younger America. Although sometimes unfairly stigmatized as peopled by eccentrics and irresponsibles, the contemporary back-to-the-land or simple life movement has much to recommend it for human closeness, the satisfaction of accomplishment through toil, the lack of ostentation, and the cooperative spirit. In our schools, the curriculum might well be modified to enhance the spirit of the closely knit group as it existed in the Jamestown and Plymouth days and on into the twentieth century in rural America. Today, even in the most disadvantaged metrocore, the need for nurturing the communal spirit within individual family groups has sustained itself under the most adverse of circumstances.

8. *Make more effective use of educational TV, packages, and school-and-home learning techniques.* At a cost of perhaps a penny a day per viewer, TV of a superior sort is one of our neglected educational resources for tomorrow's learners. The trick is to blend curricular and technical know-how with a dash of administrative skill. A most promising idea, if adopted to the U. S. scene is Britain's Open University. A mere gleam of an idea in 1969, the Open University will in a year or two provide access to continuing education for 65,000 learners.

9. *Recognizing that a measure of mutual coercion will be necessary* for the general welfare if we are to bring off and to enforce the social and educational changes that the future demands. These nine controversial curricular considerations are fraught with potential dissent, a dissent that will be based on fear. But as Gabor noted, "fear is a bad counselor and we must avoid its fatal feedback loop." As Roszak puts it, we can move

forward, "a new society piecing itself together inventively within the interstices of the old." But how?

I have previously put on the record my attempt to find an answer:

It seems reasonable to argue that, in education and in other fields of endeavor, we need new authority structures that won't dehumanize us but that also will get results. The task is to find a solid middle ground between anarchy and autocracy. To borrow an idea from Garrett Hardin, perhaps we need to work toward a form of participatory democracy in which uncoerced decisions are reached with regard to the mutual coercion that is required to protect us from ourselves. This requires a word of elaboration.

Some of us drive cars that are more of a threat to the environment than need be. An example: the $36,000 Rolls Royce that Stirling Moss road-tested last autumn —a vehicle which he said consumed almost seven [imperial] gallons of gas in one 36-mile stretch of city driving. Or consider any large Detroit product. It requires a great deal of irreplaceable material such as steel or copper and uses three or four times as much of our fossil fuel reserves as would a smaller car. Furthermore, it fouls the air to an alarming extent. Here we need to reach an uncoerced decision as to whether the world needs such extravagant and poisonous transportation. If it doesn't make sense, then we need to engage in "mutual coercion" by passing laws that limit size and gas consumption in our cars, and also begin to restore public transportation to its lost level of usefulness.

In education, too, we need to "coerce ourselves" to do more sensible things with respect to making workable the authority structure that we need. We also need to be sure that the traditions of democracy are respected in the process. But how do we achieve participatory democracy in a culture splintered by pluralism and at the same time *have* someone in control? It is pointless to debate *who* will control the schools if there is no way to *exercise* control.

John Dewey gave us an important lead in resolving this problem when, in 1903, he suggested that leadership should reside in the merit of ideas. Every teacher, he wrote, should have "some regular and representative way in which he or she can register judgment upon matters of educational importance with the assurance that this judgment (if it has merit) will somehow affect the school system. . . . " Today, we would no doubt wish to extend this concept so that the ideas of all—children, parents, administrators, teachers, and so on—can find expression in the educational free market of ideas and, when they pass coinage (i.e., when they have merit), will lead us to the *uncoerced* decisions that will provide a suitable basis for the mutual coercion needed to enforce policies.

Leadership in education must have the power to lead, including the "control" which resides in the power to coerce when enforcing an *uncoerced* group decision. Hegel wrote that "freedom is the recognition of necessity." Let us not deceive ourselves: It is a necessity that control of education, with proper restraints, be clearly vested in someone, and we need to retain and to *increase merited* respect for this duly constituted authority. Referenda and recall procedures, clearly established with respect to both *ideas* and *people,* should provide the needed protection against resurgence of a control autocracy, particularly with the independence that teachers have achieved in the past 25 years.

Time should provide many improvements to the ideas expressed here regarding mutual *coercion* based on participatory *democracy.* At the moment, however, this approach to disciplining ourselves for our own best good as we face the controversial implications of futures research impresses me as having more than enough promise to merit study and exploration.

Summary

A belief has haunted the twentieth century. It is a belief that this is a period of transition from an industrial to an automated society; from a world of abundant resources to one that must husband its resources; or else, find new and fantastic ones; from an open society to a society in which the personal and civil freedoms of the western world will be threatened if not actually compromised. The futuristic movement is an expression of this view clothed in facts and theoretical projections.

The shape of the future, however, is not thereby determined, for the course of our destiny is not shaped entirely by our minds no matter how rational. There are forces outside of ourselves that intervene to influence us in one direction or another. This does not mean, however, that people have no control over the directions in which they will move. Within the web of social conditions and trends, most of which can be known and understood, we have choices to make. This is essentially what the futurists are attempting to tell us.

The question posed for the curriculum specialist and indeed for all of us in the educational enterprise is: What should be the response of the school to the questions raised by the leaders of the futuristic movement? This chapter has presented the response of one individual who has studied the movement with care. Many other responses by educators have been made, but space does not permit us to present selections from them. If you wish to know more about the educational implications of futuristic thinking, you will find the following helpful. *Futurism in Education: Methodologies,* by Stephen P. Hencley and James R. Yates; *Futurism and Future Studies: Development in Classroom Instruction,* by Draper L. Kauffman, Jr.; *The Future of Education: Perspectives on Tomorrows Schooling,* edited by Louis Rubin; *Educational Futurism in Pursuance of Survival,* by John R. Pulliam and Jim R. Bowman; and *Educational Futurism 1985: Challenges for Schools and Their Administrators,* by Walter G. Hack and others.

Part **III**

Operative Concepts and Principles

The task of curriculum development requires that certain steps be guided by a theoretical perspective. No matter what that perspective is the curriculum worker will need to do several things: consider the objectives of instruction; reckon with the problem of what knowledge the curriculum is to contain; answer the question of balance among the various elements of knowledge; wrestle with the problem of the order of learning; consider the utility of curriculum content; and face the question of how the curriculum is to be put to work.

The following chapters address these aspects of the task of curriculum development. Each aspect is complex and controversial. While space does not permit us to present all of the pertinent literature on these aspects of curriculum development, we have attempted to select readings that present some of the more thoroughgoing considerations of the various issues. We have also provided activities that make the issues more concrete and significant as you read and study the various passages.

Chapter **7**

Aims and Objectives in Curriculum Planning

"What the heck is an unrealized basic behavioral objective."

Instructor, 84. 7 (March 1975):136.

It is generally believed that all educational personnel- especially curriculum workers, teachers, and evaluators, must be clear about both the aims of formal education and the objectives of instruction. But as soon as this claim is made certain questions arise: What are aims and objectives? How do they differ? What is the relation between them? How do they develop? How can we tell if they are clearly stated? What are some of the issues about them?

Orientation

All educational personnel envision an ideal school. Other authorities dream of an ideal economic system. For example, Adam Smith pictured a competitive system, without government interference, with a goal of maximum wealth of nations. This goal applies to the entire economic system; it is not the goal of a particular business person or the directors of a corporation. Their objectives may be to increase the profits of their enterprise without thinking about the direction of the total economy.

This is analogous to the school. What is the aim of formal education? Herbert Spencer said it is to prepare for complete living. But this may not be what a teacher has in mind as he or she faces students in science class day after day. The teacher would probably state that his objectives were to help the student learn or understand. If he teaches physics, he will formulate objectives in terms of concepts, laws, and procedures he wishes the students to acquire. If he teaches English, he will likely express his objectives as enjoyment and appreciation of literature or knowledge and skill in written and spoken expression. These objectives appear to have little if any relationship to Spencer's aims of formal education.

How do instructional objectives differ from aims? An instructional objective states what the student is expected to learn. For example, the student may be expected to develop the ability to recognize artistic quality in classical works of art; to recognize conclusions which are most consistent with a given set of facts; and to identify criteria used to justify a given judgment. An instructional system will always include stated or implied objectives.

How objectives function is a controversial area. Supposedly they are useful to the teacher as he tries to help the student understand what is to be learned; as he prepares diagnostic tests to find out what the student already knows; as he prepares tests for the purpose of evaluating the work of the student; and as he plans his own instructional activities. It is also asserted that evaluators use objectives to assess the effectiveness of a school program; and that curriculum specialists find them essential because without them he has no sense of direction for curriculum planning.

What then are the aims of formal education? Are they useful? The nature and function of educational aims have been debated throughout the history of education. There are two current conceptions of their function.

First, aims shape the content and method of the total educational system. Suppose we believe, as did Comenius, that the aim of the educational system is the cultivation of "learning, virtue, and piety." Would we not then insist that the school program comprise some of the traditional disciplines and religious and moral content? Would we not insist upon relationships in the classroom that would promote virtue and piety as we understand them? Comenius included the three R's, singing, sacred psalms and hymns, catechism, Bible history, moral rules with examples, economics and politics, physics and geography, and general knowledge of arts and handicrafts in his vernacular school. Second, consider Spencer's conception of education as preparation for complete living. Spencer would include self-preservation, citizenship, parenthood, work, and leisure as areas of activity in his school. He suggested that the way to prepare for these activities is to first understand the natural sciences.

These two examples of educational aims reflect different orientations about the role of school in a society: Comenius' is moral and religious; Spencer's is secular. There can be little doubt that Comenius and Spencer would have designed quite different educational programs.

Some have criticized this view of the function of educational aims because neither the objectives of instruction nor the content of the educational program can be logically derived from the statement of aims. According to this view, one cannot derive from the educational aims of "learning, virtue, and piety" the program laid out by Comenius. If we accept the view that one of the aims is to cultivate learning, we still have no criterion by which to decide which learnings to cultivate. According to the critics, it is certainly not clear how Comenius derived instruction in writing and arithmetic, for instance, from this particular aim. In like fashion, it is difficult to see how one can derive instruction in the sacred psalms and hymns from virtue as an aim. Instruction in the catechism, it is said, cannot be derived logically from piety.

According to some authorities, the only way in which the aims of education can be related to the objectives and content of instruction is to identify the activities associated with the aims and then to analyze these activities into their constituent parts, as one would do in a task analysis. If the educational aim cannot be clearly associated with any set of activities, then it would be deemed meaningless for curriculum development.

If we examine Spencer's aim, we can see more clearly what is meant by relating the aim to activities. There are five activity areas. To develop a curriculum by the procedure of task analysis is to analyze each of these activity areas to determine its essential elements. These would then constitute the basis for determining the objectives and content of instruction.

Some vocational education programs follow this general formula. The aim of vocational education, let us say, is ability to adapt oneself to an occupation. By assessing the labor needs of a community or region and projecting these needs over a period of time, one can determine the occupations for which the school should prepare its students. Then, by job analysis the objectives and content of the vocational program can be determined. Some authorities now claim that the same procedure can be applied to the instructional program in almost all school work areas.

In the last few years little attention has been given to the aims of education except as they enter, often implicitly, into controversies in curriculum theorizing. In sharp contrast, instructional objectives have come to the front as basic elements in curriculum planning. They have been organized into taxonomic systems and created long and heated debates about how they should be stated. In addition, efforts have been made to relate them directly to instruction through plans for individualization and for diagnosing and reteaching.

The subsiding interest in educational aims and the recent increase in interest in instructional objectives can probably be attributed to two developments. First, the researchers who developed the taxonomy of educational objectives sidestepped the question of aims by confining their deliberations to "lists of objectives found in courses of study and other educational literature." These researchers, rather than determine how objectives are derived or what they are derived from, sorted existing objectives and classified them into a taxonomy. This observation is in no way a criticism of the empirical work of these researchers. The taxonomy appealed to some curriculum workers because it was systematic and stated in language that enabled teachers to relate subject matter to objectives.

Second, the conflicts and struggles over the educational program and the severe criticism to which teachers have been subjected in the last decade has led many teachers as well as education authorities to conclude that the teaching profession has promised more than it can deliver. The profession has promised to develop good citizens and good family members. It has promised to develop individuals who would use their leisure time constructively and who would protect their health and physical well-being. It has

promised to develop democratically-oriented individuals of ethical character, capable of critical thinking. It has taken on the task of teaching about
the deleterious effects of alcohol, tobacco, and drugs and offering driver
training, hoping to reduce highway accidents.

These are not the kinds of things you will find if you look at the taxonomy
of educational objectives. Rather they are to be found in statements of
educational aims such as the Seven Cardinal Principles of Education. The
taxonomy of educational objectives call for students to acquire knowledge;
to learn to comprehend what they hear and read, to apply what they learn
in solving problems, to learn to analyze, to synthesize, and to evaluate what
they hear and read. These objectives are attainable, it is assumed, through
the study of instructional materials provided by the school.

But the exhibition of behavior entailed by good citizenship and worthy
home membership, and other aims found in educational literature, depend
upon how the student uses the knowledge and ability acquired in school
when he is in the broader society. The teaching profession cannot control
the use of the knowledge and abilities it teaches. Using knowledge and
ability is contingent on a range of factors larger than those over which the
school has control. For this reason, some teachers and curriculum workers
now think that the teaching profession is dangerously promising more than
it can deliver when it attempts to justify the school's program by recourse
to aims. Partly for these reasons, aims of formal education are considerably
less popular today than they were a few decades ago.

Taxonomies of Objectives

If aims are said to be unimportant, especially by educational technologists,
not so instructional objectives. These are to be considered elements of
curriculum planning, teaching, and evaluation. It is therefore important to
ask for a classification of these objectives. Taxonomies of instructional
objectives have been developed, one for cognitive and another for affective
learnings. Although considerable work has been done toward developing
a taxonomy for psychomotor objectives, the taxonomy is still in its incipient
stage. These taxonomies are too extensive to be presented in a brief space,
but it is possible to condense them so as to give an overview of their main
features. This overview is provided in the following passage by Ivor K.
Davies.

☐

If you examine a great number of learning objectives or even examination
questions, you will find that they can be broadly classified under one of three
main headings or domains:

Ivor K. Davies, *Competency Based Learning: Management, Technology, and Design* (New
York: McGraw-Hill, 1973), pp. 74–77. Copyright © 1973 McGraw-Hill Book Co. (UK) Ltd.
Reproduced by permission.

Footnotes have been renumbered consecutively throughout the chapter.

1. Cognitive objectives
2. Affective objectives.
3. Psychomotor objectives.

Cognitive objectives are concerned with information and knowledge; as such, realizing cognitive objectives is the basic activity of most educational and training programs. Affective objectives, on the other hand, emphasize attitudes and values, feelings and emotions; accordingly, they are the proper concern of education. Psychomotor objectives involve muscular and motor skills, or manipulation of material or objects, or some activity which requires neuromuscular coordination. Realizing psychomotor objectives is, of course, the primary concern of a good deal of industrial-vocational training.

Bloom and his colleagues at the University of Chicago have produced a most important classification or taxonomy of both cognitive objectives (Bloom, 1956) and affective objectives (Krathwohl, Bloom, and Masia, 1964). Unfortunately, they have produced no comparable scheme for the psychomotor area, although a tentative classification has been made by Simpson (1969). The taxonomy arranges objectives in the cognitive and affective domains into six major classes; these are shown in Figure 7-1. A useful way of looking at the two domains is that in the cognitive domain a teacher is interested in what the student will *do*, whereas in the affective domain, the teacher is additionally concerned with what he *does to it* or *with it*.

Figure 7–1.   Bloom's cognitive and affective domains.

	Cognitive domain	Affective domain
6	Evaluation	Organization and characterization
4, 5	Analysis and synthesis	Conceptualization
3	Application	Valuing
2	Comprehension	Responding
1	Knowledge	Receiving

An old educational axiom states that 'growth occurs from within,' and this inner growth is demonstrated in the two taxonomies by the way in which they are internally related and interrelated. The objectives in one class, for example, 'application' make use and build on the behaviors implicit in the preceding objectives, in this case, 'knowledge' and 'comprehension.' Similary, there is a great deal of correspondence between the classes in each domain; this is particulary noticeable between 'knowledge' and 'receiving' (level 1), and also 'analysis and synthesis' and 'conceptualization' (levels 4 and 5). A more detailed illustration of these relationships will be obtained by studying Figure 7-2.

Both cognitive and affective objectives are of great practical use to the teacher and instructor not only in planning, but also in exercising his organiza-

Figure 7–2.   The relationship between the cognitive and affective domains.

Cognitive objectives	Affective objectives
1. The lowest level in this taxonomy begins with the student's recall and recognition of *knowledge*,	1. The lowest level begins with the student merely *receiving* stimuli and passively attending to it. It extends to his more actively attending to it,
2. It extends through his *comprehension* of the knowledge.	2. then his *responding* to stimuli on request, willingly responding and taking satisfaction in responding,
3. To his skill in the *application* of the knowledge that he comprehends.	3. to his *valuing* the phenomena or activity so that he voluntarily responds and seeks out further ways to take part in what is going on.
4. The next levels progress from his ability to make an *analysis* of the situations involving the knowledge, to his skill in the *synthesis* of it into new organizations.	4. The next stage is his *conceptualization* of each of the values to which he is responding by identifying characteristics or forming judgments.
5. The highest level lies in his skill in *evaluation*, so that he can judge the value of the knowledge in realizing specific objectives.	5. The highest level in the taxonomy is the student's *organization* of the values into a system which is a *characterization* of himself.

Reproduced with permission from D. R. Krathwold, B. S. Bloom, and B. B. Masia, *Taxonomy of Educational Objectives, Handbook II: Affective Domain* (New York: McKay, 1964).

tional and controlling functions. The taxonomies, shown in Figures 7-3 and 7-4, serve as a complete conceptual framework, on which can be positioned any learning objective or related test question. Such a scaffold or ideational map enables the teacher to:

1. Select his range of objectives and test questions
2. Relate and interrelate his objectives and associated test questions to other objectives and questions in both cognitive and affective domains.
3. Ensure a proper balance and weight is given to objectives and questions
4. Determine that higher-order objectives are being realized, since it is only at these higher levels that the educational value of what is being accomplished is beyond dispute.

Inevitably, lower-order cognitive objectives tend to be mundane in character, and are unlikely to be particularly exciting; yet most teachers *hope* that their students will develop a continuing and growing interest in the material they have learned. Many courses, however, which start off with an interest in

Figure 7–3.   Condensed version of the taxonomy of educational objectives in the cognitive domain.

Direction	Category

Low level	1. *Knowledge.* (Remembering facts, terms, and principles in the form that they were learned.)
	(a) Knowledge of specifics.
	   (i) Knowledge of terminology.
	  (ii) Knowledge of specific facts.
	(b) Knowledge of ways and means of dealing with specifics.
	    (i) Knowledge of conventions.
	   (ii) Knowledge of trends and sequences.
	  (iii) Knowledge of classifications and categories.
	   (iv) Knowledge of criteria.
	    (v) Knowledge of methology.
	(c) Knowledge of universals and abstractions in a field.
	   (i) Knowledge of principles and generalizations.
	  (ii) Knowledge of theories and structures.
	
	2. *Comprehension.* (Understanding material studied without necessarily relating it to other material.)
	(a) Translation.
	(b) Interpretation.
	(c) Extrapolation.
	
	3. *Application.* (Using generalizations or other abstractions appropriately in concrete situations.)

Medium level	4. *Analysis.* (Breakdown of material into constituent parts.) (a) Analysis of elements. (b) Analysis of relationships. (c) Analysis of organizational principles. 5. *Synthesis.* (Combining elements into a new structure.) (a) Production of a unique communication. (b) Production of a plan or proposed set of operations. (c) Derivation of a set of abstract relations. 6. *Evaluation.* (Judging the value of material for a specified purpose.) (a) Judgments in terms of internal evidence.
High level	(b) Judgments in terms of external criteria.

Reproduced with permission from B. S. Bloom, *Taxonomy of Educational Objectives, Handbook I: Cognitive Domain* (New York: McKay, 1956).

developing positive attitudes in their students, often have their affective objectives and higher-order cognitive objectives diluted, or even eroded away, as the course loses its initial freshness and sparkle.

The vast majority of the questions in GCE O level examinations tend to be concerned with knowledge and comprehension, a few questions in GCE A

Figure 7-4.   Condensed version of the taxonomy of educational objectives in the affective domain.

Direction	Category

Low Level	1. *Receiving.* (Paying attention.)
	  (a) Awareness.
	  (b) Willingness to receive.
	  (c) Controlled or selected attention.

	2. *Responding.* (Committed and actively attending.)
	  (a) Acquiescence in responding.
	  (b) Willingness to respond.
	  (c) Satisfaction in response.

	3. *Valuing.* (Concepts are seen to have worth.)
	  (a) Acceptance of a value.
	  (b) Preference for a value.
	  (c) Commitment (conviction).

	4. *Organization.* (Construction of a system of values.)
	  (a) Conceptualization of a value.
	  (b) Organization of a value system.

	5. *Characterization of a value complex.* (Acceptance of value system.) (a) Generalized set.
High Level	(b) Characterization.

Reproduced with permission from D. R. Krathwold, B. S. Bloom, and B. B. Masia, *Taxonomy of Educational Objectives, Handbook II: Affective Domain.* (New York: McKay, 1964).

level examinations test application and analysis, and it is a very good university final examination that really concentrates on synthesis and evaluation. Once teachers and instructors, however, are appreciative of the value of using such a taxonomy when they plan their objectives and examinations, perhaps the overall quality of the work accomplished in the classroom and the examination room will improve. Since each class of objectives builds on all preceding classes, standards can be raised to more desirable level by teaching and testing a student's ability to evaluate—because this also involves teaching and testing all the other classes of objectives.

Are Behavioral Objectives Really Useful?

Those who insist that instructional objectives be stated in behavioral terms suppose that teachers either use behavioral objectives or that their instruction would be more effective if they did. Some curriculum workers and teachers doubt the validity of this supposition and assert that many teachers do not use such objectives, and that those who do are no more effective in the classroom for doing so. These claims and counter claims are set forth in the following selections.

The first passage, by Robert L. Ebel, sets forth a number of reasons why behavioral objectives may not be so useful to teachers as some authorities claim. The second excerpt, by Eliot W. Eisner, asks what research, if any, supports the claim that behavioral objectives are useful to teachers.

☐

Teachers have read books and articles which urge them to state their own instructional objectives in behavioral terms.[1] Some of them have tried to do so, and lacking clear success may feel some guilt. A few teachers actually do have statements of behavioral objectives for their courses and build their teaching efforts around them. But the number of these is small. Ammons, in fact, found *no* behavioral objectives in the 300 school systems she surveyed.[2] Some educators are not greatly concerned with this state of affairs. They see limited value in behavioral objectives and some potential danger in making behavior, rather than cognitive processes, the target of our educational efforts.

The Origin and History of the Concept

Although the phrase "behavioral objectives" has not been widely used until recent times, every program of training does in fact have behavioral objectives, whether they are stated explicitly or not. The purpose of training for a specific task is to develop the capability for the the behavior required by the task. But the broader usage of behavioral objectives in connection with educational programs is probably attributable largely to Ralph Tyler.[3] While at Ohio State University, he developed a systematic program for the specification, in behavioral terms, of the desired outcomes of a course. Usually these outcomes were a limited number of fairly specific cognitive abilities. Their emphasis was, in part, a reaction to the overemphasis on factual information in many current objective tests of achievement.

Robert L. Ebel, "Behavioral Objectives: A close Look," *Phi Delta Kappan* 52, 3 (November 1970): 171–73. Reprinted by permission of the publisher.

[1]Robert R. Mager, *Preparing Instructional Objectives* (Palo Alto, Calif.: Fearon, 1962); C. M. Lindvall, ed., *Defining Educational Objectives* (Pittsburgh, Pa.: University of Pittsburgh Press, 1964); and David R. Krathwohl, "Stating Objectives Appropriately for Program, for Curriculum, and for Instructional Material Development," *Journal of Teacher Education* (March 1965): 83–92.

[2]Margaret Ammons, "An Empirical Study of Process and Product in Curriculum Development," *Journal of Educational Research* (May-June 1964): 451–57.

[3]Ralph W. Tyler, "A Generalized Technique for Constructing Achievement Tests," in *Constructing Achievement Tests* (Columbus, O.: Bureau of Educational Research, 1934).

With the advent of teaching machines and programmed instruction, suggested first by Pressey[4] and popularized by Skinner,[5] the usefulness of behavioral objectives became more apparent, especially to the programmers. Then the cutting edge of innovation moved on to more complex models of systematic instruction. With computers prescribing individualized instruction[6] and "mastery" replacing "as-much-as-possible" as the goal, behavioral objectives remained an essential feature of innovation.

The net effect of both Tyler's leadership and recent developments has been to convince many teachers that they ought to state their objectives in behavioral terms. "Help stamp out nonbehavioral objectives" is their only half-facetious slogan.

Justifications for Behavioral Objectives

In the case of programmed instruction and the more complex learning systems, the need for specific, detailed instructional objectives is obvious. Some of these systems may be too complex to be generally feasible, and too impersonal or too inflexible to be generally effective. But where they can be used they require and make good use of behavior objectives.

But why should the ordinary non-machine-like teacher state his objectives in behavioral terms? Two justifications have been offered. The first more basic and far-reaching is that since the general purpose of all education is to change behaviors, course objectives should be stated in terms of the behaviors expected to result from the course. The second is quite different. It justifies the use of behavioral descriptions of objectives on the ground that such descriptions are more meaningful.[7]

When the purpose of instruction is to provide training for a particular task, the first justification can hardly be questioned. Even when the purpose is to provide more general, liberal education, one can argue that it is only justified if it affects behavior somehow, sometime. It may not be possible to foresee all the ways in which learning might affect future behavior, but surely some of the more probable and more important can be anticipated. On the other hand, it is quite clear that such behavioral consequences are not the real objectives of instruction. Those objectives are, rather, the knowledge and understanding, the attitudes and values which induced the behavior or made it possible. To stress behavior as the objective is somewhat inaccurate and misleading.

What of the second justification? Do behavioral objectives have clearer,

[4]S. L. Pressey, "A Simple Apparatus Which Gives Tests and Scores and Teaches," *School and Society* (March 20, 1926): 373–77.

[5]B. F. Skinner, "Science of Learning and the Art of Teaching," *Harvard Educational Review* (Spring 1954): 86–97.

[6]C. M. Lindvall and John O. Bolvin, "Programed Instruction in the Schools: An Application of Programming Principles in Individually Prescribed Instruction," in Phil C. Lange, ed., *Programmed Instruction,* Sixty-sixth Yearbook, Part II, National Society for the Study of Education (Chicago: University of Chicago Press, 1967), pp. 217–54.

[7]Ralph H. Ojemann, "Should Educational Objectives Be Stated in Behavioral Terms? Parts I, II, and III." *Elementary School Journal* 60 (February 1968): 69, 223–31; (February 1969): 229–35; 70 (February 1970): 271–78.

more definite meaning than nonbehavioral objectives in conventional class-room instruction? In one sense they do because behavior is overt and observable, whereas knowledge, understanding, ability, etc., are hidden inside their possessors. We can assess these internal qualities only by eliciting behavior that is dependent on them. But here again the overt behavioral is not the real objective. It is simply a useful indicator. To refer to it as the objective is more apt to confuse than to clarify thinking about educational goals.

Problems with Behavioral Objectives

In view of the widespread endorsement of behavioral objectives, one might expect to find many examples of their effective use. That this is not the case suggests that practical application of the concept may involve some difficulties.

One of these is the difficulty of knowing precisely what the concept means. Some use it as if the behavior in which they are interested is that of the student while he is learning, or even that of his teacher. Others use it to refer to the student's behavior on special tasks designed to show whether or not he has learned something. Still others have in mind the student's use in life, or on the job, of what he has learned in school. While these three meanings are more closely related in some subjects of study than in others, they are distinctly different. One cannot speak or even think clearly about behavioral objectives without defining which type of behavior he has in mind.

Another difficulty is that the behavior specified in these definitions is seldom the real objective of the instruction. When the behavior is that of the learner while learning, it is clearly a means to an end, not the end itself. Nor is test behavior the real objective except in those rare cases where the test is a performance test in a natural setting. Only in the third sense of on-the-job performance can behavior be the real objective. The situations in which such behavioral objectives are appropriate appear to be limited to instruction which aims at the cultivation of particular skills. Behavioral objectives seem quite inapporpriate to instructional efforts whose aim is to enable the student to respond adaptively and effectively to unique future problem situations; to equip him to make, independently but responsibly, the kind of individual choices and decisions which are the essence of human freedom.

A useful distinction can be made between training, for which behavioral objectives are often quite appropriate, and education, for which they are seldom appropriate. Educational development is little concerned with the establishment of predetermined responses to recurring problem situations. Rather, it is concerned with the student's understanding, his resources of useful and available knowledge, his intellectual self-sufficiency. It sees him not as a puppet on strings controlled by his teachers, but as one who needs and wants the help of his teachers and others as he tackles the difficult problems of designing and building a life of his own.

A third problem is that of specifying the behavioral objective in sufficent detail. Any significant behavioral act, such as the construction of an achieve-ment test for a course, consists of myriads of contributory acts. Often these are not easy to identify as separate elements in the total matrix of behavior. Often they vary from situation to situation. To identify and specify all of them may be an impossible task. But to the extent that these elements are not specified the behavior is left undefined.

A fourth problem is that of specifying an appropriate level of skill or competence in the behavior. Most significant acts of behavior cannot be said to be either present or absent, available or unavailable. They occur more or less often when appropriate, and are handled more or less well. To define them as educational objectives requires us to say not only what they are, but how well they are handled. This task also is difficult, and frequently seems to be more trouble than it is likely to be worth.

Some Limitations of Stated Objectives

There are problems in making effective use of any statement of objectives. One is the problem of validity. Simply stating that something is an objective does not make it a desirable one. True, one must think about his objectives in order to state them, and thinking is one of the best ways of working to improve them. But then one must also think about objectives when doing anything rational about educating—when developing materials, planning procedures, or preparing for evaluations. There is no reason to believe that better thinking will go into the statement of objectives than into plans for attaining them.

Another is the problem of flexible adaptability. There is always danger that stated objectives may impose a rigid formality on teaching. Stated objectives may describe what a teacher plans to do, but they should seldom prescribe what he ought to do. On Tuesday he may perceive a more important objective than he wrote into his statement on Monday. The notion that there is no further need for creative thought about objectives once they have been stated is an enemy of dynamic teaching.[8]

Finally there is the problem of effective use. What do you do with a statement of objectives once you have it? If it is a good brief summary of your general objectives you may discuss it with your students. You may refer to it from time to time to keep your teaching on course, or to keep your evaluations relevant. But if it is a highly detailed statement of specific objectives, the chances are that it will be filed "for possible future reference." It will add little of value to your own cognitive resources, to the materials you use in instruction, or to your planning of instructional procedures. If you value creative teaching, you will not try to follow it step by step.

Conclusion

Teaching is purposeful activity. Part of a teacher's effectiveness depends on his having the right purposes. Hence it is important for the curriculum builder, the textbook writer, the teacher, and the student to think hard about their purposes, about the objectives they seek to achieve.

These considerations support the belief that objectives are important. They do not suggest that objectives need to be stated explicitly or in detail. The

[8]Elliot W. Eisner, "Educational Objectives: Help or Hindrance." *School Review* (Autumn 1967): 250–60.

pedagogical issues that divide teachers, the inadequacies that limit their effectiveness, cannot be disposed of by statements of objectives. Little that is wrong with any teacher's educational efforts today can be cured by getting him to define his objectives more fully and precisely. We ought not to ask teachers to spend much of their limited time in writing elaborate statements of their objectives.

Nor should we insist that the statements be in behavioral terms. Our main business as teachers is developing the cognitive resources of our pupils, not shaping their behavior. The great majority of teachers at all levels who feel no urgent need to write out their objectives in detail, and in terms of behavior, are probably wiser on this matter than those who have exhorted them to change their ways. Too much of the current reverence for behavioral objectives is a consequence of not looking closely enough at their limitations.

What Does Research Say?

A number of questions can be asked about educational objectives that are in principle amenable to empirical study. We can attempt to determine how in fact they are formulated by various groups such as curriculum developers, administrators, and teachers, and it is possible to compare the methods used in their formulation to the recommendations of experts. We can determine the extent to which teachers have educational objectives and whether they meet the criteria for adequacy described by Tyler, Bloom, Gagné, and others. We can compare the curriculum planning behavior of those who have precise educational objectives with the planning of those who do not have precise educational objectives. We can determine the effect of clearly stated objectives on the process of instruction, and, perhaps most important, we can determine the relationship between clearly formulated educational objectives and student learning. Do teachers who know what they want students to be able to do as measured by the teachers' ability to state their objectives precisely (using criteria set forth by Mager, for example) have a greater effect on particular types of learning than teachers who do not? In short, we can ask questions about: (1) the relationship between the way educational objectives are formulated and their quality; (2) the extent to which teachers have educational objectives; (3) the effect of educational objectives on curriculum planning; (4) the effect of educational objectives on instruction; and (5) the usefulness of educational objectives in facilitating learning.

Although such questions are complex they are important objects for empirical attention. When one looks for research on these questions, one soon finds

Eliot W. Eisner, "Instructional and Expressive Educational Objectives: Their Formulation and Use in Curriculum" in W. James Popham, Eliot W. Eisner, Howard J. Sullivan, and Louise Tyler, *Instructional Objectives*. AERA Monograph Series on Curriculum Evaluation (Chicago: Rand McNally, 1969), pp. 10–14. Copyright © 1969 by American Research Association. Reprinted by permission of the publisher.

that for the most part they have been neglected. There are some exceptions however. Margaret Ammons' study (1964) of the process and the product in curriculum development is one. In that study, Ammons set about to achieve three goals; to discover whether school systems used any systematic way of formulating educational objectives, to determine the relationship between the process used in formulating objectives and their quality, and to identify the extent to which factors thought to influence teacher appraisal of educational objectives do in fact influence such appraisal. Using a questionnaire on objectives Ammons selected a sample of school systems from a pool of 359 systems where it was possible to study the responses of board members, administrators, and teachers. At the end of her study Ammons states:

The writer believes that this study has made the following contributions:
1. the discovery that some systems do not have objectives, as this is defined here, to guide their educational programs;
2. the discovery that the school systems which participated in this study do not follow a process recommended by authorities to develop their educational objectives;
3. the discovery that teachers in this study appear to base their instructional programs on what they customarily have done rather than on the system's educational objectives;
4. the discovery that while no significant relation exists betweeen process and product using the data collected for this study, there is enough relation to suggest further research before the process is discarded;
5. the possibility of using empirical tests to evaluate curriculum theories;
6. areas for further research have been identified (Ammons, 1964, pp. 451–457).

Gagné (1965) discusses the importance of educational objectives in the development of instructional systems. He refers to French's work in training apprentice Air Force mechanics and to Briggs' and Bernards' work also in Air Force maintenance training as providing evidence on the effectiveness of instructional objectives. Evidence on the effectiveness of high-level specification of objectives in educational settings is considerably more tenuous.

Although Nerbovig (1956) found that intermediate grade teachers who had participated in the formulation of objectives and who had longer experience as teachers used objectives more frequently in planning their curriculums, Ammons' findings contradict Nerbovig's.

In an interesting effort to create an instructional objectives preference list, Popham and Baker (1965) asked students to rate on a fivepoint scale instructional objectives arranged according to usefulness. One class of statements was both behaviorally stated and important, a second class behaviorally stated and unimportant, a third nonbehaviorally stated and important, and a fourth nonbehaviorally stated and not important. When the subjects' (in this case student teachers) lesson plans were surreptitiously observed with respect to the use of behaviorally defined objectives and correlated with the subjects' preferences as revealed in their ranking of objectives, $r = .25$ ($p < .05$). Although reported only as a note in the *Journal of Educational Measurement* the research by Popham and Baker appears promising; it suggests the type of inquiry needed to clarify the function of educational objectives in educational settings.

In view of the admonitions in curriculum literature to state objectives in behavioral terms, it is surprising to find such a paucity of empirical studies available. Most of the studies that have been undertaken were done in training systems in industry or in the military services. One would think—and hope —that there would be some differences between industrial and military training and education. In the *Review of Educational Research* John Goodlad (1960) wrote, "There appear to be no studies establishing an actual relationship between increased clarification of educational objectives and improved discrimination in the selection of classroom learning opportunities for students." With respect to quantitative empirical research in school settings the situation appears not to have changed much in the past eight years.

From the published studies of educational objectives one can conclude that:

1. a very limited amount of empirical data is available on the subject
2. a narrow range of questions has been asked, and
3. most of the discussion on the usefulness of educational objectives has been based primarily upon rational analysis.

Now I have no bone to pick with the rational analysis of educational issues if empirical data are unavailable or unobtainable. Indeed, in a previous paper (1967a) I explicated some of the problems concerning high-level specification of education objectives and such explication was a result of analysis rather than a result of conclusions based upon quantitative data. In that paper I identified a number of limitations in theory about high-level specification of objectives. Without elaborating on them here, they were as follows:

1. they tend to overestimate the degree to which it is possible to predict educational outcomes,
2. they tend to treat all subject matters alike regarding the degree of specificity possible in stating educational objectives,
3. they tend to confuse the application of a standard and the making of a judgment regarding the appraisal of educational outcomes,
4. they have tended to imply that the formulation of objectives should be a first step in curriculum development and hence have confused the logical with the psychological in educational planning.

In a subsequent paper (1976b), I argued further that those who have advocated high-level specification of objectives have not differentiated between establishing a direction and formulating an objective. I argued that much in school practice which is educational is a consequence of establishing directions rather than formulating objectives.

I see even more problems now. For one, if we follow Gagné's suggestion (1967) regarding the identity of content and objective, we would select or use no content which had no objective and therefore have objectives for each unit of content we selected. What would this mean in the classroom? If the suggestion is followed strictly, the teacher would have to formulate behaviorally defined objectives for each unit of content for each educational program for which he was responsible and in the elementary school he may teach as many as fourteen subject areas.

Let's assume that a teacher has one unit of content to be learned by a group of thirty children for each seven subject areas a day. Let's assume further that he has his class divided in thirds in order to differentiate content for students with differing abilities. This would mean that the teacher would have to formulate objectives for seven units of content, times five days a week, times three groups of students, times four weeks a month, times ten months a school year. He would therefore have to have 4,200 behaviorally defined objectives for a school year. A six-year school employing such a curriculum rationale would have to have 25,200 behaviorally defined educational objectives.

Expressive Objectives vs. Instructional Objectives

One of the major criticisms of the view that objectives should be clearly stated in behavioral terms is that some objectives cannot be reduced to specific behavior. According to this view, in some classroom situations the teacher involves the student in activities without having any clear idea of what the student will learn from the experiences. A kindergarten teacher, for example, may play recordings of music with no other intention than that the students express their feelings in rhythmic movements. It is claimed that in such a case to require the teacher to use behavioral objectives would be a hindrance rather than an advantage.

Before you read the following selection try to list all the reasons why behavioral objectives would not be useful to the teacher. Then make a list of the advantages of such objectives. After considering the advantages and disadvantages, what conclusion do you reach about these objectives?

☐

Aside from the question of the sheer feasibility of such a scheme, what those who object to such an approach are concerned with, I think, is that even if the scheme could be implemented, it would alter the type of relationship between the teacher and the student which they value. If a teacher focuses primarily on the attainment of clearly specified objectives, he is not likely to focus on other aspects of the educational encounter, for although clearly specified objectives provide windows, they also create walls. Those who are not enthusiastic about high-level specification of objectives are not eager, I believe, to look through the windows of those who conceive of education as behavioral engineering.

Can such differences in orientation to education be resolved when it comes to the issue of how, if at all, educational objectives should be formulated? . . .

As an institution responsible for the transmission of culture, the school is concerned with enabling students to acquire those intellectual codes and skills which will make it possible for them to profit from the contributions of those who have gone before. To accomplish this task an array of socially defined skills must be learned—reading, writing, and arithmetic are some examples of coding systems that are basic to further inquiry into human culture.

While school programs attempt to enable children to acquire these skills, to learn to employ the tools necessary for using cultural products, schools are also concerned with enabling children to make a contribution to that culture by providing opportunities for the individual to construe his own interpretation to the material he encounters or constructs. A simple repetition of the past is the surest path to cultural rigor mortis.

Given these dual concerns—helping children to become skilled in the use of cultural tools already available and helping them to modify and expand these tools so that the culture remains viable—it seems to me appropriate to differentiate between two types of educational objectives which can be formulated in curriculum planning. The first type is familiar to most readers and is called an *instructional objective;* the second I have called an *expressive objective.*

Instructional objectives are objectives which specify unambiguously the particular behavior (skill, item of knowledge, and so forth) the student is to acquire after having completed one or more learning activities. These objectives fit the scheme or criteria identified earlier. They are usually drawn from cultural products such as the disciplines and are laid out in intervals of time appropriate for the children who are to acquire them.

Instructional objectives are used in a predictive model of curriculum development. A predictive model is one in which objectives are formulated and activities selected which are predicted to be useful in enabling children to attain the specific behavior embodied in the objective. In this model, evaluation is aimed at determining the extent to which the objective has been achieved. If the objective has not been achieved, various courses of action may follow. The objective may be changed. The instructional method may be altered. The content of the curriculum may be revised.

With an instructional objective the teacher, as well as the children (if they are told what the objective is), is likely to focus upon the attainment of a specific array of behaviors. The teacher in the instructional context knows what to look for as an indicator of achievement since the objective unambiguously defines the behavior. Insofar as the children are at similar stages of development and insofar as the curriculum and the instruction are effective, the outcomes of the learning activity will be homogeneous in character. The effective curriculum, when it is aimed at instructional objectives, will develop forms of behavior whose characteristics are known beforehand and, as likely as not, will be common across students—if not at the identical point in time, at some point during the school program.

The use of instructional objectives has a variety of educational ramifications. In preparing reading material in the social studies, for example, study questions at the beginning of a chapter can be used as cues to guide the student's attention to certain concepts or generalizations which the teacher intends to help the student learn. In the development of certain motor skills the student may provide examples of such skills and thus show the student what he is supposed to be able to do upon terminating the program. With the use of instructional objectives clarity of terminal behavior is crucial since it serves as a standard against which to appraise the effectiveness of the curriculum. *In an effective curriculum using instructional objectives the terminal behavior of the student and the objectives are isomorphic.*

Expressive objectives differ considerably from instructional objectives. An expressive objective does not specify the behavior the student is to acquire after having engaged in one or more learning activity. An expressive objective describes an educational encounter: It identifies a situation in which children are to work, a problem with which they are to cope, a task in which they are to engage; but it does not specify what from that encounter, situation, problem, or task they are to learn. An expressive objective provides both the teacher and the student with an invitation to explore, defer, or focus on issues that are of peculiar interest or import to the inquirer. An expressive objective is evocative rather than prescriptive.

The expressive objective is intended to serve as a theme around which skills and understandings learned earlier can be brought to bear, but through which those skills and understandings can be expanded, elaborated, and made idiosyncratic. With an expressive objective what is desired is not homogeneity of response among students but diversity. In the expressive context the teacher hopes to provide a situation in which meanings become personalized and in which children produce products, both theoretical and qualitative, that are as diverse as themselves. Consequently the evaluative task in this situation is not one of applying a common standard to the products produced but one of reflecting upon what has been produced in order to reveal its uniqueness and significance. In the expressive context, the product is likely to be as much of a surprise to the maker as it is for the teacher who encounters it.

Statements of expressive objectives might read:

1. To interpret the meaning of *Paradise Lost,*
2. To examine and appraise the significance of *The Old Man and the Sea,*
3. To develop a three-dimensional form through the use of wire and wood,
4. To visit the zoo and discuss what was of interest there.

What should be noted about such objectives is that they do not specify what the student is to be able to do after he engages in an educational activity; rather they identify the type of encounter he is to have. From this encounter both teacher and student acquire data useful for evaluation. In this context the mode of evaluation is similar to aesthetic criticism; that is, the critic appraises a product, examines its qualities and import, but does not direct the artist toward the painting of a specific type of picture. The critic's subject matter is the work done—he does not prescribe a blueprint of its construction.

Now I happen to believe that expressive objectives are the type that teachers most frequently use. Given the range and the diversity of children it is more useful to identify potentially fruitful encounters than to specify instructional objectives.

Although I believe that the use of expressive objectives is generally more common than the use of instructional objectives, in certain subject areas curriculum specialists have tended to emphasize one rather than the other. In mathematics, for example, much greater attention historically has been given to the instructional objective than in the visual arts where the dominant emphasis has been on the expressive (Eisner, 1965).

I believe that the most sophisticated modes of intellectual work—those, for example, undertaken in the studio, the research laboratory, and the graduate seminar—most frequently employ expressive rather than instructional objectives. In the doctoral seminar, for example, a theme will be identified around which both teacher and students can interact in an effort to cope more adequately with the problems related to the theme. In such situations educational outcomes are appraised after they emerge; specific learnings are seldom formulated in terms of instructional objectives. The dialogue unfolds and is followed as well as led. In such situations the skills and understandings developed are used as instruments for inquiring more deeply into the significant or puzzling. Occasionally such problems require the invention of new intellectual tools, thus inducing the creative act and the creative contribution. Once devised or fashioned these new tools become candidates for instructional attention.

Since these two types of objectives—instructional and expressive—require different kinds of curriculum activities and evaluation procedures, they each must occupy a distinctive place in curriculum theory and development. Instructional objectives embody the codes and the skills that culture has to provide and which make inquiry possible. Expressive objectives designate those circumstances in which the codes and the skills acquired in instructional contexts can be used and elaborated; through their expansion and reconstruction culture remains vital. Both types of objectives and the learning activities they imply constitute, to modify Whitehead's phrase, "the rhythm of curriculum." That is, instructional objectives emphasize the acquisition of the known; while expressive objectives emphasize its elaboration, modification, and, at times, the production of the utterly new.

Curriculum can be developed with an eye toward the alternating of such objectives. We can, I believe, study curriculum to determine the extent to which instructional and expressive educational objectives are employed, and we can raise questions about the types of relationships between them which are most productive for various types of students, for various types of learning, and for various subject matters.

In this chapter I have argued that the problem of formulating educational objectives is not simply a question of technique but is related directly to one's conception of education. The manner in which educational objectives are couched is, at base, a value decision. Second, I have tried to provide evidence of the differences among these values by examining the metaphors used by those who have contributed to the literature of the field. Third, I have cited empirical research aimed at examining the usefulness of educational objectives. Fourth, I have distinguished between two types of educational objectives—instructional and expressive—and indicated how they function in curriculum planning. The formulation and use of these objectives have implications for the selection of learning activities and for evaluation. The consequences of their use seem to me to be appropriate subject matter for research.

Summary

All can agree that the curriculum worker and the teacher must have a sense of direction as they plan and carry on their work. The debate centers on whether or not the direction should be stated; if so, how specific and in what terms. Undoubtedly some curriculum specialists, if not some teachers, insist that educational aims always guide what we do even though we may not be aware of them. They guide us because they are expressions of our most pervasive notions of what education in general, and the school in particular, are all about. Others insist that aims are magic words; that they play no part in our curriculum planning and teaching. You will face this issue again in chapter 10 where the utility of schooling is considered.

Few will doubt the value of educational objectives. It will be readily admitted by almost everyone that the teacher no less than the curriculum worker is trying to attain more immediate ends than those expressed as educational aims. But differences of opinion arise about the character and expression of these ends. Should they be expressed in behavioral terms? Are all objectives capable of being so expressed? How are objectives used anyway? Behavioral objectives are definitely useful in programmed instruction and in all instruction where, as Eisner suggests, the behavioral outcomes match the behavioral statement of objectives. This condition likely holds for psychomotor learnings as in typing and in some mental operations such as in spelling and the fundamental processes in arithmetic. The condition would not obtain in what Eisner calls expressive objectives. Between these two extremes lies the battleground.

It should be emphasized that the issues about objectives have been discussed with little benefit of research. Much of the argument on all sides is based upon personal experiences and social and philosophical perspectives. In general, educational humanists oppose behavioral objectives and probably lean toward general aims as guides to what they advocate and do. The technological school of curriculum thought advocates behavioral objectives as essential to efficient instruction. Where would you place other curriculum theorizers, for example, those who think the curriculum should be based on the disciplines or those who think the school should prepare youth to cope with the future?

Chapter **8**

The Curriculum and the Scope of Knowledge

"We have no need for them; our kids know it all."

Today's Education. 63. 4 (November 1974): 96.

Much has been said in recent years about how pupils learn. Some authorities believe that experience is the teacher; pupils must be involved if they are to learn. Others claim that learning occurs through conditioning or reward systems. Still others believe that learning occurs when the pupil watches the behavior of others. All these views are true; individuals do learn in a number of ways.

Equally important to how pupils learn is what should pupils learn? Lay persons would probably say that pupils should learn reading, writing, arithmetic, history, and so on. An answer often given by teachers is that they should acquire facts, generalizations, attitudes, and skills. Some teachers claim that these should be learned in a problematic context so as to acquire problem-solving procedures and techniques. In addition, a few teachers who follow the humanist ideology say that the most important things pupils learn are to respect themselves and others and gain a sense of self-fulfillment.

Overview

The question of what pupils should learn is not new. Since the natural activities of children were first interfered with by formal instruction, the question of what they should be taught has been of primary interest. This question has been answered differently in different societies, and from time to time in the same society.

The student in ancient Athens studied reading, writing, manners, music, poetry, and gymnastics. Generally, the practical studies dominated the curriculum in Egypt; the linguistic studies in Judea, Greece, and Rome. The medieval world emphasized grammar, songs, and elements of religious information such as the Lord's Prayer and sacred psalms. More advanced instruction was based on the Seven Liberal Arts which were composed of two groups: the Trivium and the Quadrivium. Grammar, rhetoric, and logic comprised the Trivium while the Quadrivium was composed of arithmetic, geometry, astronomy, and music.

During the modern period the Seven Liberal Arts were expanded into a number of disciplines. Arithmetic, for example, was supplemented by algebra, and astronomy was augmented by mechanics, physics, and chemistry. Today secondary schools in the United States offer more than 900 courses, many which are expansions of the Trivium and the Quadrivium.

The shift in emphasis from one content to another is apparently associated with the spirit of the times. In a strong religious age the curriculum will emphasize the creed, music, and art of the religious institution as well as the forms of reasoning compatible with its theology. In a genteel age the curriculum will emphasize language, literature, art, and courtly manners. Curriculum in an industrial age will include science, social studies, mathematics, language, and vocational subjects.

Today the spirit of the scientific, technological society shapes the general orientation of the curriculum. It emphasizes notions of precision, promptness, material gain, competition, and cooperation. Other frame factors also influence the curriculum. Curriculum content is partly determined by social forces that impinge upon school authorities and personnel. Organized interest groups demand that the instructional program include one subject after another. Patriotism, temperance, health and physical education, American history, consumer education, and black studies, for example, have been mandated by state legislatures or demanded directly by organized interest groups.

These are all claims upon the pupils' time. However, justification for these topics is not clear. To determine what the pupil should learn is okay so long as we are not required to justify our choices. But suppose we are faced with a demand either by the student or some legitimate speaker of society to answer the question: What learnings are of most worth? How should we answer?

There is perhaps no question of greater importance for the effectiveness of an education program than the question of content. Pupils learn what they study and what they study is either beneficial, or at worst of little help, on a personal or societal level. If the educational program is to make a difference to individuals and society, it must do so largely in terms of the content it contains. This raises some basic questions:

1. What is the total range of information from which the content of the curriculum can be selected?
2. What part of this total range of information is now emphasized in the public school curriculum?

3. What are the different kinds of knowledge that make up this total body of information?

Before considering the question of what content should be included in the school curriculum we must first consider the scope of human knowledge. We must be clear about the kind of knowledge we refer to when we speak of its scope. There is much knowledge that is unsystematized. For example, one knows things about himself; he knows that he likes spinach and dislikes coffee. He knows much about his acquaintances and friends. He knows that some of them like apple pie and others do not, that some prefer one color and others another, and so on. Every individual has almost an unlimited amount of such knowledge which he uses from time to time.

When we speak of the scope of knowledge, we do not include this sort of information. Rather, we refer to the systematized knowledge that people have accumulated through the ages. Knowledge is organized into a number of categories and we frequently speak of these as subjects such as chemistry, economics, and history. It is customary to think of the school curriculum in terms of such subjects. While these categories are convenient ways to organize the instructional program, they do not give us an adequate conception of the totality of systematized knowledge.

To the Romans knowledge consisted of grammar, logic, rhetoric, arithmetic, geometry, astronomy, music, medicine, architecture, and law. If we add theology this conception of the extent of knowledge persisted throughout the medieval period and well into modern times. This conception is no longer accurate. An examination of the course catalog of any large university provides sufficient evidence that knowledge can no longer be embraced by the liberal arts and medicine, law, and theology.

In the last one hundred years, knowledge has been accumulated at an increasingly rapid pace. This massive accumulation has discouraged the development of encyclopediac minds. Instead more specialists have been produced. Today one takes pride in knowing almost everything about a small segment of human activity or the steps needed to perform specialized tasks. Yet a school curriculum based upon a survey of only a part of the domain of knowledge is likely to neglect information significant to individuals and society.

Areas of Knowledge

Recently a number of scholars have suggested categories for purviewing knowledge. Perhaps the most useful of these is the work of Tykociner. He suggests twelve basic areas of knowledge together with the knowledge categories that lie between these areas and connect them. This is readily seen in Figure 8–1 which presents the schema of these areas of knowledge. The passage from *Zetetics* that follows this diagram sets forth the twelve fields of knowledge listed in the schema and briefly describes the elements of each. Following the presentation of the knowledge areas is a table (8–2) that presents the areas ordered in a series with respect to the purposes they fulfill.

Figure 8-1. Zetetics and Zetetic systems of knowledge

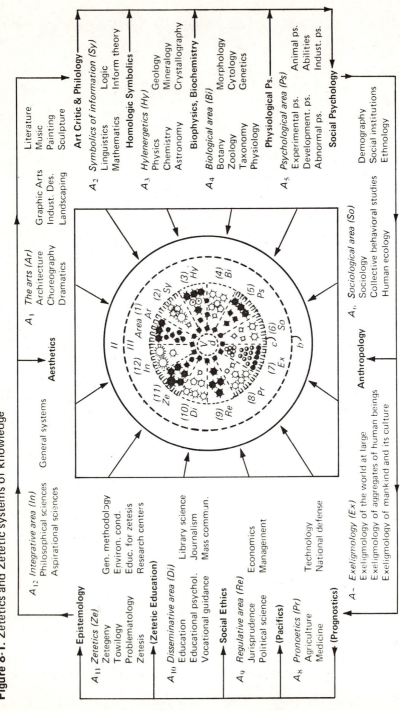

Taken from *Outline of Zetetics*, by Joseph T. Tykociner (Philadelphia: Dorrance and Company, 1966): 35-51.

174

As you study this passage and Figure 8–1, consider the extent to which the curriculum of your school matches these areas of knowledge and their purposes.

☐

Let us review briefly the twelve areas of knowledge, as represented in Figure 8–1 by sectors *Ar* to *In,* and indicate the principal links which bind these areas as a whole.

The following terms and their definitions normally included in Tykociner's diagram have been listed below:

Knowledge is the totality of information preserved by culture.

Science is the sum total of recorded systematized knowledge thus far accumulated by the human race.

Zetetics is the totality of recorded systematized knowledge related to:

Such methods of research	As lead to new problems
mental processes	stimulate creative imagination
psychological factors and	enhance selective thinking and
environmental conditions	generate original, fruitful ideas.

Zetesis is a purposeful activity aiming at the extension of the field of knowledge and experience by (a) discovering new facts and phenomena, (b) formulating generalized relations, (c) inventing mental and material devices for complementing human abilities, and (d) designing visual and auditory patterns of aesthetic significance.

A₁. The Arts (*Ar*)   The arts occupy the first sector, *Ar,* of the diagram. This area is preceded by Area 12 (the integrative area) with which it is linked by the philosophical study of aesthetics. The arts are the results of creative activity (zetesis) which, evoked by inspiration, produced unique objects of aesthetic quality. In their turn, objects of art kindle the dim light of creativity, intensify its brightness, and accelerate the development of this priceless faculty, so indispensable in the process of human evolution. Besides stimulating and sustaining zetesis, they perform a prophylactic function in overcoming boredom, which with increasing leisure is becoming a serious social problem.

It is the use of symbolic structures based on sense perceptions and appealing to the imagination which unifies the various parts of this area. Area 1 is, indeed, characterized by the use of symbolic presentation, patterned by a sequence of sounds and intervals of silence in music, or by colors distributed in various shades in painting, or by multidimensional shapes in sculpture, or by motions of the human figure in ballet.

A further characteristic which unifies all the arts is that they serve as a means of communication. The artist's role is to transmit his impressions and ideas to the public which reacts by expressing approval or displeasure.

Thus, artists and writers are concerned with symbolic patterns of light, shade, colors, sounds, words, and sentences, all forming images which, besides

Joseph T. Tykociner, *Outline of Zetetics* (Philadelphia: Dorrance, 1966), pp. 35–51. Reprinted by permission of the author and publisher.

Footnotes have been renumbered consecutively throughout the chapter.

evoking aesthetic emotions, enrich our experience and serve as a medium of communication.

This area includes (in alphabetical order):

architecture	landscaping
choreography	literature
dramatics	music
graphic arts	painting
industrial design	sculpture. . . .

As to the aesthetic element involved in art and literature, it is not entirely absent in scientific or technological creations. Mathematicians often mention the inner harmony and beauty they find in their field, and they like to speak of "elegant" solutions of their problems. Similarly, astronomers, physicists, and biologists are often impressed by the beauty, the perspectives, and the astounding horizons which their generalizations reveal.

Area 1 does not stand isolated from the other areas, but is a constituent part of a cyclic arrangement of all the areas which form a systematically interrelated whole. Art criticism and philology connect Area 1 with Area 2, the symbolics of information.

A₂. Symbolics of Information (*Sy*) The next sector, *Sy*, represents the result of a chain of developments which led from primitive attempts of communication by signs and gestures to articulated language and onward through systems of symbolic formalization to the as yet undeveloped stage of systematic concept formation.

This area also deals with symbolic structures. However, its elements are arbitrarily selected to facilitate the process of reasoning. Here the rigorous consistency of its symbolic structure is the predominant factor, while in Area 1 the originality and the aesthetic appeal are the mainsprings of creative endeavor.

The *Sy* sector includes:

> linguistics
> mathematics
> logic
> information theory.

The tendency of the first three sciences to merge is indicated in the diagram by overlapping circles. All of these sciences supply symbols, abstract concepts, and rules of operation for the purpose of ordering and communicating information in a consistent way. Because an abundance of symbols is involved, *symbolics of information* has been chosen as a suitable name for this area of knowledge. . . .

Mathematicians, logicians, and other scientists of area *Sy* are, like artists, concerned with patterns. However, the patterns they form have a cognitive character which, nonetheless, evoke feelings of elegance and beauty. Their images consist of theories, inferences, rules, and laws which are indispensable for the development of the sciences of other areas.

Since none of the known sciences of Area 2 is specifically adapted to be a direct link with the next area (A_3), the zetetic point of view requires searching for a new science to fill the gap. This led to the formulation of the science *homologic symbolics*. . . .

A_3. Hylenergetics (*Hy*)—sciences dealing with matter and energy   The area of systematized knowledge often referred to as the physical sciences is shown by the third sector *Hy*. Its basic sciences are:

> physics
> chemistry
> astronomy
> geology
> mineralogy.

Because most of the processes they exhibit lend themselves readily to mathematical treatment and to precise measurements, the first three are often called exact sciences. Figuratively, they are spoken of as fundamental blocks on which knowledge of the structure of the universe is built.

This is, indeed, an area embracing the knowledge of both the microcosmos and the macrocosmos. They study the multitudes of phenomena activated by aggregates of nuclear particles, atoms, and molecules from the tiny crystalline units to the immense units embodied in the earth, the solar system, and the galaxies. All these units act singly and in their entirety as sources of kinetic radiant energy which they interchange.

The rapid expansion of this area during the last hundred years has led to a remarkable unification of the various branches of each of its basic sciences and produced far-reaching, experimentally verified generalizations based on the equivalence of matter and energy. Such a synthesis justifies the name *hylenergetics* chosen for this area of knowledge. It is a combination of the Greek work *hyle,* signifying "matter," and *ergon,* signifying "work." It means "study of states of energy and matter convertible into each other."

In Figure 8–1 the three outer circles in sector *Hy* represent physics, chemistry, and astronomy. Two intersciences are represented by double circles—namely, physical chemistry in proximity to physics and astrophysics in proximity to astronomy. The other circles represent geology and mineralogy.

One connecting link binding this area with the next is marked by a double circle drawn on the adjacent radial line. This circle represents crystallography, a branch of mineralogy, which remotely suggests the first characteristic of living organisms, growth. There are two other double circles on the same radial line. These represent biophysics and biochemistry—links binding sector *Hy* with *Bi.*

A_4. The Biological Area (*Bi*)   The many aspects of the living world, as manifested in processes of growth and reproduction, are studied by the sciences of area *Bi.* They are often called the "life sciences" and are unified by the principle of evolution. Their subject matter ranges from the simplest units of life as they appear in single cells to complex organisms of the plant and animal kingdoms in an immense variety of forms and functions.

So great is the variety of organisms (micro, plant, and animal) that a particular science, taxonomy, is devoted to the identification and classification of biological objects into species, genus, family, etc. The wealth of information produced by the biological sciences could hardly have been obtained without application of the results of the sciences of the preceding areas. Especially helpful were mathematics, physics, and chemistry. It is sufficient to indicate, as examples, the role of optics and electronics in supplying techniques and devices indispensable in biological explorations and also the role of geological explorations which led to paleonotology—the basis of systematized knowledge of evolutionary processes.

The basic sciences are:

> botany
> zoology
> taxonomy
> morphology
> cytology
> genetics
> physiology.

They are linked with the following area (*Ps*) by physiology, which is closely connected with physiological psychology.

A₅. The Psychological Area (*Ps*)   For centuries psychology was considered the science of the soul (psyche). As represented by philosophical psychology, it developed into speculative investigations of the human mind. Introspection and observation led to a variety of psychological systems. The modern course of development was started with psychophysics when physical methods of measurement were applied to the study of quantitative relations between stimuli and responses.

The area of psychology became even more closely connected with the biological sciences when by the use of experimental methods a new field of research was opened, that is, experimental psychology which is closely related to physiological psychology. Thus, the latter became an interscience linking biology with general psychology. Application of the concepts of evolution then led to still another expansion of the field of study, namely, animal or comparative psychology. Experimental investigations suggested that each individual organism, acting as the result of integrated operations of its component organs, as a whole shows behavioral patterns of adjustment to its environment. Subsequently such studies were extended to small and large numbers of individuals acting as a group. This gave rise to group psychology, which together with social psychology, constitutes a binding link with the area of sociology. Therefore, social psychology is shown in Figure 8–1 as a double circle drawn on the border line between *Ps* and *So*.

So intimately interconnected appear the biological, psychological, and social sciences that a movement to unify all three into an area of behavioral sciences is evolving as an attempt toward further consolidation of systematized knowledge. . . .[1]

A₆. The Sociological Area (*So*)   In the area of sociological sciences, knowledge is being collected and systematized relative to the phenomena and conditions which produce, sustain, or change the many various forms of individual and group life. Sociology, originally called *social physics* and sometimes defined as "the science of society," is the basic science in this area of knowledge. . . .

The following main subdivisions of the social sciences, as represented in Figure 8–1 by circles in sector *So,* show the inherent interrelation of their subject matter with other areas of science:

1. Sociology, the study of relations between human beings, individually and in groups.
2. Collective behavioral studies, by their relation to group and social psychology, represent the link with Area 5.
3. Human ecology binds Area 6 with the biological sciences, A₄, by its connection with animal sociology and ecology.
4. Demography, the study of the vital processes and of the distribution and composition of population aggregates, supplies the necessary data for the study of human ecology and social institutions.
5. Social institutions, their structure, statics, and dynamics, form the central part of the subject matter treated by sociology.
6. Ethnology is related to cultural anthropology.

Anthropology is closely related to the next area, A₇, exeligmology, and is indicated by a double circle on the borderline drawn between sector *Ex* and sector *Pr.* It is briefly described later when links between areas are specifically discussed.

A₇. Exeligmology (*Ex*)—Sciences Dealing with the Past   For the seventh area, the word *exeligmology* has been chosen. This word, of Greek origin, means "unfolding." This area includes sciences which deal with evolution, history, and possibly other branches of the humanities. It can be briefly described as the area which binds the sciences of history, evolution, and cosmogony by their common objective: to outline stages of development and to remove gaps in knowledge which hinder the formation of a consistent perspective of the past.

In its broader sense, evolution as a science is the study of relations between phenomena which are brought about by time and space changes and developments. Related to the manifold aspects of development discovered by man's searching mind, the study of evolution may be regarded as the extension of

[1]Roy R. Grinker, ed., *Toward a Unified Theory of Human Knowledge* (New York: Basic Books, 1956), p. 375.

history into cultural, anthropological, biological, cosmological, and other developments.

History as a science is based on collections of documents and records transmitted from generation to generation and on remnants of earlier human habitations—monuments and artifacts uncovered by archaeological research. Studies in biological evolution are based on the fossils found in geological layers deposited during long periods of existence of the earth as a planet of the solar system. Still longer eons of time were involved in the cosmic developments studied by cosmology on the basis of astrophysical evidence.

What binds together these seemingly unrelated sciences of history, evolution, and cosmogony? It is their common objective, which consists in imaginative reconstruction of the past, in creating a picture of the stages undergone in the process of development, and in removing gaps of knowledge which hinder the formation of a plausible, consistent perspective of the past.

Each of the sciences within this seventh area has its specific subject matter. Each of them differs also in the type of evidence it seeks and in the magnitude of time intervals it attempts to cover.

Therefore, sector *Ex* of the diagram shows a cluster of circles divided into three groups. Group I at the periphery consists of dark shaded circles and represents branches of science concerned with cosmic evolution and the appearance of life, especially *Homo sapiens.* Group II, in the middle, consists of circles divided into a light and a dark part. These are concerned with biological and sociohistorical aspects of society. Finally, Group III, closest to the center, contains clear circles which refer to the history of human culture. There is a double circle on the borderline between the two sectors *Ex* and *Pr* which signifies that it is based on the past but looking into the future. It is the budding science for which the name *prognostics* seems suitable. In Table 8–1 branches of exeligmology are enumerated. It gives us a general picture of the development of the universe, including society and its culture.

I. The first division embraces exeligmology of the world at large as related to the cosmos and early forms of life. It includes cosmogony, geogeny, biogeny, origin and development of species, and prehistory. This group of sciences is purely evolutionary in character. On the sector diagram, it is marked by dark shaded circles.

II. The second division refers to exeligmology of aggregates of human beings and has two parallel subdivisions, marked on the diagram by circles divided into black and white zones. The subdivisions are as follows:

    a. the more general part, which is still essentially evolutionary in character. It studies the chain of development starting from the members of the human species, families, groups, and so on, up the rungs of the evolutionary ladder toward a world community;

    b. the second part, historical in character and embracing the biography of a particular individual; the history of a particular family, generation, or dynasty; the history of a particular population, ethnic group, community, state, or empire, culminating in the history of a particular federation of nations.

III. Finally, the third division embraces the exeligmology of society and its culture. It is represented on the sector diagram by clear circles.

Table 8–1:   Exeligmology

I. Exeligmology of the world at large	1. Cosmogony, a part of cosmology
	2. Geogeny, a part of geology
	3. Biogeny, a part of biology
	4. Origin and development of species
	5. Evolution and prehistory of *Homo sapiens*
II. Exeligmology of aggregates of human beings	1. a. Evolution of aggregates of human beings
	b. Biography of a particular individual
	2. a. Evolution of a family, a part of sociology
	b. History of a particular family, generation, or dynasty
	3. a. Evolution of a group (sociology and group psychology)
	b. History of a particular group
	4. a. Evolution of urban, rural, and metropolitan populations
	b. History of a particular population
	5. a. Evolution of ethnical groups, as part of anthropology
	b. History of a particular ethnical group
	6. a. Evolution of communities, a part of sociology
	b. History of a particular community
	7. a. Evolution of states, as part of political science
	b. History of a particular state
	8. a. Evolution of empires, as part of political science
	b. History of a particular empire
	9. a. Evolution toward a world community
	b. History of a particular federation of nations
III. Exeligmology of society and its culture	1. History of the development of human culture
	2. History of the development of art and literature
	3. History of the development of sciences
	4. History of the development of technologies
	5. History of the development of systems of ideas (philosophy)
	6. History of the development of aspirations

The third division could also deal with histories of particular sciences, technologies, etc. But the latter subdivisions and other fields of history have been omitted for the sake of brevity. . . .

A₈. Pronoetics (*Pr*)—Sciences Related to Sustaining Human Life   In contrast to exeligmology, which includes all the sciences related to the past, pronoetics deals with a wide area of knowledge directed toward the future. It seeks to answer vital questions which human beings encounter throughout their active life. How does one provide for the needs of oneself, one's family, the community, the state, the country, and society as a whole? How do humans survive amidst the dangers they are subjected to by their inveterate enemies: hunger, exposure, illness, ignorance, aggression, boredom, degeneration, and extinction? How can one make good use of natural and human resources, so as to create conditions conducive to a more secure, healthy, and peaceful future?

The name *pronoetics* was chosen for this area because the word *pronoe,* of Greek origin, denotes "foresight." Foresight, implemented by planning, is indeed the root out of which have grown the basic sciences of pronoetics:

> agriculture
> medicine
> technology
> national defense.

Each of these so-called "applied sciences" has a great many subdivisions. Each seeks to utilize knowledge accumulated in the preceding areas. In return, they have all made notable contributions to the sciences in those areas by supplying new instruments, materials, and techniques of research, by collecting valuable observations, opening up new domains of experience, and raising problems for many of the parent sciences.

In Figure 8–1 the sector of pronoetics, A_8, includes six circles. Four of them represent the basic sciences enumerated above. The fifth circle is reserved for recreation as a science which studies both physical and mental recuperation from the strain of occupational activities. It is now known as occupational medicine but may become itself a basic science of this area.

Finally, the sixth circle is reserved for a new development, rapidly growing in significance but not yet sufficiently systematized to be classified as a science. It includes the auxiliary techniques which supply instrumentalities for furthering research in all the other sciences. The lack of a proper name for this prospective basic science of pronoetics makes it necessary to assign to it a temporary symbol, TAZ, an acronym made up of the first letters of the phrase "Technological Aids for Zetesis." Meanwhile it occupies a temporary place in our system of knowledge as a division of technology.

A branch of national defense which is becoming of paramount importance in our time is *pacifics,* the science of peace. It attempts to discover ways for nations to live together without recourse to warfare, thus filling a wide gap in our knowledge and relating Area *Pr* to the next one, *Re,* the regulative sciences.

A_9. The Regulative Area (Social Cybernetics) (Re)   The function of this area is to study prevailing conditions and the means for harmonizing human relations for peaceful transition from past to future states of society, especially ways of balancing the distribution and exchange of the products and the services supplied by pronoetic activities.

Thus, in the ninth area, shown as sector A_9 in Figure 8–1, are included those sciences which systematize all the knowledge related to maintaining a balanced order and sustaining the degree of stability in human relations necessary for safeguarding the proper functioning of society at large. The main basic sciences in this area are as follows:

> jurisprudence
> political science
> economics
> management and administration.

The strong characteristic of this particular area of science is that it is concerned with systems of laws, rules, procedures, inventories, indices, and inducements which are designed to enable society as a whole to operate by balancing the multifarious activities and interests of individual groups and institutions. Whenever instability in any part of the sociopolitical system reaches a limit regarded as dangerous, countermeasures are, if possible, set into action in the form of social pressures and penalities which try to reestablish the disturbed balance. If the use of countermeasures is not possible, the system may be modified by complementing or changing the existing procedures or laws. In democracies, this is done by constitutional means supported by popular consent; in autocracies, by decrees.

In human made machines, such corrective regulative measures are known as "feedback mechanisms," and they are provided by nature in biological organisms. Studies of activities regulating technological and biological systems led to a science which was named *cybernetics* by Norbert Wiener.[2] The name is derived from the Greek word *kybernetes,* meaning "steerman." Therefore, the name *social cybernetics* might be appropriate for this ninth area of sciences. . . .

The connecting link which binds this area of knowledge, *Re,* with the next, *Di,* the disseminative sciences, is a branch of social cybernetics which we call *social ethics.* It is concerned with setting up moral codes to orient social behavior for the harmonious functioning of human society. It differs from philosophical ethics, which is concerned with a systematic study of the ultimate problems of human conduct in relation to their moral quality.

A$_{10}$. The Disseminative Area (*Di*)   The most outstanding feature which distinguishes the human species from the rest of living creatures is the ability to transmit from generation to generation the knowledge accumulated throughout ages of cultural development. The transmission of knowledge has grown into an activity which requires vast and costly systems of schools, institutes, and universities, employing an ever-increasing number of teachers, librarians, writers, publishers, etc. And the individual has to spend a considerable, ever-increasing part of his life acquiring this knowledge.

The tenth area of systematized knowledge is represented in Figure 8–1 by sector A$_{10}$. It contains those sciences which are related to various phases and means of disseminating knowledge, developing skills, conserving all records, and making them available for information and further research. Due to these

---

[2] Norbert Wiener, *Cybernetics* (New York: John Wiley, 1948), p. 19.

sciences, we can enjoy and utilize our cultural heritage and continue to develop the work of our predecessors.

The basic sciences in this area are:

> education
> educational psychology
> vocational guidance
> library science
> journalism
> mass communication.

A still wider objective of this area is to prepare the younger generation for creative activities by developing interest and skills necessary for the growth of the arts and the sciences. Zetetic education is the science which binds sector *Di* with the next one, *Ze,* and serves to develop awareness of the unified system of arts and sciences.

A_{11}. **Zetetics (Ze)**   For modern society, increasing in population and scope, it is not enough to record and disseminate the knowledge inherited from previous generations. New problems continually arise which require more knowledge than available at present. The sciences which study how knowledge can be increased in quality and quantity are included in sector *Ze*. They are the following:

> zetegeny
> taxilogy
> problematology
> the study of zetesis
> general methodology
> the study of environmental conditions and incentives
> education for zetesis
> organization and development of research centers.

In Figure 8–1, this emerging area of knowledge is shown as sector A_{11}, which contains circles representing the eight branches. Each of the branches studies a distinct body of subject matters. However, as a whole, the role of zetetics is to bring together and systematize available information about zetesis. Thus, zetetics binds together all the areas of knowledge, tending toward their growth and unification. It leads to the integrative area, A_{12}, which includes the study of the philosophic foundation of knowledge—epistemology. The latter represents the binding link between A_{11} and A_{12}.

A_{12}. **The Integrative Area (In)**   The culminating process in the search for what is often called "the truth" or "objective reality" is the integration of all available knowledge into one consistent system. This would represent an all-embracing synthesis which would contain not only a total picture of the world in which people live, but also a clear understanding of their role and the aims of their activities and strivings. Such attempts are implied in zetesis.

Philosophers, prophets, and other learned personalities have tried to attain such a synthesis throughout the ages, approaching the problem from various fundamentally different viewpoints. With the growth of our knowledge, this tendency has become more and more systematic and resulted in a number of sciences which may be called *integrative*.

The integrative sciences may be divided into three classes, namely:

Philosophical,   which specializes in attempts to create a consistent, universal system of abstract ideas;

Aspirational,   which embraces a large variety of ideological patterns reflecting the highest human aspirations and including all the theologies;

General systems,   which studies the general properties of every kind of system.

In Figure 8–1, sector *In* is assigned to these sciences, and the three subdivisions are represented by three circles. The upper two refer to philosophical and aspirational sciences. Their circles are surrounded by dots to indicate the many divergent schools of thought in their respective fields. The lower circle represents general systems, a new and promising field which is attracting prominent scientists interested in the main current of modern thought. . . .

Summary of Areas and Their Functions

By successive steps, aided by the sector diagram, we have succeeded in binding together the entire field of arts and sciences. We must keep in mind that the diagram represents symbolically the totality of our knowledge in a state of growth and transformation. Its dynamic quality suggests that a chain of reinforcing reactions is taking place throughout the twelve sectors of systematized knowledge in a continuous process of zetesis which tends to shape society's future as it evolves from the past.

We may summarize the twelve areas with the aid of Table 8–2 in which these areas are enumerated in five series, each distinguished by its particular function.

The first series contains two areas whose function is to facilitate communication by developing systems of symbolic representation of perceptual and cognitive activity.

The second series contains four areas which supply knowledge of facts and their basic relations in the world in which we live.

The third series, grounded on the second one, embraces four areas which extend our knowledge of the past and apply the results obtained by the second series, so as to provide and build for the future while controlling the significant fluctuations ever-present in a shift from past to future conditions.

The fourth series includes zetetic sciences, which are concerned with the growth of all the areas.

And, finally, the fifth series contains the integrative area, which represents attempts toward an all-embracing synthesis. . . .

The zetetic system of knowledge can also assist in the organization of

Table 8-2:   Functions of the areas of knowledge

Series	Areas of knowledge	Function
I.	1. Arts 2. Symbolics of information	To develop systems of symbolic representation of perceptual and cognitive activity for purposes of communication.
II.	3. Hylenergetics 4. Biological 5. Psychological 6. Sociological	To systematize knowledge of basic facts and their relations.
III.	7. Exeligmology 8. Pronoetics 9. Regulative 10. Disseminative	To systematize knowledge of the past, project future needs, and regulative activities.
IV.	11. Zetetic	To promote the growth of all arts and sciences.
V.	12. Integrative	To create an all-embracing synthesis.

education on its various levels from elementary through secondary schools and colleges.[3] It can serve as a guide for students, as well as for persons who are already active professionally, in choosing the roles best suited to make their lives meaningful, useful, and genuinely satisfactory. In the maze of modern life, orienting one's self, evaluating one's potentialities, determining one's goal, and finding one's proper role are becoming more and more difficult. A new approach, like the above, is urgently needed.

It is interesting to consider whether or not the functions of the knowledge areas are equivalent to educational aims. Are these functions simply statements of the reasons for grouping knowledge into the five series? Does Tykociner put the arts, logic, etc., together because they are used to communicate? Physics, botany, psychology, etc., because they provide basic information about our world? History, evolution, agriculture, jurispurdence, education, etc., because they provide information about future needs and how we regulate our collective conduct? Methodology, taxiology, etc., because they facilitate the creation of new knowledge? Philosophy, general systems, etc., because they enable us to build our world view? If so, do these purposes also provide a comprehensive view of the purposes of schooling?

[3]Harry S. Broudy, et al., *Democracy and Excellence in American Secondary Education* (Chicago: Rand McNally, 1963).

Tykociner speaks of the arrangement as a series. What does he mean by "series"? Is there an implied hierarchy with I being the simplest and V the most complex? Or is it implied that I is fundamental to II, II to III, III to IV, and IV to V? What curricular implications, if any, do you see in your answers to these questions?

How High School Enrollments Are Distributed

The curriculum is composed of information selected from the twelve areas of knowledge described by Tykociner. We can speak of these as subjects or disciplines when this information is organized into categories for instruction and learning purposes. These are typically grouped under general headings such as language arts, natural science, and so on. For example, natural sciences may include various subjects such as general science, biology, botany, zoology, physics, chemistry, and ecology.

The United States Office of Education survey of enrollments in the general subject areas for 1970–1971 shows the percent of the total secondary school enrollment in each area. The percent for each area is indicative of what the school personnel, the adult society, and the pupils consider to be most worthwhile knowledge. Figure 8–2 shows the number enrolled in each area. Examine the chart and the following explanatory passage. What justification do you see for this distribution of enrollments? What subject areas would you emphasize? Why? What shifts in emphasis have occurred in the last decade? Do you agree with the explanations given in the reading?

Estimated course enrollments in the subject areas of English language arts, health and physical education, and social sciences each exceeded 100 percent of total school enrollment. Such rates emphasize that (1) school authorities almost universally require a course in each of these areas for each pupil, and (2) with short courses and a heightened interest in these areas of study, pupils frequently enroll in more than one course in each area during the period of a school year. In the count of enrollments, these pupils are included more than once—one time for each course in which they enrolled.

In the three subject areas with course enrollments exceeding 100 percent of all 1970–71 secondary school pupils, a large segment of the enrollments was concentrated in generalized grade-specific courses. Enrollment in such courses made up 63.2 percent of all enrollments in the English language arts and 54.1 percent of all enrollments in the social sciences. Graded physical education courses and graded combined health and physical education courses together constituted 78.0 percent of all course registrations in health and physical education.

Diane B. Gertler and Linda A. Barker, *Patterns of Course Offerings and Enrollment in Public Secondary Schools, 1970–71.* DHEW Publication No. (OE) 73–11400 (Washington: U.S. Government Printing Office, 1972): pp. 2–8.

Figure 8-2. Course enrollments in each subject area as a percent of total secondary school enrollment: United States, 1970-71.

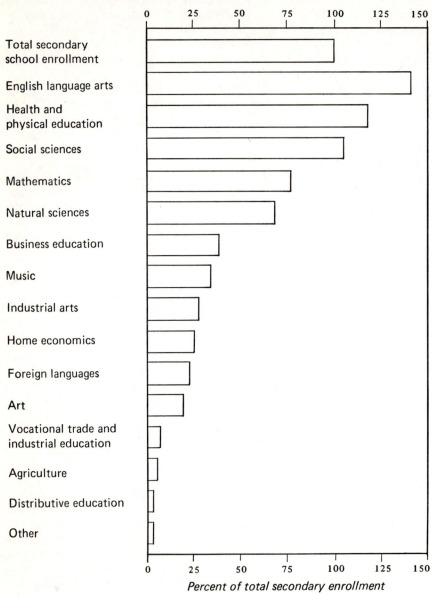

Percent of total secondary enrollment

Source: Table 1
OE/INCES

Note. Subject/area totals of course enrollments may exceed the number of individual pupils, since a pupil may enroll in more than one course within a subject area during a school year.

Mathematics   Within the subject area of mathematics, 35.1 percent of all enrollment was in seventh- and eighth-grade general mathematics. Upper-level general mathematics courses represented only 18.3 percent of total mathematics enrollments. The single upper-level mathematics course showing the largest enrollment was elementary algebra (16.5 percent of all mathematics enrollment). When totaled together, elementary, intermediate, and advanced algebra courses accounted for 27.7 percent of the course enrollment in mathematics.

Natural Sciences   First-year biology attracted the greatest number of pupils enrolled in the natural sciences, accounting for 21.4 percent of the enrollment in that subject area. The second most popular science course was grade 9–12 general science, representing 13.3 percent of all enrollment in the natural sciences. General science courses enrolled about the same number of pupils as a decade ago; yet, a decade ago they represented 56.6 percent of natural science enrollments, while in 1970–71 they comprised 36.4 percent. This downward trend in general science enrollments is balanced by increases in the more specific areas of earth science and physical sciences.

The fifteen courses claiming the highest percentages of pupils enrolled have been ranked from highest to lowest, with comparative rank as of the preceding survey indicated in Table 8–3.

Table 8–3: Survey results

| | 1970–71 | Ranking[a] | |
Course title	Percent of pupils	1970–71	1960–61
General Mathematics, grades 7–8	27.0	1	1
English, grade 9	20.5	2	2
English, grade 10	17.3	3	3
U.S. History, grade 9–12	16.7	4	4
Biology, first year	14.8	5	10
English, grade 11	14.3	6	5
English, grade 7	13.7	7	11
English, grade 8	13.6	8	6
Elementary Algebra	12.6	9	12
General or Fine Art (grades 7, 8, and 9)	11.9	10	7
Health	11.6	11	19
Physical Education, grade 9	11.4	12	20
Driver Education (classroom phase)	10.6	13	28
General Music	10.3	14	8
Typewriting, first-year	10.2	15	17

[a] The ranking may not be absolute, because there is a slight discrepancy between the aggregation of reported courses in the two surveys.

Four of these courses (first-year typewriting, health, ninth-grade physical education, and the classroom phase of driver education) ranked below fifteenth in the 1960–61 survey. The most spectacular change in rank was demonstrated in driver education. Four other courses (grade 8 general science, grade 9 general science, grade 7 or 8 U.S. history, and world history) included among the first fifteen in the earlier survey have dropped to a lower ranking in the 1970–71 pretest survey.

Some of the greatest increases in the number of courses offered were noted in Engligh language arts and social sciences. An examination of the titles of the courses reported indicates that many of the new courses are intended to offer pupils a choice of studies and answer their contentions that the school curriculum is not relevant to their daily lives and concerns.

The pretest further reveals a trend toward substitution of specific courses for traditional combination offerings, particularly at the upper high school levels. For example, while enrollment in grades 9–12 world history dropped from 12.5 percent of total enrollment in 1960–61 to 9.2 percent in 1970–71, more particularized courses such as world cultures, Asian and African studies, and anthropology have replaced it in the current curriculum. Enrollment in these more specialized courses more than offset the decrease in enrollment in world history. In 1960–61, American literature was considered to be a component of eleventh-grade English, and was so shown in the published survey. The 1970–71 data show Amercian literature now to be an individual course in its own right, in which 6.7 percent of all secondary school pupils enroll. At the same time, enrollment in traditional eleventh grade English declined slightly, indicating that the emphasis is no longer placed on covering all facets of the English language arts in a single course. Instead, pupils enroll in separate composition, literature, and reading classes, as their individual abilities, needs, and interests dictate. . . .

Curriculum Trends

Perhaps the most notable general developments in course offerings and enrollments in the past decade have been (1) the greater variety of courses offered, (2) the extent to which advanced or college level courses are made available to pupils in high school, and (3) the offering of traditionally upper-level high school courses to younger pupils, particularly in mathematics and natural sciences.

Another finding of the pretest is that a multiplicity of *short courses* have been introduced into the curriculum. The average number of courses per pupil rose from 6.4 in 1960–61 to 7.1 in 1970–71. The *higher number of courses* taken by the average pupil during a school year has undoubtedly been made possible by a lengthened school day and by flexible class scheduling plans in a number of schools.

How the Scope of Curriculum Compares to the Scope of Knowledge

If we match the subject areas in Figure 8–3 with the total scope of knowledge set forth in Tykociner's categories, it will be readily seen that certain areas of knowledge are almost completely neglected while others comprise the bulk of the curriculum. A reference to the function of the various areas will indicate that some of the basic functions of knowledge are either un-

Figure 8-3. Matrix of secondary school subject areas and Tykociner's categories

	Integrative	Zetetics	Disseminative	Regulative	Pronoetics	Exeligmology	Sociological	Psychological	Biological	Hylenergetics	Symbolics	Arts
English language arts												
Health education												
Physical education												
Social sciences												
Mathematics												
Natural sciences												
Business education												
Music												
Industrial arts												
Home economics												
Foreign language												
Art												
Vocational trade and industrial education												
Agriculture												
Distributive education												
Other												

recognized by the school or seriously neglected. Figure 8–3 will assist you in comparing the two sets of categories. Check the cells in which the subject areas and the knowledge areas coincide. You may need to review Tykociner's categories and the subject areas offered in the secondary school as you check the cells. Which of Tykociner's categories do the schools omit? Which components in his areas of knowledge are either short changed or omitted? Which functions in Table 8–2 are slighted? As you consider these questions, you should remember that only the large high schools provide a comprehensive program of studies.

Recently much has been said about providing a balanced curriculum. What light, if any, does your analysis throw on the problem of balance?

Summary

As the range of knowledge continually expands so too does the school curriculum. Old areas grow and new ones emerge from time to time. These developments give rise to new perspectives, new goals, and new ways of attaining old goals.

In the last century, the science of genetics developed from Mendel's experiments in cross fertilization of peas. This, in turn, led to the improvement of food production. The new science found its way into the curriculum. As a result today more individuals are gaining new views about food production, human diseases, human behavior, and longevity.

Subjects taught in school are made up of selected elements of these areas of knowledge. Unfortunately, some areas are neglected making the range of information available to pupils far less adequate than is needed to cope with life today. One of the duties of the school personnel, especially curriculum workers and teachers, is to evaluate the curriculum constantly, being sensitive to both the cognitive demands that society places upon its members and the adequacy of the areas of knowledge to the curriculum.

Chapter **9**

The Curriculum and Types of Knowledge

Instructor 82. 5 (1973) 128.

"Mr. Sottle, it's not as much that I'm an under-achiever as you are an over-expecter."

1. Attitudes and Imperatives
2. Value Concepts
3. Normative Knowledge and the Curriculum
4. Concepts: Building Blocks
5. Laws and Law-Like Statements
6. Facts: Statements of Particulars
7. Can You Recognize Types of Knowledge?
8. Forms of Knowledge and School Subjects
9. Reminder

In the last two decades new emphasis has been placed on teaching concepts. Specialists in each field—social studies, science, and so on—have been busy selecting concepts and telling us how to teach them. Values have also received a major share of attention: Witness the development of a taxonomy of affective objectives and the development of widespread interest in values clarification. Other forms of knowledge, however, have lingered in the background, little noticed by either specialists or teachers. Yet these neglected forms—moral principles, descriptive principles, and so on —are essential to intelligent behavior. This chapter presents the types of knowledge, discusses their characteristics, and indicates their relations to the disciplines.

Knowledge can be classified either into areas or into school subjects. It can also be broken down into cognitive types such as concepts, facts, and values. We frequently claim that we are teaching these elements of knowledge when we teach courses. When we say we want pupils to study history, English, science, and the like, what we usually mean is that we want them to acquire these forms of knowledge. Upon analyzing examinations, or the taxonomies of objectives, we see that these are what we expect pupils to learn. We test for their ability to state and use concepts, principles, procedures, and so on. To master a subject is to master the types of knowledge that comprise it.

Among the types are attitudes, values, rules, concepts, laws, law-like principles, and facts.

An attitude statement. I like geometry. *Knowing that*

A value. This knife is good.

A rule. In passing another automobile on the highway keep to your right.

A concept. Water is an odorless, tasteless liquid composed of two parts hydrogen and one part oxygen.

A law. The volume of a confined gas varies inversely with the pressure if the temperature is constant.

A law-like principle. If a person is frustrated, his behavior regresses.

A fact. The thermometer reads 70° Fahrenheit.

These types of knowledge are referred to as "knowing—that." To possess such knowledge is to know *that* such and such is the case—*that* a liquid with this and that property is called water, *that* this particular knife is rated highly, *that* the thermometer reads 70°, and so on.

Another kind of knowledge concerns the question of how something is done and is referred to as "knowing-how." One knows how to type, to test soil, to balance a bank account, and to do any number of things. This form of knowledge includes what are typically referred to as procedures and skills.

Why should curriculum workers and teachers understand the types of knowledge? For one thing, the utility of what is learned in school depends on the type of knowledge emphasized and on which items of a given type are selected. For example, facts have no explanatory power, but they are useful because they enable us to establish relationships among variables and serve as data by which to test law-like statements. The layperson no less than the scientist or professional uses facts to defend his claims and actions.

In sharp contrast, laws and law-like statements have explanatory power. Gas laws explain why a pneumatic tire has more pressure when it is hot. If the volume of the tire remains approximately constant and the temperature of the air in the tire is increased, the pressure increases. According to gas laws, the pressure varies directly with the temperature when the volume is constant. This type of knowledge enables us to relate variables when we are called upon to give an explanation or to make a decision. Just as other forms of knowledge are not equally useful so are laws and law-like principles not of equal utility.

It is obvious that the utility of knowledge depends on the character of the knowledge and the population. The knowledge used by a physician will not be used by the general population. Every specialized field has its own domain of information about which outsiders know little. But domains intersect. Everyone buys medical services at some time. The public frequently uses knowledge about health insurance, its purchase and coverage.

Moreover, some knowledge is so much a part of our day-to-day thinking that we are scarcely aware of it. For example, take the concept of the earth's shape. It would be extremely difficult to ferret out the ways in which this concept enters into our daily life. Just try to imagine the difference in orientation between a person who thinks of the world as being flat with four corners and one who thinks of the earth as round. Many concepts which are not only crucial but also frequently used lie between the concept of the earth's roundness and those which we seldom use. The curriculum worker, therefore, has a dual task with respect to the selection of knowledge. The first is to decide the amount of emphasis to be placed upon the various types of knowledge and the second is to decide within a given type which members of that type are the most useful.

The curriculum worker and teacher should understand the types of knowledge because the difficulty of the curriculum is related to the density of the knowledge types. By "density" we mean the ratio of a given type to other types. If the density of facts is so out of proportion that the student must remember many details, the program may be both uninteresting and difficult because of the burden placed on sheer memory. The same observation can be made about any of the various types of knowledge. The density of concepts, for example, can be so heavy that the student is overburdened with concept attainment.

The types of knowledge are significant for still another reason. The performance required to teach a procedure in physics, for example, would not be the same as that required to teach the concept of density. To teach a pupil how to organize data gained from doing an experiment requires a teaching performance that is considerably different from that of teaching a concept. It is interesting to note that Taba's well-known levels of teaching are simply moves from one knowledge type to another.

Attitudes and Imperatives

Strictly speaking, utterances of attitudes are not forms of knowledge, but expressions of psychological states such as hate and desire. Yet attitudes convey information from which the listener infers the feelings of the speaker. Utterances of attitudes are easily mistaken for values because, in the final analysis, they are components of the criteria of value judgments. While this point will become clearer as you study the passages on attitude statements and values, a glimpse of it can be gleaned from the fact that individuals often disagree about the worth of things. When they do, the disagreement can usually be traced to differences in the way they feel, typically reflected in the reasons they give to support their choices.

The following passage, discusses attitude and imperative statements together. This helps to classify the meaning of each.

☐

... 'Serve God, and honor the king!', 'Down with the aristocrats!', 'I hate Communists,' 'Let us love all men as brothers,' 'I feel humble in a cathedral.' These statements form a class on their own, because they are either not

John Wilson, *Language and the Pursuit of Truth* (Cambridge: At the University Press, 1956), pp. 56–58. Reprinted by permission of the publisher.

Footnotes have been renumbered consecutively throughout the chapter.

verifiable at all, or only in a trivial way. . . . They are not the sort of statements intended to be true or false, except in a trivial sense: they are rather expressions of attitude, or commands. Thus 'Serve God!' is not true or false: we just do not want to apply those standards to it. In one sense, it is not a statement at all; (although it is a sentence); it is a command. 'I hate Communists' is true or false in the unimportant sense that either I do hate Communists or I do not; but the main use of the statement is to express my attitude. I might just as well have said 'Down with Communists!', without really altering the meaning of the statement.

These statements, or sentences, are important, because they represent the intrusion of what I called poetic communication. They are not intended to state facts, or to give information about the world: they simply express the speaker's feelings or desires. They are, therefore, of no possible value in argument or discussion, because in these activities we are trying to get at the truth, not to express our feelings. But they are of interest to us, chiefly because what appear to be other kinds of statements may really be imperatives or attitude statements in disguise.

For example, a statement like 'All men are equal,' or 'All men are born free' looks like a straightforward indicative statement, whose use is to convey certain information about the world. They look parallel to statements such as 'All men are mortal' or 'All men are born with two eyes in their heads.' But if we examine them more closely, we can see that they are not used in the same way at all. For what sort of information is conveyed by the statement 'All men are equal'? Is one supposed to verify such a statement by measuring the various properties of men—their height, their intelligence, their virtue, and so on—and seeing whether they are equal? In what particular respects are they supposed to be equal? Again, how do you verify the statement 'All men are born free'? What counts as being 'born free' and not being 'born free'?

Such statements are really disguised attitude statements; though of course other uses may be found for them, these will be secondary uses. 'All men are equal' is used rather as the attitude statement 'Down with privilege!' is used. In history we find that people make such statements as protests against particular types of privilege which disqualify them from doing certain things: for instance, against class privilege, the color bar, the privileges of the wealthy, and so on. Similarly 'All men are born free' is a protest against various types of tyranny or compulsion, and is used to mean 'Away with this tyrannical behavior!' These statements do not really give information at all: they express attitudes.

We have to pay attention to the context of such statements, before we can decide upon their use. Even then we may not be certain: but at least we can ask the speaker what he intends to convey, and how his statement is supposed to be verified. But in most cases the attitude is sufficiently obvious for us to classify them as attitude statements. When the French revolutionaries, for instance, insisted on the value of liberty, equality, and fraternity, they did so as a protest against certain forms of tyranny practised by the nobles (lack of liberty), the nobles' privileges (lack of equality), and their ill treatment and discourtesy at the nobles' hands (lack of fraternity). Most statements about liberty, equality, and fraternity are disguised attitude statements, protesting against certain behavior.

It is often difficult to decide whether certain statements are attitude statements or not. This is particularly true in the case of religious or 'metaphysical' statements. . . . But we can always discover how a statement is to be treated by discovering how it is to be verified. Thus 'God is a loving father' *might* be an attitude statement, meaning 'Let us love each other as brothers' or 'Let us feel grateful for the good things of life.' Alternatively, it might be giving information, in which case we should want to know what sort of information, and how to tell what counts as evidence for its truth. The onus of giving an account of the meaning and verification of a statement which purports to give information lies on the person who makes the statement. If he cannot do this, we may feel inclined to say that it does not really give information, and is not the sort of statement to call true or false: that it is just an attitude statement.

Value Concepts

Another type of knowledge is referred to as values. What are values? Sometimes the term "value" is used synonymously with "attitude." Suppose a pupil says he does not like biology. Sometimes such a statement is interpreted to mean either that the pupil has a negative attitude toward the subject or that he does not value it. In fact, the student has uttered his attitude toward the subject. The statement of a value is not the same as an expression of an attitude. "Poor old Jones" expresses an attitude; "Jones is a good tennis player" expresses a value. In the expression "poor old Jones" we do not say anything about the person. We simply express our feeling. In the second case, we say something about Jones. We may or may not like Jones; we may not know him personally. But we rate highly his performance as a tennis player. This rating is a value judgment.

Behind the judgment is a set of criteria by which we decide Jones to be a good tennis player. These criteria determine the category of tennis player in which we place Jones and others—whether we call a given player good, poor, or average. From this standpoint values are particular kinds of concepts; namely, those whose criteria can and often do entail such attitudes as likes or dislikes, hopes or fears, desires or aversions, neutrality or commitments. To include values in the curriculum is to include a particular kind of content. In the following selection you will find a discussion of value statements and how they differ from expressions of attitude. In the latter part of the passage you will find a lucid discussion of the problem of establishing the truth of value statements.

When we use evaluative words and make value statements, we are commending something or somebody. But this is not just adopting an attitude toward

John Wilson, *Language and the Pursuit of Truth* (Cambridge: At the University Press, 1956), pp. 65–70. Reprinted by permission of the publisher.

the subject of our commendation. To say 'Joe is a good man' is not like saying 'Good old Joe!' The former is a value statement, the latter an attitude statement. The former has a method of verification, the latter has not. Value statements are not attitude statements. It is undoubtedly true that when we make value statements, we are adopting an attitude of approval: but it is not our only or even our main object to express this attitude when we make the statements. We are also *assigning value*. We do this on the basis of certain criteria; and if challenged, we could give reasons for our belief. We could answer the question 'How do you verify this statement?' by saying 'Well, with me a "good man" is someone who is so and so and such and such. If he passes these tests, I consider my statement verified.'

As with other statements, so with value statements: the most important thing is to agree about the proper method of verification. This entails agreeing about the appropriate criteria. In many cases we are agreed: we all have the same criteria for good knives, for instances—that they should cut well, stay sharp, not break, and so on. Consequently the statement 'This is a good knife' can be profitably discussed, because we all want the same method of verification used. We simply see whether the knife in question passes the established tests or not. If it does, we agree to call it 'good.' Exactly the same applies to our judgments of men, actions, motives, and societies, though these judgments are *moral* judgments, unlike our judgment about knives. They are both *value judgments*, however, and they both depend for proof on established methods of verification, or agreement about what criteria to use.

Unfortunately we do not always agree about the criteria or method of verification appropriate to our value statements. Some people may have one set of criteria for what counts as a good person, other people may have a quite different set. Good behavior is different in Russia and in America, in the Victorian Age and in the twentieth century. If I were arguing over some question of value with a caveman, for instance, it would become evident that we held entirely different sets of criteria for value. Until we could agree to use the same set, our argument would be ineffective. He would call a man who clubbed women over the head and stole whenever he got the chance a 'good' man. I would call a man who was courteous to women and only stole when he could not get food any other way a 'good' man. There would be an impasse.

We might, of course, proceed a little further with the argument, by arguing not about what men counted as good, but about which of our two sets of criteria was the better. This is a more difficult business: we should really be discussing which method of verification is more appropriate to our value statements about people. In order to settle the question, we should have to employ higher criteria, or we should have to agree about a method of verification to verify which method of verification was the more appropriate. For instance, I could argue with the caveman thus: 'If you accept human happiness as valuable, then you must accept not stealing as valuable, because stealing does not bring happiness; and if you accept that, you must accept a man who does not steal as valuable or good, at least in that particular respect.' This argument would only work if he shared my higher criteria for value—namely, whether something brings happiness. If he did not share this, of course, I could not convince him.

We can always go on questioning our criteria or methods of verification: but we shall only get a satisfactory answer if we have some higher criteria or verification in terms of which way to answer the question. If we have none, then we shall not know how to answer it at all. In this as in other cases, verification is all important.

The distinguishing feature of value statements lies in the importance of the criteria for verifying them. If I make an empirical statement, such as 'This man has taken property which is legally another's,' such a statement can be conclusively verified by observation and experience. But if I make a value statement, such as 'This man has acted wrongly,' we need to do more than just observe what in fact he has done in order to verify it. By observation, we may be able to *describe* what he has done perfectly, and two people might agree that the description was accurate. But it would still be possible for those two people to disagree about the *value* of the action. They would so disagree if they did not share a common set of criteria for the value of actions of this sort. Unless they do share these criteria, no amount of facts or accurate descriptions can prove that the action is good or bad.

This difference between empirical and value statements can be made clear if we consider the two statements 'Poppies are red' and 'Abraham Lincoln was a good man.' Suppose somebody chose to deny the first statement, and asserted that poppies were green. We could refute him by pointing out that the vast majority of people had agreed to call them red, that scientists could measure the distribution of wavelengths in the light they reflect, and show them to be similar to that in the light given off by other red objects, and so on. We would probably end up by saying that he was color blind. In other words, we have a standard and agreed method of verifying whether something is red or not, and if somebody ignores or goes against this method, he is simply making a mistake. But if somebody denied the statement 'Abraham Lincoln was a good man,' we could not necessarily convince him by the same method. We could, certainly, tell him what Abraham Lincoln did, and describe his life in detail, and this might convince him, if he had not known it before. But equally it might not. He might accept all the facts, and still disagree about the values. His view might be curious, but it would not be logically curious, as it would be logically curious if he accepted all the facts about poppies but still thought they were green.

This is because the meaning of descriptive words, and the truth of empirical statements, is tied down to the established method of verification. We are all agreed about what it is to count as red, flat, square, and so on, and if somebody goes against this agreement, he is talking nonsense, because our language has been tailored to fit this agreement. 'Red' means something which most people think red, and which gives off light of a certain wavelength. If somebody calls poppies green, he is not just expressing a difference of opinion, but misusing words. But a man who called Abraham Lincoln 'bad' would not be misusing words: for evaluative words like 'good' and 'bad' are not tailored to fit any one system of verification at all. They are simply used by people in accordance with their criteria, and different people have different criteria. We could put this by saying that people agree about the reasons for describing things, but that they have different reasons for commending or valuing things.

Provided we hold the same set of criteria as another person, however, the facts of the matter are very important. For the argument then turns simply upon whether the subject of the value statement does or does not satisfy the criteria. Thus if *A* and *B* were agreed that a man who told the truth and did not deceive people was to be called 'good,' *A* could point out that Abraham Lincoln, as a matter of fact, did satisfy these criteria: and *B* would then have to admit that he was good. The verification of value statements thus depends partly upon experience or knowledge of the facts, and partly upon criteria of value. . . .

Value concepts and statements are of particular interest to those concerned with social studies, literature and other art forms, history, ecology, and other studies that treat questions of social and political consequences. In the preceding pages some of the problems of establishing the dependability of value statements have been noted. The problem of agreeing about matters of value is a crucial one in curriculum development and instruction. Often it is not understood as a cognitive question and hence is treated as a matter of personal opinion. In this case values are not viewed as a kind of knowledge that provides a content of instruction to be dealt with rationally. Rather they are considered to be subjective; modifiable by group influence, subliminal techniques, and other unobtrusive procedures. In sharp contrast is the view expressed by Wilson that values are forms of knowledge involving criteria based upon experience and ultimately upon the consequences of acting upon them. These contrasting views give rise to different conceptions of the curriculum and instructional procedures, especially in areas that are full of valuative concepts and statements.

Normative Knowledge and the Curriculum

Another form of knowledge consists of rules. There are many different kinds of rules and their function is to tell us how to do something or what to do in various circumstances. In our daily activities we need to know that such and such is the case, that certain events and happenings can be explained by laws or law-like statements, or that the value of events, objects, persons, and so on can be determined by reference to criteria. We also need to know the most effective way to attain a given end, or what is the right and proper thing to do in a given situation.

It is important to notice at this point that rules are not the same sort of knowledge as values and value statement. Values have to do with the worth of objects and events. They do not tell us how we should behave nor do they carry with them an impelling force to do something. Rules, on the other hand, range from statements telling us what to do in a given circumstance, if we want to attain a desired end, to expectations which place upon us the responsibility for behaving in certain ways because such behavior is recognized as the right and proper thing to do.

It is well to note that in some cases the rules are almost entirely *ad hoc.*

If a group, say a class of students, is formed and it wishes to regularize its procedures, it formulates rules by which the members are to conduct themselves. The validity and utility of these rules may be limited for specific purposes determined by the particular group. Other rules, however, have general utility. This is so for rules that regulate the behavior of individuals in any large group such as parliament or a labor union.

If we think about rules we recognize the fact that a great deal of our day-to-day conduct is governed by rules. We drive automobiles in accordance with rules; our food is cooked according to rules; we dine and dance by rules; we conduct our courts by rules; we run bureaucracies by rules; and in fact there is hardly an activity of any consequence that does not involve some form of direction and regulation by rules. It is also important to note that we judge the morality of conduct by rules, and that in the final analysis the moral person is one whose conduct conforms to the rules of behavior that have evolved through the centuries.

Harry S. Broudy et al. discuss the various types of rules and their relationship to the process of schooling and the curriculum.

☐

A half-century ago, a great deal of emphasis was placed upon the valuative and normative content of education. Stories in elementary school readers were selected because they illustrated moral lessons. Copybooks were based on maxims. Moral notions made up a great deal of the content of English and social studies, and even the natural sciences were tinted with moral views.

A revolt occurred against this direct way of teaching valuative content. For one thing, it was alleged that such instruction tended to be merely verbal—mere rote learning. For another, as behavioristic psychology gained ascendancy, emphasis was placed more and more upon the development of attitudes and overt ways of behaving instead of on ideas. This meant that in the realm of moral conduct it was conceived to be far more effective to develop right attitudes and habits of behavior than to deal with the concepts and rules of such behavior.

As a result of these counterforces, the curriculum came to be stripped of much significant normative and valuative content. Activities of a gross sort, designed to develop in the individual both moral and democratic ways of behaving and to induce the attitudes appropriate to them, became the major emphasis. Student government and other sorts of extracurricular activities were justified on the grounds that they developed proper attitudes and democratic behavior. In this view, it was hardly necessary for the individual to develop *concepts* of right conduct and to learn the norms of such behavior; it was only necessary that he learn to behave in approved ways. Or, it was believed that such concepts would be acquired incidentally but nonetheless effectively as a by-product of the behavior.

This way of handling problems of moral conduct and civic behavior has

Harry S. Broudy, et al., *Democracy and Excellence in American Secondary Education* (Chicago: Rand McNally, 1963), pp. 139–41, 150–53. Reprinted by permission of the publisher.

tended to develop individuals who are unable to give justifications for their behavior, except, of course, those derived from common sense. Youth as well as adults are conservatives without knowing why, or liberals without knowing why. They believe democracy to be the best way of life, but are unable to defend it effectively when challenged by those who hold contrary views. Indeed, they are often unable to tell whether or not another view affirms or denies democracy. It seems clearly evident that the time has come for the curriculum to give primary consideration to the study of the values and norms by which individual and social conduct are regulated and justified.

Three kinds of norms should be taken into account as the content of the curriculum is selected. These are the norms of efficiency or prescriptive rules, regulatory norms, and moral norms.

From time to time, each individual is engaged in activities which require that he perform in specified ways in order to attain certain ends. A baker bakes cakes; a gardener grows flowers; a carpenter squares corners; a mechanic replaces a tire. Each of these tasks is performed in conformity with some sort of procedural rule which we call a prescription or recipe. The rules for baking a cake tell the baker the ingredients to include, the order in which they are to be mixed, and so on. The midwestern gardener knows that he should not uncover his roses until the forsythia bloom in the spring.

The educational program contains a large number of such prescriptive rules. Thus, the rules of rhetoric and grammar tell how to attain certain effects in written expression. The same thing can be said of rules having to do with how to achieve certain effects in painting or in music.

It is characteristic of rules of this sort that there is an end to be attained, and that the rule tells the individual how to attain the end in the most efficient way. There are no penalties for failing to follow such rules, save that the individual may fail to achieve the result he desires. But the consequences are of his own doing.

The individual is often involved in situations in which his conduct is expected to conform to certain regulations. In such situations he is bound by what may be called regulatory rules. If he is driving an automobile on the highway, his behavior must conform to the traffic rules. If he is taking a test, he must conform to rules governing the examination. There are rules for classroom behavior, for behaving in the school, and in society generally. Some of the latter are laws, or legal regulations. These rules are not designed for the attainment of some particular end, as in the case of prescriptive rules. Unlike prescriptive rules, they are put into effect or enforced, and there are penalties for breaking them.

Many of the individual's activities are controlled, in one way or another, by regulatory rules. In fact, the individual lives and carries on his ordinary activities within a system of such rules. Every institution with which he is associated has its own set of rules governing the activities for which it is responsible. And what is called bureaucracy in modern society is little more than institutions in which the behavior of individuals responsible for carrying on the work of these institutions is thoroughly and systematically governed by certain regulatory rules. To understand social institutions is in large measure to understand the different activities which these institutions carry on and the rules by which they are governed. Partly for this reason, some critics of the school claim that the curriculum has given too little attention to those rules of conduct established and enforced by authority.

Finally, there are the rules of morality and prudence. The individual is often in situations in which the question of what is the moral thing to do arises. Over the centuries society has worked out certain norms of conduct to which people are to conform in their dealings with one another. These rules make up perhaps the most basic elements of human culture. They lie at the base not only of social institutions, but ultimately of regulatory rules themselves and of the choice of ends which are served by prescriptive rules. They have to do with such virtues as honesty, sincerity, justice, charity, fairness, and brotherhood. Moral rules are not put into effect and enforced as are regulatory rules. Neither are they passed and put into operation by convention or authority. They cannot be rescinded. Nor do they provide formulas for attaining given ends. They rest in man's higher conscience and are not capable of proof by empirical procedures.

The curriculum must be designed to teach the student not only to conform to selected sets of these three types of rules, but also to be aware of the rules themselves. To attain these ends, the school curriculum should contain selected examples of human behavior which can be analyzed and studied from the standpoint of the norms which they involve.

Moreover, the student needs to be taught in such a way that he understands the nature of these rules. He should see clearly that the criteria of acceptability for such norms are quite different from the criteria used in deciding the acceptability of descriptive statements and principles.

It is one of the tasks of the schools not only to teach the individuals to do that which is right and wise, but also to know why it is right and wise. The school cannot teach choices and decisions, but it can teach the facts, the value definitions, and the valuative principles on which right and wise decisions are based. It can, of course, inculcate habits of behaving in certain ways. But on analysis, even these habits turn out to be incipient principles as well as ways of behaving. This can be seen from the fact that habits are always exercised in certain conditions and in certain times and places. When the conditions are specified verbally, together with the mode of action appropriate to them, the whole formulation is a principle. The trouble with sheer habit is that the individual does not understand the circumstances under which it is performed, and this may easily render it outside the range of his intelligence and so not subject to deliberate modification.

Concepts: Building Blocks

We have already noted that teaching of concepts has been a recurring topic of discussion during the last two decades. The attention it has received can probably be attributed to the fact that concepts function in two fundamental ways. They enable us to interpret the objects and events about us and to formulate principles and laws. When we look at an object in our environment and classify it as one of a kind of things, we say that we understand it. In fact, our concepts are the categories into which we classify the objects and events of our world and thereby render them intelligible.

Concepts also enable us to formulate laws and principles. If you analyze any law in physics or chemistry, or any other science, you will find that it consists of a number of concepts that make up the conditional part of the law, and another set of concepts that make up the consequent part of the law. Consider the law-like statement: If an individual is constantly frustrated, his behavior will become more primitive. The first part of this statement consists of two concepts: individual and frustration. The second part, that is the consequent part, consists of two concepts: behavior and primitive. If the conditions denoted by the set of concepts are present, we would expect primitive behavior to follow. Moral principles and rules are also made up of concepts and so are statements of fact. Indeed, the great bulk of the content of any curriculum consists of conceptual knowledge.

What are the different kinds of concepts? There are many classifications. Concepts can be classified in terms of subject matter fields as when we speak of the concepts of physics, the concepts of mathematics, the concepts of economics, and so on. From a curricular standpoint it is important to be able to classify concepts in this way and to decide their relative value for either general or specialized education. Concepts are also classified in accordance with their linguistic form. Thus we can speak of conjunctive concepts, disjunctive concepts, and relational concepts. These sorts of concepts have been revived in pedagogical literature by Jerome Bruner's work. The following passage sets forth their general characteristics.

☐

It is usually the case for one to infer identity or some other significate not from a single attribute exhibited by an instance but from several attributes taken together. That is to say, we do not attempt to infer illness *only* from abnormal body temperature, but from a whole set of clinical signs taken in combination. The question of how attributes or cues are combined for making inferences now concerns us. The principal distinction we wish to make is between *conjunctive, disjunctive,* and *relational* concepts, each involving a different mode of combining attributes.

To render more concrete the description of types of categories, we refer to the array of instances contained in Figure 9–1. Each instance is made up of figures and borders. The figures vary in shape (square, circle, or cross), in color (red, green, or black), and in number (single, double, or triple). The borders vary in number (one, two, or three). Thus, the instances comprise the combinations of four attributes, each with three values. Each instance in the array exhibits one value of each of the four attributes. We may speak of a "category"

Jerome S. Bruner, *A Study of Thinking* (New York: John Wiley, 1956), pp. 41–43. Copyright © 1956 John Wiley & Sons, Inc. Reprinted by permission of the publisher.

of instances or a concept in terms of the defining properties of some subset of the instences. For example, "all cards with one red figure" is a concept, so too "all cards with two figures and/or with circles," so too "all cards possessing the same number of figures and borders." The three examples turn out to be drastically different kinds of concepts, and we turn now to a consideration of their difference.

A *conjunctive category* is one defined by the *joint presence* of the appropriate value of several attributes. A typical conjunctive category in the universe of Figure 9–1 may be defined by the *conjunction* of three figures, redness, and circles, i.e., all cards containing three red circles. Three exemplars of this category are to be found in the figure. All others fail to qualify. Most experiments on concept attainment deal with such conjunctive categories, and procedures such as the Vigotsky Test and the Wisconsin Card Sorting Test are based on them as well.

The *disjunctive category* may be illustrated by that class of cards in Figure 9–1 that possess three red circles, *or* any constituent thereof: three figures, red figures, circles, three red figures, red circles, or three circles. The class comprises fifty-seven instances. Any fraternal or civic organization with a membership requirement such as "Anyone residing in *or* paying taxes in Altavista shall be eligible for membership" exemplifies a disjunctive category. A strike in baseball is also disjunctive. A strike is a pitch that is across the plate and between the batter's knees and shoulders *or* it is any pitch at which the batter strikes but fails to send the ball into the field. Similarly, a "walk" occurs either when four balls have been pitched *or* when a pitched ball strikes the batter.

The difficulty with disjunctive concepts is their arbitrariness; the lack of any apparent relation between these attributes which can substitute for one another. This feeling of arbitrariness may be one source of resistance to the categories used by clinical psychologists. A concept such as "stable personality" or "serious disturbance" can only be defined disjunctively, with sometimes one set of signs serving as the cue and sometimes others. Hammond (1955) and Todd (1954) have commented on the role of such vicarious functioning of cues in clinical judgment.

The relational concept or category is one defined by a specifiable relationship between defining attributes. Thus in the universe of Figure 9–1, we may define as a class all those instances containing the *same* number of figures and borders, or those cards with fewer figures than borders. Income tax brackets (after deduction), each specifiable as a class, are defined in terms of the relationship between number of dependents and level of income. "Effective stimulus" is defined in psychology as an energy change at a receptor surface capable of discharging the receptor: a relationship between two states.

It is sometimes possible to describe the same grouping or class of instances in terms of two different combinations of attributes. One way of combining attributes may prove to be equivalent to another in terms of the groupings that result by use or application, i.e., it may turn out that one rule for combining attributes may prove to be equivalent to another. Such cases are of interest, particularly in the sciences where they are capable of generating theoretical controversy of the kind that produces more heat than light.

Figure 9-1. An array of instances comprising combinations of four attributes, each exhibiting three values. Plain figures are in green, striped figures in red, solid figures in black.

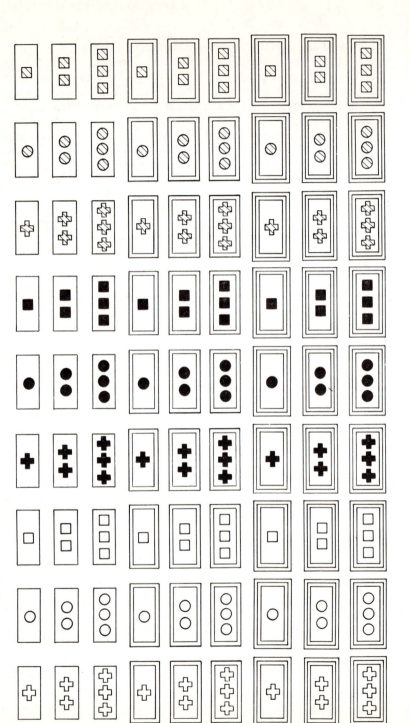

Laws and Law-Like Statements

Another type of knowledge consists of condition-consequence generalizations. The physical sciences are replete with this sort of knowledge. One readily thinks of the law of gravity, the gas laws, and Ohm's law. Laws are made up of clearly defined concepts, and they have high explanatory and predictive power. The life sciences contain fewer such generalizations and the social sciences have almost no such laws. The curriculum of the social sciences, nevertheless, provides explanations of social and political events by reference to law-like generalizations.

For example, the early migration of some people to North America is explained by saying that they came for religious freedom. The law-like character of this claim becomes evident when cast in an if-then form. "If people of such and such character are not allowed to worship as they choose and there is free land to which they can go, they will migrate to the new territory."

Generalizations of this type are constantly used, implicitly to be sure, in the social studies to explain events of the past and present. There is perhaps no way to avoid using them as social, political, and economic happenings are discussed. Pupils as well as teachers want explanations, and when laws are not available law-like generalizations and even weaker claims must be resorted to. But the curriculum can provide for pupil experiences in the examination of the sort of data that would be required to verify law-like generalizations and to consider the sort of theoretical conceptions on which they hang.

The next selection, from a conceptual analysis of the social studies curriculum, sets forth the nature of laws and law-like generalizations and explores their meaning in both a social and physical context.

It is not altogether clear what constitutes a lawful regularity in either the natural or social sciences. Basically laws are claims that some phenomenon in the natural world is consistent in its behavior without respect to time or place. Thus gravitational pull affects bodies here and on the moon, and that was as true 2000 years ago as it will be tomorrow. This criterion would suggest that most statements in the social sciences and history are not law-like (law-like meaning those propositions that have the potential to be laws even though they have not yet been given that status).

In history, for example, one finds many generalizations like the following: "By 1890 the frontier in America was closed." This statement serves to summarize various conditions and facts that are descriptive of a particular time and place. This generalization is synthetic and thus testable assuming that the concepts "frontier" and "closed" are definable in a way that permits meaningful selection of evidence. However, as stated, the proposition could not possibly

Gary Wehlage and Eugene M. Anderson, *Social Studies Curriculum in Perspective* (Englewood Cliffs, N.J.: Prentice-Hall, 1972), pp. 62–66. Copyright © 1972 by Prentice-Hall. Reprinted by permission of the publisher.

offer a regularity of nature, rather it serves to summarize or colligate information about conditions in a particular context. Because of this characteristic these synthetic generalizations are often referred to as past tense generalizations.

The term "past tense" is in no way a technical or precise term, and in fact generalizations stated in present tense grammar can be summaries of past situations. Assume for the moment that one is doing research on the political structure of early Indian tribes in North America, and, after examining various tribes, the following conclusion is stated: "Decisions are made in fairly democratic fashion by a large number of chiefs."[1] This is essentially a statistical past tense generalization because it refers to a particular group over a particular time (even if unstated). In other words the grammatical tense of a statement does not determine the nature of the claim.

Generalizations about events at a particular time in the past are not law-like because they cannot make any claim about events beyond the particular setting to which they refer; they are bound by time and place. One characteristic of law-like statements is their timelessness. A law asserts a claim that is good for tomorrow as well as yesterday, and because they are timeless laws are stated in present tense form: e.g., "All copper expands when heated." However, as just pointed out, it is not sufficient to formalize generalizations in the present tense to obtain law-like propositions. Yet a leading textbook in social studies education implies as much in the discussion of inquiry in social studies: "A generalization in its final form is usually stated in the present tense in order to facilitate wide application in all times and places."[2] Certainly the discovery of repeated patterns of relationship descriptive of the future as well as the past hangs on more than the tense of a verb.

As previously stated, the requirements for a generalization to be a law are not absolutely clear. Laws of nature essentially claim a regularity to be universal in the sense that given certain specified conditions the regularity exists without respect to time or place. Laws may be either uniform or statistical. The following is a law expressing a statistical regularity: "The half-life of radium is 1700 years. (The probability is 50 percent that a particular radium atom will disintegrate within 1700 years, or 50 percent of the atoms in a piece of radium will disintegrate in 1700 years.)" Much of modern science is based on probability or statistical regularities, and the notion held by some individuals in the social sciences that for a proposition to be a law it must assert a uniform regularity is untenable. It appears that virtually all empirical work in social science results in statistical statements, and for the foreseeable future any social science laws will be statistical in form.

Statistical laws are basically of two types. First, there is the *a priori* probability of mathematics which allows (with certain assumptions) the precise calculation of probability. For example, the probability of a coin coming up heads on each successive toss is 1/2; or the odds of drawing any spade from a deck

---

[1]Mindella Schultz, *Teacher's Guide for Comparative Political Systems: An Inquiry Approach* (New York: Holt, Rinehart and Winston, 1967), p. 12.

[2]Byron G. Massialas and C. B. Cox, *Inquiry in Social Studies* (New York: McGraw-Hill, 1966), p. 120.

of cards are 13/52. The second major category of statistical propositions results from quantifying the relative frequency of an event. The death rate of 30-year-old men, or the percentage of smokers as opposed to nonsmokers who develop lung cancer, is each expressed in a statistical generalization that indicates the probability that a member of the group will possess the characteristic. The statistical generalization cannot tell us if a particular member will develop cancer if he smokes, but for the population a probability figure can be offered concerning an individual's chances of getting cancer. It is the relative frequency generalization that is of most interest in the social sciences.

Philosophers of science have devoted considerable attention to the concept of scientific law. One way to get at the nature of scientific laws, and at the same time clarify the implications of the inquiry process, is found in the analysis of Richard Braithwaite. He begins by pointing out that the only specific agreement on criteria among philosophers is a generalization. However, he argues that only those generalizations occurring in established scientific deductive systems can be called laws. For him, laws must have two kinds of support: first, empirical support in the way of evidence, and second, deductive support. The latter is obtained when a proposition is deductible from higher level generalizations in some theoretical system. It also occurs when a generalization relates theoretical terms which are in turn related to other theoretical concepts within a deductive system.[3]

Braithwaite's case of the black ravens helps clarify the implications of this position. He argues that

> the blackness of all ravens is surely "accidental" if no reasons can be given for such blackness; and this is equivalent to saying that there is no established scientific system in which the generalization appears as a consequence. If a reason can be given for the blackness of all ravens by exhibiting such a scientific system, this generalization will be regarded as law-like.[4]

Thus even though a proposition may have considerable empirical support (every observed raven has been black) this alone is not sufficient for it to be called a law. The point is that lawfulness implies much more than a body of empirical support. The likelihood that the next raven one meets will be black is very high, but this represents only an isolated fact. The goal of science is to develop broad ranging theories to account for events. Isolated propositions about the blackness of ravens or any other phenomenon does not do this.

Part of the process of developing theories is constructing theoretical concepts. Carl Hempel emphasizes the role of these concepts in his discussion of laws. He indicates there are two levels of scientific inquiry: "the level of *empirical generalization,* and the level of *theory formation.*"[5] The early stages of inquiry into a subject usually result in the discovery of regularities about directly observable phenomena. These generalizations are descriptive of ordi-

[3]Richard B. Braithwaite, *Scientific Explanation* (Cambridge: At the University Press, 1953), pp. 301–2.

[4]Braithwaite, *Scientific Explanation,* p. 304.

[5]Carl G. Hempel, *Aspects of Scientific Explanation* (New York: Free Press, 1965), p. 178.

nary events such as "Wood floats in water," or "People repeat behavior they find rewarding."

At the level of theory, however, unobservable concepts are employed that provide higher level laws that account for lower level empirical propositions. The goal of theory formation is eventually to subsume a wide variety of empirical generalizations under a very few theoretical laws. Examples of unobservable or theoretical concepts are molecule, atom, ego, id, drive, status, and other terms under which a variety of directly observable behaviors can be included. It is essential that theoretical concepts be developed to broaden the applicability and power of systematic inquiry. Often empirical generalizations have exceptions which cannot be accounted for until theoretical terms and laws have been formulated. Take for example these generalizations: "Wood floats in water; iron sinks in it." As they stand they have important exceptions, as when wood becomes waterlogged and when iron floats upon being an appropriate shape. By moving to the level of theory, however, these observable generalizations and their exceptions can be taken into account by introducing a theoretical concept. In this case the concept is density which is defined as the quotient of a body's mass and volume ($I = M/V$). Using this concept the following generalization (a corollary of Archimede's principle) can be stated: "Any body floats in a fluid if its density is less than that of the fluid." One is now in a position to understand why some wood does not float and why ocean liners made of steel do not sink.

Efforts to develop theoretical concepts and generalizations in the social sciences have not been as successful as in the natural sciences. Furthermore, when social science attempts to move from low-level observational generalizations to theoretical propositions, there is a tendency to come up with propositions of high probability and low information value. Such generalizations are almost certainly true in some sense but do not say anything specific about events. Sociologist George Homans refers to these propositions as *orienting statements*.[6] As an example of this kind of generalization, Homans offers the Marxian generalization that the organization of the means of production determines the other features of society.[7] Homans argues that this proposition does not specify the nature and amount of change in society resulting from a change in the means of production. At best an orienting statement allows one to say that some abstract factor is related to some other abstract factor in some unspecified way. These statements are helpful in pointing one in a direction and giving him some clues as to what to look for, but as they stand such generalizations are unable to say anything specific about the world.

In keeping with the position expressed earlier that a generalization must be part of a deductive system to be considered a law, orienting statements do not qualify as laws. In other words, propositions that express a relationship between theoretical concepts are not necessarily sufficiently informative to be considered a law, if they are not deductively related to more specific generalizations. In the final analysis, the goal of a science is to provide a body of knowledge that has high information value. In Homans' words, "sooner or

[6]George C. Homans, *The Nature of Social Science* (New York: Harcourt Brace Jovanovich, 1967), pp. 14–18.

[7]Homans, *The Nature of Social Science*, p. 14.

later a science must actually stick its neck out and say something definite. If there is a change in *x,* what sort of change will occur in *y?* Don't just tell me there will be *some* change. Tell me *what* change."[8]

Facts: Statements of Particulars

The word "fact" is used frequently in educational discourse. We are often told that we should not teach so many facts; that we should use more thought-provoking queries such as why questions. But we are seldom told what is meant by the word "fact." It is used in several senses, generally to denote something that is true. In this sense, to say that a statement is a fact is to express a judgment about the validity of the statement. We speak of the law of gravity as being a fact, that is to say, true. Or we say of the statement, "Thomas Jefferson died on July 4, 1826," that it is a fact, meaning that this statement is true.

In these two instances we have judged the validity of two sorts of knowledge—a law and a particular. But when we speak of fact as being itself a form of knowledge, we use the term in a different sense. Here the word "fact" means a statement of a particular. It is a statement about an act, a happening, or anything that we observe directly with a minimum of inference. In short, a fact is what in scientific discourse would be referred to as a datum. When we say truly that it is four o'clock in the afternoon, or the thermometer reads 70 degrees Fahrenheit, we are stating facts.

There are few passages in the literature that set forth the meaning of "fact." However, the following passages give as clear an indication of the uses of "fact" as can be found. The first is a simple discourse that indicates the meaning of "fact" and distinguishes it from inference. It is taken from an introductory book in logic by W. Little, Harold Wilson, and W. Moore.

> The word *fact* is often used somewhat loosely to refer to any statement believed to be true. We shall use it here, however, in a more limited sense, to refer to a thing which has been demonstrated to be true without inference or interpretation. Learning to distinguish between statements of what happened and interpretations of what happened is a part of the basic training of the careful thinker. It is this distinction newspaper editors have in mind when they urge their cub reporters to "get the facts." In 1944 the city of Chicago was plagued by a series of incendiary fires in apartment houses on the south side of the city. In one of these, in which several persons lost their lives, firemen found mattresses burning at the foot of both the front and rear stairways in the building. The cub reporter would be stating a fact should he write: "Firemen found mattresses burning at the foot of both the front and rear stairways of the building." But he would be bringing in something else should he write: "The fire was started by an arsonist who tried to murder the inhabitants of the building by blocking both exits with burning mattresses." In this latter statement the reporter would be making an inference about the origin of the fire and the motive of the person starting it.[9]

[8]Homans, *The Nature of Social Science,* p. 18.

[9]W. W. Little, Harold W. Wilson, and W. Edgar Moore, *Applied Logic* (Boston: Houghton Mifflin Company, 1955), pp. 152–53.

This use of the term fact is similar to that set forth by Morris Cohen and Ernest Nagel when they say:

> We sometimes mean by "facts" certain discriminated elements in sense perception. That which is denoted by the expressions "This band of color lies between those two bands," "The end of this pointer coincides with that mark on the scale," are facts in this sense. But we must note that no inquiry *begins* with facts so defined. Such sensory elements are *analytically sought out by us*, for the purpose of finding reliable signs which will enable us to test the inferences we make. All observation appeals ultimately to certain *isolable* elements in sense experience. We search for such elements because concerning them universal agreement among all people is obtainable.[10]

Cohen and Nagel go on to set forth other uses of "fact."

> "Fact" sometimes denotes the propositions which *interpret* what is given to us in sense experience. *This is a mirror, That sound is the dinner bell, This piece of gold is malleable,* are facts in this sense. All inquiry must take for granted a host of propositions of this sort, although we may be led to reject some of them as false as the inquiry progresses.

It must be emphasized that fact, in this sense, is an interpretation of our observations. The interpretative character of "This is a mirror" is made evident simply by saying "This object we see here is an instance of the class of things we call mirrors." When we have identified the object as one of a kind of things, we have thereby interpreted it. This is frequently the meaning of "fact" in pedagogical literature.

Cohen and Nagel distinguish still another use of "fact" commonly found in pedagogical discourse. In this case, "fact" denotes an instantial generalization. As they say,

> "Fact" also denotes propositions which truly assert an invariable sequence or conjunction of characters. *All gold is malleable, Water solidifies at zero degree Centigrade, Opium is a soporific,* are facts in this sense, while, *Woman is fickle,* is not a fact, or at least is a disputed fact. What is *believed* to be a fact in this (or even in the second) sense depends clearly upon the evidence we have been able to accumulate; ultimately, upon facts in the first sense noted, together with certain assumed universal connections between them. Hence, whether a proposition shall be called a fact or a hypothesis depends upon the state of our evidence. The proposition *The earth is round* at one time had no known evidence in its favor; later, it was employed as a hypothesis to *order* a host of directly observable events; it is now regarded as a fact because to doubt it would be to throw into confusion other portions of our knowledge.

According to this use of "fact," it is true that not only a particular piece of gold is malleable but all objects belonging to the category of gold have this same property. Thus the instantial generalization "All gold is malleable" is a fact.

---

[10]Morris R. Cohen and Ernest Nagel, *An Introduction to Logic and the Scientific Method* (New York: Harcourt, Brace, 1934), pp. 217–19.

In our discussion of concepts we noted that conceptual knowledge consists of a category and criteria by which to decide what is included in and excluded from the category. We now see that two uses of "fact" are related to conceptual knowledge. One use denotes that a particular satisfies a criterion: "This piece of gold is malleable," "This sample of water freezes at zero degrees centigrade." The other use denotes propositions which assert that all instances satisfy a particular criterion. The latter is an instantial generalization. Thus we see that both the interpretative and the generalization uses of "fact" overlap conceptual knowledge.

Can You Recognize Types of Knowledge?

One of the ways of finding out how well we understand the different forms of knowledge is to try to recognize them in classroom discourse. We often understand things in the abstract but are unable to recognize them in concrete form. If we can identify the types of knowledge in classroom discourse, we have good assurance that we have a working knowledge. The following exchange between students and teachers represents five different subjects: language arts, social studies, literature, history, and biology. To the right of the discourse are columns representing the different types of knowledge. Study the verbal exchanges between teachers and students and check the column that you think represents the type of knowledge being discussed. Then underscore the teacher-student utterances that correspond to that type of knowledge. When you have finished your analysis, compare and discuss your judgments with two or three other persons who have also made the analysis.

	Skills	Facts	Laws or Law-Like Concepts	Rules	Values	Attitudes
T: Let's review just briefly the words that we took yesterday that are often confused. Give us a pair of words that you think you will remember and use correctly, though they are often confused. S: "There" and "their."						
T: You'll have to spell them. S: There are three of them.						
T: All right, you tell us about one of them. S: T-h-e-i-r. That means like "their house." It means ownership.						
T: Right. S: And t-h-e-y apostrophe r-e. That means they are.						
T: Right. S: And t-h-e-r-e. That usually is put at the beginning of a sentence or something.						

	Skills	Facts	Laws or Law-Like Concepts	Rules	Values	Attitudes

T: Sometimes it introduces a sentence, and then it's called an expletive.
S: Is it usually an adjective?
T: It's not an adjective. It's usually a word of place as "here." "There" and "here" are place words.

S: What's the difference between manslaughter and murder?
T: Intent is involved in murder. The person intends to do it. You would say something like you said that you were going to do it, then you did it. Or, you went ahead and did it with malice aforethought. In the other case, you would kill someone while you were performing or doing some illegal act. As Bryan mentioned, suppose you were driving in a car at an illegal rate of speed, and in doing so, you ran over someone, whereas if you had been driving at a legal rate of speed, this wouldn't have happened. When you started out you hadn't intended to kill a person. You hadn't done it willfully, yet through some criminal negligence on your part, or some criminal act on your part, you had incidentally killed a person. Not intentionally, but through some other violation it happened.

T: All right. Now, the chief function of any kind of fiction is to entertain, isn't it? Do you feel that in this book, *Cry, the Beloved Country,* the author is actually entertaining you?
S: Well, in a way.

T: Are you enjoying this story?
S: Yes.
T: Do you enjoy this story itself? Are you concerned with what Steven Kumalo is doing? Do you care whether or not he is able to rescue Absalom?
S: I think that we are looking for two points in this book. One point is for entertainment—the story. The other is what the author is trying to do—what he's trying to teach you.

	Skills	Facts	Laws or Law-Like	Concepts	Rules	Values	Attitudes

T: Now, what do we call the device of spreading a particular doctrine or point of view?
S: Propaganda.
T: Propaganda. Is propaganda a nice word?
S: I think so.
T: When I say "propaganda" to you, do you like it? Good or bad? Quick, react!
S: Bad.
T: It's not a good word, is it? Now, the word itself means, any kind of organized or any concerted movement to spread a particular doctrine or information.

S: What's a "tariff wall"?
T: All right, both sides have tariffs. One side puts up a wall. Why does a nation have tariffs?
S: Well, I don't understand what a *wall* is.
T: Why does any nation have a tariff?
S: To equalize the price of the incoming trade?
T: All right put that another way.
S: So we can keep competition from the foreign countries from competing with ours.

T: Let's begin with the lowest part of the brain.
S: The medulla.

T: All right. Where is that located?
S: It's right above the spinal cord in the back, kind of in the lower part of the skull.
T: You say it's above the spinal cord?
S: It's right beside, yes.

T: Well what relation is it—what is the relationship between the medulla and the spinal cord?
S: It's just an extension of it.

T: Yes, the medulla is just an extension of the spinal cord, and what is on the other end of the medulla—the top end, you might say?
S: The cerebellum.

Forms of Knowledge and School Subjects

School subjects are composed of the six discussed forms of knowledge. In fact, the difference between one subject and another is partly a difference in the amount and kind of forms each contains. Some forms are to be found in all subjects. Conceptual knowledge is a case in point. Concepts such as center of interest and perspective are to be found in art, score and note in music, sentence and paragraph in language, and order and number in mathematics. In the physical sciences one finds such concepts as density and atoms, and in biological sciences mammals and genes. In history there is feudalism and nationalism, and in the social studies, crime and government. In physical education one finds fatigue and recreation. One can easily think of other subjects and other concepts. No subject is apparently without them. Perhaps the same thing can be said of facts.

One of the ways to explore your understanding of curriculum content is to check the cells in the following grid.

You will note that one dimension of the grid provides the different kinds of knowledge and the other dimension provides a few of the subjects that make up the program of studies. As an example, consider history. All agree that history contains facts and concepts, but many of us would debate the question of whether or not history contains law-like statements. We could all agree perhaps that it contains no strict empirical laws. But does it contain rules? Some would probably say that it does, although they may be hard pressed to give examples. Perhaps value statements and value concepts could be found in history but would one find expressions of attitudes. And what skills and procedures would be included in the content of history? If one understood history from this standpoint and was able to give examples of the various kinds of knowledge that make up its content, he would be in a position to consider the question of the relative importance of these various forms of knowledge and the amount of emphasis to be placed upon them.

As an exercise in grappling with the substance of the curriculum, the reader may wish to consider each of the various subjects from the standpoint of the knowledge it contains as suggested in Figure 9–2. A study of textbooks used in elementary or high school in connection with this diagram should be rewarding.

As you check the cells in Figure 9–2 you may wish to remember that the substance of a discipline is related to the question of whether the discipline is empirical or not. The assertions of an empirical discipline depend for their validity not only on logical consistency but also verification of their deductions by direct observation. The natural sciences, psychology, and some aspects of the social sciences are examples of empirical studies. The propositions of nonempirical studies do not depend upon direct observation and manipulation of the environment as a test of their validity. Instead their claims rest upon logical rigor and convention. Among these are language, mathematics, logic, and the general area of discursive symbolism.

Figure 9-2. Areas of study and types of knowledge.

	Facts	Concepts	Laws or law-like rules	Values	Attitudes	Skills
History						
Social studies						
Typing						
Agriculture						
Physics						
Chemistry						
Art						
Music						
Mathematics						
Home economics						
Biology						
Metal work						
Physical education						
Etc.						
Etc.						
Etc.						

Reminder

We have identified and discussed six forms of knowledge. We have provided readings that describe how we predict and explain with laws; interpret with concepts; rate things with values; support our points with facts; express our feelings as attitudes; decide when to do things, and what is the right and proper thing to do by rules; and perform tasks with skills. We teach one or more of these forms of knowledge when we teach any subject, or, for that matter, when we teach anything. One of the curriculum worker's responsibilities is to see that these various knowledge forms be adequately represented in the curriculum, and that the methods and materials appropriate to each are adequately provided.

The disciplines differ from each other primarily with respect to the knowledge forms they contain. For example, mathematics is composed primarily of rules, procedures, and concepts; physics is made up primarily of concepts, laws, and procedures; grammar consists largely of concepts and rules. To know a subject is to master the forms of knowledge that comprise it.

Chapter 10
The Utility of Knowledge and Schooling

"And now to the most important point about teaching . . . relevance."

Instructor 84, 4 (December 1974) 96.

Curriculum workers and teachers intend the knowledge in the curriculum to be useful to students. In fact, the claim made to justify every curriculum is utility of learning. Few persons, if any, would wish to say that the content of the curriculum should be of no use to anyone. The problem of what content to teach does not arise from disagreement among teachers and curriculum workers about whether or not the content should have utility. Rather the difficulty is attributable partly to the fact that no generally accepted criteria exist for deciding whether a given bit of knowledge is useful, and partly to the lack of research on the utility of schooling. For this reason, it seems appropriate to explore the meaning of utility and to distinguish utility from other concepts with which it may be easily confused. In general, knowledge has utility if it satisfies the desires of, or serves as a means for, individuals or groups, or influences society in desirable directions. If a bit of knowledge does not function in any of these ways, it has no utility.

Orientation

The utility of knowledge must be distinguished from objectives of instruction. Instruction strives to teach concepts, principles, rules, procedures, values, and so on. It is expected that children will learn how to read, how to multiply and do other arithmetic processes; it is expected that they will learn some of the concepts and laws of natural science; that they will come to understand some of the social concepts and law-like principles used in explaining social events; and so on. As means of satisfying some need or rendering some societal benefit these learnings have utility. If they satisfy the needs of individuals to check their bank accounts, to estimate their expenditures, or to satisfy their curiosity about phenomena in the physical and social environment, they can be said to be beneficial.

Utility is easily confused with objectives. When we say that our objective is to develop good citizens, or more efficient workers, or to improve society in some particular way, we are not stating objectives of instruction; we are making assertions about the utility of what is to be taught. It is important for the curriculum worker as well as the teacher to distinguish clearly between objectives and utility. If this distinction is not understood curriculum workers and teachers are likely to make false promises about the school's products. This is true for several reasons.

First, the benefits that society derives from schooling are not always associated with a particular body of knowledge. It may be that the economic prosperity of a nation is more closely associated with the amount of schooling its members have than the subjects they study in school.

Second, the performance of individuals in the family may bear little relationship to any knowledge the school can teach, although we have claimed for at least fifty years that the school should develop individuals for worthy home membership. Finally, teachers have neither the pedagogical know-how nor the political power to determine the ends for which students will use the knowledge they acquire in the classroom.

The utility of knowledge can be considered in several different ways. The utility of concepts, laws, facts, values, and so on can be considered without regard to the disciplines to which they belong. By looking at utility from this standpoint we are thinking of how instances of the category of knowledge called concepts, of the category called laws, and so on, function in thought. For example, regardless of the discipline from which concepts are taken, they are used always to interpret something.

The utility of knowledge can be considered in another way. We can ask for the uses of the content of a given discipline. How is the content of arithmetic used? How is geographic knowledge used? Both of these senses of utility will be considered later. They are of great importance, and curriculum workers and teachers should take all ways of considering the utility of knowledge into account in selecting content.

Another approach to the question of utility is to consider for whom the knowledge is useful and for what. Particular jobs or tasks require both knowledge about *how* to do something and knowledge *that* such and such is the case. For example, an automobile mechanic must have conceptual knowledge because he must diagnose car troubles. He must know that if such and such is the case, the trouble is so and so. If the ignition system is not working, what is wrong with it. Once he has determined the problem, he must rely upon his knowledge in order to solve it. This is knowing-how. Job analysis will ordinarily reveal the knowledge that should be taught to persons who are going to perform the particular job. Thus the curriculum in vocational and professional education is typically composed of knowledge necessary to perform adequately on the intended job. In such cases the content of the curriculum is derived from the demands of the particular job.

Another approach is found in studies that ascertain the knowledge used by laypersons in their everyday activities. Some studies not uniquely related to preparation for particular vocations are considered important to almost everyone. Arithmetic, history, geography, and language arts are examples. It is generally held that everyone regardless of their future occupations should be schooled in these studies. But what should they know about them? Consider arithmetic. Everyone will agree that the student should learn the fundamental processes. But should students be taught to extract the square root? To calculate compound interest? And what about geography? Should students be taught the capitals of each of our fifty states? The depth of Lake Michigan? How can the curriculum worker decide what elements of such studies are to be learned by all students and to what ends? Current educational research has attempted to answer questions of this sort. Data on the daily activities of individuals—obtained by questionnaires and interviews—have been analyzed to determine what knowledge the layperson uses from day to day with respect to these fields.

Still another approach to the question of utility is to consider only the student and his interests. This approach uses the criterion of personal satisfaction as a measure of utility. Whatever curriculum satisfies the intrinsic need of the individual for learning and development is said to have utility. If an individual feels the desire to play a piano or to paint, it is argued that he should be encouraged to learn to do these things, and that the knowledge he thereby gains has utility in the sense that it satisfies his legitimate desires. Such learning may have no financial remuneration nor make any particular contribution to society or to the happiness or enjoyment of others. Nevertheless it has utility for the individual in that it gives him satisfaction. This way of looking at the utility of knowledge is at the base of almost all those who believe that the content of the school program should be relevant to the individual. Relevance in this sense means that the knowledge satisfies the individual's personal desires for certain kinds of information or activities. The justification of almost all humanistic emphases in the curriculum has rested on this criterion of utility. And it has been put forth as one of the supreme aims of education; namely, the development of the individual.

Thus far we have considered the utility of knowledge. It is important to think about the utility of schooling separately. We can think of schooling in terms of how long one attends—ordinarily 180 days a year for twelve years. We can also think of schooling in terms of thoroughness—how much knowledge and how many skills the students acquire. It seems reasonable to assume that the quality of life in a community is related to the level of schooling—its amount and thoroughness—enjoyed by its members. The more time an individual spends in school, as well as the thoroughness of his schooling, benefits the community where the individual lives.

One can also look at the utility of schooling from a societal standpoint. Is it reasonable to assume that the productivity of a nation whose citizens have completed high school would be greater than the productivity of a nation of people who had had little or no schooling? The production and consumption of goods and services is probably related to the level of schooling of a society. There are doubtless several other features in a social system which are enhanced by the advanced levels of schooling. This aspect of utility will be explored in the latter part of this chapter.

Uses of Cognitive Forms

In Chapter 9 we explored the different kinds of knowledge and how they comprise the curriculum. In this chapter we try to answer the question of how these cognitive forms function in the behavior of the individual. It is easy to see how skills are used. If one has learned to type, it is readily evident that this know-how is used in typing letters, manuscripts, and so on. The same can be said about knowing how to spell, how to do arithmetic operations. However, the use of such knowledge forms as concepts, values, and laws is not so evident because it is not observable in overt behavior. Watching a TV repairman work on a TV, for example, does not tell us the concepts he uses to detect the trouble and to remedy it. What is true in this case is also true of almost all the disciplines included in the educational program.

Whether one studies history, biology, or sociology, utility is not stamped on the knowledge forms acquired. Nor will a curriculum worker or teacher be able to cite any uses of these knowledge forms unless they understand how they function in the direction and control of behavior. This is one of the reasons why it is important to consider the various forms of knowledge separate from the disciplines. The generic uses of the various knowledge forms should be clearly understood by both teachers and curriculum workers.

One of the most thoroughgoing treatments of this topic is by Harry S. Broudy.

☐

Suppose you learned the multiplication table when you were in grade school. How do you use this learning? You use it whenever the situation calls for multiplication: 6 times 7 = ? 4 x 7 = ? If you learned the table by rote, your answer is automatic: 42 or 28. You have *replicated* the original learning pretty much as you learned it in the first place. Reading, writing, spelling, computational procedures in arithmetic are all used replicatively. The items that are used most often come into mind automatically when needed. Items that are not used frequently, e.g., the succession of English kings, the dates and terms of treaties, the atomic weights of the chemical elements, are forgotten quite soon after the learning has been completed.

Accordingly, many items studied in school cannot be recalled in later life

Harry S. Broudy, *General Education: The Search for a Rationale* (Bloomington, Ind.: The Phi Delta Kappa Educational Foundation, 1974), pp. 37–46. Reprinted with permission of the publisher.

Footnotes have been renumbered consecutively throughout the chapter.

or even in later schooling, if they have not been used frequently. If we give high school and college graduates tests in history, science, or literature five or ten years after graduation, the amount they can recall is distressingly small. Such test results seem to make general education a waste of time or lead to the verdict: The schools have failed.

Suppose in your school days you read poems and stories about English kings and in adult life you go to see a movie about Henry VIII. Do you recall all the facts you learned about Henry VIII? Do you recite all the poems and stories you read about this period in English history? Could you? Probably not. Yet much of the movie seems familiar. Somehow the store of images, ideas, and words related to this topic are activated by seeing the movie, and these associations weave themselves in and around the images projected on the screen. Would an aborigine of the Australian bush "see" what you see in the movie?

This use of school learning we might call *associative.* Often we are no more aware of what is in our subconscious cellars of memory than we know the contents of our attics, but given the right occasion and stimulus we find to our surprise many items there that we had completely forgotten about.

For a third use of school, the *applicative,* imagine yourself confronted with problems such as: (a) deciding whether to invest your money in stocks, bonds, or real estate; (b) deciding whether to support candidate A or B in an upcoming Congressional election; (c) deciding on how to solve the energy shortage without increasing pollution of air and water.

Each type of problem presents a situation that presumably is giving trouble, and a good solution would change the situation so as to reduce the trouble. How can we use our schooling to help make the right decisions? Suppose we have passed with decent grades several formal courses in economics, political science, physics, biology, and chemistry. Can we apply these disciplines to our practical·problems? The chances are overwhelmingly against our being able to do so unless our vocational specialty has immersed us in problems of this sort at the operational level, i.e., worked in a bank or a brokerage house; been involved in political campaigns or in projects operated by the government; employed as an engineer in some phase of the energy field.

To solve a problem requires not only an understanding of the relevant principles, but an intimate and extensive acquaintance with the phenomena of a field. One has to know the people involved, the relevant research studies, the solutions that have been tried and how they have worked; the various side effects of a given solution. This knowledge only the specialist has. Furthermore, unless a technology has been invented that translates the principles of physics or economics into operations, knowing the principles has no effect on solving the problem. Thus a technology for using lasers in surgery makes the laser principle useful, and price controls make certain principles in economics applicable to controlling the market. The layperson, the educated generalist, lacks both the familiarity with the phenomena and the technology.

Finally, there is the *interpretive* use of schooling. We can use the same examples as in the applicative use. The study of the various disciplines by themselves cannot be used applicatively, but they can be used to understand, i.e., to interpret the problems. Indeed, application of schooling presupposes interpretation, but there can be interpretation without application.

With this general sketch of the uses of schooling in mind, we can now ask what general education can reasonably be expected to accomplish. With regard to replication, relatively little. Certain skills and facts will be retained for long or short periods depending on how often they are used. Historians use certain dates frequently; architects may not; hence architects will forget facts that the historian keeps on the tip of his tongue.

The long exposure of the pupil to the basic disciplines, however, forces him to repeat or rehearse certain facts and principles many times, so that some data tend to be retained and used replicatively. But with the explosion of knowledge, there is little hope that many of us can master and retain any significant proportion of it. Instead we rely on handbooks, encyclopedias, digests, and the like for the facts, if and when the need for them arises.

Yet even to use these manuals intelligently requires an understanding of what knowledge would be relevant. For example, in what part of the encyclopedia or digest would one go for facts relevant to the problem of a controlled versus a free market economy? What data would be relevant to decide the merits of developing nuclear or fossil sources of energy for the year 2000?

On the associative dimension, we can expect a great deal from general studies. If you have visited Europe, for example, what did you expect to see when you first came to London or the Lake District or Stratford-on-Avon or Dover? How much of what you saw in France, Italy, and Germany was prefigured in what you had studied about these countries in school? English history and literature; Roman history and Latin—how much of these could you now recall with sufficient accuracy to pass an examination in them? Yet can you doubt that these studies colored the lenses through which you first saw these countries and the "famous" places in them?

How much of our ideals of manhood and womanhood has been shaped by the literature and art we have studied? How much of our value system seeped into our experience in the same way? True, we do not now recollect the details of those early studies, but that they have made a difference in our imagic store is apparent the moment we visit a culture with a wholly different tradition, for example, Japan or India.

The educated Indian citizen thinks about the physical world pretty much as does his counterpart in Britain because both have to think with the categories of modern physics and chemistry. But the significance of trees and animals and soil may be quite different for them because of the difference in the images they have absorbed from religion, mythology, and philosophy.

What is "richness" of experience, if not associative resources? Not all enrichment comes from schooling. Ordinary experience, as has been noted earlier, is far richer in our country than it ever has been, thanks to the mass media and ease of travel. Yet just as there is a difference between common sense science and educated science, so is there a difference between the richness contributed by the mass media, by the impacts of daily life, and that contributed by formal study of religion, literature, and other arts. And this is so precisely because formal studies are concerned with form, and formality means order and selection so that effects are concentrated and intensified. Formal science brings principles into sharp focus; literature uses language with precision and sensitivity; serious art, especially as it has been selected and preserved over long periods, gives vivid expression to extraordinary feats of imagination. By comparison the effects of ordinary experience are diffuse and erratic.

And somewhat the same sort of thing can be said in behalf of formal studies in the interpretive uses of schooling. Men will interpret their experience somehow, whether they have gone to school or not; whether they have had general education or not, much or little. Interpreting is as native to us as seeing, hearing, or tasting. To "understand" x or y is to recognize it as this sort of thing and that it is related in such and such a way to other things. To understand an earthquake is to interpret it in terms of shifting substrata of earth and rock; to understand inflation is to interpret rising prices in terms of the supply of money, goods, customers, etc.

Interpretation can be habitual, routine, stereotyped, or it can be sophisticated, creative, imaginative. Education is supposed to nudge the individual toward the latter levels of interpretation. We speak of the educated person as having broader *perspectives* than the untutored one; of being able to put events and problems into the proper *context;* to be aware of the complexity of and the limitation of solutions. Why can we claim this for the educated person? Because he is interpreting "with" ideals and associations and feelings that have been reflected upon by the best minds over centuries. They have withstood thousands of debates, have been refined in thousands of soul searchings, and held up to critical scrutiny at every turn. Presumably they are "better" than uneducated interpretations, and they certainly are different.

Perhaps the matter can be put in still another way. We are familiar with stencils—patterns cut out of paper or board. When the stencil is put on another surface the pattern shows through the cutouts. To interpret experience is to see it through stencils. Some are formed out of daily routines and expectations; out of the common sense judgments and mores of the group in which we carry on the transactions of daily life. But some are the stencils of science, history, literature, philosophy, and the other products of the disciplined mind.

An educated person is recognized by the stencils that shape his interpretation rather than by the shape of his action or the strength of his passions. Suppose one were to pick out ten people at random from a crowd attending a horse race or a race riot. Outwardly their actions could be distinguished with great difficulty. Even their attitudes might be similar. However, when they begin to discuss the riot or the race we get an inkling as to their differing stencils of interpretation. And by the differences in the language and concepts of these stencils we can make a shrewd guess at the level of schooling from which they emerged.

It is, therefore, as misguided to expect general education to produce a peculiar type of action as it is unrealistic to expect the generally educated person to "apply" knowledge. The school tries to reinforce the ideals which the community professes. The citizenry are often unhappy with the school when its "products" do not live up to these ideals and embarrassed when they do. But anyone who has reflected on the matter knows that the quality of conduct exhibited by individuals has far less to do with their schooling than with the kind of conduct the group will tolerate or reward. For there is no technology, no mechanism, that enables us to "apply" moral principles to conduct. Understanding human conduct and moral principles heightens sen-

sitivity and reflection, but it does not automatically grind out specific decisions. . . . Understanding affects the inner quality of conduct only when it
unites with feeling and commitment. The public has a right to demand that
pupils use the stencils of interpretation they were taught in school, because
over these the school has a large measure of control. The same cannot be said
for commitment.

If the interpretive and the associative uses of schooling—for which alone
general education can take the responsibility—do not directly affect action,
how can we clarify their usefulness to its recipients? The answer lies in the
power of general education to enlarge or vary the perspective or the context
in which action takes place. In a modern interdependent technologically dominated culture the demand for specialization of function and breadth of perspective grow at about the same rate, albeit in directly opposite directions.

In the vocational life, the replicative and applicative uses of specialized
vocational training need no elaboration. But in every profession practitioners
are faced with the demand that they take into account the broader social and
moral perspectives in which their work is done. Scientists have been plagued
by this for a long time, but especially since the invention of the atomic bomb.
Engineers are worrying now whether the products they design will have undesirable effects on the environment. Class actions in behalf of consumers, for
example, are a recent development in legal practice.

But when a profession tries to broaden the context of its practice, it runs
into disciplines that had not been included in the professional curricula. Engineers, for example, are not too familiar with the way sociologists and anthropologists view the very people for whom bridges, locomotives, and
automobiles are being designed. Indeed, much of the difficulty encountered by
schools in dealing with the children of the inner-city stemmed from the teachers' lack of understanding of a culture other than their own.

As far as citizenship is concerned, general studies are virtually indispensable
if one wants to play the role of the free citizen in a modern technological
society that has not given up its democratic ideals. But whether a given citizen
wants to or not is another matter; general studies, one might expect, would
predispose him to try, but the counterforces are very strong—too strong even
for many well-schooled individuals. In citizenship general studies function in
two ways: first as stencils of interpretation of problems, e.g., foreign policy
decisions, taxes, etc.; and second, as inclining people toward critical examination of issues, a desire for logical coherence, and a tendency to see problems
in many contexts.

Finally, with regard to the quality of personal life, general studies affect the
self-concept, its ideals and aspirations. But even more, perhaps, they furnish
stencils for evaluation of conduct. The efforts to reduce marriage, love, politics,
peace, and prosperity to a set of skills have had limited success. They work
pretty well when the larger context is already understood, but they are no
substitute for that understanding. Only honest people can play skillful politics
safely; only people genuinely in love can use a sex manual without substituting
it for love; only those who are committed to social justice can safely experiment
with social engineering. People believe in general studies because they believe
that they can or should supply the knowledge of which the larger contexts of

life are constructed. And that is why they want it for their children even when the exigencies of life may turn them in the direction of more specific training that will yield more immediate economic returns. The simultaneous desire for general and highly specialized schooling, therefore, is not an anomaly. . . .

Assuming Broudy's view of the utility of schooling to be correct, which knowledge forms would have great utility? Little utility?

Benefits of Schooling

Some benefits of schooling accrue to the student as an individual. He learns to know and to do those things required to communicate, understand, enjoy, and cope with the simpler aspects of his environment. These benefits appear to depend on elementary knowledge of particular subjects—reading, arithmetic, arts, science.

There are other benefits which accrue to the individual as a member of a community. Some also accrue to the community or the society as a whole. Little consideration has been given to these advantages of schooling except by economists who have recently begun to consider education as a form of human capital. But in addition to the economic benefits of schooling, there are also many other benefits to be considered such as political and military advantages, and the general enrichment of community and national life.

Curriculum workers and teachers have seldom been concerned with these sorts of utilities, but it is becoming increasingly clear that some basic issues rest upon the question of whether or not schooling contributes to the quality of life. Issues such as compulsory schooling, alternative forms of schooling, and the financial support of schooling hinge upon the question of whether or not school makes a significant contribution to the quality of community and national existence.

The excerpt that follows summarizes succinctly some of the considerations that go into the question of determining who benefits from schooling in the broader sense as well as on an individual basis.

☐

To determine the utility of schooling, it is necessary to collect and organize data on the benefits of schooling to the individual and society. To escape subjective biases, data should be collected by public criteria. The determination of these criteria is a complex process, and the collection and organization of relevant data are perhaps even more taxing. All that can be done here is to

B. Othanel Smith and Donald E. Orlosky, *Socialization and Schooling* (Bloomington, Ind.: Phi Delta Kappa, 1975), pp. 61–78. Reprinted with permission of the publisher.

set forth some of the criteria found in the current literature and to indicate in a general way what their use would probably lead to.[1]

These benefits can be classified as follows:

1. Benefits that accrue to the individual
   a. Admission to the labor force
   b. Increase in income
   c. Multiplication of options
   d. Personal development
2. Benefits to other individuals
   a. Advantages to employers
   b. Enrichment of community activities
3. Benefits to society
   a. Advantages to a market economy
   b. Contributions to economic growth
   c. Contributions to political behavior
   d. Contributions to social cohesion.

The Criteria Problem: Admission to Work

The first issue to be considered is the utility of basic knowledge and skills. There is little question about the desirability of fundamental learning. Almost everyone agrees that children should be taught to read, write, calculate, and to understand basic concepts and principles. Anyone who fails to acquire these abilities risks exploitation throughout his life and an inferior level of life in his personal and social existence. These abilities are important to a nation whose populace works in a wide range of occupations and makes decisions about personal and societal issues. The school should guarantee that all pupils reach minimum levels of achievement in fundamentals. Exceptions to this standard should include only those few pupils whose learning potential is severely hampered by physical, mental, or emotional characteristics that render them incapable of achieving the minimum levels. These pupils should be included in as much of the school program as might be beneficial to them.

The level of achievement the school should accept as its goal must be determined. . . .

Perhaps the most common criterion for deciding the school's success in teaching fundamental skills and knowledge is the grade norm. It has been employed to determine whether the benefits of schooling are equitably distributed among the regions and social groups of society. By isolating a target group, for example, the American Indian, and comparing its average achievement to the average of the total group, it can be determined if the school is

---

[1]John Vaizey, *The Economics of Education* (New York: The Free Press of Glencoe, 1962), pp. 37–53, 125–35; Burton A. Weisbrod, *External Benefits of Public Education* (Princeton, N.J.: Industrial Relations Section, Department of Economics, Princeton University, 1964), pp. 69–99; George Psacharopoulos, *Returns to Education* (San Francisco, Calif.: Jossey-Bass, 1973), pp. 1–35; 111–25; Mark Blaug, *An Introduction to the Economics of Education* (London: Allen Lane The Penguin Press, 1970), pp. 23–101, 101–20; Charles Benson, *The Economics of Public Education* (New York: Houghton Mifflin, 1961), *passim.*

adequately preparing the target group in basic skills. In this approach those above the grade norm are regarded as adequately served by the school. The pupils whose performance is below the norm are considered to be those on whom the school's influence has been less desirable. If a large proportion of a target group falls below the norm (say, 70 percent), it is concluded that the school is failing with that group. . . .

Grade norms assume that pupil performance establishes standards against which to compare the achievement of individuals and groups. Schooling that results in higher grade norms is typically judged to be better. But reliance solely on an achievement criterion begs the question. The preference for greater achievement is left without justification except for the claim that achievement is good in itself. This position provides no external standard for judging schooling or for deciding how much formal learning a society should provide for its members. To ask if a particular level of pupil achievement is adequate is to ask an incomplete question; one must also question for what is it adequate. Without an external criterion, the answer must be that achievement is adequate in itself. This answer is pointless. To escape this circularity, an external standard for assessing pupil achievement must be found. The most satisfactory approach is to look for a measure of utility.

The matter can be put differently. The criterion should not be one that compares an individual with the average achievement of his age group. Rather, it should address the question of how much and what kind of learning the society should require of all individuals. Aside from societal maintenance and well-being, the purpose of schooling is to induce learning sufficient to enable the individual to assume an adult role. The criterion should specify an achievement floor in basic knowledge and skills below which none would be permitted to fall, except for cases of extreme disability. . . . This floor should be the threshold to the realm of work. Those who reach it would thereby be admitted to the labor market without penalty for inability to read, write, calculate, and use fundamental knowledge.

Unfortunately, there is no empirical basis for such a criterion, although the utility of certain knowledge (arithmetic operations, for instance) was a subject of much interest in the early years of educational research.[2] Nevertheless, it is possible to approach it by using the judgment of competent persons. If the performance expectations of everyday life can be decided upon by a board of judges and the ability of pupils to perform these expectations can be measured by tests, then it would be possible to begin the development of a criterion of utility such as is suggested here. As pupils progress through school they would advance toward this floor each year. With an improved program it could be established empirically that by a specified time every pupil will reach the level of achievement agreed upon by competent judges. . . .

Once the individual enters the labor market, his income is associated with the amount of schooling he has had. It is to be understood that this relationship is based on averages and is not necessarily true for particular individuals. For

---

[2]Guy M. Wilson, "A Survey of the Social and Business Uses of Arithmetic" *Teacher College Contributions to Education,* No. 100 (New York: Teachers College Bureau of Publications, 1919); see also his *What Arithmetic Shall We Teach?* (Boston: Houghton Mifflin, 1926).

large numbers, however, it is quite clear that income and schooling are positively correlated.

The individual forgoes wages while he is in school and thereby invests in his own schooling. On the other hand, he stands to gain higher earnings with schooling. Is there a point of maximum economic return from his investment? Perhaps few individuals look at their schooling in this way, but there is such a point. Some authorities report that on the average the greatest rate of returns on the individual's investment is derived from elementary school, the next from high school, and, finally, from college.[3] The maximum rate of return is apparently derived from elementary schooling. Of course, the rate of return will vary with the individual's ability, energy, and social status. Obviously, if an individual invests in schooling, and social barriers preclude the use of his learning for economic gain, his investment is depreciated.

Schooling also increases the individual's options along a number of dimensions. It enhances his job opportunities. The band on the spectrum of occupations from which an individual may choose to seek employment widens with increased schooling. One who has just reached the achievement floor in basic knowledge and skills will be restricted in the jobs he can expect to get, while the individual who has completed more advanced levels has a wider range of job options.[4] In some cases schooling can also restrict the individual's chances of employment. A highly specialized person may find his job opportunities greatly restricted. A professional engineer may not be able to find employment in a job market oversupplied with engineers as readily as a person with only a high school diploma. Unable to find employment in his profession, the engineer will seek alternative jobs at a salary commensurate with his ability. Anything less would be a sacrifice of his training and ability as well as of the values of his lifestyle. He is likely to seek work in service activities for which his specialized training is more of a handicap than an asset. The employer is apt to look askance at one who is overtrained for the level of occupation in which he seeks work. If this analysis is correct, there is a level of schooling at which job options are maximized.

Schooling not only increases employment opportunities but also options of lifestyles. Many patterns of life are possible in an industrial society. For example, one can live a "life of carefree wholesome enjoyment," of "meditation and study," of "group participation and group enjoyment," and of "sympathetic concern for others."[5] On the average the range of choices among these styles is contingent upon the amount of schooling one has had. Ordinarily a high school graduate will have more options than an elementary school graduate, and a college graduate will probably have more than a high school graduate. Again the relation between schooling and lifestyle options is probably not linear. There appears to be no good reason to suppose that continuous increase in years of schooling will indefinitely multiply one's choices among ways of life. Perhaps one who settles for a bachelor's degree will have as many options, other things being equal, as one who completes a doctor's degree. Although

[3]Psacharopoulos, *Returns to Education,* pp. 17ff.

[4]Weisbrod, *External Benefits of Public Education,* pp. 23ff.

[5]Charles Morris, *The Open Self* (New York: Prentice-Hall, 1948), pp. 73–96.

one can hypothesize that a college graduate has more options, four years of high school may be as near the maximum as a college degree, for all we know. The individual benefits from schooling in still another way. The school contributes to his development as a person. Every individual possesses potentials. The richer and more open the society the better are his chances to actualize his potentials. The school is dedicated to this end. This is a moral aim of schooling and is discussed as a form of equality in the last part of this chapter. Its utility is the individual's satisfaction resulting from his growth. This utility is associated with the humanistic tradition, which emphasizes schooling as a means of self-actualization, self-direction, and adequacy, although personal development may accompany all forms of learning regardless of their utility. The individual pursues knowledge because it gives him satisfaction. If self-fulfillment is the realization of one's aspirations through his own efforts, this benefit is associated with no particular knowledge or skill—academic, vocational, or otherwise. It all depends upon the individual's private sense of satisfaction. In the pursuit of learning for this benefit, is there a point of diminishing satisfaction with the expenditure of one's energies? Theoretically there is. But it could be true only for knowledge about particular things since one's appetite for learning shifts from time to time from one thing to another and is perhaps insatiable except for specific ends.

The individual is not the only recipient of the benefits of schooling. Others also benefit from it.[6] The profits of schooling spill over into various activities that affect other individuals. The employer who must depend upon the performance of his employees benefits from the work of the school. The success of his enterprise often depends as much upon the abilities and sincerity of those who work for him as upon his own efforts. The individual's schooling not only increases the quality of his labor but also helps to enrich the experiences of his neighbors. Their aesthetic life, as reflected in clubs, choral groups, art and flower shows, landscaping, care of the home, and social life are heightened in some measure by his schooling. A neighborhood of persons who have completed high school would be likely to be rated higher in terms of the quality of its culture than one whose schooling did not exceed the elementary grades. . . .

Schooling can be beneficial to society as well as to the individual and his neighbors. The society can benefit in two ways: collectively and distributively.[7] In the first case the advantages accrue to society as a whole, but they affect individuals differently. In the second case the society benefits as a whole, and at the same time all individuals are affected in the same direction. Neither form of utility takes into account the needs of individual members of society.

A form of schooling that produces scientists and technicians to build an efficient military machine can work to the advantage of the society as an aggregate in its struggle with other nations. This can have differential effects on individuals, assuming limited funds for education. The lower classes can be affected deleteriously by this policy, since their learning may be neglected. The

[6]Weisbrod, *External Benefits of Public Education,* pp. 30–39.

[7]Vilfredo Pareto, *The Mind and Society* (New York: Dover Publications, 1963), Vol. IV, pp. 1456–1500.

more affluent classes can profit because of the educational and economic advantages enabled by military education.

Educational policies that affect the nation collectively are likely to be controversial. If a nation faces the problem of whether to support extensive expenditures for the production of scientists and technicians to strengthen its position in relation to other nations or to emphasize schooling for the masses, the matter is likely to be unsettling. If one considers the nation's security and nothing else, he will decide that the sacrifice of the masses' schooling is beneficial. On the other hand, if another person takes into account only the benefits to the masses, neglecting any indirect benefits they may gain, he will conclude that sacrificing their schooling is morally wrong. It is nonsense to ask who is right in the absence of a criterion for rendering the two opinions comparable. In the absence of such a criterion, any discussion of the issue will only produce rationalizations that cover up the real motives.

A change in schooling can increase the school's utility for society and at the same time can benefit all individuals. This is utility for the society distributively. The expenditure of public money under the Smith-Hughes Act to advance vocational education was beneficial both to the society and all individuals. The society was strengthened in its relationship to other societies since a trained labor force enhances production. At the same time every member of society benefits, assuming an increased supply of consumer goods and a higher national income resulting from a more productive labor force. A change in the school that results in an increase in the gross national product would be beneficial to the society, and each individual would also benefit from the improved economic conditions. If the school were to increase the amount of political participation, it would thereby benefit the society distributively. In this form of utility, changes in the school can increase the advantages to individuals when affecting the society as a whole.

A polity will necessarily be concerned with the societal benefits of schooling. It assumes that the establishment of schools will enhance the society. In its early periods of development a polity is not likely to support schools merely for personal benefits such as self-actualization. When the concerns of the polity for societal benefits have been satisfied, the advantages of schooling for the individual can then be more readily sanctioned. It is likely that personal utility for everybody *per se* is possible only under special circumstances of great wealth and optimum distribution, a condition that few societies are approaching. In technological societies, and in those that aspire to be so, the policy of gearing the school to the needs of society itself dominates.

The American government has tended to place great emphasis upon schooling for economic production and defense. This is evident in the various educational acts of the national government. The Morrill Act to support colleges, the Smith-Hughes Act to support vocational education, the Smith-Lever Act to diffuse information about agriculture and home economics, the Reserve Officers Training Corps, Army Training Programs, and recent efforts to launch a program of career education support this statement. In addition, states have enacted laws exercising control over the curriculum in the interest of collective advantages. For example, many states require American history in the schools to preserve traditions and promote patriotism. Meanwhile, school personnel and educational theorists were committing the school to the production of certain societal results, expressed generally in the Cardinal Principles of Secondary Education: command of fundamental processes, worthy home membership, vocational efficiency, citizenship, worthy use of leisure, ethical character, and health.

The failure to distinguish between objectives of instruction and utility is a constant source of confusion in educational literature. All but one of the cardinal principles are utilities and not objectives. Achievement in the fundamental processes is not a utility, but learning that is useful because of what it enables the individual to do in life. The other objectives are societal benefits. The school can teach knowledge and skills that might enable an individual to be a worthy member of a home, a good citizen, and an efficient worker, but it can have only limited influence on the development of the kind of person who will use the knowledge and skill to these ends. This confusion lies at the base of the issues about the accountability of the school. The school can be held accountable for whatever can be tested, such as knowledge and skills. But it is not accountable for the uses they are put to, for the teacher cannot control the ends for which knowledge will be used.

Some of the societal ends to which schooling contributes, theoretically at least, . . . [are] maintenance of a market economy, economic growth, political wisdom, and social cohesion.

The market system in an industrial society is dependent upon the transmission of information. The vast system of communication—newspapers, books, magazines, and other media—by which human wants are stimulated and channeled underwrites the distribution of goods and services. This system is possible because of widespread literacy. What people want and what they strive to get is what they know about. The better informed they are, the more likely they are to choose wisely. They can thus affect the market itself. It is likely that this benefit begins to decrease at an undetermined level of schooling. For all that is known, little advantage along this line may result from schooling beyond the secondary level. But an extensive study of consumption patterns of different educational strata and their effects on marketing practices should probably illuminate this aspect of the school's utility.

For more than forty years the primary measure of the economy's status has been growth in the national income or the gross national product, which is approximately the same. One societal goal is to increase, or at least maintain, economic growth. Does schooling contribute to this end? Considerable research has already been done on the relation of schooling to this goal. While the research has not produced conclusive evidence on the relationship, it has given approximations and pointed the way to more adequate methodological procedures. How much does schooling contribute to economic growth? The amount of the contribution depends upon the level of the society's development. Roughly speaking, the investment in schooling in advanced nations enjoys about the same returns as investment in physical capital. In developing nations the payoff of investment in physical capital is less than for investment in schooling. The highest percent of return is from elementary schooling, while higher education yields the lowest.[8]

[8]Psacharopoulos, *Returns to Education,* pp. 87ff.

These estimates of the contribution of schooling to growth take no account of the content of schooling except as it is reflected in the educational levels. It is safe to assume that the content of elementary schooling consists in fundamental skills and knowledge. At the secondary and higher education levels, content can be extremely varied. Apparently the content of elementary schooling has a high payoff economically, since elementary schooling accounts for almost half of the contribution of schooling to economic growth.[9] At higher levels the comparative efficacy of one kind of content is indefinite. Using influence on economic growth as a criterion, data from a few developing countries faintly indicate no superiority of technical over general secondary schooling.[10]

An open society depends upon the political behavior and wisdom of its members. Their political beliefs and practices are acquired from a number of sources: participation in neighborhood and community activities, newspapers and other media, family associations, and so on. It is widely held that the school also helps to develop awareness of social and political issues, national goals, and basic values. In addition it is claimed that the school develops the ability to participate in the democratic process. The development of the individual along these lines presumably contributes to a stable, progressive society and thus benefits the social system as a whole as well as individuals.

Is this claim true? Does schooling enhance political behavior? Measures of political behavior are in their infancy, and their capacity as indicators of a healthy democracy is not yet determined. The indices are chiefly concerned with participation in political activities. Some of these are active membership in political organizations, attendance at political meetings, support of candidates, voting, and influencing the vote of others. Data bearing on these indices show that the higher the level of schooling the individual attains, the more likely he is to become engaged politically in these ways.[11]

A society must have some degree of social unity in order to carry on its various functions.[12] It can undergo one dissension after another as long as there is common ground on which to stand while the struggles over issues and conflicting commitments are being settled. In an open society some of the ingredients of the common ground are commitment to procedure, belief in common virtues, traditions, ideology, and taming all forms of power. Whatever values may characterize a society, it is watchful of its unity. A society always attempts to safeguard its cohesion by force, by control of communication, by schooling, and by such other means as may from time to time appear to be effective. The belief that schooling contributes significantly to the cohesion of society is deep seated in advanced countries. It partially explains state

---

[9]Ibid., p. 13.

[10]Ibid., p. 70.

[11]V. O. Key, *Public Opinion and American Democracy* (New York: Alfred A. Knopf, 1961), *passim.*

[12]Louis Wirth, "Preface" to Karl Mannheim, *Ideology and Utopia* (New York: Harcourt, Brace, 1936).

laws specifying that American history and patriotism be taught in the public schools of the United States.

Does schooling contribute to the cohesion of American society? Leaders of the teaching profession sometimes claim that it does. It is said that the school teaches social values, that it inculcates a way of life, and that it disciplines youth in the procedures for identifying and criticizing values and resolving conflicts. These are what the school supposedly teaches. But that is not at issue. The basic question is: What are the indices of social cohesion? Clues to indicators of cohesion are hard to come by in the literature. Only a few suggestions can be given here. The degree of social cohesion may be indicated by the ability of a society to meet its internal and external conflicts constructively, the amount of like response to symbols, the amount of consensus on ideals, the ability to stand together in a social crisis, and the similarity of outlook across generations.

The contribution of schooling to social cohesion is probably conditioned by its purpose as much as by its quantity. A program of schooling that emphasizes economic returns on one's investment in schooling rather than other utilities is likely to yield a disintegrative effect in a prolonged or severe crisis such as the Great Depression of the 1930s. Furthermore, if this utility is highlighted in justification of higher education, a large supply of highly trained people who cannot find employment commensurate with their training can be a source of dissension and bitter opposition to the system.

The general problem of social utility can now be restated. Knowledge, skills, and attitudes are taught in the school. These entities are testable, except perhaps for attitudes, and thus teachers can determine how effective their instruction is. Assume that the instruction induced the desired learnings. At this point, the school is successful, judged by its internal standards. But is it successful when social dividends are considered? At the present time this question can be partly answered for economic utility; for other social returns the answer cannot be given. It is possible to state something of what an empirical answer would require. Assume that the goals of a society are identified. Assume also that the maximum and minimum effects of schooling upon society's progress toward these ends are determined. If numerical indices are then assigned to different levels of schooling that approximate the point of maximum return, it can be said that these indices are a measure of the utility of schooling.

To sum up, it is well to bear in mind that the suggested list of utilities is only partial and is not as important as the problem posed. An exhaustive list of possible utilities is not needed. The aim of research should be to establish a few crucial criteria by which to determine what schooling is most beneficial to society and the individual. Issues concerning what programs the school should provide, whether general or technical schooling is better, how much schooling should be compulsory, alternative forms of schooling, or alternatives to schooling itself are being discussed in a data vacuum. In the absence of external criteria to guide the collection and interpretation of data on these issues, one hears arguments based on personal experience, random observations, sentiments, and pedagogical and social doctrines. At best these issues are considered in the light of data bearing on dropout rates, achievement of poverty groups, equality of educational opportunity, adolescent interests and problems, changes in the character of school populations, and the like. Until research has established criteria for determining the benefits of schooling, basic educational policies will continue to be decided by idle and inconclusive arguments and inadequate data.

Some fundamental questions could be answered were a breakthrough on this problem to occur. How many years of schooling should be required? What should be the minimum level of achievement in basic skills and various areas of knowledge? What is the school accountable for? How much emphasis can be given to schooling for self-realization? Consider an abstract society in which progressive changes in the school continue to increase the level of schooling of the total population. Would the crucial social utilities of schooling reach a maximum? Theoretically, they would. The maximum would be the point where the benefits would no longer be increased by an increase in schooling for the populace. At this point there would be no reason to improve or extend the school for these utilities. The nation would then enjoy educational prosperity.

What about personal utility in this abstract society? An approach to this question can be made if it is assumed that the society must have economic and social well-being before it can devote energy to the ideal of self-cultivation on a universal scale. If this assumption were allowed, the society could turn to the utility of schooling for the personal development of every individual after the maximum of social utility is in sight. At last education could become its own end.

Social Utility of the Disciplines

We have seen how the generic forms of knowledge are used as one deals with his environment. When these various forms take on a content their use becomes specialized. We interpret social events by social science concepts and not by the concepts of other disciplines. This does not mean that cognitive forms such as concepts and laws function differently from one content area to another but rather their use is restricted by the nature of the phenomena to be dealt with.

Several ways have been devised for ascertaining the utility of the various disciplines. These have either sought the knowledge demanded by various jobs and tasks, or else, the knowledge which is used by individuals in their daily activities as family members, citizens, and so on. It has been found that some words, arithmetic skills, geographic and historical facts, and grammatical constructions are used more frequently than others. These findings have led to the elimination of relatively useless material from the curriculum, rendering the curriculum more beneficial to individuals as they perform their out-of-school responsibilities. In this sense, much knowledge has specific utility for the individual. The individual can do tasks involving simple arithmetic, spell commonly used words, find locations on maps, and do other things too numerous to mention.

However, the specific knowledge for collective societal benefits is not so easily specifiable if indeed it can be identified at all. What specific knowledge, for example, distinguishes the good citizen? What specific knowledge, if taught to all individuals, will increase national productivity or increase military effectiveness? What knowledge will sustain social cohesion? Perhaps these ends are attained by the amount and thoroughness of schooling rather than by particular disciplines. At any rate this is the question considered in the following selection. The argument of this selection may not be sound, either logically or empirically. After you examine it carefully, try to formulate your thoughts about it. If the argument is acceptable, what difference would it make in the curriculum were we to follow it?

☐

Three basic dimensions of the school program can be identified: amount of schooling expressed as time spent;[13] kinds of subject matter expressed as scientific, humanistic, and technical; and thoroughness of instruction and learning expressed as measures of achievement. Although these dimensions can be combined in a number of ways, the most plausible hypotheses to be generated from them are as follows: The societal benefits of schooling are maximized by increasing (1) the amount and thoroughness of schooling or (2) the amount and thoroughness of schooling in specified subjects. These hypotheses differ in that the first proposition makes the school program flexible since no particular subjects are required, and the second prescribes particular kinds of content.

Certain considerations favor the view that the utility of schooling for either the individual or society is independent of any particular content once the achievement floor has been attained. On first view, however, the proposition that various utilities of schooling can be affected by the content of instruction appears to be true. What can be more certain than that one's behavior is changed by the knowledge he acquires? If a pupil learns to type, obviously he will perform differently when he wants to use a typewriter from what he would have done previously. If a pupil learns the elementary concepts and principles of mechanics, he will be able to talk about mechanical efficiency, whereas before he probably could not have done so.

If individual behavior is changed by particular knowledge, why are the social utilities of schooling not also affected? The answer is not far to seek. Some behavior is content-specific. If an individual practices medicine, works as a secretary, or is a dairy farmer, a competent analysis can readily identify much of the knowledge he possesses. But if the individual engages in political activities as a citizen, his knowledge is not as evident. Assume . . . that the

B. Othanel Smith and Donald E. Orlosky, *Socialization and Schooling* (Bloomington, Ind.: Phi Delta Kappa, 1975), pp. 113–20. Reprinted with permission of the publisher.

[13]For an exploration of the importance of this factor see J. B. Carroll, "A Model of School Learning," *Teachers College Record* 64 (1963):723–33; and David E. Wiley, *Another Hour, Another Day: Quantity of Schooling, A Potent Path for Policy,* Studies of Educative Processes, Report No. 3 (July 1973).

amount of participation varies directly with the amount of schooling. How much of his participation could be attributed to learning acquired in the social studies program? It seems reasonable to assume that such behavior can be attributed to the content most closely associated with it. But what is reasonable is not necessarily the case. Political participation could be associated with a mass of information acquired from different disciplines. It could be generated by knowledge derived from scientific sources, the study of literature and other art forms, or from the whole complex of school studies.

In fairness, however, it should be noted that history and civics have been required of every pupil for several decades. Increased political participation with increased schooling may be attributable to involvement in these studies. It would seem that elementary school graduates participate less than high school graduates because they have had less exposure to history and civics. However, the connection between the content of these studies and political behavior is tenuous. One must ask why individuals participate in political activities. Is it because of a sense of duty generated by instruction in history and civics? Is it because of the knowledge of history and government they acquired in school? Do they participate because of the network of economic and social connections in which they are involved as citizens and workers? When one considers the vast complex of forces that play upon the individual, it seems improbable that a few hours of instruction in one or two school subjects could account for his political behavior. Nevertheless, the question must remain open, for relevant data are not available.

Some social utilities are not dependent upon the behavior of individuals *per se* but rather are social phenomena involving countless kinds of behavior of myriad individuals. Economic utility is an example. The chain of influence linking it to any particular content is long and devious—if indeed the chain exists at all. Claims are often made that certain academic knowledge classified as general education has universal value and thus should be required of every pupil. The available evidence, scant though it is, lends no support to such claims when measured against the criterion of economic growth.[14] It is likely that the *level* of schooling attained in a society is more closely associated with economic growth than is a particular *kind* of schooling.

Social cohesion is another utility that does not depend upon the behavior of individuals. There is apparently no cohesive behavior *per se*. At first glance, however, it would appear that social cohesion is associated with schooling that emphasizes social values and political knowledge. A great deal has been made of the importance of values and the contribution of the humanities to the development of a value system, but it is a far cry from this claim to social cohesion. Commonly held values are undoubtedly essential to a society's stability. It does not follow, however, that such values are either generated or sustained by instruction in the humanities. Rather, common values are in all probability developed by participation in conjoint activities and sustained by institutions.[15] Furthermore, social cohesion may depend upon the image of society possessed by its members. The development of such an image may be

---

[14]Psacharopoulos, *Returns to Education,* p. 70.

[15]William Graham Summer, *Folkways* (Boston: Ginn and Company, 1906), pp. 1–119.

influenced more by the total school program than by a particular part of it. The following observation by Louis Wirth helps to elucidate this point:

> A society is possible in the last analysis because the individuals in it carry around in their heads some sort of picture of the society. Our society, however, in this period of minute division of labor, of extreme heterogeneity, and profound conflict of interests, has come to pass where these pictures are blurred and incongruous. Hence we no longer perceive the same things as real, and coincident with our vanishing sense of a common reality we are losing our common medium for expressing and communicating our experiences. The world has been splintered into countless fragments of atomized individuals and groups. The disruption in the wholeness of individual experience corresponds to the disintegration in culture and group solidarity. When the bases of unified collective action begin to weaken, the social structure tends to break and to produce a condition which Emile Durkheim has termed *anomie,* by which he means a situation which might be described as a sort of social emptiness or void. Under such conditions suicide, crime, and disorder are phenomena to be expected because individual existence no longer is rooted in a stable and integrated social milieu and much of life's activity loses its sense and meaning.[16]

If Wirth's analysis is correct, there can be no doubt of the need to strengthen the forces of social integration. The task appears to be of such magnitude that one must question the contribution that a particular content of the school program can make. The matter cannot be settled until measures of social cohesion are available and ways of ascertaining the advantages of schooling have been worked out.

What about methods of teaching and curriculum designs? Do they influence the utility of schooling? If they influence achievement, perhaps they do. Types of curricula and methods of instruction are repeatedly advanced as significant influences upon achievement. A number of surveys of research literature contravene this claim. Walker and Schaffarzick have made one of the most extensive analyses of curriculum research, covering twenty-three studies made since 1957.[17] They strongly suggest that the new curricula are not superior to the traditional curricula when the content bias in the achievement tests is taken into account. They observe that "different curricula are associated with different patterns of achievement" found in the curricula themselves.

Their guarded conclusions are in agreement with those reached by others, particularly by Wallen and Travers, who reviewed research on methods and found that methods apparently made no difference,[18] and by Stephens, who concluded that such variables as methods, team teaching, programmed instruction, and a host of other variables fail to show consistent differences in

---

[16]Louis Wirth, "Preface" to Karl Mannheim, *Ideology and Utopia* (New York: Harcourt, Brace, 1936).

[17]Decker F. Walker and Jon Schaffarzick, "Comparing Curricula," *Review of Educational Research* 44, 1 (Winter 1974):83–111.

[18]N. E. Wallen and M. W. Travers, "Analysis and Investigation of Teaching Methods," in *Handbook of Research on Teaching,* ed. N. L. Gage (Chicago: Rand McNally, 1963), pp. 448–505.

achievement.[19] While these analyses do not show conclusively that such variables have no influence upon achievement, they certainly indicate that fundamental conceptual analyses and empirical studies based thereon must be made before one can be reasonably certain about the effects of curriculum types and methods of teaching. In the meantime, it seems wiser to assume that neither of these factors is associated with individual or social utility of schooling.

It is interesting to note what Walker and Schaffarzick have to say about content:

> If the designers of the studies we have reviewed realized that the curricula they were comparing would have different patterns of outcomes, why did they try to compare these outcome patterns with an agglomerate achievement test yielding only one composite score? And why ... is there no systematic apparatus at local, state, regional, or federal levels of school policy making for considering the merits of various items of content that might be included in the school curriculum or in tests used to judge the success of students, teachers, or curricula? Why is it virtually impossible to find research which attempts to discover the consequences of studying different items of content, when there is so much research on the consequences of different media, methods, or strategies of teaching? And why do schools and funding agencies spend so much on organizational and technological innovations that have not been shown to produce different patterns of achievement and relatively little on innovations in curriculum materials?[20]

The relation of particular types of subject matter to the social utilities of schooling is a fundamental curriculum question, and one on which much research must be done. It is not improbable that the use of various criteria of utility against which to evaluate curriculum content would go a long way toward answering the perennial question: What knowledge is of most worth? It could turn out that some information now in the curriculum has little utility and that some not included has great utility. It seems just as likely, however, that the total impact of the school determines the social utility of schooling rather than any specifiable content.

Summary

One of the perennial problems that the teacher and curriculum worker faces is the out-of-school usefulness of what is taught. The question of utility involves the relationship, if any, between what is learned in school and the functions that the individual performs out of school. It seems clear that the individual in his daily activities will interpret and explain aspects of his environment as the need arises regardless of whether he is schooled or not. Even the illiterate primitive individual, shaped in the ways of a primitive tribe, will interpret and explain his environment to himself and others. The differ-

---

[19]J. M. Stephens, *The Process of Schooling* (New York: Holt, Rinehart and Winston, 1967). Stephens reached about the same conclusion from an analysis of research studies made in the first three decades of this century. See his *The Influence of the School on the Individual* (Ann Arbor, Mich.: Edwards Brothers, 1933).

[20]Decker Walker and Jon Schaffarzick, "Comparing Curricula," *Review of Educational Research* 44, 1 (Winter 1974):98.

ence between the individual who is schooled and the one who is not lies in the kinds of concepts and principles employed to interpret the world. The individual who is schooled will use more sophisticated concepts and principles and will be more skilled in the use of them than ihe unschooled individual. There is a sense, therefore, in which the function of the school is to provide the individual with more sophisticated concepts with which to understand things and human beings.

But when we go beyond the interpretative use of schooling and jump to the conclusion that schooling will improve the individual as a member of a family, as a citizen, and as one who will use his leisure properly and care for his health we leap a chasm. There is no halfway station; we cannot negotiate it in two leaps, as Clemenceau said of Wilson's League of Nations. The accomplishments of schooling and the ends of life are not the same; often there is a deep gorge between the two.

While the impact of the teacher and the school may shape in some measure, perhaps less than we wish to think, the kind of person who will choose the ends we desire, it is by no means clear that the school can guarantee that the individual will use what he has learned for these purposes, nor that it would be desirable were the schools able to do so. To urge the belief that the individual can be educated to use knowledge for out-of-school purposes envisioned by teachers and curriculum workers is tantamount to urging that the teaching profession control the individual if not the society.

The foregoing argument has been put rather bluntly for the purpose of challenging you to examine with far more care than is usually done claims about the usefulness of what is taught. We should consider with care the question of whether or not in fact we are teaching knowledge that improves the interpretative capacity of our students. We should certainly consider, indepth, the question of whether or not the content of the curriculum and our methods of instruction are capable of achieving such aims as worthy home membership, good citizenship, correct or humane conduct toward others, worthy use of our leisure time, and a host of other aims with which most of us are familiar. We are not condemning our efforts to attain the lofty ideals of education, but on the contrary inviting you to examine our claims about the curriculum's utility to be sure that we are standing on solid ground.

Chapter **11**

The Perennial Problem of Sequencing

Instructor. 83. 2 (October 1973):188.

"What with a systems approach, teacher-pupil planning, and experience units, we should be able to pull off this curriculum each day and still be home for the 11 o'clock news."

The question of how to arrange knowledge to maximize learning arises anew with almost every change in curriculum theory and practice. At least since the time of Comenius we have been told that instruction should move from the simple to the complex, or from the concrete to the abstract. Several other ways to answer the question of sequencing developed with the emergence of child study in this century. Under the influence of evolutionary theory we were told that the child's development recapitulates the history of the race . This was interpreted to mean that children should learn about primitive life, and read about and do the things that characterized the earlier stages of human development before they were engaged in the more complex activities and learnings of the modern world. This theory has long since been abandoned, but developmental theory still influences the way we sequence knowledge and instruction.

Overview

Recently we have been referring to Piaget's stages of development, using them to guide our ordering both instructional activities and materials. Thus we are told that the child moves from a sensory-motor stage to a preoperational stage. This is followed by a stage of concrete operations, and finally by the fourth stage—formal operations.

Bruner, on the other hand, recognizes three stages: enactive, iconic, and symbolic. These roughly correspond to action, imagery, and symbolic thinking. All these are refinements, however important, of the time-honored pedagogical prescription suggested by Comenius and a host of others in the course of educational history.

Another view of sequencing knowledge and instruction stems from the belief that the school should enable children to become self-directing, and that the best way to accomplish this is to free the child of subject matter requirements. This obviates the problem of ordering knowledge and instruction. Children are to become involved in situations. As they learn to cope with situations they acquire whatever knowledge is needed in whatever sequence is appropriate to their individual needs. In this view, the question of how to arrange knowledge to maximize learning is answered automatically and is of no particular pedagogical concern.

A third answer to the question of how to arrange knowledge is rooted in the notion of prerequisite learnings. The arrangement of knowledge for learning in this case is determined by ascertaining the heirarchy of knowledge involved in the attainment of a particular objective. This position stands or falls on the question of whether or not there are learning hierarchies and whether the steps in learning that lead to the objective can be delineated.

Sequencing According to Need

When the curriculum is considered a process of living; that is, coping with situations as they arise, it is pointless to try to order knowledge for learning. All that can be said is that the learner will select information he needs as he confronts the situation.

The view that the curriculum is a process of living is currently embraced in the psychosocial humanistic orientation. But it is a well-established position, dating back at least to the eighteenth century. This position and its implications for the selection and organization of knowledge and learning has never been better stated than by William Heard Kilpatrick. His view about the curriculum as a process of living follows.

☐

Some who still think of the curriculum as specified content will be troubled at seeing it here called a process of living. This shift from the static outlook of content to the dynamic outlook of process is but part of a very inclusive modern tendency permeating the development of thought for now nearly three centuries. It is the fault, not the virtue, of education that it has adhered so tenaciously to static conceptions. The shift to the dynamic is long overdue.

We begin accordingly with life as an ongoing and developing interaction between the organism and its environment. For us here there are two sides to the process: on the one hand, a child growing up; on the other, the surrounding

William Heard Kilpatrick, *Remaking the Curriculum* (New York: Newson and Company, 1936), pp. 46–53. Reprinted with permission of the author and publisher.

Footnotes have been renumbered consecutively throughout the chapter.

group and cultural life amid which the child thus develops and in which he is increasingly to share. We who are interested from both angles wish, as regards the child, that as he lives and grows he may live fully and happily; and, in behalf of the group, that he may ever share more responsibly and helpfully in carrying forward the common social life.

The curriculum becomes then all of the child's life for which the school carries responsibility. In our democratic society certain aims immediately emerge for guiding the work of the school. We aim that our children, as they grow up, shall increase in intelligent self-direction and in richness of personality. We wish them to share ever more fully in the group life on a basis of ever more adequate and responsible consideration of all concerned. As regards the culture of the surrounding life, our youth must . . . learn it as they share ever more fully in that life. They must, however, so learn this culture as, on the one hand, to escape ever better from its mere domination and, on the other hand, to be ever more able and disposed to share in the continuous process of remaking it as the need shall continually arise. The task of the curriculum is to help each child so to live and grow that these several aims may be progressively realized.

A New Type of Curriculum Unit

From our organismic conception the unit element of such a curriculum becomes, not a specified lesson of subject matter to be learned, as was formerly held, but a person facing an actual situation. That is, the unit is an actual instance of child living—this, for the teacher, to be educatively conceived and educatively directed. That this conception demands the thoroughgoing reconstruction of any remaining traditional type of school practice is here consciously intended. It is hardly possible to overemphasize the radical character of the transformation sought. Many elementary schools, especially for the early years, have already gone far with this transformation. Few secondary schools, however, have, so far as this writer knows, been able as yet to see beyond specified separate subjects. Most still think in the old terms.

Let us examine more closely how the educative process is carried on in such a curriculum unit; more specifically, how study and learning go on when a child faces an actual situation to deal effectively with it. The effort at this point is to see the educative process going on in and through an instance of actual child directed living.

(1) Suppose a child faces a situation. First of all there is in him that which makes this a situation for him, and second there is in the environment something that so stirs him that he is moved to act. Only as these things happen together does a child face an actual situation.

So stated, many will properly see the old doctrine of interest presented in new dress. The aim here is to reaffirm that doctrine. By interest in any full or desirable sense we mean that the child as he faces an actual situation is so unified within that he is, as we say, centered on the thing at hand. Positively he is stirred to act zealously; negatively he is not so divided within as to be unable or unwilling to give himself intently and determinedly to what he is doing. Admittedly there are degrees of such interest; we wish it as wholehearted as possible. Some will at once ask, "But suppose the children are not interested?" For answer we say that unless children are ill or have been miseducated, they are eager to be actively engaged. Their active interests may not of course be what we should prefer. In such case we have to do the best we can. But we must start where the child's interests now are, help him to choose the best among them, and then help these to grow into something better. Many teachers, willfully, will not have it so. They still insist on beginning with subject matter. Their danger is that by suppressing the child they develop the bad instead of the better. Children used to the old dictation-of-subject-matter-from-above, like pathologic cases everywhere, require careful treatment; but tact and wisdom along better lines will usually pay increased dividends.

(2) Facing thus an actual life situation, the second step is to analyze it, partly to set up or clarify ends, partly to get materials for the planning that comes next.

(3) The third step is to make one or more plans and choose from among them, for dealing with the situation. In a developing situation the plan will be in process of making from step-to-step as the situation develops. Planning is clearly an imaginative and creative step, but the imagination is checked and molded by the hard facts of the situation.

(4) Then comes the step of putting the plan into operation, watching meanwhile to see how it works, so that if need arise revision may be made.

(5) If the plan succeeds, a final stage is the backward look to see what has been done and how it might be done better another time.

We are to think of the foregoing not so much as separate chronological steps, though they may be so, but rather logical phases that enter into any instance of dealing with an actual situation, whether it be building a campfire or writing a play. The thing most to be valued is how the child, or the group, is active, dynamic, thinking, feeling, pushing ahead, moving forward physically—all these are taking place at each step and phase. And note that the process is self-directed and in general contains its own inherent testing. The children run it and learn by the practice. The campfire has to burn. The play has to go as a play. The children have to learn as they go.

How Study and Learning Enter

It is easy to see that study enters at each of these stages, most definitely perhaps after the first. In fact, study takes on new meaning when, as here, we see it as the effort to grapple intelligently with an ongoing process that may stall or run away from us if we do not give it the best thought of which we are capable.

Learning also enters at every stage and phase whenever we undertake to deal with a developing process. Life presents continual novelty. In relation to each such novel element and moment two things result: (1) in each succeeding new phase the mind has to do new and creative thinking, slight though it often may be; and (2) in each such phase the organism as a whole has to choose, either to accept or to reject, what it will do. These two elements exactly constitute learning, as we have seen.

In learning, then, the organism first contrives (creates) for itself something new, a new response. It may be a new idea, a new feeling in this relation, a new fact in relation, a new move in such a connection. Of course, neither thinking, nor feeling, nor moving ever goes simply alone. Always the other aspects also of the whole organism are involved in spite of our choosing to name one for especial consideration. Then comes the second aspect or phase of learning. In a novelly developing experience continual choices are necessary. Rival possible significances present themselves, rival hypotheses as to what are the facts, rival tendencies toward feeling or acting. We must choose. We accept one (at least to act on), we reject the others (at least for the time). Then occurs the miracle earlier referred to: whatever one accepts to act on is *by that very fact* built into one's very being, and there it abides on substantially equal terms with what was therein beforetimes included. Learning has taken place. The creation (first phase) and the incorporation (second phase) together constitute learning.

And all that was consciously weighed in making the choice is learned in the sense and degree that it was accepted or rejected, each along with the peculiar limitations and emphases that entered into the decision. And the decision there made is somehow registered in the nervous system to determine, unless later experience shall change the verdict, one's subsequent attitude toward using it and toward the selective conditions on which it will be used. And in this verdict thinking, feeling, impulse, bodily action, and all the rest concur. The learning is effected by, and is registered in, the whole of the organism.

These considerations show both the practical and the moral advantage of learning in situations that do in fact connect thinking properly with doing. What is thus learned, whether of idea or distinction, was accepted in and for action and so is learned (stored up) also for future action. To keep thought and action joined thus effectually together—the thought guiding the act and the act testing the thought—is precisely the way to build effectual character, both moral and prudential or practical. It is from such considerations that the proponents of this general position start with *a person facing a situation* and base their procedure on *acting on thinking*.

Macrosequencing: Its Developmental Basis

We refer to macrosequencing as the organization of knowledge and the formulation of instruction to coincide with the different stages of the individual's development. For a long time teachers have arranged the knowledge of instruction roughly in accordance with the development of the child. Examining the existing program of studies of almost any school proves that it corresponds roughly to the child's development.

The school program begins with simple experiences in nursery school and kindergarten. These roughly correspond to the preoperational stage of child development. At this level the child engages in activities that enable him to relate his experiences to his actions. The child also acquires linguistic forms. This stage continues into the more conventional school; that is, what is referred to as the lower grades. Here the program of studies emphasizes the development of the ability to handle symbols that represent objects, relationships, and intuitive concepts. While it is true that the school program has often emphasized the ability to acquire and interpret symbols such as words and pictures to the neglect of experiences with real things, the program has roughly corresponded to the preoperational stage, the stage represented by the movement from intuitive perceptions to the expression of thought in symbolic form.

Following this stage of development the school program, at least in its most progressive form, has emphasized learning through the manipulation of concrete things and the verbal formulation of experiences. In addition, the program also stresses classification and the acquisition of knowledge through symbols.

In the upper grades and the high school the program emphasizes logical reasoning through abstract symbols and through the native language. The amount of manipulation of concrete things becomes relatively less important in the instructional program, although the recent tendency has been to emphasize this aspect of development.

In the following excerpt Bruner suggests some educational implications of Piaget's stages of development. As you read his analysis reflect upon the school's program as you know it. Try to list the different defects in the program as judged against Piaget's stages. In what respects, if any, does that program need to be changed to make it conform more nearly to Piaget's stages of development? What bearing, if at all, do Piaget's stages have on the notion of prerequisite courses? Consider the order of courses now given in the elementary school. Is instruction arranged according to Piaget?

Intellectual Development. Research on the intellectual development of the child highlights the fact that at each stage of development the child has a characteristic way of viewing the world and explaining it to himself. The task of teaching a subject to a child at any particular age is one of representing the structure of that subject in terms of the child's way of viewing things. The task can be thought of as one of translation. The general hypothesis that has just been stated is premised on the considered judgment that any idea can be represented honestly and usefully in the thought forms of children of school age, and that these first representations can later be made more powerful and precise the more easily by virtue of this early learning. To illustrate and support this view we present here a somewhat detailed picture of the course of intellectual development, along with some suggestions about teaching at different stages of it.

The work of Piaget and others suggests that, roughly speaking, one may

Jerome S. Bruner. *The Process of Education* (Cambridge: Harvard University Press, 1960), pp. 33–40. Reprinted with permission of the author and publisher.

distinguish three stages in the intellectual development of the child. The first stage need not concern us in detail, for it is characteristic principally of the preschool child. In this stage, which ends (at least for Swiss school children) around the fifth or sixth year, the child's mental work consists principally in establishing relationships between experience and action; his concern is with manipulating the world through action. This stage corresponds roughly to the period from the first development of language to the point at which the child learns to manipulate symbols. In this so-called preoperational stage, the principal symbolic achievement is that the child learns how to represent the external world through symbols established by simple generalization; things are represented as equivalent in terms of sharing some common property. But the child's symbolic world does not make a clear separation between internal motives and feelings on the one hand and external reality on the other. The sun moves because God pushes it, and the stars, like himself, have to go to bed. The child is little able to separate his own goals from the means for achieving them, and when he has to make corrections in his activity after unsuccessful attempts at manipulating reality, he does so by what are called intuitive regulations rather than by symbolic operations, the former being of a crude trial-and-error nature rather than the result of taking thought.

What is principally lacking at this stage of development is what the Geneva school has called the concept of reversibility. When the shape of an object is changed, as when one changes the shape of a ball of plasticene, the preoperational child cannot grasp the idea that it can be brought back readily to its original state. Because of this fundamental lack the child cannot understand certain fundamental ideas that lie at the basis of mathematics and physics— the mathematical idea that one conserves quantity even when one partitions a set of things into subgroups, or the physical idea that one conserves mass and weight even though one transforms the shape of an object. It goes without saying that teachers are severely limited in transmitting concepts to a child at this stage, even in a highly intuitive manner.

The second stage of development—and now the child is in school—is called the stage of concrete operations. This stage is operational in contrast to the preceding stage, which is merely active. An operation is a type of action: it can be carried out rather directly by the manipulation of objects, or internally, as when one manipulates the symbols that represent things and relations in one's mind. Roughly, an operation is a means of getting data about the real world into the mind and there transforming them so that they can be organized and used selectively in the solution of problems. Assume a child is presented with a pinball machine which bounces a ball off a wall at an angle. Let us find out what he appreciates about the relation between the angle of incidence and the angle of reflection. The young child sees no problem: for him, the ball travels in an arc, touching the wall on the way. The somewhat older child, say age ten, sees the two angles as roughly related—as one changes so does the other. The still older child begins to grasp that there is a fixed relation between the two, and usually says it is a right angle. Finally, the thirteen- or fourteen-year old, often by pointing the ejector directly at the wall and seeing the ball come back at the ejector, gets the idea that the two angles are equal. Each way of looking at the phenomenon represents the result of an operation in this sense, and the child's thinking is constrained by his way of pulling his observations together.

An operation differs from simple action or goal-directed behavior in that it is internalized and reversible. "Internalized" means that the child does not have to go about his problem solving any longer by overt trial and error, but can actually carry out trial and error in his head. Reversibility is present because operations are seen as characterized where appropriate by what is called "complete compensation"; that is to say, an operation can be compensated for by an inverse operation. If marbles, for example, are divided into subgroups, the child can grasp intuitively that the original collection of marbles can be restored by being added back together again. The child tips a balance scale too far with a weight and then searches systematically for a lighter weight or for something with which to get the scale rebalanced. He may carry reversibility too far by assuming that a piece of paper, once burned, can also be restored.

With the advent of concrete operations, the child develops an internalized structure with which to operate. In the example of the balance scale, the structure is a serial order of weights that the child has in his mind. Such internal structures are of the essence. They are the internalized symbolic systems by which the child represents the world, as in the example of the pinball machine and the angles of incidence and reflection. It is into the language of these internal structures that one must translate ideas if the child is to grasp them.

But concrete operations, though they are guided by the logic of classes and the logic of relations, are means for structuring only immediately present reality. The child is able to give structure to the things he encounters, but he is not yet readily able to deal with possibilities not directly before him or not already experienced. This is not to say that children operating concretely are not able to anticipate things that are not present. Rather, it is that they do not command the operations for conjuring up systematically the full range of alternative possibilities that could exist at any given time. They cannot go systematically beyond the information given them to a description of what else might occur. Somewhere between ten and fourteen years of age the child passes into a third stage, which is called the stage of "formal operations" by the Geneva school.

Now the child's intellectual activity seems to be based upon an ability to operate on hypothetical propositions rather than being constrained to what he has experienced or what is before him. The child can now think of possible variables and even deduce potential relationships that can later be verified by experiment or observation. Intellectual operations now appear to be predicated upon the same kinds of logical operations that are the stock in trade of the logician, the scientist, or the abstract thinker. It is at this point that the child is able to give formal or axiomatic expression to the concrete ideas that before guided his problem solving but could not be described or formally understood.

Earlier, while the child is in the stage of concrete operations, he is capable of grasping intuitively and concretely a great many of the basic ideas of mathematics, the sciences, the humanities, and the social sciences. But he can do so only in terms of concrete operations. It can be demonstrated that fifth grade children can play mathematical games with rules modeled on highly advanced mathematics; indeed, they can arrive at these rules inductively and learn how to work with them. They will flounder, however, if one attempts to force upon them a formal mathematical description of what they have been doing, though they are perfectly capable of guiding their behavior by these rules. At the Woods Hole Conference we were privileged to see a demonstration of teaching in which fifth grade children very rapidly grasped central ideas from the theory of functions, although had the teacher attempted to explain to them what the theory of functions was, he would have drawn a blank. Later, at the appropriate stage of development and given a certain amount of practice in concrete operations, the time would be ripe for introducing them to the necessary formalism.

What is most important for teaching basic concepts is that the child be helped to pass progressively from concrete thinking to the utilization of more conceptually adequate modes of thought. But it is futile to attempt this by presenting formal explanations based on a logic that is distant from the child's manner of thinking and sterile in its implications for him. Much teaching in mathematics is of this sort. The child learns not to understand mathematical order but rather to apply certain devices or recipes without understanding their significance and connectedness. They are not translated into his way of thinking. Given this inappropriate start, he is easily led to believe that the important thing is for him to be "accurate"—though accuracy has less to do with mathematics than with computation. Perhaps the most striking example of this type of thing is to be found in the manner in which the high school student meets Euclidian geometry for the first time, as a set of axioms and theorems, without having had some experience with simple geometric configurations and the intuitive means whereby one deals with them. If the child were earlier given the concepts and strategies in the form of intuitive geometry at a level that he could easily follow, he might be far better able to grasp deeply the meaning of the theorems and axioms to which he is exposed later.

But the intellectual development of the child is no clockwork sequence of events; it also responds to influences from the environment, notably the school environment. Thus instruction in scientific ideas, even at the elementary level, need not follow slavishly the natural course of cognitive development in the child. It can also lead intellectual development by providing challenging but usable opportunities for the child to forge ahead in his development. Experience has shown that it is worth the effort to provide the growing child with problems that tempt him into next stages of development. As David Page, one of the most experienced teachers of elementary mathematics, has commented:

In teaching from kindergarten to graduate school, I have been amazed at the intellectual similarity of human beings at all ages, although children are perhaps more spontaneous, creative, and energetic than adults. As far as I am concerned young children learn almost anything faster than adults do if it can be given to them in terms they understand. Giving the material to them in terms they understand, interestingly enough, turns out to involve knowing the mathematics oneself, and the better one knows it, the better it can be taught. It is appropriate that we warn ourselves to be careful of assigning an absolute level of difficulty to any particular topic. When I tell mathematicians that fourth grade students can go a long way into "set theory" a few of them reply: "Of course." Most of them are startled. The latter ones are completely wrong in assuming that "set theory" is intrinsically difficult. Of course it may be that nothing is intrinsically difficult. We just have to wait until the proper point of view and corresponding language for presenting it are revealed. Given particular subject matter or a particular concept, it is easy to ask trivial questions or to lead the child to ask trivial questions. It is also easy to ask impossibly difficult questions. The trick is to find the medium questions that can be answered and that take you somewhere. This is the big job of teachers and textbooks.

One leads the child by the well-wrought "medium questions" to move more rapidly through the stages of intellectual development, to a deeper understanding of mathematical, physical, and historical principles. We must know far more about the ways in which this can be done.

Microsequencing Based on Prerequisite Knowledge

It has long been recognized that sometimes learning one item of knowledge requires knowledge of another item. This is implicit in the notion that mastery of one course is considered essential for success in another course. While this notion is easily misconstrued and misused for administrative convenience, it is nevertheless true. In order to succeed in second-year French one must have a knowledge of first-year French, or in order to do algebra one should first have mastered certain elements of arithmetic.

However, the amount of prerequisite knowledge needed to continue studying a subject is probably much smaller than is generally supposed. It is almost impossible to establish enough specific prerequisite knowledge in history or social studies to justify a fixed sequence of knowledge within a unit of instruction let alone courses. The same is perhaps true for English, but a stronger case can be made for prerequisite knowledge in the sciences, foreign languages, and mathematics.

Under the influence of programmed instruction the problem of sequencing has become a primary consideration. No one has studied this problem more thoroughly than Robert Gagné. He has developed a theory of hierarchical learning in which the lower items of knowledge in the hierarchy must be mastered prior to attainment of the next echelon, and so on, until the end product has been attained. This ordering has given rise to a theory of diagnosis and remedial instruction. By giving pretests designed to test the students' knowledge of the various items in a hierarchy, the places at which the individual will have difficulty in progressing toward the end result can be identified. These are the places where his knowledge of the prerequisite elements is insufficient. By instructing him in deficiencies he overcomes his difficulty.

Gagné's theory has been criticized on the grounds that it fails to take into account Piaget's work on child development. This criticism is too extensive to include it as a reading in this volume, but you can easily refer to it.[1]

[1] Robbie Case, "Gearing the Demands of Instruction to the Developmental Capacities of the Learner," *Review of Educational Research* 45, 1 (1975):59–87.

In the following excerpt from one of Gagné's articles on this subject, you will be able to see what is entailed by the establishment of a hierarchy and how it can be used in instruction.

Some Initial Observations In a previous study of programmed learning (Gagné and Brown, 1961) several kinds of learning programs were used in the attempt to establish the performance, in high school boys, of deriving formulas for the sum of n terms in a number series. Additional observations with this material led us to the following formulation: In productive learning, we are dealing with two major categories of variables. The first of these is knowledge, that is, the capabilities the individual possesses at any given stage in the learning; while the second is instructions, the content of the communications presented within the frames of a learning program.

In considering further the knowledge category, it has been found possible to identify this class of variable more comprehensively in the following way: Beginning with the final task, the question is asked, What kind of capability would an individual have to possess if he were able to perform this task successfully, were we to give him only instructions? The answer to this question, it turns out, identifies a new class of task which appears to have several important characteristics. Although it is conceived as an internal "disposition," it is directly measurable as a performance. Yet it is *not the same* performance as the final task from which it was derived. It is in some sense *simpler,* and it is also *more general.* In other words, it appears that what we have defined by this procedure is an entity of "subordinate knowledge" which is essential to the performance of the more specific final task.

Having done this, it was natural to think next of repeating the procedure with this newly defined entity (task). What would the individual have to know in order to be capable of doing *this* task without undertaking any learning, but given only some instructions? This time it seemed evident that there were two entities of subordinate knowledge which combined in support of the task. Continuing to follow this procedure, we found that what we were defining was a *hierarchy* of subordinate knowledges, growing increasingly "simple," and at the same time increasingly general as the defining process continued.

By means of this systematic analysis, it was possible to identify nine separate entities of subordinate knowledge, arranged in hierarchical fashion (see Figure 11–1). Generally stated, our hypothesis was that (a) no individual could perform the final task without having these subordinate capabilities (i.e., without being able to perform these simpler and more general tasks); and (b) that any superordinate task in the hierarchy could be performed by an individual provided suitable instructions were given, and provided the relevant subordinate knowledges could be recalled by him. . . .

Figure 11-1. Hierarchy of knowledge for the task of finding formulas for the sum of *n* terms in a number series.

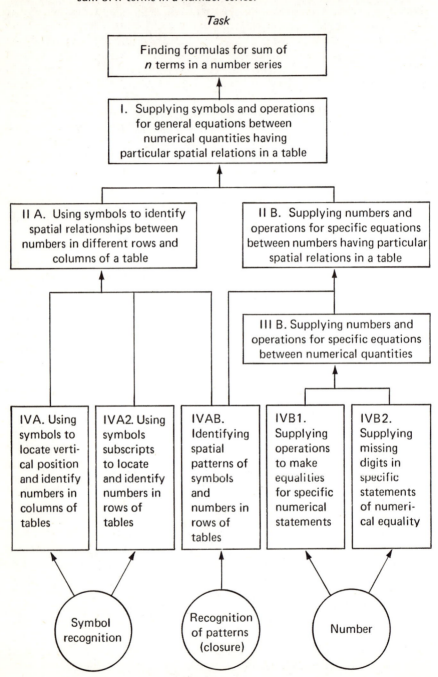

Subordinate Capabilities: Learning Sets   When one begins with the performance of a particular class of tasks as a criterion of terminal behavior, it is
possible to identify the subordinate learning sets required by means of the
procedure previously described. The question may be stated more exactly as,
"What would the individual have to be able to do in order that he can attain
successful performance on this task, provided he is given only instructions?"
This question is then applied successively to the subordinate classes of tasks
identified by the answer. "What he would have to be able to do" is in each case
one or more performances which constitute the denotative definitions of learning sets for particular classes of tasks, and totally for the entire knowledge
hierarchy.

A theory of knowledge acquisitions must propose some manner of functioning for the learning sets in a hierarchy. A good possibility seems to be that they
are mediators of positive transfer from lower level learning sets to higher level
tasks. The hypothesis is proposed that specific transfer from one learning set
to another standing above it in the hierarchy will be zero if the lower one
cannot be recalled and will range up to 100 percent if it can be.

In narrative form, the action of the two classes of variables in the acquisition
of knowledge is conceived in the following way . A human learner begins the
acquisition of the capability of performing a particular class of tasks with an
individual array of relevant learning sets, previously acquired. He then acquires new learning sets at progressively higher levels of the knowledge hierarchy until the final class of tasks is achieved. Attaining each new learning set
depends upon a process of positive transfer, which is dependent upon (a) the
recall of relevant subordinate learning sets, and upon (b) the effects of instructions.

Experimental Predictions and Results[2]

Using the procedure described, we derived the knowledge hierarchy depicted
in Figure 11–1 for the final task of "deriving formulas for the sum of n terms
in number series."

As mentioned previously, it contained nine hypothesized learning sets. . . .
Each of these subordinate knowledges can be represented as a class of task to
be performed.

Measuring Initial Patterns of Learning Sets   It is predicted that the presence
of different patterns of learning sets can be determined for individuals who are
unable to perform a final task such as the one under consideration. To test this,
we administered a series of test items to a number of ninth grade boys. These
items were presented on 4" X 6" cards, and the answers were written on
specially prepared answer sheets. This particular method was used in order to
make testing continuous with the adminstration of a learning program to be
described hereafter. Each test item was carefully prepared to include instructions having the function of identification of terminal performance and of
elements of the stimulus situation.

[2]The author is grateful to Bert Zippel, Jr., for assistance in the preparation of learning
program materials and in the collection of a portion of the data.

Beginning with the final task, the items were arranged to be presented in the order I, IIA, IVA, IVA2, IVAB, IIB, IIIB, IVB1, and IVB2. For any given subject, the sequence of testing temporarily stopped at the level at which successful performance was first reached, and a learning program designed to foster achievement at the next higher level (previously failed) was administered. . . .

A particular time limit was set for each test item, at the expiration of which the item was scored as failed. If a wrong answer was given before this time limit, the subject was told it was wrong, and encouraged to try again; if the correct answer was supplied within the time limit, the item was scored as passed. It is emphasized that these time limits, which were based on preliminary observations on other subjects with these tasks, were *not* designed to put "time pressure" on the subjects, nor did they appear to do so.

The patterns of success achieved on the final task and all subordinate learning set tasks, by all seven subjects, are shown in Table 11–1. The subjects have been arranged in accordance with their degree of success with all tasks, beginning with one who failed the final task but succeeded at all the rest. Several things are apparent from these data. First of all, it is quite evident that there are quite different "patterns of capability" with which individuals approach the task set by the study. Some are unable to do a task like IIA (see Figure 11–1), others to do a task like IIB which is of course quite different. Still others are unable to do either of these, and in fact cannot perform successfully a task like IIIB. All seven of these subjects were able to perform IV-level tasks successfully, although in preliminary observations on similar tasks we found some ninth grade boys who could not.

Second, the patterns of pass and fail on these tasks have the relationships predicted by the previous discussion. There are no instances, for example, of an individual who is able to perform what has been identified as a "higher level" learning set, and who then shows himself to be unable to perform a "lower level" learning set related to it.

If learning sets are indeed essential for positive transfer, the following consequences should ensue:

Table 11–1: Pattern of success on learning set tasks related to the final number series task for seven ninth grade boys

Subject	Task									
	Final	I	IIA	IIB	IIIB	IVA1	IVA2	IVAB	IVB1	IVB2
WW	–	+	+	+	+	+	+	+	+	+
WC	–	+	+	+	+	+	+	+	+	+
PM	–	–	–	+	+	+	+	+	+	+
GR	–	–	–	+	+	+	+	+	+	+
DJ	–	–	–	–	+	+	+	+	+	+
JR	–	–	–	–	–	+	+	+	+	+
RH	–	–	–	–	–	+	+	+	+	+

Note: + = Pass; – = Fail.

1. If a higher level learning set is passed (+), *all* related lower level tasks must have been passed (+).
2. If *one or more* lower level tasks have been failed (–), the related higher level tasks must be failed (–).
3. If a higher level task is passed (+), *no* related lower level tasks must have been failed (–).
4. If a higher level task has been failed (–), related lower level tasks may have been passed (+). The absence of positive transfer in this case would be attributable to a deficiency in instructions, and does not contradict the notion that lower level sets are essential to the achievement of higher level ones.

The relationships found to exist in these seven subjects are summarized in Table 11–2, where each possible higher, lower level task relationship possible of testing is listed in the lefthand column. It will be noted that there are several relationships of the type higher (–), lower (+), as listed in Column 5. These provided no test of the hypothesis regarding hierarchical relations among learning sets. The instances in the remaining columns do, however. The + + and – – instances are verifying, whereas + – instances would be nonverifying. As the final column indicates, the percentage of verifying instances is in all cases 100 percent. . . .

The division in the teaching profession about the way to handle sequencing content and instruction is rooted partly in ideologies. Some teachers insist that there should be no sequencing of content. On the contrary, they believe that the teacher should create an environment in which there would be a multiplicity of learning sequences. According to this view, sequencing content will be automatically cared for by the students as they take advantage of the opportunities created by the teacher.

Table 11–2: Pass-fail relationship between related adjacent higher and lower level learning sets for a group of seven ninth grade boys

Relationship examined	Number of cases with relationship				Test of relationships	
	Higher+ Lower+	Higher– Lower–	Higher+ Lower–	Higher– Lower+	N (1+2+3)	Proportion (1+2)/ (1+2+3)
Final task: I	0	6	0	1	6	1.00
I: IIA, IIB	1	5	0	1	6	1.00
IIA: IVA1, IVA2, IVAB	2	0	0	5	2	1.00
IIB: IIIB	3	2	0	2	5	1.00
IIIB: IVAB, IVB1, IVB2	5	0	0	2	5	1.00

Note: + = Pass; – = Fail.

On the opposite side is the conventional notion that there is an order in the disciplines, and that this order should not be vitiated by the sort of loose construction that will result from following the opportunistic procedure. Consider the question of sequencing in your own area of specialization. Which of the positions do you find most compatible with your view of your field? What justification do you have for your opinion?

Types of Curriculum Structure

Sequencing content and instruction is only one aspect of the broader problem of determining the form of curriculum structure most conducive to learning. Curriculum structure has been considered not only from the standpoint of its vertical dimension but also in terms of the horizontal relationship among elements of knowledge such as is implied in the concepts of integration and correlation. Furthermore, each of these dimensions has been considered from a number of different angles. For this reason we have included a reading which systematically lays out the various types of curriculum structure.

☐

Curriculum theorists have repeatedly stressed the importance of providing for structure in the curriculum (Bruner, 1960; Gagné, 1971; Goodlad and Richter, 1966; Johnson, 1969; Taba, 1962; Tyler, 1950). Many theorists have not only exhorted curriculum developers to structure their curricula but have identified factors related to the extensiveness of curriculum structure. Such factors have included "continuity," "sequence," and "integration" (Tyler, 1950); "spiraling" (Bruner, 1961; Schrader, 1972); "hierarchical arrangement" (Briggs, 1968; Gagné, 1971); "flat" versus "vertical structure" (Briggs, 1968); "kinetic" versus "static structure" and "commonality" versus "progression" (Anderson, 1971); and "coherence" (Schrader, 1972).

With such diverse terms as these in the literature and little or no attempt made to relate one to another, a synthesis is needed (a) to summarize these notions and (b) to suggest a parsimonious set of concepts for thinking about curriculum structure extensiveness encompassing the range of structuring factors mentioned above.

Curriculum and Its Elements

Curriculum, for the purpose of this paper, is defined as "a structured series of intended learning outcomes" (Johnson, 1967, p. 130). A curriculum, according to this conception, consists of a series of intended learning outcomes (ILOs) organized into some structural arrangement. The basic unit of a curriculum

George J. Posner, "The Extensiveness of Curriculum Structure: A Conceptual Scheme," *Review of Educational Research* 44, 4 (Fall 1974):401–406. Copyright © 1973, American Educational Research Association, Washington, D.C. Reprinted by permission of author and publisher.

is, thus, an ILO, or a microcurriculum element. In contrast to microelements, macroelements are classes or categories of ILOs.

Curriculum can be conceptualized at different levels of generality depending upon whether structure involves micro or macroelements. Microelements (individual intended learnings, i.e., cognitions, performance capabilities, or affects) can be inferred from an analysis of classroom discourse and textbooks, or can be derived directly from lists of objectives and major ideas. Macroelements (categories of microelements) can occur at different levels of generality, ranging from a lesson, to a unit, to a course, to a whole program and are described in syllabi, curriculum guides, course offerings, and program sequences.

Curriculum Structure in the Literature

Although curriculum structure has been discussed by many writers, the work of four investigators is particularly useful. These four have provided explicit definitions of various structuring factors allowing one to compare and contrast their conceptions of structure. Therefore, the present review focuses primarily on the notions of these theorists.

The chart in Table 11–3 summarizes the structuring factors defined by Anderson (1971), Briggs (1968), Schrader (1972), and Tyler (1950).

Convergence can be found in the ideas of these four writers through their common conception of curriculum structure. All four either implicitly (Briggs, 1968; Tyler, 1950) or explicitly (Anderson, 1971; Schrader, 1972) view structure in curriculum as dependent upon the number and degree of relationships between curriculum elements. Although some overlap is thus evident, the factors identified by these four writers are obviously not equivalent. The problem, then, is to develop a scheme based on these factors but not specific to any one writer's conceptions. In this way, the scheme may help to synthesize these seemingly diverse conceptions into a unified framework.

A Scheme for Curriculum Structure

Curriculum structure extensiveness can be conceptualized along two dimensions, namely, the commonality and the temporality of the relationships between curriculum elements.

Commonality The first factor, commonality, refers to the degree to which pairs of elements are identical versus independent (Anderson, 1971). A continuum can be imagined along the dimension of commonality. Pairs of elements with the greatest degree of commonality are those in which the elements are identical or *repeated*. At the other end of the continuum are pairs of elements in which the elements are completely *unrelated*. Between these two extremes are those pairs in which the elements are neither identical nor independent but are *related* in some way.

Temporality The second dimension of curriculum structure in this scheme is the temporal quality of the relationship between elements. Elements in this

Table 11-3: A summary of structuring factors described by four major researchers

Tyler (1950)	Schrader (1972)	Anderson (1971)	Briggs (1967)
Continuity "vertical reiteration of elements"	*Continuity* measured by "... the number of consecutive... tasks in which [a given] ... theme is present"	*Commonality* "contiguous units with matching elements"	*Vertical Structure* "dependence of each vertically ordered element on the one immediately preceding"
Sequence "build on previous experience but going more broadly and deeply"	*Spiraling* measured by "... the number of total appearances of [a given theme] ... in more complex form"	*Progression* "contiguous units with unmatched elements"	*Hierarchical Structure* "the teaching of component skills in association with more complex ones"
Integration "horizontal relationship of curriculum experience"	*Coherence* representable as a ratio of the number of pairs of tasks which have a given theme in common, to the number of pairs of tasks with a prerequisite relationship		*Flat Structure* "independence of elements"
	Integration measured by "... the total number of distinctively different... areas or topics represented in the hierarchical levels of the task analysis"		

scheme can be either (a) vertically related (i.e., one element temporally subsequent to another) or (b) horizontally related (i.e., two elements temporally concurrent). In addition, vertically related elements can be either contiguous (i.e., one element related to another element directly following the first) or noncontiguous (i.e., one element related to another, temporally separated from the first by one or more unrelated elements). Since the distinction between contiguous and noncontiguous elements implies that elements are temporally separated, it does not apply to horizontally structured elements.

To reiterate, the commonality and the temporality of the relationship between elements together comprise the major dimensions of curriculum structure extensiveness. These two dimensions are summarized in Table 11–4.

Examples of curriculum structure in terms of these dimensions are presented in Table 11–5.

Using this scheme, one can translate commonly used terms in the literature reducing them to the dimensions of structure discussed above. For example, "continuity" (Schrader, 1972; Tyler, 1950) and "commonality" (Anderson, 1971) refer to the repeating of vertically contiguous elements. "Sequence" (Tyler, 1950), "spiraling" (Schrader, 1972), and "vertical structure" (Briggs, 1968) are terms for the relating of vertically contiguous elements. "Spiraling" (Bruner, 1960) can be considered the relating of vertically noncontiguous elements. "Integration" (Tyler, 1950) is equivalent to the relating of horizontal elements. "Flat structure" (Briggs, 1968) and "progression" (Anderson, 1971) both refer to unrelated elements, the former in the horizontal direction and the latter in the vertical direction.

Implications for Research

If the curriculum is defined as "a structured series of intended learning outcomes" (Johnson, 1967, p. 13), then it is appropriate for curriculum theory and research to be concerned with the selection and the structuring of intended learnings. Although more work is still needed, schema have been devised organizing intended learnings according to both type (Bloom, 1956; Krathwohl, Bloom and Masia, 1964) and substance (Phenix, 1964; Schwab, 1964; Tykociner, 1964). These schema may provide concepts suitable for framing research questions regarding the learning outcomes that should be pursued by educators.

Table 11–4: Dimensions of curriculum structure extensiveness

			Commonality		
			Repeated	Related	Unrelated
Temporality	Vertical	Contiguous			
		Noncontiguous			
	Horizontal				

Table 11–5: Examples of curriculum structure

		Commonality		
		Repeated	*Related*	*Unrelated*
Temporarlity	Vertical	*Macro:* Repeating American history until passed *Micro:* French class two days in a row deals with same part of speech	*Macro:* Intermediate algebra after elementary algebra *Micro:* Different systems of numeration taught successively	*Macro:* Geometry follows algebra *Micro:* Spelling lesson follows analysis of a poem
	Horizontal	*Macro:* Health and biology courses both teaching seventh graders about reproduction *Micro:* Neatness stressed in the dress, penmanship and grooming of all eighth grade English students	*Macro:* A historical novel about the Civil War studied in English concurrently with an analysis of civil war battles *Micro:* Lecture and text present F=ma while lab demonstrates a concrete example	*Macro:* Medieval history studied concurrently with arithmetic *Micro:* Memorization of the Declaration of Independence concurrently with the composition of the atmosphere

Table 11–6: Examples of variables for research in curriculum structure

I. Independent variables
    1. Extent of curriculum structure on microlevel
    2. Extent of curriculum structure on macrolevel
II. Dependent variables
    1. Student recall, retention, transfer, cognitive differentiation, etc.
    2. Student interest and satisfaction with course
    3. Student perception of structure
    4. Student awareness of program goals and learning objectives
    5. Teacher satisfaction with course
    6. Ease of instructional planning
    7. Ease of evaluation planning

Likewise, conceptual frameworks for curriculum structure are needed by curriculum workers. The few experimental studies that have been carried out in this area have only dealt with microlevel structures as independent variables and with student achievement as the dependent variable (see, for example, Anderson, 1968; Trindade, 1972). However, macrolevel curriculum structures are presumed important in every program with prerequisite courses and prescriptions for courses to be taken concurrently. Also, curriculum structure, whether macro or microlevel, presumably have affective consequences for students and affects the teacher's evaluation and instructional planning. Table 11–6 summarizes these potential research areas.

Summary

We have noted three different conceptions of sequencing. One, that the learner orders his own learning as he deals with a situation from moment to moment. He selects what he wants to know as the need arises. If he makes a mistake in the selection he simply goes through the process again until he finds that which satisfies his present need. This is an opportunistic notion of sequencing but those who advocate it maintain that it is psychologically sound.

Two, to maximize learning content must be ordered in accordance with the development of the individual. Because development is conceived of in stages that cover two or more years, the developmental notion gives little guidance to the teacher in his day-to-day task of sequencing content and instruction. Nevertheless, the macro approach is important in arranging the program of studies. You may wish, however, to examine this claim more closely and to determine for yourself whether or not the developmental approach is useful on a day-to-day or moment-to-moment basis in the classroom.

Three, is microsequencing. This assumes that for any learning task there is a hierarchy extending from the very simple to the more abstract and complex elements which lead to the attainment of a specified objective. This notion of sequencing is useful to the teacher as he deals with the students from moment to moment in his classroom. It affords a basis for diagnosing and remediation on the assumption that the hierarchy of knowledge is real and that the failure to learn is to be attributed to deficiency of knowledge at some point in the hierarchy.

These conceptions of sequencing are the source of much controversy in pedagogical circles, and the teacher, as well as the curriculum specialist, should be thoroughly aware of each one and its implications for curriculum development and instruction. In addition, it is important to be aware of the different ways to think about curriculum structure, both in its vertical and horizontal dimensions. Much is written about integration and correlation of learning, and it would be difficult to deny the significance of these concepts in curriculum development. The article by Posner opens up the area of curriculum structure for your exploration.

Chapter **12**

Putting the Curriculum to Work

"Well, it finally happened! The new curriculum we have developed is the same one we gave up 15 years ago."

The phrase "curriculum design" is often used in educational literature but is seldom clearly defined. As a consequence, discussions of curriculum design often are difficult to contrast with discussions of curriculum planning or curriculum decisions. Perhaps the most straightforward way to define curriculum design is to simply consider it as the "organization that puts the curriculum to work." But even such a "simple" statement is ambiguous. The introduction to this chapter attempts to reduce the confusion about curriculum design and to prepare readers to study curriculum design from a common orientation. The discourse and examples that follow have been provided to serve this purpose. Curriculum designing is organizing activities, personnel, and materials that support learning. Analogies and illustrations help clarify this definition of curriculum design.

Orientation

The term "design" is usually used in construction. An architect who designs a building takes ideas (symmetry, balance), products (steel, glass, cement), and function (place to work, live), and combines them into a form that accommodates these elements. The structure that combines these may be a house, an office building, a bridge, or a ship. When schools are organized into a structure they also comprise ideas (content), products (materials), and function (acquisition of knowledge) and combine them into a form that enables the schools to be effective. The architect's planned construction depends on his views about the elements regarded to be important.

The curriculum designer's task is similar. Curriculum design depends on the view of those who make decisions and the organizational arrangements they regard to be most useful. For example, when the core curriculum was recommended for the junior high school it represented one curriculum design. The core curriculum assumed that certain basic or "core" learnings could serve as an essential starting point for learning the breadth of the curriculum. In most cases the broad fields of social studies and language arts became the origin of the interrelationships among the subjects adolescents were taught. This basic premise lead to organizational decisions to "design" a school arrangement to accommodate the rationale of the core program. Some of these characteristics included (1) longer classes than the usual fifty minutes, (2) combined language arts and social studies within a class, (3) teachers trained in language arts and social studies, (4) emphasis on the relationships between language arts and social studies rather than teaching each as separate subjects.

The traditional approach to curriculum design in the secondary school assumes that high school students need to be taught by a specialist in each subject. It also assumes that students should be assigned in groups to teachers responsible for teaching a single subject in a fifty-minute period for one period each day of the week. This plan of organizing content and personnel constitutes two of the elements that determine the traditional design.

This chapter presents variations on curriculum designs and their rationale. These variations arise because different curriculum directors regard different factors to be important and/or regard different organizational arrangements to be effective. Furthermore, the orientation of the curriculum worker provides the "force" that influences curriculum design decisions.

Even when curriculum planners share a common orientation they may devise a different curriculum design. For example, those who advocate alternative schooling opportunities may recommend alternate schools on the one hand or alternates within a school on the other. Both approaches are an attempt to promote more student options in the school curriculum and each leads to a quite different design. The reader should be alert to the differences that arise in the design, or means, advocated by those whose results, or ends, are expected to be the same. The entire question of design and its importance is raised with this issue. Some may even argue that effective teachers will be successful in any reasonable design and incompetent personnel will not improve by merely organizing the schools differently. The reader should study each article in this chapter and determine the means and ends intended by the various designs. The reader should also attempt to classify the design by identifying the distinguishing characteristics such as organizational patterns, arrangements of personnel, or point of view about the content to be studied.

Curriculum designs are not easily classified as discreet types, however. The components of the curriculum are numerous and different people cooperate to plan and implement curricular design. This mixture of ideas and different viewpoints from curriculum workers adds heavily to the difficulty of reaching agreement on the optimum design to use. Teachers, for example, may vary their behavior according to their individual orientation, and usually they adapt to a given design by adjusting it to their own preferences. A school may elect to design the curriculum around a concept like team teaching and design the curriculum accordingly. Within team teaching, one member of the team may emphasize an inquiry approach in group discussion; another may stress individualized instruction and learning stations. Individual variations in curriculum implementation can, and often do, contribute another dimension to curriculum design, and curriculum planners must face decisions about combinations and options such as nongraded schools, alternative schools, team teaching, individualized instruction, fused curriculum, vertical planning, horizontal planning, structure of content, types of knowledge, and an unusually extensive list of options. The organization of these components constitutes the problem that faces the curriculum designer.

Curriculum design poses at least one other major question: How to "package" content? Some may emphasize cognitive knowledge, others may view affective learnings to be most important, and others reject both and focus on the method or structure of the subject of study. The question of how to sequence the intended learnings and what the major thrust of the curriculum should be constitute two of the most important concerns about the curriculum. The design of the content by (1) selecting the learnings considered most important, (2) establishing a sequence that is effective, and (3) relating that sequence to other variables such as the maturation of learners and correlation with other knowledge is a major concern in curriculum design. This chapter presents different viewpoints about how to include content variations in the design of the curriculum.

Design for Humane Education

The following article presents the view that schools are designed to cope with a narrow spectrum of human behavior. This narrowness is evidenced by the failure of the schools to take more of the categories of developmental psychology into account when questions about the role of schools are asked. It is possible to systematically categorize the operational goals of teaching according to those psychological categories of development and to identify critical areas in which appropriate questions should be asked. The next article provides a discussion and explanation of how to proceed from the rationale that humaneness should be incorporated in curriculum design.

☐

The eloquent writing of the past few years on the theme of the humane school could result in yet another educational fad, with its accompanying rituals, jargon, and ultimate disillusionment. This theme, especially, invites pompous nonsense, and we have already heard enough.

Arthur W. Foshay, "Curriculum Design for the Humane School," *Theory Into Practice* 10(June 1971):204–7. Reprinted by permission of the author and publisher.

Footnotes have been renumbered consecutively throughout the chapter.

Let's hope it won't happen. That the schools are in many ways inhumane is easy to demonstrate. The idea that they need not be is one of the most inviting now on our minds. To avoid another disillusioning fad, we need to begin the process of turning our big shambles of an institution into the kind of nurturing social tool we have always intended it to be. And to do this, we need tools.

One such tool is an approach to curriculum design and evaluation that explicitly relates the human condition to the necessary goals of teaching. The purpose of this paper is to offer such an approach for the consideration of the profession.

To begin, we have to cope somehow with the word, "humane." How shall it be understood? Socially? Theologically? Physically? Since the beginning of civilization, the classicists have asked "What is Man?" and their answers are spread before us in the history of ideas, in literature, in the arts. The question is so broad that it seems beyond us educationists; we wait for some agreement among the authorities, but we know it will never come. Under these circumstances, lest we merely wait, we have to nerve ourselves and make an answer of our own—one we can use until a better one appears. One source we have often used has been developmental psychology, which has served us well: it underlies the kindergarten and nursery school curriculum, which many of us feel has been our most successful attempt at curriculum design. It has nourished the growth of guidance programs. We turn to it repeatedly as we attempt to design other programs. Where would some of the best current programs be, for example, without Piaget? Let us turn to it again.

Research in developmental psychology falls into recognizable categories. According to such research, people develop intellectually, emotionally, socially, aesthetically, spiritually, and physically. . . .

For our purposes, these categories have certain advantages. They do not grow from any particular philosophical or theological system, and need not conform to any particular set of limiting assumptions. They are open-ended and pragmatic. Most important, they define themselves empirically. Since what we try to do in schools is open-ended and pragmatic, and since we try to act according to what appears to happen instead of only in terms of what ought to happen, these categories may well serve to hold the term "humane" still for us long enough to carry on some work. Let's try them out here, at least in principle, and see what they yield. We'll come back to what they mean in a moment.

Before we do so, however, let us consider another set of categories, for in the interaction of the two sets we may find a helpful approach to curriculum design and evaluation.

The Operational Goals of Teaching

This second set of categories deals with the intentions teachers have that are independent of the subject matter they are working with at any given moment. We shall consider four: fluency, manipulation, confidence/value, and persistence.

Fluency   One goal of any teacher is that students become familiar with the symbol system, vocabulary, media, and the typical phenomena associated with the content he seeks to teach. . . . Fluency does not necessarily precede every-thing else in teaching—it may grow through time and experience—but it is always a necessary operational teaching goal.

Manipulation   Teachers also seek to lead students to manipulate the data out of which content is made. . . . To read is to draw understanding from a page —to manipulate the symbol system in such a way as to interpret it. An art experience does not consist of becoming familiar with the various art media and their properties. It consists of manipulating them in such a way as to make an art object. And so on. The ability to manipulate the data, which we often call "understanding," is a universal teaching goal.

Confidence/value   Teachers also seek to instill confidence in students—confidence that they can manipulate the data on their own. At the same time, teachers hope students will value the ability they acquire. . . . When we are teaching the way we know how to, we build confidence and value by repeatedly putting students on their own in the content, while calling their attention to the satisfactions associated with being on their own. We make the whole affair rewarding.

Persistence   If a student is fluent, has learned to manipulate the content, and has developed confidence and value, then we hope he will persist in "doing" the content after formal instruction has stopped. We hope the student who has learned to think historically will continue to do so, and that the budding pianist will play for pleasure on his own, later. While our failures in this area are grievous, they are not universal. The attrition of budding pianists is shocking; so is the attrition of budding mathematicians. But many children who learn to read go on reading, and there is much evidence that life-long persistence is kindled in school in science, the arts, athletics, and other fields.

The Psychological Categories

Now let us reconsider the categories of developmental psychology mentioned earlier. Each of them must be understood in some operational manner, if they are to be used operationally—and that is our intent here.

Intellectual   Bloom's *Taxonomy of Educational Objectives: Cognitive Do-main* serves as an elaboration of what this category includes. Most of us can claim a considerable acquaintance with it: we recognize the difference between Scheffler's "knowing that" and "knowing how"; we accept Bloom's "higher" and "lower" intellectual activities. . . .

Emotional   The idea that there is an emotional life that is not merely a pollution of the intellectual life is of our century. Samuel Johnson's *Dictionary* (1755) defines passion merely as a disturbance of the reason; we know better. The emotional development of children and young people has been a major preoccupation of the researchers and observers in developmental psychology for more than two generations. For us educationists, it is a familiar domain, though still in need of extensive exploration. . . .

Aesthetic   The idea that there is such a thing as aesthetic development came to prominence much more recently than did the ideas of intellectual, emotional, and social development. . . . In general, to borrow from Harry Broudy, aesthetic development consists of increasingly finer discriminations in the sensuous, formal, technical, and expressive meanings of art objects, whether produced by oneself or others, and whether visual, tactile, dramatic, poetic, or kinesthetic. . . .

Spiritual   By "spiritual" we refer to what people do about awe. We are awestruck creatures: we can ask questions that cannot be answered intellectually, emotionally, socially, aesthetically, or physically—questions that require not an answer, but a confrontation and an acknowledgment. The meaning of human existence, the possibility of a conscience, the concept of infinity ("Where is the end of the sky?"), Job's questions, all are examples. . . . All people are spiritual, even if not religious. One dare not deny this quality of what it is to be human.

Physical   The significance of the fact that we are physical beings has not been examined in nearly the depth the fact demands. Anyone who has worked with children has had to recognize the fact that they need to come to terms with their own bodies. As they mature, their "body image" changes, and with it their view of themselves. Years ago, in a book called *Children's Social Values,* I reported that some children saw themselves as physical creatures, from the neck up. Others have made similar findings. But an adolescent clearly sees himself in a full-length mirror. We offer little or no help to children's sense of themselves as physical beings, except (and for a small minority) in athletic programs. However, for the purposes of our analysis here, we should acknowledge that the physical self is a prominent part of the whole self, and call for more research on its significance as it interacts with the other qualities that enter into the human condition.

A Model for Curriculum Design and Evaluation

All this leads us to a design for the construction and evaluation of the curriculum. The six elements of the human condition from developmental psychology and the four elements of the operational goals of teaching may be arranged on a grid as follows:

A grid for curriculum design and evaluation

	Fluency	Manipulation	Confidence/ value	Persistence
Intellectual	1a	2a	3a	4a
Emotional	1b	2b	3b	4b
Social	1c	2c	3c	4c
Aesthetic	1d	2d	3d	4d
Spiritual	1e	2e	3e	4e
Physical	1f	2f	3f	4f

Where these qualities intersect, curriculum questions are raised. For example, cell 1a raises the question, "How does fluency in a given field contribute to the intellectual growth of a student?" Cell 3c raises the question, "How does confidence and value in a given field contribute to the social growth of a student?" Cell 4f raises the question, "How does persistence in a given field contribute to the sense of physical self of a student?"

All together, there are twenty-four cells in the grid, hence twenty-four questions to be confronted by the curriculum planner and the curriculum evaluator. Note that the great preponderance of our current curriculum design and evaluation efforts deal with only two of the cells—1a and 2a. That is, we ask in the main only that our curriculum efforts answer the question, "How do fluency and manipulation in a given subject field contribute to the intellectual growth of the student?" Our failure to deal with the other twenty-two questions implied by this analysis explains in some degree why students are "turned off" by the curriculum, and why the stereotype of the academic person held by the public is so pejorative. . . .

One thing the grid tells us is that we have projected a monstrous version of the human condition by our failure to examine seriously twenty-two out of the twenty-four elements that belong in comprehensive curriculum design and evaluation. No wonder we are concerned with making the school humane!

Another observation to be made about the grid is that there are areas of it about which we know very little. We know much less about the aesthetic, spiritual, and physical aspects of growth than we do about the others. Our current evaluation schemes tend to leave out the areas of confidence/value and persistence. That whole quadrant of the grid that includes cells 3d through 3f, and 4d through 4f, is difficult to deal with for this reason. By contrast, the quadrant that includes cells 1a through 1c, and 2a through 2c, is much more familiar to us and correspondingly easier to deal with. The diagonal from 1a to 4f is a line of increasingly sparse knowledge and increasing difficulty. It obviously would repay researchers and curriculum developers to attend to it.

What does it mean to be human? We have answered that question here with the principal dimensions of the research in developmental psychology. What does it mean to teach? We have answered that question here with a four-category analysis. Where the two intersect, we have found questions, some of them perplexing, that offer a kind of map for curriculum development and evaluation for those of us who would develop a curriculum for the humane school we all seek. This is a proposal for analysis, nothing more. It will be interesting to see where it takes us.

Organizing Content for Instruction

A more detailed design is described in the next article in which the learning experiences are organized to optimize cumulative effects in a single field of study. This article introduces a close relationship between substance and objectives through a revised design of the curriculum. The article is an excellent example of how to analyze a field of study and convert that analysis into a curricular pattern. Study the article and identify the variables that influence the decisions and recommendations that are offered.

☐

Students in graduate curriculum classes and workers in the field often find the organization of learning experiences one of the most difficult and complex aspects of curriculum construction. But difficult as it is, without it, learning experiences do not provide for the cumulative effect which brings about major educational changes in students.

To aid in this explanation, I have prepared a *partial* list of curriculum elements for a K-6 English curriculum and an example of both a fifth and sixth grade learning experience with the objectives they were planned to further. (The numbers after both the elements and the objectives refer to classification numbers used in the *Taxonomy of Educational Objectives Cognitive Domain* and the *Taxonomy of Educational Objectives Affective Domain.*) *The elements included are neither a complete nor an ideal list; nor are the objectives and the learning experiences; their purpose is to provide a point of reference for illustrating and explaining aspects discussed later.*

Curriculum Elements in an English Curriculum for K-6
Concept Elements
    Regarding Language (Oral and Written)
        Language has pattern (sound patterns, sentence patterns)
        Language is arbitrary

Knowledge of rules for capitalization, punctuation, and word usage (1.21)
Knowledge of criteria for judging personal letters (1.24)
Ability to use rules for punctuation, capitalization, and word usage in writing personal letters (3.00)
Ability to write personal letters that are effective and easily understood (5.10)
Ability to formulate appropriate standards for evaluating the content of a personal letter (5.20)
Ability to evaluate personal letters in terms of selected criteria (6.20)
Interest in writing personal letters (2.2)

The learning experience grew out of the fifth grade's concern for a classmate who had suffered a broken leg and arm in an automobile accident. The children were shocked by the accident and wanted to do something for the injured child. After much thought and many ideas, they decided to give him a "letter shower" during the four days he would be in the hospital.

The teacher pointed out that their letters would be more enjoyable to the sick child if they met certain criteria or standards. The list of criteria that finally resulted included:

Mary Lee Marksberry, "Organizing Learning Experiences," *Elementary English* 52 (May 1975):653–9. Copyright © 1975 by the National Council of Teachers of English. Reprinted by permission of the publisher and author.

Tell about your own ideas, feelings, or experiences.
Say what you have to say in a clear, honest way.
Tell what you have to say in an orderly way.
Choose words that say what you mean.

To help those children who might need it, the teacher put the form of a model letter on the board. She also suggested that they write down their ideas first without worrying too much about spelling, punctuation, and capitalization and assured them that these aspects would be corrected later.

As each letter was finished, the child and the teacher read it over together, discussing it in terms of the standards previously set up and making needed changes. Then, with the teacher's guidance where necessary, the child recalled and applied known rules in correcting the mistakes in mechanics.

After clean copies of the letters had been made, the addressing of an envelope was discussed. A model was developed and each child used it in addressing the envelope. Final activities involved figuring out how many and determining who would send letters each day.

Sixth Grade Learning Experience   This learning experience took place early the following school year and was planned to advance eight objectives listed in the Sixth Grade Curriculum Guide:

Knowledge of rules for use of the English mechanics in written compositions (1.21)
Familiarity with criteria for evaluating clarity in a composition (1.24)
Ability to apply known rules of English mechanics in written compositions (3.00)
Skill in writing compositions using good organization of ideas and statements (5.10)
Ability to formulate appropriate standards for evaluating a written composition (5.20)
Ability to apply given criteria in the judgment of written compositions (6.20)
Ability to apply given criteria in the judgment of one's conduct when evaluating written compositions (6.20)
Desire to participate in activities concerned with written compositions (2.2)

To reestablish communication lines within the group and also to reintroduce writing, the students spent one class period discussing how they felt about writing and why they found it difficult—or easy.

The next day each child was given an individual copy of a short composition written by a sixth grade student of the year before describing a personal experience, or an excerpt from a well-known story describing a personal experience of a character in the story.

During the few minutes spent in reading these handouts there were many appreciative giggles and sharing of choice bits. This spontaneous sharing led to a discussion of similar personal experiences. At the peak of the discussion the teacher interrupted and said, "The experiences you are sharing are too good to lose. Take out a piece of paper and write down one of the experiences these handouts have made you think of. Write it so it is told just as clearly as it would be if you were telling it to the person you're talking with now."

Plenty of time was given for completing the stories. The teacher collected them, and before the next class period read each story and marked errors in the mechanics of writing.

The next day the teacher began the class by saying, "Before we go on with our work today we need to make some class decisions about how we will share our stories. What possibilities do you see?" Discussion brought out the possibility of the teacher reading all of the stories, each child reading a story, and making exceptions for those who did not want their stories read.

After much discussion it was decided to use all of the ideas. Those who wanted to read their stories could do so, those who would like to share their stories but keep their identity a secret could give them to the teacher to read, and those who did not want to share their stories in any way could write "Personal" across the top of their papers. After organizing the papers so that the plan could be followed, one other decision was made, a person reading a paper should be allowed to read straight through to the end without being interrupted.

The teacher reminded the students that since the purpose of this first writing assignment was to tell a personal experience clearly, the discussion following each paper should be concerned with whether or not this was done. To get thinking started she asked, "What are some questions we might consider to help us decide whether or not a personal experience has been told clearly?" After considerable discussion and some prompting, the pupils came up with the following list:

Is the author telling about something he knows?
Is the story clear? If not, what needs to be added or left out?
Is the story told in an orderly way so that the time the events took place is clear?
Which of the parts are told especially well? Why do you say this? Are there any unusually good sentences? Why are they especially good?

They also recalled that in the fifth grade they had worked out and used standards for their own conduct during the evaluation of written work:

A critic—
Remembers that the person who wrote the paper did the best he could.
Is considerate and helpful. Tells what is good as well as what is not good.
Thinks about what the writer is really trying to say.
Gives suggestions in a polite way.
Tells in what ways a paper is "good," "interesting," or "poor" because general statements are not helpful to a writer.

They further agreed that the person whose paper was being criticized should receive comments graciously and, if in disagreement, defend politely what was written.

Plenty of time was given to reading and evaluating each story (with the exception of those which had "Personal" written on them). The discussions roughly followed the questions that had been developed to help in making judgments about whether the purpose of the assignment had been met. A summary statement of the strengths and weaknesses was written on each paper. (The teacher also wrote a summary statement of strengths and weaknesses on each paper marked "Personal.") In all of these discussions the teacher, by well-directed questions or carefully worded comments, kept the discussions at an objective level.

After all the papers had been considered, the students evaluated their discussion against the standards for being good critics and good receivers of criticism, and talked together about how they could improve their next discussion.

The following class period was spent revising the papers. Students first made the revisions suggested in the class discussions. Then they classified mechanical errors into categories such as paragraphing, spelling, sentence fragments, capitalization, punctuation. This made it possible to find appropriate pages in the language text when they could not recall needed rules. The teacher was available at all times to assist those who needed help in applying rules.

After revisions were completed, students took the paper to the teacher for a final check. Then it was copied in their best handwriting and either filed in a writing folder or put on a special bulletin board for further enjoyment by the class.

Rationale for Organization of Learning Experiences

As a basis for my clarification of difficult aspects of organization, I will first summarize Ralph W. Tyler's widely known statement on the function of organization and procedures for attaining it. It is found in his book *Basic Principles of Curriculum and Instruction. . . .*

Organization is the arranging or ordering of learning experiences in such a way that they reinforce each other. It involves a careful consideration of two kinds of relationships, vertical and horizontal. Vertical organization refers to relationship over time, and horizontal organization refers to relationship from one subject area to another.

To achieve vertical organization, two criteria must be met, continuity and sequence. Continuity refers to the reiteration of major curriculum elements within a field of study. Sequence includes continuity but goes beyond it. It emphasizes the importance of each subsequent experience building on earlier ones so that curriculum elements do not remain at the same level but instead increase in breadth and depth.

The criterion for achieving horizontal organization is integration. It refers to the utilization of curriculum elements from one subject area to other subject areas of the curriculum. For example, a concept element of English such as "Effective language is clear and honest," can be utilized in social studies, science, mathematics, music, and other areas.

Curriculum elements are the threads which tie the curriculum together. They are major long-range items to be emphasized throughout the entire length and breadth of the instructional program. Concept elements, skill elements, and value elements are threads often used. These are three types illustrated in the partial list of curriculum elements given for the English curriculum.

As was mentioned earlier, the criteria for effective organization (continuity, sequence, and integration) are achieved only as the elements are stressed throughout the breadth and depth of the curriculum. Merely stressing them, however, is not enough. They are more meaningful to students if they are systematically organized throughout the learning experiences according to carefully considered principles of organization. Various organizing principles have been used. Among these are chronological, simple to complex, increasing range of activities included, increasing breadth of application, use of description followed by analysis, concrete to abstract, and the part-whole principle of organizing content.

Since elements are the large concepts, skills, values, and the like, of such importance and complexity that they need to be threaded throughout the curriculum from the early years to the later years, they are usually stated at a level representative of their mature development. This necessitates having a clear understanding of the relationship between objectives and elements. Briefly stated, the learning experiences designed to further the objectives at each level carry the elements. If the elements and objectives are classified according to the classification scheme of the *Taxonomies,* the relation between "intellectual abilities and skills objectives" and "skill elements," and between "affective domain objectives" and "value elements" can be easily seen.

Explanation of Organization Procedures Using English Curriculum Illustrations

Let us consider the skill elements in the example of an English curriculum given previously. Since the classification number from the appropriate *Taxonomy* has been written by each skill element and by each objective for the learning experiences, it is easy to see the relation between the intellectual abilities and skill objectives and the skill elements. The same is true for the affective domain objectives and the value elements.

This can be more clearly explained by using, as an example, the skill element "Ability to put together elements from various sources so as to create a new product or structure in the area of English" (5.00). Because it is a general statement of the synthesis category in the *Taxonomy* it is classified as 5.00. Two of the objectives for the fifth grade learning experience and two for the sixth grade learning experience as previously explained, contribute to its growth because they too are classified in the synthesis category. The fifth grade objectives are "Ability to write personal letters that are effective and easily understood" (5.10) and "Ability to formulate appropriate standards for evaluating the content of a personal letter" (5.20). The sixth grade objectives are "Skill in writing compositions using good organization of ideas and statements" (5.10) and "Ability to formulate appropriate standards for evaluating a written composition" (5.20). Since provisions are made for furthering each of these synthesis objectives in one or the other of the learning experiences it can be said that the element is being promoted. . . .

Concept Elements

The objective, "Knowledge of rules for capitalization, punctuation, and word usage" (1.21) used in the fifth grade learning experience, and the sixth grade objective, "Knowledge of rules for use of the English mechanics in written compositions" (1.21) are both carrying the concept element "Desirable language has a doctrine of correctness" through the activities provided for their development in the respective learning experiences. The rules students are to remember in both cases help the learner understand the meaning of the "doctrine of correctness." Since the concept element is obviously reiterated, the criterion of continuity is being met. . . .

The activity planned in the fifth grade learning experience to further the objective "Knowledge of criteria for judging personal letters" (1.24) is also carrying a concept element regarding language. This time, however, the element is "Effective language is clear and honest" because the criteria to be remembered give some meaning to it. . . .

Skill Elements

In the fifth grade learning experience, the activity involving setting up standards was planned to further the objective "Ability to formulate appropriate standards for evaluating the content of a personal letter" (5.20). Later in the same experience, when the children actually wrote letters, the objective, "Ability to write personal letters that are effective and easily understood" (5.10) was advanced. Since each of these objectives is an aspect of synthesis, both are carrying the synthesis skill element "Ability to put together elements from various sources so as to create a new product or structure in the area of English" (5.00).

In the learning experience for the sixth grade the objective "Skill in writing compositions using good organization of ideas and statements" (5.10) was furthered by the activity of writing stories about personal experiences. This, too, is a synthesis objective so it is also carrying the synthesis element, "Ability to put together elements from various sources so as to create a new product or structure in the area of English" (5.00). This reiteration of the synthesis element indicates that the criterion of continuity is being met. Since the second learning experience provided a new situation and a new response, the learners are getting a broader and deeper skill and the criterion of sequence is being met. Another activity in the sixth grade learning experience, the one concerned with formulating questions to guide the evaluation of their stories, was designed to advance the objective, "Ability to formulate appropriate standards for evaluating a written composition" (5.20). It, too, by providing a new situation for formulating appropriate criteria met the criterion of sequence. The organizing principle being used to meet continuity and sequence of this skill element is "increasing range of activities included." . . .

Value Elements

In the fifth grade learning experience, an effort was made to structure the activities in such a way that students would succeed and would enjoy what they were doing. If this was realized, students would obtain satisfaction from practicing the behavior inherent in the various knowledge and intellectual abilities and skills objectives. Through this satisfaction, a willingness to respond should be developed, and the objective, "Interest in writing personal letters" (2.2) would be realized. Through its realization, the value element, "Continuing interest in literature and in improving communication" (2.0) would be furthered. . . .

Integration of Curricular Elements

Illustrations of the horizontal criterion of organization, integration, is more difficult because space does not permit giving examples of learning experiences in other subject areas. A more general explanation will have to suffice.

The two concept elements used in the illustration given, "Desirable language has a doctrine of correctness" and "Effective language is clear and honest," are concepts that can be furthered in all other subject areas of the elementary school: mathematics, science, social studies, etc. If emphasis is placed on such concept elements in these particular subject areas as well as in English, the criterion of integration would be met.

In a similar way, if the skill elements and the value elements are emphasized in other subject areas than English with the content appropriate to that area, students will get a unified view of the elements and not see them as tied to one particular subject area.

I have used only two learning experiences and selected elements to illustrate how the criteria for effective organization may be achieved. In actual practice, each of the elements must run through many learning experiences at each grade level if the cumulative effect which brings about major educational changes is to be provided. Such an organization of learning experiences involves careful planning throughout the curriculum.

The Technology of Curriculum Design

Thus far we have presented curriculum designs based partly on evidence, partly on theory, and partly on "best hunches." Can a more rigorous approach to curriculum design be employed? Can decisions about curriculum design be based on data and include reasonably high predictability? These questions are addressed in the next article which attempts to create a conceptual structure in which the dimensions and consequences of curriculum are more systematically and stringently planned.

☐

The need for increased rigor in the planning and design of curricula is acute and generally well recognized. The rationales for the planning and design of

G. L. Oliver "Toward Improved Rigor in the Design of Curricula," *Educational Technology* 10 (April 1970): 18–23. Reprinted by permission of the author and publisher.

curricula have historically dealt with the development of surveys intended to identify, describe, analyze, and order the opinions of experts in fields of general societal needs, occupational and/or disciplinary needs, and the needs of learners themselves.

These rationales and related techniques have, however, drawn a good deal of criticism, for the following reasons: They are, at best, based on unrelatable and value-laden statements of the beliefs and attitudes of a limited number of experts in a given subject matter field. In many instances, they are based entirely on rationally derived rather than hard empirical data. Parochial in their preoccupation with specific occupational or disciplinary issues, these rationales and techniques fail to generalize to the needs of the curriculum field as a whole. They are not subjected to rigorous programs of diagnosis and assessment, designed to establish their empirical validity. They lack descriptive and analytical sophistication in the manner in which their various dimensions are identified, analyzed, and ordered. And, most important, they are not, in general, based on any comprehensive theoretical position as to the nature of education, training, curricula, or instruction. The result, especially of this latter condition, has been the proliferation of a number of unrelated and unrelatable rationales and techniques—that have left the field without a viable conceptual structure upon which it can build.

Curriculum Design as a Crude Technology

... There is, of course, certainly nothing new about the notion that the fields of curriculum and instruction, being praxiological in their outlook, are concerned with identifying what ought to be done, with describing and implementing the necessary strategy for doing it, and with evaluating the results. In spite of this, however, the literature in these areas continues to be primarily concerned with the scientific studies of the psychologist or sociologist. When technological issues are dealt with in the literature they are generally on a technologically unsophisticated, anecdotal, and prescriptive basis. Given the technological nature of instructional goals, it seems that more attention should be given to developing more sophisticated technological descriptions of curricular and instructional design processes.

In order to demonstrate the crucial differences in the theoretical focus provided by these two decision systems, let us briefly review the essential differences in their content, goals, functions, and evaluative criteria:

1. While science focuses on investigating the behavior of components in abstract and surrogate environments in order to minimize variability and confoundedness, technology investigates the behavior of components in real world septic environments in order to maximize these factors.

2. The goals of science include the control, explanation, and understanding of phenomena, whereas those of technology are focused on optimizing the control of environments. As Fogel (1963, p. 4) points out, the scientist "does to know" while the technologist "knows to do."

3. The scientist processes data in a manner calculated to lead him from a set of causal conditions to a related set of effects, and the technologist

reverses this order. Starting with a desired effect, the technologist attempts to identify the required set of independent causal conditions. The scientific process by which this former activity is carried on is referred to as "discovery" and the latter is generally referred to as "invention." In the former case, the processes of induction, deduction, and hypo-thetico-deduction are commonly employed. In the latter case, such logic and rationality give way to stochastic decision structures for relating means and ends. These structures are developed by analogical and meta-phorical extension and by criterion tradeoffs based on intuition and common wisdom, as well as on empirical science.

4. The power of scientific theorizing depends primarily upon empirical sensory data inputs, whereas technological theorizing depends primarily upon the "hunches" of the technologist.

5. While the outputs of the scientist are inductive and deductive explanatory statements, those of the technologist are forecasts that attempt to indicate in advance the extent to which a state of affairs can be anticipated by means of some set of independently selected variables (Finan, 1963, p. 530).

6. Finally, scientific theories are evaluated in terms of their relative power for relating facts within a theoretical network, but technological theories are evaluated in terms of the probability of their forecasts. In the first instance, the criteria for evaluation include reliability and validity in explanation and prediction. In the second instance, reliability and fidelity in interpretation and forecasting are the criteria for evaluation.

If the instructional enterprise were to give prerequisite attention to the development of a more sophisticated technological methodology rather than to scientific theorizing, the following innovations might logically be expected: There would be renewed emphasis on the study of task, learner, and instrumental variables associated with the acquisition of meaningful human capabilities as opposed to emphasis on the learning of capabilities of surrogate subhuman species. The study of the "how" of instruction might be emphasized more than the "why" of human behavior. A primary concern could be the invention of powerful instructional strategies, not the discovery of logical inductive or deductive systems of explanation. More emphasis might be placed on the compilation of handbooks containing artful, heuristic, and highly operational, as well as scientific, theories of curriculum and instruction. The development of techniques for testing the forecasting and interpretive power of specific curricular and instructional design methods might take priority over testing the reliability and validity of principles and theories of instruction.

The Romans built fine bridges and roads, not because of their scientific sophistication in explanation and prediction, but because of their technological sophistication in interpretation and forecasting. Their inductive and deductive explanatory theories, judged by our present level of scientific know-how, were primitive indeed. Yet, on the other hand, their technological output in bridge and road building was equivalent in many ways to our own. The difference is probably due to the prerequisite attention given by the Romans to technological theorizing.

A review of aims, objectives, and procedural statements that provide the substantive content of curricula leaves the reviewer with the uneasy feeling that all is not well. Not only do such descriptions and analyses of what ought to be done, and how to go about doing it, appear to be plagued with problems of terminology, but they appear to be oversimplistic and fragmented in the range of critical events that must logically come under the control of the curriculum planner and designer.

Clearly, the application of the principles of operationalism to the defining of curricular aims and objectives has been immensely beneficial in the improvement of their semantic meaningfulness; epistemological and ontological issues related to these same statements have seldom been subject to rigorous theoretical investigations.[1] It seems abundantly evident that if the general rigor and forecasting power of curriculum designs are to be improved, the theorist must start with a study of the necessary and sufficient events that must be controlled by the designer before he can proceed to develop techniques for assuring their semantic meaning. In short, the key question at this stage in the development of the curriculum field is *not* "How ought curricular events to be identified, described, analyzed, and ordered?" *but* "What curricular events ought to be identified, described, analyzed, and ordered?" . . .

Summary

Curriculum designs can be developed through a variety of ways: administrative changes, content analysis, response to psychological knowledge, or theoretical orientation. Examples of each way have been illustrated in this chapter. Two factors stand out: (1) the design of the curriculum is influenced by identifiable factors; and (2) the actual design of the curriculum is the consequence of decisions that are within the control of the schools. Regardless of which authority one follows, the eventual design of the curriculum will reflect the views held by decision makers in the schools.

The design of the schools becomes a tangible plan that is clearly demonstrable. When an administrator organizes the schools into a team teaching approach, it is clearly different from a traditional single-teacher-single classroom relationship. These are different curricular designs and are reflected in the organizational and content decisions that are planned to implement the curriculum. The curriculum worker should recognize that ideas and decisions about curricula are useless until they are implemented. Implementation occurs according to a plan to organize the critical variables, and that organization 1s called curriculum design.

[1]Westbury (1969, pp. 4–5); one of the few to deal with these theoretical issues and to suggest their methodological implications for the curriculum field, points out that only five out of 178 works cited in the *Review of Educational Research* (1966) on curriculum are directed at basic theoretical issues.

Part IV
Curricular Change

It is easier to convince people today than previously that change does take place. New developments everywhere make it obvious that today is different from yesterday. Furthermore, the future will probably change at an accelerated rate compared to the past, and today's generation accepts this premise. Whether one is persuaded by Toffler's *Future Shock* or simply draws comparisons between the present and the past, it is apparent that society and its components have changed. These changes occur in all important factors of our lives. A few examples illustrate the areas in which change has had far-reaching implications.

Impressive technological developments have drastically altered peoples' lifestyles and viewpoints. Fifty years ago the typical entrepreneur would not have considered doing intercontinental or transoceanic business. Travel and communication constraints made interaction so difficult that only a few major enterprises could conduct business at great distances. Today traveling to places that were previously impossible to reach is routine. Airplanes that travel at mach 2 or faster and a communication system of telephones, cables, and telex stations have made international business possible. The transportation and communication industries have enabled major changes to take place. Placing a phone call to a distant location in a few seconds, traveling two or three thousand miles in four to six hours, or watching a political convention the instant it happens in another state would be unimaginable to the average person at the turn of the century.

Another example clearly recognized are major changes in the traditional family. As this nation approaches zero population growth, with 20 percent or more of the population moving annually from one neighborhood to another, and as the grandparent-parent-child trilogy diminishes, new lifestyles emerge. These new lifestyles cast aside the tradition that sometimes imprisoned family members, but imprisonment stabilized a large segment of the population. This "release" from conformity has been especially difficult for many because of certain unique human characteristics. When people lose their traditions they have few if any "instincts" to tell them what to do. People learn to behave according to their surrounding environment (social, physcological, familial, etc.). When that environment lacks consistency or traditional cues, then people fend for themselves. Those who cope well with this freedom are often exhilarated by the opportunities presented. Those who fail to handle these opportunities may have little to support them and become confused, anxious, and disoriented. The current communal living, paired living without marriage, and marriages without children are only a few of the differences that exist today more frequently than in the past. Changes in family life and new purposes for families are products of changes in our traditions.

Developments in other fields such as medicine, agriculture, chemistry, and astronomy are no less dramatic. All these fields have taken giant strides. The polio vaccine has contributed immeasurably to the health of the nation and relieved anxiety and suffering that took place during the epidemics before research led to a cure to this crippling disease. Chemists who have discovered new ways to combine old elements to create products and solutions that range from frying pans that won't stick to house paint that fights mildew are everyday developments we now take for granted. Astronomers have undertaken the gigantic task of communicating with others somewhere in the universe, even though a message may take twenty thousand years to arrive. Imagine launching a forty thousand year project a mere hundred years ago. It is difficult enough today, but the project is underway and reflects a visionary viewpoint and technical development that did not exist in the last century. And scientists in the same field have provided us with the assurance that the universe will continue to expand for at least thirty billion years. They are even saying it may expand forever. Think how long "forever" is and the sophisticated scientific procedures required to issue such a statement. The changes in scientific developments are impressive by most anyone's standards.

Changes in family life, in communication and transportation, and scientific endeavors are only a few of the areas in which volumes about change have been written. But everything is not necessarily changing, and certainly everything is not changing at the same rate. In addition all changes are not improvements, and many changes that result in improvements also create new problems. In some areas changes are required for survival, but also some of the most stable elements of our society are the most permanent whether it be the path of a river or the Constitution of the United States. Some of the common developments which benefit nearly everyone, such as the automobile, also have some of the most disastrous side effects—highway deaths, injuries, and pollution. Change for the sake of change is not worth promoting. Change often has negative side effects, and the consequences of change are often unpredictable.

Given these few brief statements about change let us relate the notion of change to the schools. The purpose of the previous discourse was not primarily to illustrate the kind of changes we have seen. (Most of you already knew this information and could write your own list of changes.) The point of this discussion was to contrast the attitude we have about change in the familial, scientific, communication, or transportation fields with the attitude we have about social and educational change. We readily admit that changes have taken place and will continue to take place in many of these other areas of endeavor. There is a different attitude generally when schools and society are included in this discussion.

One hears comments that we can split an atom but cannot dissect and study an inferiority complex. Or we can create the means for communication but the lack of meaningful communication is one of our greatest problems. For 2000 years human frailties have included greed, envy, avarice, aggression, selfishness; little progress has been made in changing these characteristics. The stereotype of the politician on the take, the unscrupulous businessperson, the child batterers, wife beaters, and criminals who commit acts of violence are all with us. The questions of whether society today is unchanged from the barbarism of primitive society, the slavery of a century ago, or the cruel sweatshops, prisons, and mental institutions of yesteryear may be debatable. Perhaps the improvements still leave us short of perfection and the discrepancy piques our conscience and good sense. And certainly the society has not provided preparation and opportunity for all to engage in work with dignity as fully functioning members. Perhaps, for these reasons, we are discontent with societal changes, and that leads us to complain that society has changed very little.

Though this book is not looking at the whole of society it is important to draw parellels between societal change and change in the schools. Among society's attempts at solutions are the institutions intended to alter the hardened and destructive tendencies of its people. One of the institutions is the school. The school has been charged with lagging twenty, thirty, or more years behind the times. The schools are described by one quipster as the only place Rip Van Winkle would have found familiar surroundings when he awoke from his famous nap. Though change and improvement occur, the difference between high expectations and hard reality often contributes to our discontent with the schools and society. Unrealistic expectations and shortfalls in accomplishments are difficult problems to combat. But high expectations and slow change are both relative. The gap between what we desire and what we have depends in large measure on the viewpoint of the observer and the factors that are under consideration. The factors we are examining in this book are those factors that relate to the school and its curriculum and the viewpoint of those who have studied and written about change in the curriculum are presented throughout this section.

The curriculum of the schools must compete with other agencies for support, endorsement, and status. And when the school's curriculum is compared to other developments, its contribution often pales against the sensational results of scientific payoff found in space flights, heart transplants, jet airplanes, and nuclear energy. The contrast between rapid change and progress in some sectors of society and alleged stagnation of the schools poses an interesting paradox.

The dramatic changes in society require knowledge for their creation. They also require capable and solvent people for their support and consumption. Where does this necessary knowledge and intelligent decision making come from? Surely the schools, the only institution established for the transmission of systematic knowledge, must deserve some of the credit. The extreme position that scientific development and some other endeavors are dynamic and changing and that schools are lethargic and moribund is an exaggeration. The accomplishments in schools are more like social changes that are slow and deliberate than the dramatic breakthroughs of science and technology. But changes do take place. In fact, the difficulty in schools is both a problem of changing *per se* and a problem of promoting appropriate change. The appropriateness of curricular change is addressed throughout this book, particularly in the chapters on educational theory. The fact of change and the question of why and how changes occur are topics addressed in this section.

Three chapters are presented on change. The first chapter provides evidence of change and speculation about anticipated changes. The second chapter raises the question of why change occurs at all. The final chapter discusses the question of how change takes place and the role of those individuals and forces that promote change.

Chapter **13**

Evidence of Change

"I'm going to take Ancient History-they can't change that."

Today's Education 62. 5(May 1973): 53.

This chapter only contains a small sample of the literature on change. To make the point that educational change does occur, we present excerpts from articles describing new education developments, future plans, and comparisons of present and past curricula. The purpose of this collage is to provide information about different kinds of changes and to allay, or at least modify, the view of the skeptics who charge the schools with a terminal case of stagnation.

The readings that follow provide a quick trip through a few instances of change in the schools and particularly in the school's curriculum. However, a chapter that included only selections that list and praise the dynamic side of schools would be a distortion. The balance between those articles that identify changes and those that claim little has changed are both included. There is no claim here that all changes that have taken place are desirable. The curriculum worker should realize that changes are possible but not certain. The opposite view that change is impossible is dispiriting and inaccurate. The readings that follow provide information about both sides of these issues.

Planned vs. Automatic Change

In the first selection the controversial position whether planned change is possible or if society is a victim of evolving developments and its own inertia is raised. Lester F. Ward and William Graham Sumner were the foremost early proponents of these opposing views. Read this next article and then identify at least one educational change that exemplifies each of these two opposing views.

☐

Policy makers, social scientists and social practitioners in America are not more agreed about the proper direction and management of social change in 1960 than they were at the turn of the present century. But the focus of the controversy has shifted. In 1900—in America at least—the issue was typically stated in sweeping ideological terms. Should or should not men seek, through deliberate and collaborative forethought in the present, to mold the shape of their collective future? Or should confidence rather be placed in a principle of automatic adjustment, operating within the processes of history to reequilibrate, without human forethought yet in the interest of progress and human welfare, the inescapable human upsets and dislocations of changing society?

Lester F. Ward was one of the earliest social scientists in America to proclaim that modern people must extend scientific approaches into the planning of changes in the patterns of their behaviors and relationships. He was well aware that people were already utilizing their accumulating collective and scientific intelligence deliberately to induce changes in their nonhuman environment. And he saw a major role for the emerging sciences of man in extending a similar planning approach into the management of human affairs.

> Man's destiny is in his own hands. Any law that he can comprehend he can control. He cannot increase or diminish the powers of nature, but he can direct them ... His power over nature is unlimited. He can make it his servant and appropriate to his own use all the mighty forces of the universe ... Human institutions are not exempt from this all-pervading spirit of improvement. They, too, are artificial, conceived in the ingenious brain and wrought with mental skill born of inventive genius. The passion for their improvement is of a piece with the impulse to improve the plow or the steam engine ... Intelligence, heretofore a growth, is destined to become a manufacture ... The origination and distribution of knowledge can no longer be left to chance or to nature. They are to be systematized and erected into true arts.[1]

Ward's proclamation seemed foolish boasting, if not downright sacrilege, to many among his contemporaries. William Graham Sumner was one of the leaders in sociology who emphasized both the folly and sacrilege of prophecies like Ward's.

Kenneth D. Benne, Warren G. Bennis, and Robert Chin, "Planned Change in America," in *The Planning of Change: Readings in the Applied Behavior Sciences* (New York: Holt, Rinehart and Winston, 1961), pp. 28–30. Copyright © 1961 by Holt, Rinehart, and Winston. Reprinted by permission.

[1]Quoted in Henry Commager, *The American Mind* (New Haven, Conn.: Yale University Press, 1950), pp. 208, 210, 213–14.

Footnotes have been renumbered consecutively throughout the chapter.

If we can acquire a science of society based on observation of phenomena and study of forces, we may hope to gain some ground slowly toward the elimination of old errors and the reestablishment of a sound and natural social order. Whatever we gain that way will be by growth, never in the world by any reconstruction of society on the plan of some enthusiastic social architect. The latter is only repeating the old error over again, and postponing all our chances of real improvement. Society needs first of all to be free from these meddlers—that is, to be let alone. Here we are, then, once more back at the old doctrine *laissez faire.* Let us translate it into blunt English, and it will read—Mind you own business. It is nothing but the doctrine of liberty. Let every man be happy in his own way.[2]

It may be fortunate or unfortunate that American controversies today over the direction and management of social change seldom take the form of sweeping societal prescriptions and counterprescriptions or ideological debates—a form which Ward and Sumner, along with their contemporaries, gave to them. In any event, the form of the controversies has shifted. In large measure subsequent events have foreclosed the factual basis for Sumner's argument. *Laissez faire* has been widely abandoned in practice as a principle of social management, whatever ghostly existence it yet enjoys in political platforms and pronunciamentos. Human interventions designed to shape and modify the institutionalized behaviors of people are now familiar features of our social landscape. "Helping professions" have proliferated since Ward's and Sumner's day. Professions of industrial and public management have taken shape. The reasons for being of all of these is deliberately to induce and coach changes in the future behaviors and relationships of their various "client" populations. This is most apparent in "new" professions such as psychiatry, social work, nursing, counseling, management, and consultation in its manifold forms. But older professions too, such as medicine, law, teaching, and the clergy, have been pressed increasingly to become agencies of social change rather than of social conservation. Resistances to assuming the new role have, of course, developed along with the situational pressures to enact it.

Behavioral scientists, neo-Sumnerians among others, have been drawn, with varying degrees of eagerness and resistance, into activities of "changing," such as consultation and applied research. "Helping professionals," "managers," and "policy makers" in various fields of practice increasingly seek and employ the services of behavioral scientists to anticipate more accurately the consequences of prospective social changes and to inform more validly the processes of planning designed to control these consequences.

Schools Do Change

The combination of planned change and "natural developments" tend to coalesce if we look at the educational changes that have occurred during the history of schools in the United States. The description of these changes is provided in the next article by John Goodlad. The list of changes can be interpreted against the position stated by Ward and Sumner. The reader

[2]Quoted in Commager, *The American Mind,* pp. 201–2.

should consider which of these two positions offers the best explanation of how change takes place; furthermore, you should be alert to the charge that schools are unchanging and determine if it seems true that schools are rigid and stagnant.

☐

It often is said about education, as about many other things, that nothing changes but the appearance of change. It might also be said, however, that one's view of change depends to a considerable degree on the perspective of time. Looking in the 1970s for widespread, authentic implementation of the innovative ideas contained in the cant and rhetoric of reform in the 1960s suggests little movement. Only a small part of each successive wave of recommended change rubs off onto practice. Perhaps this is not all bad, since it protects us from the excesses of those who make reputations by being more daring than their contemporaries. But some features which cause schools to seem inevitably and forever the same hang on stubbornly—telling and questioning as the main form of teaching, daily instruction chopped into arbitrary slices of time, long spells of student immobility, textbooks, and copybooks, to name only a few. Nonetheless, in the sweep of 200 years since independence, much of the tone and reality of American education is conveyed accurately by the word "change" in aims, in substance, in access to schooling, and in where and how education occurs.

The saga is a captivating one, particularly the last 150 years of it, during which schooling has advanced from the privilege of a few to a widely accepted right of all. The whole of it often is described as "the great American experiment in mass education." Only a few rather visible threads of change are discussed here, beginning with goals and concluding with the march toward equality of opportunity and a learning society. The central focus is on schools, since we have attached so much importance to them but there is some attention to education conceived more broadly.

Today, two central thrusts characterize most widely accepted statements of goals for education in this country: the full development of the individual and identification with an ever-widening concept of social and cultural responsibility. A statement emanating from the 1970 White House Conference on Children and cast within a framework of "the right to learn" juxtaposes these two thrusts in seeking to answer the question: What would we have twenty-first century man be?

We would have him be a man with a strong sense of himself and his own humanness, with awareness of his thoughts and feelings, with the capacity to feel and express love and joy and to recognize tragedy and feel grief. We would have him be a man who, with a strong and realistic sense of his own worth, is able to relate openly with others, to cooperate effectively with them toward common ends, and to view mankind as one while respecting diversity and difference. We would want him to be a being who, even while very young, somehow senses that he has it within himself to become more than he now is, that he has the capacity for life-long spiritual and

John I. Goodlad, "An Emphasis on Change," *American Education* 11, 1(January-February 1975): 16ff.

intellectual growth. We would want him to cherish that vision of the man he is capable of becoming and to cherish the development of the same potentiality in others.

Early goals for education were spare and stark in comparison with such a sweeping, almost ethereal statement. Going back to colonial days in Massachusetts we find little concern for individuality and much for responsibility in the admonition to town leaders that they take account of children's "ability to read and understand the principles of religion and the capital laws of the country." Although there was, a century later, some expression of concern for practical preparation for jobs in agriculture, navigation, shipbuilding, surveying, and trading, the commitment to moral instruction and love of country remained central. With the passage of another hundred years (bringing us well past independence and into the middle of the nineteenth century), the emphasis still was on responsibility—a degree of education that would enable one to perform all social, domestic, civic, and moral duties.

Paralleling humanistic stirrings in Europe, there were, of course, expressions of concern over this pervading sense of education only for responsibility, and they resulted in a few innovative deviations during the second half of the nineteenth century. But it is this continued domination of the moral and nationalistic over a period of 250 years that makes John Dewey's emphasis on the meaning of individual human experience so dramatic. Historian Lawrence Cremin interprets Dewey's definition of education—the reconstruction or reorganization of experience—as "a way of saying that the aim of education is not merely to make citizens, or workers, or fathers, or mothers, but ultimately to make human beings who will live life to the fullest."

There was no immediate and general acceptance of that concept. In fact, this and related ideas of Dewey were attacked for decades afterward and remain controversial today. . . .

Gunnar Myrdal has pointed out that Americans "are at bottom moral optimists." A sense of sin arises out of our self-recognized inability to live up to the precepts of our idealism. Cultural unity, says Myrdal in *An American Dilemma,* arises out of "this common sharing in both the consciousness of sins and the devotion to high ideals."

Perhaps it is the tension thus created that provides the drive for our educational preoccupation with curricular reform. . . .

Courses on curriculum construction have been common in our universities for only a few decades, books on the subject for only a few more. Perhaps, then, exponents of "sound principles of curriculum planning" should not be too upset when publishers and teachers pay little attention to them. Until recently, publishers of educational materials concerned themselves almost exclusively with textbooks and with whether the content was acceptable and reasonably within pupil understanding. Ramifications pertaining to children's interests, appropriate recognition of sexes and races, objectives to be achieved, readability, and the like followed some years—and usually decades—after the appearance of goals stressing the individual in education and self-realization. And the addition of social and psychological considerations to subject matter vastly complicated the curriculum building process.

Knowledge of goals is about all one needs in order to guess the content of early school programs in this country. In the second half of the seventeenth century, the school day was occupied with reading, spelling, and instruction in the Bible. The hornbook, a board with a handle, was inscribed with the alphabet and the Lord's Prayer. The first New England Primer (1690) contained epigrams, prayers, questions and answers about the Bible, and spelling lessons. . . .

By the time of independence, the curriculum was more crowded and planning was becoming complex. Provisions for vocational skills and more complicated arithmetic teaching had to be fitted in. And with separation and initial unification effected, the content of citizenship education and the teaching of national loyalty changed dramatically. The schools were having to change with the times, just as they have been exhorted and constrained to respond ever since.

With industrialization, urbanization, and rapid expansion in population during the second half of the nineteenth century, the schools shook themselves out the seventeenth- and eighteenth-century molds and created new structures which held with surprising firmness until past the middle of the twentieth. It is reasonable to suggest that it is those highly visible characteristics of egg-crate buildings, graded classes, compartmentalized subjects, and rigid time units brought into being in the 1860s and 1870s that have provoked the image of tortoise-like change in schools. But these things, too, shall pass—and are, indeed, passing, like the Dame School, the circuit school, and the Lancaster Plan before them.

But within these familiar rubrics curriculum change (much but not all in the form of accretions to what already existed) went on apace. Vocational training in both skills and attitudes was needed for work in the factories; physical and health education made their common appearance early in the 1900s. The elementary school curriculum of the 1920s and 1930s included arithmetic, spelling, reading, handwriting, grammar, composition, nature study, geography, history, singing, drawing, painting, and perhaps some shop and cooking for the upper years. Secondary schools commonly included algebra, geometry, some arithmetic; English composition, grammar, and literature; Latin, French, and sometimes a little German; civics, history, geography; health and physical education; physics, chemistry, and biology; and a clutch of electives in the arts, technical subjects, and home economics, depending on local resources.

Methods of teaching reading became (and continued to be) a controversial matter with the introduction of whole-word recognition approaches and "controlled vocabularies" in the late 1920s. Progressive education is blamed or credited, depending on one's point of view, with a rash of experiments with fused, integrated, or core curriculums; society or community-oriented approaches; life adjustment education; and child-centered education all blossoming in the 1930s and fading in the war-torn years of the 1940s. By the 1950s, there were many who believed the time was come to have done with our progressive follies and, in the light of the United States' new found status in the world, to tighten and prune, to cut the fat out of curricular accumulations, and to replace outworn content with the fast-ripening fruits of a knowledge explosion. It was time for and, indeed, the social and civic responsibility of academicians to bestir themselves from their more scholarly activities in order to jack up the ailing curriculums of America's schools.

Emphasis on structure of the disciplines, supposedly both disciplining and freeing the mind simultaneously, though highly visible was not the only emphasis in the ensuing reform movement. Assumptions about the nature of learners loomed large; psychological considerations had been part of the fabric of curriculum and instruction for some time. Even very young children were credited with ability to learn basic mathematical and scientific concepts, to extrapolate from data and experiments, and to make intuitive leaps. The young child was "discovered educationally," the significance of cognitive development taking its place beside traditional concerns for emotional, social, and physical development for nursery school youngsters at least in the view of a handful of influential leaders.

Although these emphases were brewing in the 1950s, they came to a boil in the 1960s, spewing out all over the stove in 1965. Sputnik had touched that nerve of sin again. We flayed our schools as we once flayed witches. Our schools had gone soft, we said and a few obligingly enterprising television cameramen soon "proved" it. We were not quite ready to say that we, the American people, had gone soft, however. . . .

The immediate aftermath of Sputnik is fascinating and deserves an analysis within the historical context of our nation beyond what it has as yet received. We already had inordinate expectations for our schools, for more than one hundred years linking them virtually in a cause and effect relationship with individual well-being and national welfare—regarding them, as Robert M. Hutchins observed, as "the foundation of our freedom, the guarantee of our future, the cause of our prosperity and power, the bastion of our security, the bright and shining beacon that was the source of our enlightenment. . . ." How we sought to polish up the beacon and step up the candlepower after Sputnik!

A veritable host of many long-standing traits, movements, tenets, and ideologies of American education came tumbling together in The Education Decade. The innovative character, which some observers from abroad have identified as our most notable contribution to educational advancement generally, was dominant. We innovated all over the place: with new approaches to curriculum content; with programmed and computerized instruction; with modular scheduling, modular buildings, and acoustically treated walls, ceilings, and floors; with nongrading, team teaching, and flexible grouping; with films, filmstrips, multimedia "packages," and televised instruction. . . .

We updated our long-standing ambivalence about teachers and teaching as a profession by proposing "teacher-proof materials," while revering the newly emerging professorial jet set. Members of this new elite were much sought after: as advisors and consultants to the federal government, publishers, school systems, special projects, and foundations, and as speakers everywhere. Research became so revered that "no teaching the first year and then only a seminar in your specialty" was as significant as the unprecedented salary going with a much-publicized appointment at a prestigious university. . . .

The Elementary and Secondary Education Act of 1965 (ESEA), which both brought the pot of reform to a boil and spilled out the brew across this nation, ranks with those great federal acts of faith which gave us our land grant universities and assured that we would not forget the vocational arts (Smith-Hughes Act) in our pursuit of the liberal arts and sciences. . . .

The ESEA represents not only a high—perhaps the zenith—in our history of faith in education and our ability to effect constructive change in schools, but also a significant watershed in the post-Sputnik frenzy. Ironically, it also symbolizes the dangers of disillusionment inherent in expecting too much of our schools. President Lyndon B. Johnson was both right and wrong in his statement before Congress to the effect that education is at the heart of all problems, if one looks deeply enough.

Our schools have served us well, in spite of their shortcomings, in the face of unreasonable expectations. But they simply cannot be expected to correct those many acute problems associated with rapid growth, urbanization, and socialization which are, perhaps, more amenable to solution by human engineering: technological displacement of labor-intensive employment, urban decay, pollution, and the like. That education would solve them was the expectation of the 1960s, however—at least, so one might judge from the rhetoric of legislators, educators, and previously neglected groups in our society calling for recognition and equity. The expectation simply was not and could not be met. . . .

It is overly simplistic to cite only unrealistic expectations as the cause of considerable, widespread criticism of schools at the beginning of the 1970s. The country was weary of war and the young bitter about it; our expanding economy appeared to be checked; an increasing imbalance of imports over exports was beginning to challenge the phrase, "as sound as a dollar"; our resources no longer seemed limitless; the alarm of conservationists over environmental rape was clanging more loudly; inflation and recession were twin devils; daily life was complex; our urban problems seemed as bad as before; ethnic minorities had come a long way but the road to further progress was not at all clear; women were men's burden of conscience; many things seemed not to go right. We had used and abused schools as the vehicle to improve or change all this and they had been found wanting. A Ford Foundation report was interpreted to say that the much-touted reforms had not worked; campus stress and tumult were near dormant; shrinking enrollments suggested caution, not boldness; research grants were hard to get; the professorial jet set had dwindled to a few, now older. With some communities confronting the unfamiliar problem of consolidating or closing elementary schools, there were those prognosticators who solemnly declared teaching to be dead as a profession! But it is unlikely that education or educators will roll over.

Among those aspects of life celebrated on the 200th anniversary of the United States of America, schools loom large. While some hear only hollowness in the words of tribute, those who know our history best are appropriately stirred and are neither carried away nor turned off by the rhetoric. They know that our schools never have lived up to the most extravagant claims nor deserved the most scathing criticisms. Our institutions of learning have mirrored the strengths and weaknesses, successes and failures, of the surrounding society, overly praised when all seemed well in the land and overly cursed when little seemed to be going right. . . .

It probably is healthy, therefore, that the middle years of the 1970s find us between cycles, with neither the worst fears nor the most grandiose proposals of the past two decades realized. We did not deschool our society. Neither Pygmalion nor computers took over in the classroom. That new generation about which we were so excited goes no more to the polls and no less to prison (or *vice versa*) than its predecessors. Our schools are not nearly as good as the predictions of 1966 said they would be by now, nor as bad as many said they were in 1972. It appears that our schools are marked at least as much by stability as by change. Between cycles, then, we are at one of those stable periods when reflection might provide the needed perspective before we move again. What better time than on our 200th anniversary?

The long look at yesterday, today, and tomorrow suggests that extending opportunity for education has been one of the most significant areas of change, and yet it remains the area of greatest need and challenge. It has two parts: access and appropriateness. The struggle for more general access, for fulfillment of the right to learn, has been carried on under the rubric of equality of opportunity. It has taken place previously in the political arena and in the courts. The drive for appropriateness has been more person-centered, drawing upon growing knowledge about individual differences and humanistic concern for the individual. . . .

With the addition of individual development to the stated aims, free public education simply to prepare for entry into the labor force is not sufficient. Likewise, a common curriculum is regarded today as a Procrustean anachronism. With the U.S. Supreme Court having established in the 1954 *Brown* decision the right of all children to attend the same integrated local schools, the issue of what constitutes equality is more complex: Is bus-aided integration (or its absence) equal opportunity? Is the right to establish a tax-supported bilingual school equality? Is access to many "schools of choice" equality? In regard to equality within a given locality, gross disparities in the ability of local communities to support schools have resulted in court challenges to the legality of property taxes as the prime base for financing schools.

Such issues are likely to be the motivation for and at the heart of educational change for some time to come. The issue of who shall be educated is caught up in expressions such as "lifelong" and "recurring" education. Change will be toward extending opportunity downward to younger ages and upward to older ones. . . .

What will continue to trouble us is how to provide simultaneously for individuals "to do their thing" and for all to acquire the education they need for performing "all social, domestic, civic, and moral duties." The sense of sin perceived by Myrdal and our fear of sloth, if nothing else, will protect against losing sight of one or the other of these twin, traditional goals.

The immediate road ahead will see us attempting to restore some of our old sense of *community* in regard to schooling and education. Breaking out of the egg-crate building and the 9 a.m. to 3 p.m. schedule into the larger community and the itinerant day will become *de rigueur* among innovative schools. There will be new partnerships among schools, museums, public health agencies, industry, and public media—especially television—for educational purposes. Community involvement will be more widespread; more people will be part-time teachers (and, of course, part-time students). But *citizen involvement,* after a cyclone of rhetoric and a short whirlwind of activity, will fall far short of today's predictions. This is but one of those short cycles which will move us, nonetheless, one step more toward that visionary goal of a learning society. Some good almost always rubs off from such cycles of enthusiasm and excess.

There will be changes in the ratio of federal, state, and local support for education, with the proportion paid by the first two increasing and that of the third declining. The courts will continue to play a significant role in the adjustments. Accompanying these changes will be tension regarding authority to make decisions. This tension will carry the controversy far beyond the issue of decentralization versus centralization into the finer nuances of what is better centralized and what decentralized. The stirring of this pond will keep it muddy—to a degree, deliberately. Some of the fun is taken out, along with challenges to candidates for public office, when lines of authority and responsibility are defined too rationally. Change in our society and, therefore, in education, has seldom been strongly motivated by desire to remove ambiguity, even though we tend to place rationality high on our scale of values.

Seventy-Five Years of Change

The following passage asks several questions about educational innovations. Do they persist? Do they leave a residue when they wash out? Who initiates innovations? What factors are associated with their tenure? While many of these are not curricular innovations, it is nevertheless interesting to review a wide spectrum of changes within which curricular modifications are made.

This study suffers from the bias of subjective judgments. But efforts were made to reduce the bias as much as possible. The authors independently classified the changes, then compared the results of their work. Agreement on the inside-outside dichotomy was 88 percent; for the post-pre 98 percent; for the success-failure categories 68 percent (no differences exceeded one scale point); and for the focus of the change, 72 percent. Differences were resolved on the basis of evidence that supported the rating.

The purpose of this essay is to report a study of educational changes attempted during the past seventy-five years, examine the efforts to put these ideas into practice, rate the efforts to install them as successful or unsuccessful, attribute that success or failure to particular factors, and make recommendations to those who promote educational change. The changes selected are broad, macrochanges rather than narrow and specific changes. Also, many changes have

Donald E. Orlosky and B. Othanel Smith, "Educational Change: Its Origins and Characteristics," *Phi Delta Kappan* 53 7(March 1972): 412–14. Reprinted by permission of authors and publisher.

been attempted during this period for which there is no record, but on the whole it may be assumed that the changes which are included in this account are of general significance.

Four categories were used to classify changes according to their degree of success or failure. The symbols used and the descriptions for degrees of success were:

4. A change that has successfully been installed and has permeated the educational system.

3. A change that has successfully been installed and is sufficiently present that instances of the change are obvious.

2. A change that has not been accepted as a frequent characteristic of schools but has left a residue that influences educational practice.

1. A change that has not been implemented in the schools and would be difficult to locate in any school system.

Changes that were rated 3 and 4 were regarded as successes and changes rated 1 and 2 were regarded as failures. The changes were also classified according to the aspect of the educational system that was the focus of change. The symbols employed in this classification were: A—instruction, B—curriculum, and C—organization and administration.

Each idea for change was classified according to its origin. Some changes originated outside the school setting and others arose within the field of education. The changes were classified as internal or external, using these symbols: I—internal origin, within the education field; and EX—external origin, outside the education field.

The fourth distinction made was between changes proposed recently and those proposed some time ago. Changes initiated after 1950 were regarded as recent; all others were listed in the pre-1950 era.

Table 13-1 provides an alphabetical listing by categories of the changes included in this report.

It is important to observe in Table 13-1 that a large number of changes (49) originated within the school system, compared with a small number (14) originating from external sources. The schools initiated changes at a ratio of 3 1/2 to 1, compared with individuals or agencies outside the schools. External changes were invariably in the areas of curriculum (8) or organization and administration (6). The external ideas had a higher success percentage (93) than the internal ideas (64). These data suggest that when an idea has both outside group and school support, success probability is high.

It should not be inferred from the lower success rate of ideas originating within the field of education that ideas are likely to fail because of their origin. For instance, all efforts to alter instructional behavior originated within the education field, but it is notoriously difficult to change teaching habits. Also, the lower percentage of success is quite likely due to the fact that the professional literature reports a larger number of internal change attempts. Failures that originate outside education are less likely to remain long enough to be recorded as an effort to change at the macro level studied.

Table 13–1: Changes listed according to date of origin, source, rating of success, and focus of change

Change	Post-1950	Source	Rating	Focus
Ability grouping		I	3	A
Activity curriculum		I	2	B
Adult education		EX	4	C
British infant school	X	I	3	B
Carnegie unit		I	4	C
Community school		.I	2	B
Compensatory education	X	EX	3	B
Compulsory attendance		EX	4	C
Conservation education		EX	3	B
Consolidation of schools		I	4	C
Core curriculum		I	1	B
Creative education	X	I	1	B
Dalton plan		I	1	A
Desegregation	X	EX	3	C
Driver education		EX	4	B
Elective system		I	4	B
Environmental education	X	EX	3	B
Equalization procedures		I	4	C
Extra-class activities		I	4	B
Flexible scheduling	X	I	2	C
Guidance		I	4	A
Head start	X	EX	3	C
Home economics		EX	3	B
Individually prescribed instruction	X	I	3	A
International education		I	3	B
Junior college		I	4	C
Junior high school		I	4	C
Kindergarten		I	4	C
Linguistics	X	I	3	A
Look-and-say method		I	3	A
Media and technology		I	4	A
Microteaching	X	I	3	A
Middle school	X	I	3	C
Mid-year promotion		I	1	C
New leadership roles		I	4	C
Nongraded schools	X	I	3	C
Nursery schools		EX	3	C
Open classroom	X	I	3	A
Phonics method		I	3	A
Physical education		EX	4	B
Platoon system		I	1	C
Programmed instruction		I	3	A
Project method		I	2	A
Safety education		I	4	B
School psychologist	X	I	3	C

Table 13-1: Continued

Change	Post-1950	Source	Rating	Focus
Self-contained classroom		I	3	C
Sensitivity training	X	I	2	A
Sex education	X	EX	2	B
Silent reading		I	4	A
Social promotion		I	4	C
Special education	X	I	4	B
Store front schools	X	EX	3	C
Student teaching		I	4	A
Team teaching	X	I	2	C
Testing movement		I	4	C
Tests and measurements		I	4	A
Thirty-school experiment		I	1	B
Unit method		I	2	B
Unit plan		I	2	A
Updating curriculum content		I	3	B
Visiting teacher		I	2	A
Vocational and technical education		EX	4	B
Winnetka plan		I	1	A

Changes were successfully implanted in instruction, curriculum, and organization and administration. None of these three categories was immune. Likewise, failures in all three areas suggest that each area had resisted changes or was unable to accommodate some of them. All of the successful changes in instruction came from within the education field, two-thirds of the changes in organization and administration originated within education, and half of the curricular changes came from within the field. Thus it appears that the public school is more responsive to change than is generally conceded.

Government influence was evident in such programs as Head Start, which required heavy financial support, and in compulsory attendance, where the legislative branch produced change through law.

The successful pre-1950 ideas usually involved school organization and administration. It appears to be easy to try and discard changes in curriculum and instruction, but when the machinery of organization and administration is modified, the change is relatively permanent.

It should be noted that there are factors and agencies not categorized in this analysis that bear on change and are influential in the determination of educational practice. They cannot be regarded as the basis for any particular change but affect the entire spectrum of educational practice. Four such factors within education are (1) educational research, (2) school personnel (teachers, administrators, state departments, and university personnel), (3) educational commissions and committees, and (4) professional and extra-legal organizations. The elements outside the field of education that should be taken into account include (1) state and federal constitutional requirements, (2) court decisions that rule on educational practice, and (3) pressure groups in society.

Planned change should be based on a combination of past experiences, current theories, and analysis of all aspects of the field of education. The conclusions that follow encourage such an approach and can serve as guides to those who promote educational change.

1. Changes in methods of instruction are apparently more difficult to make successfully than changes in curriculum or administration.

2. Changes in instruction are most likely to originate within the education profession. In no case in the past did a successful change in instruction come from outside education. Changes in ways of teaching and organizing instruction are neither the result of legislation nor of social pressure, but rather are the outcome of professional wisdom and research. This is attributable partly to the fact that the teacher's behavior in the classroom is shaped by factors considerably removed from social concerns, partly to the stability of teaching patterns, and partly to the intellectual character of teaching about which the public has little information.

3. A change that requires the teacher to abandon an existing practice and to displace it with a new practice risks defeat. If teachers must be retrained in order for a change to be made, as in team teaching, the chances for success are reduced unless strong incentives to be retrained are provided.

4. Specific curricular changes such as the establishment of the elective system are often initiated from within the field of education. Successful changes in curriculum can originate either within the profession or from the outside. Neither point of origin monopolizes ideas for curricular change.

5. Curricular changes involving the addition of subjects or the updating of content are more permanent than changes in the organization and structure of the curriculum. Efforts to change the curriculum by integrating or correlating the content, or by creating new category systems into which to organize the content, are made at great risk. Complete or considerable displacement of an existing curriculum pattern is not likely to be permanent even if the faculty initially supports the change. This can be attributed partly to cognitive strain on the faculty, partly to upsetting the expectations of pupils and consequent parental distrust, and partly to faculty mores which tend to become stronger when threatened by change.

6. Changes in the curriculum that represent additions such as new subjects or changes in the substance of subjects can be made most securely with support from legislation or organized interest groups. The failure of curricular changes to be permanent may be attributed either to lack of social support or to resistance to displacement of the existing curriculum pattern. If school authorities are successful in finding social backing for the addition of a subject to a curriculum, the change can be made with little risk of failure. On the other hand, if social opposition is pronounced, the probability of the change not being made is very high, or if it is made it is likely not to persist.

7. Efforts to alter the total administrative structure, or any considerable part of it, are likely to be unsuccessful.

8. Changes that represent additions or extensions of the educational ladder, such as junior college, are more likely to be lasting than changes that entail general modifications of the administrative organization, such as flexible scheduling.

9. The lack of a diffusion system will lead to abortive change. A change initiated in a particular school, in the absence of a plan for diffusion, no matter how loudly it may be acclaimed, is not likely to become widespread nor to be permanently entrenched.

10. Changes that have the support of more than one critical element are more likely to succeed. Compulsory education, with legal, social, and educational support, did not have to overcome as much resistance as it would have if only educators had supported it.

11. Changes will be resisted if they require educational personnel to relinquish power or if they cast doubt on educator roles. Accompanying legislative, legal, and financial impetus increases the probability of success in such changes.

12. The weight of the cognitive burden is one of the significant factors that determine the permanence of a change. If the cognitive load is light, i.e., if not many people are required to learn many new facts and procedures, a change is more likely to persist than if the burden is heavy. The weight of the burden is proportional to the number of factors entailed in the change. For example, if the total administrative structure is the object of change, the chances for successful innovation will be low. The same observation can be made about changes in methods of instruction or curricular changes.

13. The initiation of change may come from a number of sources—professionals, social groups, government, and so on—and changes may arise from research, as in the case of ability grouping, or from ideologies, as in the case of the core curriculum, or from professional wisdom, as in the platoon system. The source of the change appears to have far less to do with its staying power than the support the change receives and the strain it places upon the school personnel. The core curriculum and creative education are constant drains on the time and energy of a faculty and they consequently tend to disappear even though each may enjoy faculty support. On the other hand, international understanding tends to be more persistent as a curricular change. It requires far less time and energy of the teacher and has enjoyed no greater support from the faculty then either the core curriculum or creative education.

14. The federal government, as a change agent, will have optimum success if it takes certain facts into account. In the first place, the government acts in two ways. It passes enabling legislation empowering various federal agencies to do specified things to attain certain goals. In the second place, it acts through the courts to interpret laws, to establish norms, and to order certain actions by school officials. Programs of the U.S. Office of Education are based largely upon enabling legislation. In the development of its programs the USOE is subject to the same conditions of success as any other change agent. For example, its efforts to induce changes in methods of teaching are likely to be less successful than efforts to change curriculum content or to extend or modify the educational ladder; its efforts are likely to be more successful if it has the support of commission recommendations, organized groups, and professional personnel.

The data set forth in this report are too broad to provide insight into the sort of situational analysis that successful change entails. More refined data can be secured by intensive case studies. A few well-chosen case studies can be made to explore the underlying variables whose manipulation and control can give a change agent greater assurance of success.

The educational system in a dynamic society cannot remain stagnant. We should expect changes to be proposed that will alter the school system, since the United States is undergoing rapid change. The idiosyncracies of a particular situation may not always conform to the patterns revealed in this study, but it is likely that an understanding of the characterisitcs of the changes proposed over the last three-quarters of a century will be helpful in the development of successful procedures in the installation of educational changes.

Curriculum as an Instrument for Social Change

The attempt to promote nationwide adoption of the metric system of measurement illustrates two characteristics of curricular change. The first characteristic is the tendency of the schools to be influenced by developments in the society. As the world's society "shrinks" and the metric system comes closer to the United States, the schools are viewed as the agency to provide instruction on the metric system. The second characteristic is the huge difficulty encountered in bringing about changes in all the necessary components to install metric measurement. Both of these characteristics should become obvious as the reader studies the current state of metrication in the schools. The next article describes attempts at a massive change. The inclination of the schools to resist changes that require development of materials, facilities, training personnel, and other factors is evident in the attempt to install the metric system as common practice in our society.

☐

The United States is now moving toward nationwide adoption of the modernized metric system of measurement, i.e., the International System of Units (SI), as it is technically called. Adoption will entail complex social and technological changes and will exert a pervasive impact upon American education. However, until recently, the nature of this impact and its specific effects upon educational policies and practices were largely a matter of speculation. In order to develop preliminary answers to these questions, the National Institute of Education in 1973 funded an exploratory study of the metrication process and the resulting educational problems encountered by five English-speaking countries currently engaged in transition to SI as their official measurement system: Great Britain, Australia, South Africa, New Zealand, and Canada.[3]

Albert B. Chalupsky and Jack Crawford, "Preparing the Educator to Go Metric," *Phi Delta Kappan* 57, 4 (1975):262–65. Reprinted by permission of the author and publisher.

[3]Albert B. Chalupsky, Jack J. Crawford, and Edwin M. Carr, *Going Metric: An Analysis of Experiences in Five Nations and Their Implications for U.S. Educational Planning,* National Institute of Education Project No. 3-2173, Final Report (Palo Alto, Calif.: American Institutes for Research in the Behavioral Sciences, 1974).

The rationale underlying the study was simple. In metric conversion, the United States occupies a unique position in the world—and indeed a unique position in our own recent history. Together with Brunei, the Yemen Arab Republic, and the Yemen Peoples' Democratic Republic, we are well behind every other country, something we have never experienced in modern times.

However, this tardiness provides at least one benefit. We can profit from five nationwide experiments in changing measurement systems. Although each has common features, there are notable differences in method and schedule. Systematic study of these "living laboratories" can supply valuable source data for the formulation of U.S. educational policies and programs.

Recent History

In one form or another, the metric system has been with us since 1795, when France legalized the metric system, using the new unit of length, a meter. While most of the major European nations gradually adopted the metric system, it was not until recently that nations of the British Commonwealth began to convert.

Britain began its metrication program in 1965 with the hope of becoming substantially a metric country by 1975, a goal which proved unattainable. In 1966 the South African government decided to convert, expecting to be 85 percent metric by 1975. Through a carefully planned and forcefully scheduled program, South Africa remained on or ahead of schedule. Australia launched its ten-year metrication program in 1970 and has been moving generally on schedule, due in no small part to lessons learned by observing Britain's problems. Also apparently on target is New Zealand, which began its seven-year program in 1970. While Canada announced its decision to convert in 1970, progress in the early years was slow, due in large measure to the lack of metric activity in the U.S., its main export market. Nevertheless, progress in the past year has quickened considerably; specific schedules have been established in the hope of conversion by 1980.

In the U.S., the argument over whether the metric system should be adopted as the single official system of weights and measures is perhaps one of our longest continuing controversies, dating back to the administration of George Washington. Historically, our metric controversy has been characterized by high emotionalism and by "more intense and virulent prose than an attack on the sanctity of motherhood"[4] This controversy is documented in detail in a 1971 U.S. Department of Commerce publication.[5]

Despite the long controversy, the U.S. Congress enacted a law in 1866 which made use of the metric system legal but not mandatory; in 1893 the secretary of the treasury issued an order to establish the international meter and kilogram as "fundamental" standards of length and mass for the U.S. For over

[4]Frank Donovan, *Prepare Now for a Metric Future* (New York: Weybright & Talley, 1970).

[5]U.S. Department of Commerce, *A History of the Metric System Controversy in the United States,* National Bureau of Standards Special Publication 345-10 (Washington, D.C.: U.S. Government Printing Office, August 1971).

80 years, the yard and the pound have been officially defined as ratios of metric units.

Following this legislation, there was little real progress toward metrication until 1968, when the Metric Study Act became law. As a result, the National Bureau of Standards directed a study of the views of representatives of business, labor, trade associations, consumer groups, educators and the professions —as well as the general public—toward metric conversion. The Metric Study Group concluded that eventually the United States would join the rest of the world in using the metric system and that it would be in the best interests of this country to effect such a change under a coordinated national program. . . .

Since 1971 there have been several attempts to enact federal legislation establishing a national metric conversion board charged with developing a comprehensive plan for changeover. As of November 1975, we are still waiting.

Even though no specific metric conversion law was passed, a bill establishing national policy in metric education did become law in 1974. The Education Amendments of 1974 specify that "increased use of [a] metric system in the United States is inevitable, and [it] will become [our] dominant system of weights and measures." The law further states: "It is the policy of the United States to encourage educational agencies and institutions to prepare students to use the metric system of measurement with ease and facility as a part of the regular education program."[6] In support of this policy, the commissioner of education has been authorized to spend $10 million for each of the fiscal years ending prior to July 1, 1978 for grants and contracts to encourage educational agencies to prepare students to use SI.

Metric progress is even more evident at the state level. According to a survey by Jeffrey Odom, director of the Metric Information Office of the National Bureau of Standards, forty-nine states had some type of formal metric education under way by mid-1974. . . .

Numerous teachers' workshops have suddenly emerged. Such activity by educators, despite the lack of federal legislation, can be traced to the fact that progress in industry is quickening to the point where the question of *will* the U.S. convert has very largely been replaced by the questions of *how* and *when.* . . .

This growing snowball of activity in the federal, state, and business arenas raises a multitude of questions concerning how educators in the U.S. can cope effectively with the problems of going metric. It was to these questions that the AIR study was addressed, and the answers were to come from study of the five target countries.

Policy Issues

The Education Profession's Role in Early Planning   Educational associations and professional groups tend to exert a positive and sometimes a major force for metrication. The extent of their support and the roles played by particular specialties within education vary widely. The associations of science and math

---

[6]P.L. 93-380, Education Amendments of 1974, Section 403, Education for the Use of the Metric System of Measurement.

educators are usually in the forefront, followed by support from industrial and vocational educators. Social studies and language groups often remain aloof or are ignored in initial planning. . . .

Commitment of Scheduling South Africa and Great Britain are the extremes in adherence to announced schedules. South Africa announced and followed a tight calendar for conversion, with mandated milestones. Great Britain's schedule, although announced, was allowed to slip again and again. Some groups met the original schedule but found they were too far ahead for useful coordination with others and were unable to proceed. . . .

Although education was rarely responsible for conversion slippage in the countries studied, it nevertheless felt the impact when other sectors of society failed to meet their schedules. Students, by design, will learn SI before the general public is using it. If conversion across the country lags, students will be immersed in one measurement language in school for years while being forced to cope with a different language out of school.

Metric conversion scheduling within the educational system itself also raises problems. The independence of higher education as well as the degree or departmental autonomy within universities is conducive to uneven progress. An area of particular concern to students is the degree to which SI will be emphasized in college entrance exams. Textbook publishers and developers of standardized achievement tests for all grade levels are faced with similar transition difficulties.

The Need for Continuing Communication and Coordination Metrication is a pervasive and interdependent network of changes among all sectors of society. Adequate communication about SI and current policy to all organizations *and* to all educators is crucial, but may require a sizable investment. Overseas evidence points to the need for advance information on the rationale for conversion, the advantages and consequences. . . .

Problems in Teaching SI

Metric Materials The intense demand for metric materials generates a flood of inaccurate and inadequate products. Materials produced under pressure to meet the new demand frequently contain serious errors. They are often unsuitable for classroom use and are not related to any explicit teaching learning objectives. A common oversight overseas was the failure to provide for materials evaluation until classrooms were loaded with ineffective and error-laden junk. The United States appears to be heading rapidly toward a similar plight. There is a rising tide of new materials but a general lack of evaluation efforts. As overseas staffs became experienced in metric instruction, they discovered many ways to produce inexpensive, teacher-made, and student-made materials. For them, it was a slow trial-and-error process. U.S. educators can capitalize on this achievement.

Teacher Training All school staffs require training in SI. Frequently, the math or science teacher feels he or she already knows SI. It was found that these teachers knew only a smattering of metric measurement—some of which was inappropriate or incorrect under SI. More learning was required.

One necessary component of teacher training is an initial awareness of the purpose and need for conversion and how it will influence the professional and daily life of the target audience. Most teachers will need reassurance that the change will not be too difficult or threatening and that adequate training and support will be provided.

Failure to see the implications of SI outside math and science instruction may be commonplace. However, conversion to SI presents even more problems to vocational education. The recalibration and replacement of expensive equipment can be a major problem. In the social sciences the conversion of geographic measures and map units to SI can be complex.

Explicit and covert resistance to change can be expected among teachers as well as other adults. The need to identify and cope with resistance issues (e.g., "I'm too old to change") was repeatedly emphasized by our respondents. Frequently, teachers overemphasize the problem of learning SI. It can be unnecessarily cumbersome if exact conversion from customary to metric units is emphasized. This is counterproductive and makes learning unnecessarily complicated. A training strategy found effective in the countries we surveyed is to demonstrate, using familiar objects, how easy the metric system is when you plunge directly into it.

Classroom Practices and Teaching Strategies   As with teacher training, the reliance on conversion from customary units to SI and vice versa can seriously impede instruction. All overseas evidence stressed the importance of early immersion in SI and direct measurement of common objects with metric units. Dual labels are false comforts; the longer they are used, the more they complicate and block new learning. . . .

An important aspect of the SI system is learning the rational relationships among units. The relationships along a single measurement dimension can be readily taught—for example, how a cubic decimeter can be built from, and shown equivalent to, a thousand centimeter cubes. However, the relationships among SI units of volume, area, and mass, as well as their relationships to length units, are not as apparent to students or teachers. Instruction in these relations can be an important part of teacher training workshops. . . .

Temptation for Unnecessary Precision   The decimal notation used in SI fosters the adding of unnecessary digits far beyond useful accuracy. Students can be appalled by the fact that one pound equals 453.594 grams or that one mile equals 1.609 kilometers. An Australian newspaper describes a fugitive as between 175.2 cm and 180.3 cm in height. Recognizing that .1 cm is equivalent to a thick pencil stroke, this was much the same as describing a person's age as between 25 years, two months, three days and 30 years, four months, one day.

Impact on Teaching Time   Throughout the countries studied, claims for savings of class time and effort with SI are pervasive. These claims include estimated savings up to 25 percent of the time that students currently spend on arithmetic in grades one through eight and up to $500 million each year.[7] The claims are often quoted as based upon established evidence. However, our overseas search turned up *no* evidence supporting or refuting such claims. If such claims are true, their potential impact on education is sizable. If erroneous, the fraud should be stopped as we attempt to persuade U.S. educators to go metric. In all fairness, many teachers justifiably expect some economy of time as a result of metrication, because it eliminates a second system, is simple, and reduces time spent on fractions.

Where Do We Go from Here?

Recent National Projects A variety of metric research and development projects have been funded at the federal level during the past three years. In 1972 the U.S. Office of Education funded a Western Michigan University project for development of industrial-vocational teacher education materials. In 1973 the National Science Foundation contracted with the University of Minnesota to conduct a technology assessment study of alternative strategies for going metric. In 1974 a number of new metric projects of interest to educators were started. . . .

Suggested Future Projects We recommend the following activities:

1. A thorough study of costs versus benefits of metrication. There is no better vehicle for such a study than the five English-speaking countries now undergoing conversion.
2. A close scrutiny of the timetables planned and followed by these other countries, together with an assessment of schedule-related problems and their solutions.
3. Identification and analysis of resistance sources. What needs and values are placed in jeopardy by the change? What incentives are used to work through or prevent unnecessary resistance to conversion?
4. Materials evaluation. Such a service, conducted on a national basis and broadly communicated to schools, could provide a useful guide to metric programs.
5. Identification of blocks to teacher training, and a description of strategies to reduce them.

To and Fro of Curriculum Change

While the attempt to introduce metrication into the schools proceeds slowly and unevenly, changes in curriculum sometimes occur rapidly and then

[7]U.S. Department of Commerce, *U.S. Metric Study Interim Report, Education,* National Bureau of Standards Special Publication 345-6 (Washington, D.C.: U.S. Government Printing Office, July 1971).

retrench before starting in another direction. Since 1957 no part of the curriculum has received as much attention as science education. One might think the massive efforts to improve and change the science curriculum would, by now, provide firm answers to the role and teachability of science in the school programs. But such is not the case. A recent article by Blumenfeld traces the effort to revise the science curriculum and suggests the current state of the scene and future directions to consider.

☐

As we look at the science curriculums in our schools today, we note that we are often still using educational programs that were successful for a society less oriented toward rapid change. For the most part, we don't see new programs responsive to the consequences, both desirable and undesirable, of modern science and the technology growing out of it.

The textbooks and curriculums of the past emphasized the didactic. Students were expected to gain an appreciation of the natural world through memorization of facts and principles. Consideration of contextual relationships was almost nonexistent. Fortunately, some scholars in the field had the foresight to recognize the influence that science and science education could and would have on culture and society. Their insight was the basis upon which effective modern science education is founded. . . .

The major criticism of science education in the 1950s was that students were entering college poorly prepared in science. Some specific criticisms of science education below the college level included the following:

1. Science was being taught predominantly through technological application.
2. Science courses were predominantly fact-oriented.
3. Science courses did not develop unifying concepts.
4. Laboratory work was not open-ended, that is, not inquiry-oriented.
5. Modes of instruction were authoritarian, primarily teacher-centered.
6. Teachers were often poorly trained.

With the support of the National Science Foundation (NSF) and with the cooperation of educators and educational institutions, scientists began to plan curriculum reform in science education. Curriculum commissions, study groups, and others undertook the development of programs to update classroom teachers in their subject and develop new teaching materials and strategies.

The form and structure of the NSF-sponsored programs were based upon the principles set forth at the 1959 National Academy of Sciences Conference at Woods Hole, Massachusetts. The Conference developed two themes:

Fred Blumenfeld, "Science—Yesterday, Today, and Tomorrow," *Today's Education* 63, 3 (September-October 1974):86–89. Reprinted by permission of author and publisher.

1. The underlying principles that give structure to a subject should be the basis for the curriculum of that subject.
2. Curricular activities should allow students to approach science in the manner of a working scientist.

The Biological Sciences Curriculum Study (BSCS) program, for instance, uses three different schemes to develop the structure of biology. The so-called "yellow" version develops the structure through a cellular approach; the "blue" version, through a molecular theme; and the "green," through an ecological scheme.

Similarly, the structure of chemistry was approached either through the Chemical Systems or Bond Approach (CBA) or the Chemical Education Material Study (CHEMS). . . .

These developments in high school science quickly indicated the need for better science program in the junior high and elementary schools. Such programs as Introductory Physical Science (IPS). Earth Science Curriculum Project (ESCP), Time, Space, and Matter (TSM), Intermediate Science Curriculum Study (ISCS), and others were designed for the junior high school. In the elementary schools, learning theory was more carefully considered in developing the science programs. The programs initiated at this level were Science—A Process Approach (SAPA), Science Curriculum Improvement Study (SCIS), Elementary Science Study (ESS), and many others. . . .

All these K-12 projects in science education are still widely in use, although in many cases for high-ability students only. In addition, many of these high school science programs, some supported by NSF, have had a major impact on the design and content of many science texts and curriculums.

Most of the above programs assume that the same content and instruction are valid for students interested in science-related careers and also for those seeking only general education in the subject. As a matter of fact, such programs, while excellent for students selecting a vocation in science, have fallen far short of meeting the needs of those interested in general education. Neither have they changed the attitude of the general public toward science. The findings of the 1970 President's Task Force on Science Policy indicate that, in fact, the citizens' confidence in science has been eroded, in part because of a lack of understanding concerning how science improves the quality of their daily lives.

Education is a constantly changing endeavor. The needs of fifteen years ago are not the needs of today. No one questions our ability to produce scientists and engineers. Today, however, the need is to produce an informed citizenry, one capable of making decisions in a world beset by technological and social problems. Our current high school science programs often fail to meet this need. . . .

It now appears that we must modify the thesis set forth in the 1959 Woods Hole Conference. Jerome Bruner, the Conference chairman, later said in an article in the September 1971 issue of the *Phi Delta Kappan*:

> If I had my choice now, in terms of a curriculum project for the seventies, it would be to find a means whereby we could bring society back to its sense of values and

priorities in life. *I believe I would be quite satisifed to declare, if not a moratorium, then something of a deemphasis on matters that have to do with the structure of physics, the nature of mathematical consistency, and deal with it [a curriculum project] rather in the context of the problems that face us. . . . We might put vocation and intention back into the process of education much more firmly than we had them there before.*

We must, therefore, take a hard look at our present science curriculums. . . . To this end, the curriculum committee of NSTA (National Science Teachers Association) has offered a blueprint for the future in its *Position Statement on School Science Education for the 1970s.* In part, the document states:

> All teachers, and especially science teachers, are challenged to educate young people to expect, to promote, and to direct societal change—
> Awareness of the social aspects of science includes—
> Perception of the cultural conditions within which science thrives.
> Recognition of the need to view the scientific enterprise within broad perspectives of culture, society, and history.
> Expectation that social and economic innovations may be necessary to improve man's condition. . . .

The implications of this statement are quite clear. Science courses should no longer be tied, inexorably, to a single discipline, isolated from a societal setting, and rarely touching on other relevant academic areas. . . .

NSF's Advisory Committee for Science Education had endorsed this position a year earlier in their report, *Science Education—The Task Ahead, for the National Science Foundation,* which states:

> The articulation of mathematics with science, of science with technology, and of technology with the future of man and society poses the greatest challenge we face in the area of curriculum. Without this articulation, we will continue to suffer from a long list of educational ills which threaten both the future of science and of society. . . .

The unified mode of instruction would enable students to gain a more complete understanding of the total setting of a problem or system under study. For example, a consideration of the population problem could involve study in such areas as birth control (biology and political science), housing and food supply (social studies and economics), and energy needs and pollution (physics and ecology). . . .

In the traditional science class, all pupils begin at the same point; follow the same path; and finish supposedly with the same result, depending upon the educator's point of view. Is this a realistic expectation? I do not think so, especially if we are obligated to ensure that every individual attains maximum potential.

In our efforts to develop the full potential of students, we must first provide them with many optional learning activities. To do this, we must eliminate the notion that the only way to learn a subject is to study it for a full year. One method of removing the lockstep schedule of programming and at the same time increasing the alternatives and interest in science courses is through the individualization of instruction. . . .

Presently, there are several places where a full or partial individualized instruction program is in existence, including Millburn, New Jersey; Barringer High School in Newark, New Jersey; and Shawnee Mission, Kansas.

Autotutorial schemes, minicourses, college school activities, and career-oriented programs are alternative teaching practices currently in use. We must recognize, of course, that all options require flexible scheduling which provides teachers and students with essential blocks of unstructured modules.

Whatever the teaching strategies, it is now evident that the teacher's function is altered. The educational environment is now teacher-managed instead of teacher-oriented. The instructor guides students, arranges to have instructional materials available, is involved with individual and small group interaction, and generally serves as a resource person. . . .

How well can new teachers entering the profession and those presently in the classroom cope with these novel approaches? Will communities be inclined to support inservice programs to retrain and reeducate teachers? Will teacher educating institutions be willing to restructure courses so that new science teachers are prepared to promote alternative instructional programs?

These questions cannot be resolved quickly, for it is no easy task to provide a meaningful educational program. However, articulation of the science program in grades K through 12 must be ensured so that the best development approach to science is obtained. To do this, we must increase communication between classroom teachers and those who prepare them. We must also increase our efforts to seek both governmental and private support for programs that provide aid to science education in all its aspects.

Now is the time to face the educational challenges of the future with commitment and conviction. For yesterday's learned experiences structure today's realities which, in turn, formulate tomorrow's creativity.

What's the Worth of Curricular Change?

This short trip through changing times in the schools should emphasize that change in the schools does and can occur. The evidence of change is strong. The complexity of change, and the time and resources to bring about change are also obvious factors to take into account. And perhaps the most compelling issue is the answer to the question: "When does a change also constitute improvement?" Can we be sure that the changes in science instruction have improved the quality of science or the scientific literacy of the public? And how certain are we that metric measurement will bring about improvements that are worth the effort? These and other questions should come from thoughtful reading and analysis of curricular change.

Chapter **14**

Why Changes in Curriculum Take Place

"Just when I learn to spell library, they change its name!"

Phi Delta Kappan 54, 7 (1973): 485.

1. A Pebble in Space Creates Demands for Curriculum Change
2. Forces that Promote Change
3. Example of Forces for Change: Vocational Education
4. Information Sources and Curricular Changes
5. Social Justification of Curricular Reform
6. Summary

It is helpful to know why changes in the school curriculum are attempted. Understanding the change process enables curriculum workers to capitalize on change when the time and circumstances are ripe. It also helps avoid attempts at change that require inordinate amounts of effort because the conditions for change are lacking. There is no sure formula for knowing when or under what arrangements change can be successfully undertaken. But past attempts to make changes serve as lessons: there is a time for change and there is a time when change should not be attempted.

For example, during the 1920s and 1930s S. L. Pressey attempted to promote "teaching machines" as a way to improve school's effectiveness and efficiency. He drew on personal energy and finances but finally had to halt his efforts when the nation's economy slowed and the energy and resources he had expended for fifteen years gave out. About twenty years later, "teaching machines" and programmed instruction rose rapidly in stature and acceptance. By 1960 programmed instruction including linear and branching programs had emerged, and rather sophisticated computerization had been employed to capitalize on these developments.

Other illustrations of truncated efforts at change can be drawn from the testing movement, life adjustment education, compensatory schooling, and career education. Acceptance of changes depends on timing and quality of the idea as well as on an accurate assessment of the frame factors. In addition, it is important that ideas for change appeal to those who wish to correct shortcomings in the school. Many of the changes in school organization arise from dissatisfaction with existing arrangements.

Developments that grew from ideas about better ways to solve school problems include the junior high school in early 1900, the emerging middle school today, team teaching, nongraded schools, individualized instruction, open classrooms, and the recommendation that society should be de-schooled.

This chapter presents examples that illustrate the stimulus for change and some of the variables that come into play when changes occur. As the reader examines these changes it would be a good idea to pinpoint the problem the change is intended to solve and the circumstances that aid or prevent the change from occurring.

A Pebble in Space Creates Demands for Curricular Changes

The first article describes an event unparalled in history—the successful launching of the first satellite. As you read this article, assess the strength of this stimulus to bring unified action to promote changes in the school's curriculum.

☐

. . . . The Soviet Union had successfully launched the first man-made satellite "Sputnik,"—short for "Iskustvennyi Sputnik Zemli," meaning "artificial traveler around the earth."

Almost as astonishing as the fact that the Russians had gotten Sputnik into orbit at all, the reports noted, was its weight: more than 150 pounds heavier than Vanguard, the most frequently mentioned American entry in what the newspapers dubbed the race for space.

. . . The three-stage Russian rocket that had pushed Sputnik aloft was nearly 20 times more powerful than that planned for Vanguard, and that Sputnik's polar orbit—against the earth's rotation—was deemed far more difficult to achieve than the east-west orbit contemplated for the American launching. . . .

Few had imagined that Russian science had advanced so far. The signals had nevertheless been coming in. There had been the report in 1955, for example, that the Soviet Union had trained some 1,900,000 teachers by that year, as contrasted with the American total of 1,360,000; and that more specifically, the Russians were preparing young people for careers in science at a rate of some 126,000 annually as compared with our 59,000.

"In America," reporters were told by a Russian scientist attending meetings being held in Washington at the time of the Sputnik launching in connection with the International Geophysical Year, "you have trouble recruiting young men to study science. In the Soviet Union we have trouble turning them down. With us, science is a matter of pride, and everybody wants to be a scientist." Added Dr. Vannevar Bush, then chairman of the corporation of the Massachu-

Mark Travaglini, "In the Wake of Sputnik," *American Education* 11, 1 (January-February 1975): 26–28. Reprinted by permission of the author and publisher.

Footnotes have been renumbered consecutively throughout this chapter.

setts Institute of Technology, "If there's a youngster with talent for science, they make sure he gets all the education he can take. We still have bright boys who can't afford to go to college. There ought to be some kind of program for making sure our boys get all the education *they* can take."

While Dr. Bush's remarks would require some desexing to make them digestible today, his views struck a responsive chord. Others quickly echoed them. In 1955, it was pointed out, one-third of all high school students qualified for college had failed to continue their education because of lack of funds, and more particularly, higher education had for that reason been denied to half of those scholastically ranked among the top 30 percent. And as the Sputnik-stimulated conversation broadened, this skimming-off process was revealed to be only one among a broad range of problems.

Surveys showed, for example, that the colleges and universities were having grave difficulties in filling faculty vacancies. Moreover, the proportion of top quality faculty members was declining. In the 1953–54 academic year, whereas 40 percent of all college teachers held doctoral degrees, only 31 percent of the new faculty members hired that year held doctorates and by 1956–57 the figure was down to 23 percent. Part of the problem was that relatively few institutions of higher education even offered doctoral programs—only 160 as of 1957, and of that total sixty awarded fewer than ten such degrees a year.

Nor, as many educators pointed out, were the trouble spots by any means limited to higher education. Though the United States took pride in being the leading nation in a world community in which English was but one among a couple of dozen major languages, only Spanish and French were being studied by any appreciable segment of American high school students. Overall, less than 15 percent of the public high school population was studying a modern foreign language (not a surprising figure, really, since fewer than half of the nation's secondary schools offered such courses) and the same percentage held true for the three million students attending college. And Russian was particularly neglected. Witness a New York *Times* editorial arising from the fact that shortly before the launching of Sputnik the U.S. Office of Education had received copies of the mathematics and science books used in Soviet elementary and secondary schools. Even ten months later, the *Times* pointed out, the Office had still been unable "to find persons with dual competence in Russian to make comparisons from partial translations with American school texts." The situation did not seem destined to improve. Scanty though high school foreign language courses were, the supply of teachers prepared to conduct them was nevertheless 25 percent below the demand, and meanwhile the number of college students training to teach foreign languages was steadily dropping.

And there were other shortages as well. With only 26,000 full- and part-time guidance counselors available throughout the nation's entire elementary and secondary school system, experts said an additional 15,000 were needed in the high schools alone to achieve anything approaching adequacy. According to HEW Secretary Marion B. Folsom, the nation needed at least 159,000 additional classrooms just to keep up with the expanding population, not to speak of dealing with overcrowded schools and half-day schedules. Though the direct responsibility for the conduct of education lay with the states, only six had full-time supervisors of mathematics and science, and only two had supervisors for foreign language instruction.

Such shortfalls and the need to give education a boost had not gone unnoticed, In a special message to Congress in January 1956, President Eisenhower had called attention to critical shortages "in medicine, teaching, nursing, science, engineering, and other fields of knowledge," and a few months later he told a meeting of the National Education Association that "our schools are strong points in our national defense. . . . more important than Nike batteries, more necessary than our radar warning nets, and more powerful even than the energy of the atom." Former Senator William Benton returned from a tour of the Soviet Union to tell reporters that "education has become a main feature of the cold war. . . . Russia's classrooms and libraries, her laboratories and teaching methods may threaten us more than her hydrogen bombs. . . ." General Nathan F. Twining, Chief of Staff of the U.S. Air Force, declared that "the security of our nation in the years ahead depends as much on the wisdom and skill of our engineers, scientists, and technicians as it does upon the courage of our fighting men . . ." James B. Conant, former president of Harvard, agreed that education needed help but insisted that it should be extended across the board and not just in the areas of science and engineering. What was needed, he said, was "not more Einsteins but more Washingtons and Madisons."

Spurred by such comments from national leaders, concern for strengthening the schools and colleges began to gather momentum. Ultimately the call came from several quarters for the federal government to lead the way by enacting supportive legislation. That proposal quickly ran into firm opposition. By failing to mention education, it was argued in and out of Congress, the Constitution reserved responsibility for its conduct to the states, and thus the federal government had no business getting involved. Moreover, the opponents declared, federal aid to the schools and colleges was a sure path to federal control over them.

The advocates of federal assistance responded by dwelling on the vital part played by education in the nation's progress and security, and on the proposition that since the problems were national in scope they required national attention. Moreover, they argued, there was precedent for this kind of assistance—notably in such legislation as the Morrill Act of 1862 creating the Land Grant Colleges, the Smith-Hughes Act of 1917 addressed to vocational education, the Cooperative Research Act of 1954, and the Library Services Act of 1956. What proved to be the most stirring stimulus to action came on that Friday evening in the fall of 1957 with the announcement from Moscow that put the word "sputnik" into American dictionaries.

The convening of the 85th Congress three months later brought on the introduction of a rash of federal aid to education bills—ultimately reaching some 150 in all. The most acceptable proved to be HR 13247, introduced in the House by Representative Carl Elliott and paired in the Senate with S 4237, introduced by Senator Lister Hill. Having passed both houses by wide margins, the bill was signed into law by President Eisenhower on September 2 as the National Defense Education Act of 1958, designed "to strengthen the national defense and to encourage and assist in the expansion and improvement of educational programs to meet critical national needs; and for other purposes."

Meanwhile there had been the launching of the initial American satellite, Explorer, and the United states was off on a series of unparalleled ventures into space that were to lead some eleven years later to the triumphant touchdown of Apollo 11 on the lunar surface. By that time the National Defense Education Act had recorded some noteworthy achievements of its own.

More than 1.5 million men and women had been enabled to pursue higher education under NDEA's Title II National Student Loan Program. Title III, originally written to strengthen elementary and secondary instruction in science, mathematics, and modern foreign languages, had been broadened to include 50-50 matching grants to the states covering a wide range of subjects. The Title IV graduate fellowship program was expanding the supply of teachers and raising the quality of college faculties by enabling more than 15,000 men and women each year to complete their doctoral programs. Title V had provided more than $158 million to the states for guidance and testing and had helped raise the number of full-time counselors by more than 260 percent, to 44,000. Under Title VI (by this time also broadened) the skills of some 122,000 teachers and education specialists had been sharpened at NDEA-supported institutes offering advanced training not only in counseling and foreign languages but in such areas as reading, history, English, civics, and geography. Thanks in large part to Title VII, the schools were making greater use of such products of technology as television, computers, motion pictures, and tape recorders. And under Title VIII, more than 85,000 young people had been trained in such fields as electronics, drafting design, and data processing, while the number of institutions offering technical education had grown from 262 in 1959 to 1,100 a decade later. All in all, by the time Neil Armstrong stepped on the moon, the federal investment in education through NDEA had reached nearly $3 billion.

Among the various people who had commented on the launching of Sputnik was Chancellor Franklin D. Murphy of the University of Kansas, and this is what he said: "The message which this little ball carries to Americans, if they would but stop and listen, is that in the last one-half of the twentieth century . . . nothing is as important as the trained and educated mind." Clearly his fellow citizens *had* stopped and listened, and the message had come through loud and clear.

Forces that Promote Change

Change is not always stimulated by an event of space exploration magnitude. Obviously, events of this importance are not everyday occurrences, although everyday efforts at curriculum change do take place. What are the more constant forces that promote change? In the next article, Ronald Doll lists four factors he regards to be significant variables that promote curricular reform.

Ronald C. Doll, "The Multiple Forces Affecting Curriculum Change," *Phi Delta Kappan* 51, 7 (March 1970): 382–84. Reprinted by permission of the author and publisher.

☐

Four forces affecting curriculum change have become especially prominent: (1) the drive for power; (2) the appeal of the dollar; (3) growth in knowledge, with corresponding efforts at evaluating acquisition of knowledge; and (4) the needs and concerns of people in schools, within surrounding social and cultural milieus.[1]

The Drive for Power

Consider people's drive for power over the curriculum. During the forties, for instance, this drive revealed itself in the urge of a person or a group to speak loudly, to alert other citizens to an alleged danger, to become nationally prominent, or, as we say today, "to shake up the troops." Sometimes the drive had a helpful end; often it seemed only a quest for power for power's sake. During eras of attack on the curriculum, school people tend to think of a person's natural drive for power as being malicious and threatening. During quieter, saner moments, they think of the drive for power as a force which could possibly result in improvement.

Within recent years we have seen several major attempts at shifting loci of power over the curriculum. Among them are the following:

1. A push by scholars in the subject fields, often at the expense of professional educators and especially curriculum leaders, to give elementary and secondary school pupils choice content from their fields and, whether incidentally or not, to enhance their own status as curriculum workers.

2. Prods from the far left to promote particular brands of political education, with countering prods from the far right against alleged dangers like sex education and sensitivity training.

3. Militancy by teachers' organizations, which have learned that when one begins to talk about teacher welfare, he must soon discuss organization of schools and children's curricula, both of which matters have previously been in the preserve of boards of education and their administrative staffs.

4. The increasing strength of highly localized community groups, especially in the big cities, at the expense of centralized control of schools.

5. The militant behavior of youth, beginning in the colleges and moving to the secondary schools.

6. The new thrust of quasi-governmental regional or national agencies, like the Education Commission of the States, which have developed prestige and sometimes real power.

7. Forays toward control of the curriculum by the U.S. Office of Education and other federal agencies, at the expense of state departments of education and local school districts.

[1]Students in the course 76.701, Supervising and the Improvement of Instruction, winter semester, 1969–70, at Richmond College have helped in defining these forces.

8. Campaigns for a black curriculum and, to a minor degree, a red curriculum, a Puerto Rican curriculum, a Mexican-American curriculum, and so on.

While systems and formal arrangements for decision making about the curriculum have not materially changed during the 1960s, the persons who have initiated and sanctioned curriculum ideas have often come from groups other than teachers, administrators, and school board members. Power has shifted, in part, to scholars in the subject fields, conductors of summer inservice institutes, people who complain most loudly, those who have special programs to promote, the inner councils of teachers' unions and associations, self-appointed community leaders, paraprofessionals, and other climbers on career ladders, designers and reviewers of project proposals, bureaucrats at state and federal levels of government, and specialists at sitting-in, impeding, and taking over meetings for decision making. These individuals and groups have sought power in obvious, open ways. Other, quieter participants in a new drive for power, like owners of wealth and persons high in the power structures of communities, have also been at work. . . .

The Appeal of the Dollar

A second fundamental force which has affected curriculum change in the United States is the strong appeal which money has for curriculum makers in a materialistic society. Always in need of funds to do what they have wanted to do for children, curriculum personnel have found a bonanza in grants-in-aid, which have frequently proved to be mixed blessings. Whereas under a time-honored arrangement school boards and administrators waited for all their funds to be sent them by tax collectors, state finance officers, and (sometimes) federal agencies, school officials have become seekers of special grants to augment school district income. . . .

While grants have emphasized, for example, particularized cognitive development and special attention to poverty areas, producers of educational materials have sought financial profit through new educational ideas and the increase in child population. The appeal of the dollar for these producers has brought a flood of instructional materials which are conditioning, increasingly, what children learn. Thus one may say that both the curriculum hobbies of grantors and the sales promotion schemes of businesspeople are now having unprecedented impact on curriculum decision making. Priorities in the curriculum have been realigned as control has continued to follow the dollar.

Growth in Knowledge

A third force persistently affecting curriculum change is growth in knowledge, which formerly occurred slowly and quite steadily but now shows marked, erratic bursts of speed. The teacher is no longer able to "cover the book." Instead, many books now cover the teacher. The eight-to-twelve year doubling of knowledge in the natural sciences which Robert Oppenheimer noted has not been duplicated in other subject fields. Nevertheless, knowledge abounds embarrassingly in all fields, so that Herbert Spencer's question, "What knowledge is of most worth?" becomes more and more pertinent. Against a backdrop of educational objectives, curriculum planners are forced to seek new answers to Spencer's question. . . .

With increased growth of knowledge have come definite attitudes toward the effects of its growth. While one of these attitudes has been concern with how to sort out elements of knowledge and place them within the curriculum, another has been fear that even the former elements are not being learned. Hence a flurry of effort at evaluation and assessment. Enter, for instance, national assessment, research and development centers, and new contracts for firms which develop and sell tests.

Proponents of national assessment have declared its purpose to be evaluation of educational performance as a means of gauging strengths and weaknesses in schooling and of assisting research. It could, under the wrong conditions, become a direct determiner of the curriculum in the same way that Regents Examinations have been one of the determiners of the high school curriculum in New York State. Dangers in the current anxiety about evaluation may well include confusion of means and ends in the curriculum, pressures which pupils and teachers feel in preparing for major examinations, and a tendency to sacrifice all-round development of children to a new set of remote goals. Though the elementary and secondary schools obviously did not cause the current burgeoning of knowledge, they are seriously caught up in its effects.

The Needs of People in School

A fourth major force affecting curriculum change is the needs and concerns of pupils, teachers, administrators, parents, and other persons who work together to provide the best education for children. To dedicated educators, this is the most satisfying, meaningful force with which they deal. Always the real needs and concerns of people have part of their foundation in societal, subcultural, and community milieus. Therefore, parents and other community members should be expected to contribute to inschool education and to education beyond the confines of the school. The experiences children have in schools must be related increasingly to the life space of youngsters throughout the day. . . .

The Interrelationship of Forces

Curriculum leaders find that the four prominent forces which have been discussed above sometimes become merged and blurred because human motivation is almost never single or pure. Actions which are taken by professionally minded teachers for the good of children may be aided, for instance, by teaching devices manufactured by profit seekers and by ideas developed by power hungry community groups. Is it possible that when a society begins to age and to become more complex, the impact of single forces on the curriculum of its schools become less clear-cut and distinctive by combining at times into a major, fused force? If so, discussions of "outside forces" versus "inside" or institutional ones become unreal, and efforts to identify separate forces according to any criteria become more difficult.

Example of the Forces for Change: Vocational Education

Vocational education is an excellent example of a major change in the schools that incorporates each of the four factors identified by Doll. In the next article look for links between the forces that promoted vocational education and the factors Doll cited as forces for change.

☐

Austria's Archduke Francis Ferdinand had been assassinated almost three years earlier. World War I was at the height of its fury and the United States was on the brink of entering the conflict. Soon it was not only to send waves of doughboys to the trenches in France but to become, thanks to a rush toward industrialization that had seen manufacturing surpass agriculture as the chief source of the nation's wealth, a crucial source of material in a new, mechanized form of warfare.

Against this background of a convulsive struggle abroad and a growing need for skilled workers at home, the Congress passed and President Woodrow Wilson signed on February 23, 1917, the landmark Smith-Hughes Act. Introduced by Senator Hoke Smith and Representative Dudley M. Hughes, both of Georgia, the new law broke with a centuries-old tradition by which preparation for work was excluded from the school curriculum. Culminating years of effort on the part of numerous individuals, organizations, and government agencies, it provided federal support and leadership for establishing vocational education in the nation's high schools. . . .

At the time of our nation's founding and for most of the decades since, the training of workers predominantly took the form of apprenticeship. Job skills were inculcated by father instructing son and mother teaching daughter, or by arrangements under which a beginner worked as a helper to a journeyman or master craftsman. Vocational education as such, however, was regarded as somehow less worthy than other aspects of learning and therefore not appropriate as a classroom enterprise. In *A History of the Problems of Education,* John Brubacher sees this attitude as a remnant from Athenian culture. The Greeks excluded vocational training from the school curriculum, he says, because the "industrial arts were too closely connected with the ancient institution of slavery" and thus carried "a servile stigma." In any case, education and work were seen as being in unrelated realms, a point of view that was to persist over the centuries.

That they ultimately began to come together was primarily a consequence of the Industrial Revolution, which caused production to be shifted from the home to the factory and from handcraft to power-driven machinery. Whereas early craftspersons learned the entire manufacturing process, from obtaining the raw material to turning out the finished product, the machine worker was seldom exposed to more than a fractional part of what his job was all about. In addition, whereas the apprentice served a master who had a traditional and

Edwin L. Rumpf, "The Vocational Education Breakthrough," *American Education* 11, 1 (January–February 1975): 22–25, 28.

often legal responsibility for his training, behavior, and welfare, the neophyte factory worker saw his employer as a faceless corporation or a far-removed capitalist who didn't so much as know the employee's name and had no particular obligation to him.

Thus a gap developed, with training for a vocation ceasing to be attached to production and instead being left up to the individual. The schools were identified as the logical institution to fill that gap and help meet the nation's economic needs by producing workers able to handle the increasingly complex industrial machinery and processes. There were also social pressures for the schools to take on a job-training function—so that they might respond more realistically, for example, to the educational needs of the great mass of young people. In 1910, to take a representative year, only one of every four boys or girls continued their education beyond elementary school—in large part, many parents claimed, because the high school curriculum was geared to students bound for college and did little or nothing for those who wanted to prepare for the new kinds of jobs that were opening up. Organized labor charged that the high schools served only a small segment of the society and were short-changing the sons and daughters of working people. Many observers pointed to the Land Grant College Acts of 1862 and 1890, which provided federal support to establish and maintain state colleges focused on agriculture, the mechanical arts, and the domestic sciences. If the federal government could support such instruction in the colleges, they insisted, it could do no less at the secondary level. . . .

National pride also became a consideration, with the publication of the report of a Commission on National Aid to Vocational Education . . . in 1914. "In this whole country," it declared, "there are fewer trade schools than are to be found in the little German kingdom of Bavaria, with a population not much greater than that of New York City. There are more workers being trained at public expense in the city of Munich alone than in all the cities of the United States, representing a population of more than 12,000,000."

The proposed new law nevertheless generated considerable opposition, pre-dictably on the basis of the costs involved but more especially as a matter of principle. Aid such as that called for in Smith-Hughes, it was claimed in the Congressional debate, not only posed the threat of federal control of the schools but would "cause the states to lean upon the national government for the support of their own educational systems" (as President Buchanan had said in vetoing a predecessor to the Land Grant College Act of 1862). The bill's proponents dismissed these arguments and dwelt on such matters as equity, increased farm production, strengthening the work force, and individual at-tainment. . . .

The proponents carried the day, and thus was adopted "an Act to provide for the promotion of vocational education; to provide for cooperation with the states in the promotion of such education in agriculture and the trades and industries; to provide for cooperation with the states in the preparation of teachers of vocational subjects; and to appropriate money and regulate its expenditure." While Senator Smith and Congressman Hughes were basking in the glow of their achievement, Mrs. Hughes pointed out to her husband that the bill said nothing about training traditionally of interest to women.

Promptly thereafter the reference to "agriculture and the trades and industries" was broadened to include "home economics."

Ancillary to carrying out its objectives, the Act contained several provisions that have had a lasting impact on federal support not only of vocational education but of education generally. To deal with the issue of "federal control," for example, its administration within each state was placed in the hands of a State Board of Education. Toward deterring the states from tending to "lean upon the national government for the support of their own educational system," appropriations under the law bear the condition that for each dollar of federal money expended, the state or local community or both shall spend at least an equal amount. (Currently the states and localities are overmatching the federal contribution by a ratio of more than five to one.) And to ensure adequate planning and accountability, each state was called upon to develop a state plan outlining how it intended to proceed, and to submit annual reports of how the available money was being spent and what progress was being achieved. . . .

The federal vocational education laws enacted over the years since Smith-Hughes have become progressively broader in their provisions, offering the states greater administrative flexibility, giving them more options, and enabling them to afford wider educational opportunities to youth and to adults as well. There has at the same time been established an educational mechanism that can be quickly responsive in times of national emergency, as witness the 7.75 million people who were prepared for industrial jobs during World War II.

With enrollments in occupational training programs approaching 15 million and with annual expenditures for them of nearly $3 billion—almost 85 percent of the amount from state and local sources—vocational education is now recognized as a vital component of the school curriculum, not only building a foundation for economic progress but broadening the career horizons of individual citizens throughout the nation. And Smith-Hughes showed the way.

Information Sources and Curricular Changes

This chapter presents both a clear and ambiguous answer to the question of why curricular changes occur. The clear answer is that changes arise because the society is discontented with the ways schools function. As a consequence, support for change including legislative, legal, or financial inducements, builds up. These inducements seem quite clearly to contribute to curricular reform. The ambiguous answer involves several points: (1) how to identify entry points for change; (2) how to change individual behavior; and (3) how to identify such variables as the critical mass for change; (4) how to identify the target for change; and (5) how to maintain change once the initial steps have been taken. These factors and other subtle elements are imbedded in the operation of the schools.

The analysis of educational change in the field of mathematics described in the next article presents these five subtle points as schools undertake the difficult task of altering their programs. The article alerts the reader that there is no predictable and generalizable simple road to reform. Examine the evidence presented in this article and then ask where you would first turn to introduce and promote a major change in the schools. Would you depend on workshops, text materials, social pressure, change agents, or administrative edicts?

☐

James B. Conant noted in an address before the Sixteenth Annual Association for Supervision and Curriculum Development Conference that the trial and error method of advancing practical knowledge is successful only to the degree that the experimenter can make a valid judgment as to the outcome of the experiment. He must be in a position to decide whether the outcome of the experiment improves conventional practice in some manner. Accumulated experience and skill developed by long practice are essential in making such judgments in fields where the theoretical component is still small.

In the middle ages, Conant observed, it was the skill and experience of the metal-making artisan alone which supplied the basis for a decision. Some cities became famous for the quality of their products during this period; their fame was an outcome of the successful crude evaluations of experienced artisans. Today, chemistry and physics supply concepts and techniques which enable a metal maker to speak with precision about better and worse procedures for making better or worse metallic products. The introduction of a theoretical component from these fields has resulted in substantial improvement in the criteria for passing judgment on the outcome of an experiment.

The history of medicine in this century provides another excellent example of the use of fruitful trial and error experimentation. Tests of specific hypotheses in the context of extensive practical know-how contributed to widely held theory. The relation of bacteria and virus to disease is an obvious example.

The writers were intrigued by Conant's view of change. They wished to relate his perspective to the "advancement of practical knowledge" within the field of education. A generous grant from the Charles F. Kettering Foundation enabled them to implement a study of the educational change phenomenon, stressing influences of selected information sources, influences of channels used to communicate innovations, and characteristics of information users. The study is based upon data gathered from interviews of a representative random sample of educators who were drawn from a representative cross-section of education's knowledge diffusion structure.

A Systematic Study of Educational Change

Recently, more than 600 educators were asked to describe innovations (i.e., practices, products, and ideas which were new to the person) newly adopted

W. C. Wolf, Jr., and A. John Fiorino, "Some Perspectives of Educational Change," *The Educational Forum* 38, 1 (November 1973): 79–84. Reprinted by permission of author and publisher.

within their practice, about to be adopted in their practice, or which were considered but not adopted in their practice. These individuals were employed in elementary schools, secondary schools, and institutions of higher education as teachers, counselors, and administrators primarily.

At least one innovation was adopted by 70 percent of the subjects; at least two by 24 percent; and at least three by 7 percent. Similar results were obtained for innovations earmarked for adoption and innovations considered but not adopted. The majority of these educators seemed interested in changing their practices. They sought alternatives, considered available options, and most important, were willing to make changes. Three aspects of their efforts to change were studied indepth: first, the nature of change undertaken by them; second, factors that influenced these changes; and third, the impact of selected information sources upon change.

The subjects interviewed were randomly selected from among individuals exposed to specified publications, brief assemblages, and extended assemblages. . . .

Given the nature of sample selection, this population is probably biased in the direction of innovative activity. . . . Unfortunately, this bias only strengthens subsequent results.

Data obtained permitted two levels of analysis. All possible sources of information mentioned were related to efforts by the subjects to change their practice, and the twenty specific sources of information selected were related to changes in the practice of these individuals. In order to illustrate the nature of these changes, one kind of innovation—the subjects' accounts of new mathematics programs geared to the elementary school level—has been selected for analysis. Specific references are made to mathematics innovations throughout the following sections of the article.

The Nature of Change

The interviews revealed that many subjects were engaged in the process of changing their elementary school mathematics programs. . . . These changes were prompted by dissatisfaction with existing programs and a desire to expand current practices.

Few innovations could be attributed to the imagination of the person being interviewed. Rather, these educators learned about alternatives to their practice from other people. Their initial awareness may be traced to attendance at a professional meeting, to a particular college course or workshop, to a newspaper or journal article, or to contact with a field representative of a publishing house or school supply company. This initial awareness was sustained if an innovation didn't cost too much, if it could be adopted without too much fuss, and if it seemed to improve or extend the current practice. Simply substituting one kind of mathematics practice for another accounted for more than half of the innovative interventions mentioned. These substitutions were quite incidental to the operation and financing of an existing educational program.

Like the middle-age artisan, educators interviewed relied upon their skill and experience to judge an innovation. Nearly half of the subjects adopted one or more mathematics innovations . . . without benefit of any kind of trial period. Those who employed a trial period generally relied upon observation of the innovation over time. . . .

Innovations calling for minimal program alteration and modification of pedagogical behavior were most likely to be adopted. These kinds of practical considerations, rather than evidence about an innovation based upon disciplined inquiry, were of paramount importance both in trying out a mathematics innovation and in eventually adopting the innovation within practice.

Given the fact that the study sample is well-educated, rich in experience, and employed in leadership roles, it is somewhat disappointing to report that much —if not most—of the subjects' energies were being expended in behalf of mathematics innovations not apt to alter markedly the status of conventional practice.

When educational role, prior experience, and level of training were related to changes within the mathematics programs, two generalizations worthy of comment emerged. Responses of teachers and bachelors degree holders consistently reflected maintenance of an educational status quo. On the other hand, responses of teacher educators consistently reflected efforts to alter conventional practice. These differences related directly to educational role and somewhat to level of training, but they were unrelated to prior experience.

Factors Influencing Educational Change

Every effort was made to document what subjects did from the time of their initial awareness of a new mathematics innovation to the time they adopted or rejected the innovation. Characteristics of information sources were related to the ultimate fate of these mathematics innovations. Also, the researchers attempted to identify specific stages in the educational innovation adoption process in order to contrast these stages with stages recognized by rural sociologists as pertinent to the diffusion and utilization of agricultural innovations.

Definitive information about the *form, duration,* and *audience size* of various kinds of diffusion strategies were gleaned from the subjects' interviews. Innovative subjects became aware of and extended their interest in mathematics innovations primarily through colleague contact, meetings and workshops, institutes, and courses, all of which provided for personal interaction and involvement. Personal, direct involvement forms related more directly to innovativeness than any other forms of diffusion. Forms requiring less than one week's involvement accounted for most of the responses extending interest in mathematics innovations. Publications, speeches, workshops, and so forth were most influential in getting subjects to consider seriously changing aspects of their mathematics program. Most of these influential forms were offered in a building where the subjects practiced or at a site in the subjects' communities.

Subject exposure to sources of innovation ranged from a one-to-one experience reading a periodical to attendance at an annual meeting of a professional association along with hundreds or thousands of other educators. Audience size related significantly to involvement with mathematics innovations in only one respect—hardly any subjects credited large group forms, where fifty or more participants were gathered, with either awareness of or extending interest in mathematics innovations.

Analyses of the interview data revealed mathematics education practices at the elementary school level changed in three stages. This model was at variance with the widely held five-stage model set forth by rural sociologists for agricultural change. The first stage combines awareness of and continuing interest in a mathematics innovation (the data analyzed revealed little difference between responses to these two factors). The second is similar to the evaluation stage —which amounts to personal judgment to go ahead—described by rural sociologists, whereas the third is the adoption stage. The most conspicuous difference between the educators' and the rural sociologists' change schemes is the absence of a trial stage in the former group's pattern.

The Impact of Selected Information Sources upon Change

Perhaps the most devastating outcome of this inquiry emerged from analyses of the degree to which the specific publications, brief assemblages, and extended assemblages influenced subjects' mathematics programs. Nine in ten subjects interviewed failed to relate—in any way—mathematics innovations discussed to these specific sources of information (even though their exposure to these diffusion strategies accounted for subject inclusion in the study). The researchers are unable to explain these data.

When changes in mathematics programs were viewed in terms of the specific information sources considered, variation in performance became apparent. . . . Three ASCD regional institutes, one NDEA academic year institute, and one publication attracted the most innovative subjects among those interviewed. Conversely, three NDEA summer institutes and two publications harbored the least innovative subjects among those interviewed. . . .

When form, duration, and audience size were considered, no clear-cut pattern emerged to distinguish the most fruitful from the least fruitful diffusion strategies. . . .

Discussion

. . . What sources did the subjects utilize? A wide variety of sources were identified, but utilized in what appears to be a fortuitous manner. When one stands in the path of a shotgun blast—even at long range—he is probably going to feel the effects of some of the "shot." Much of the educational communication network seems to operate as a shotgun aimed at an amorphous target audience almost out of range of the weapon. Hence, a significant loss of information occurs at the practitioner level.

Agencies interested in the diffusion of educational innovations need to consider factors such as personal involvement, small group experiences, and follow-up when they plan professional programs. Purposes set forth for large group regional and annual meetings need to be considered. So do purposes for periodicals and other widely distributed publications.

Subjects did not rely upon either a trial stage or scientifically gathered information in the process of innovation adoption. They seemed to be "turned on" by an innovation for practical reasons and then followed it through to the bloody end, called adoption, with little variation. Once adopted, innovations became a fixture within the subjects' practices. . . .

Today's practitioner seems driven toward change for the sake of change. Often he lacks knowledge of prior educational practice, and he certainly doesn't employ disciplined inquiry techniques. What has resulted from his efforts is hardly an improvement upon the style of the middle-age metal worker. If anything, his evaluation capabilities probably are inferior to those of the artisan.

Social Justification of Curricular Reform

A global treatment of conditions that lead to curriculum reform is provided by Richard Burns and Gary Brooks. They have taken the position that changes in society can be pinpointed, and the implications of these changes and developments for the schools can be addressed. Their list of factors presents changes in society that can be translated into decisions about school curriculum. You may consider some of these factors less important than others. See if you can create your own list of factors, ordered by priority, and defend the emphasis you give to each of these developments.

☐

. . . Since 1950, various individuals, groups, and organizations have sensed the need for changes in our curricula. As a result, improvements have been made, especially in mathematics, biology, physics, chemistry, English, and foreign languages at the high school level. To a lesser degree, reforms have been made in high school music, economics, and geography. Elementary education, preschool education, reading, mathematics, and special education have experienced some reform. Unfortunately, *none of the reforms have gone far enough to produce the curricula needed for today's education.*

Science instruction today is leading the way in recognizing the *process deficiency in education.* Learners need to know more than mere information —they need to know how information is gathered, identified, and transformed; in short, they need to know how information is *used.* Learning must involve more than the mere memorization of facts and principles. Learning must involve an understanding of the methods by which fields of knowledge have been constructed. Learners should know the "hows" and "whys"—the whole structure of the sciences, mathematics, and social sciences. Learners must develop skill in using the same processes that physicists, historians, zoologists, economists, and others use to study and pry information out of our natural

Richard W. Burns and Gary D. Brooks, "The Need for Curriculum Reform," *Educational Technology* 10, 4 (April 1970): 8–12. Reprinted by permission of author and publisher.

and social environment. Learners need to know the methods, the ways—*the processes*—by which factual information, once gained, is transformed into generalizations, concepts, principles, and laws. Learners need to know how to learn, how to use what they have learned, and how to communicate about what they have learned.

Fourteen reasons why our curricula need changing are identified and outlined below. No order of importance is intended.

1. We are living in a global society.
2. We are living in a rapidly changing world.
3. Our culture is experiencing an information explosion.
4. Present curricula are information-oriented rather than process-oriented.
5. There is a lack of relevancy between inschool education and out-of-school life.
6. There is a prohibitive time lag in education between the discovery of new techniques and the incorporation of these techniques into educational practice.
7. General education and core curricula are presently too survey-oriented.
8. There are new technical innovations for which new curricular patterns can be designed.
9. Urban living, a decreasing emphasis on family structure, and the increasing mobility of the population demand greater individual responsibility.
10. There is an increased recognition of the needs of minority groups and minority group problems.
11. Our knowledge of what is true is constantly changing.
12. There is an increased understanding of how people learn.
13. The behavioral definition of learning products has revealed deficiencies in our present curricula.
14. Productivity has released people from the necessity of long labor.

A Global Society

People use the expression "my world" to mean the environment in which they operate. For many people, the world in which they live is extremely small and isolated. In times past what people did in other "worlds" had little effect on people in their "world." Provincialism and isolationism are rapidly becoming dead ideologies. Events in Egypt, Japan, Vietnam, Peru, and hundreds of other places directly or indirectly affect "home." War, atomic energy, space travel, germ warfare, communications satellites, and dozens of other phenomena eventually affect the welfare of each individual on this planet. The effects of global pollution of atmosphere and water are influencing every living thing on earth. The problems which face society now and in the future will not be solved from a state of ignorance. The population explosion, for example, can only be solved by the intelligent behavior of every adult the world over.

A Rapidly Changing World

Perhaps 90 percent of all scientists who have ever lived are now alive. What will future generations call this age? Whatever the designation, it will imply "change." Within the lifespan of many individuals, our society has progressed from the horse and buggy to Apollo spacecraft, and Apollo is only the beginning. Scientists and engineers have changed and are changing our world far beyond the wildest futuristic dreams of the individual citizen.

Change is a difficult phenomenon to accept and even more difficult to prepare for. How do we educate for change? Logically the answer lies in (1) the efficient learning of basic materials which will have wide transfer value and (2) acquiring ability to learn independently, outside the classroom. In a changing world, the curriculum can afford few frills; it must be flexible; it must be constantly changed and augmented; and it must prepare the learner for *change*. It may well be that the test of an educated person in the near future will be his or her ability to adapt to change. . . .

The Information Explosion

The world is currently experiencing an information explosion, the import of which we are just beginning to realize. Knowledge is increasing at a geometric ratio. Thus, it is inconceivable that learners can be educated by the daily feeding (in most states, 180 days) of *bits* of information. The role of information and its relationship to education should be intensively reexamined. There is no intent to exclude information; in fact, much more information is going to be needed and utilized by learners. The bulk of this information, however, will not be stored in the minds of learners but rather in computers or comparable devices. Modern information storage and retrieval systems will make it possible for learners to have at their fingertips an infinite amount of information which can be utilized in problem solving. Information *usage* must be emphasized in the curriculum, rather than the mass acquisition of information. This shift in emphasis will not only radically affect the learner but also will result in a redefinition of the role of the teacher. Teachers will no longer *tell*, lecture, and present lessons, but will assume roles akin to counseling, consulting, and guiding. . . .

Information Orientation of Curricula

Present curricula and present teaching methods emphasize *information* learning rather than discovery, problem solving, data analysis, data gathering, and related activities. Textbook learning, teacher telling, lectures, and factual achievement tests all indicate the overwhelming emphasis placed on the mastery of information in our present system. The complex nature of today's world demands the acquisition of behaviors other than those classified as *knowledge*. Learners also need to develop understandings, motor skills, processes (mental skills) and affective traits—attitudes, interests, and appreciations. It has already been observed that learners need to be prepared for "change" in a rapidly changing world. It is no longer conceivable that learning (and getting an education) can be pinpointed to the acquiring of a specific set of finite behaviors containing the exact amount of information which will serve the learner to meet his present and future needs.

Lack of Relevancy

Many teachers hate to admit it, and school administrators frequently act as if they had never thought of the problem, but a little soul searching will force almost all educators to realize that the content taught in most classrooms is not relevant to the lives of the learners. The more "different" the student, the greater this problem becomes and the easier it is to see.

It is fairly easy to see, for example, that a young Huk child in the Philippines or a Montagnard youngster in the mountains of Vietnam would have little use for a lesson in literary criticism of *Beowolf,* a laboratory exercise in disecting crayfish, or a mathematics lesson dealing with the relative rates of two trains traveling between Chicago and New York. It is more difficult to admit that a Navaho learner in Utah or Arizona might not profit from *The Scarlet Letter* or need to know how to draw the pores on a starfish. Minority education in a Los Angeles slum district just might be conceived as having to be different from the equivalent grade level education needed in Winnebago, Iowa. Once we accept the idea that an education might necessarily be different if the pupils are to profit from their learning, we must come to an attack on the problem of relevancy. . . .

The Time Lag

There are so many reports of the time lag between discovery and application, all of them negative, that one is hard pressed to decide if twenty or one hundred years is the proper descriptive term. In education, competent observers report that the time lag is even more serious than in other segments of society.

Curricula must be updated and integrated with methods which will maximize learning. Materials for learning should be empirically designed, behaviorally-oriented, up-to-date, intensive, adapted to the learner, and relevant to his environment. Multisensory approaches should be used—students should work with things, instruction should be based on reality, and the classroom and environment should be brought closer together. . . .

Survey Orientation of General Education and Core Curricula

Pursuing a general education degree should not imply the learning of a little bit about a lot of things. A general education should develop behavior competencies just as well as does its opposite, special or technical education. The difference in behaviors is one of kind and not degree.

Many courses of study for survey, core, introductory, orientation, and general courses reflect a "let's cover the whole thing" type of organization. The result is that the "learner knows a lot about nothing." This expression implies that the learning is too shallow to be functional. Survey, core, orientation, introductory, and general courses need to cover fewer topics—and cover them well. The topics covered should reflect the "core," "general," or "survey" title. That is, the topics should be basic, fundamental, and representative of a broad area. The topics studied should be carefully selected and then studied as intensively as topics in other courses. The behavioral outcomes should be functional and useful. For instance, a course in "Survey of Literature" need not attempt to cover all literature. Rather, the selections should be carefully selected; they could be representative of various literary types or styles. Each selection should be studied indepth, with behavioral goals reflecting the acquiring of a general literary criticism ability. Poorly organized core and general courses waste many hours of valuable learning time; those responsible for their presence at all levels of education should hasten to revise them. . . .

New Curricular Patterns for Technical Innovations

Many of the possibilities for new curricular patterns can barely be imagined since only meager beginnings have been made. However, there are four major ways in which technology can directly affect curricula. First, technology can be a tool used to improve the design and organization of curricula. . . . Second, technology can be an area of study in itself, thus adding to what is to be learned in a given curriculum. Third, technology can provide new sources of materials, making it possible to devise curricular problems either currently superficially studied or altogether absent from the curriculum. CAI provides a good illustration of how a technological innovation can be harnessed to facilitate problem solving. . . . Fourth, technology can provide "on the spot" coverage of history in the making, thus eliminating both the time lag and inaccuracies which are often characteristic of historical reporting. The most dramatic examples of this point were the TV and radio coverage of the Apollo 11 and Apollo 12 flights to the moon. . . .

All of these major influences of technology on curricula should be fully exploited. Learners should be brought into visual and audio contact with government, business, religious, social, and military leaders. The environment of faraway places should be brought into the classroom. Efficient learning materials must be designed that are guaranteed to result in learning *if used properly.* Children should be trained in computer language, computer skills, and similar functions so that they can use technological aids in learning.

Urban Living, Family Structure, Mobility, and Individual Responsibility

Should schools stress individuality and individual freedom, or should they train individuals to become effective members of groups—such as families, communities, states, and nations? *They should do both.* Should schools educate students to develop their personal role, their unique talents, or should schools develop good citizens, with a high degree of interest and responsibility in public affairs? *They should do both.*

Urban living, giant industries, huge federal programs, increased mobility of the population, large tax burdens, military service, and changing moral values cause individuals to become lost, isolated, and alienated.

Minority Group Needs and Problems

One important aspect of the subgroups within any culture is their tendency to develop unique communication systems. This phenomenon results in isolation of the groups from outsiders. . . .

Our nation's schools are faced with the problem of training individuals to acquire an appreciation of other cultures, to become tolerant of people who are different from them, and to understand the concept of brotherhood. . . .

Truth Is Changing

Our understanding of what is *true* is constantly undergoing change as new information is discovered. Constant revision and updating curricular content is required if learners are to "know the truth." As examples, we *used to believe:*

1. The earth was round.
2. The atom was indivisible.
3. Wet feet caused colds.
4. The earth was approximately two billion years old.
5. Permissiveness was the key to child rearing.
6. The American Indian was a blood-thirsty savage.
7. Infants thrived best on regular feeding schedules.
8. It would be difficult to walk on the moon.

Some measure of the degree of this problem, especially with textbook-centered learning, is provided by the realization that curricular materials are frequently out-of-date. We are led to believe that in any decade people discover as much or progress as far as from the beginning up to the initial year of the decade. If this is true, and it requires two years to develop a textbook, a third year to get it commonly accepted in the market, and schools use the book for an additional five years (a common practice), then as much as forty percent of what we might know about a topic could be excluded from the learning at the eighth year. . . .

An Increased Understanding of How People Learn

Significant advances have been made in learning theory—which have *not* been applied to classroom practices to any significant degree. A good illustration is furnished by the concept of individual learning. Even though individualized instruction is commonly recognized as a valid *principle,* very little has been accomplished by way of making it a classroom *practice.* Numerous techniques and innovations, including tutoring, pupil-pupil assistance, teacher aides, the contract method, supplementary assignments, individualized lesson assignments, flexible scheduling, programmed instruction, television, and data retrieval systems are available as ways of implementing individualized learning. What is holding us back? . . .

Behavioral Objectives and Curricular Deficiencies

The analysis of learning in terms of changes in behavior has progressed remarkably in the past decade. The best instructional materials now on the market are a result of the careful delineation of the terminal behaviors, or specific objectives expected to be achieved by the learners.

In the past, educators, especially teachers, have tended to rely on broad, vague, and general statements of goals. The reasons for this dependence on the more or less useless, general statements about learning stem from ignorance of how to develop specific objectives, general satisfaction with present accomplishments, a vague feeling that being "pinned down" would disclose deficiencies, and a hazy notion that general goals provide room for "on the spot" adjustments which are necessary in light of learner interests and learner contributions. . . .

The lack of stated goals for any course of instruction can only mean that the learner has a fuzzy notion of what is to be accomplished. This undoubtedly accounts for some of the student unrest which impinges upon the educational process. Many students are confused about what they are to learn—in fact, students have often been observed leaving final exams and remarking to each other, "Did you know what he wanted?" or "So *that's* what he wanted!" . . .

Increased Leisure

Science and technology have contributed to increased personal productivity to a degree which presently affords the individual in our culture the prospect of eventually being free of drudgery. During the 1970s, the average worker will probably spend less than forty hours per week gainfully pursuing a living. Many people already have achieved relative independence from the time clock. Each person, to the degree that he is free from work, needs recreational skills; especially leisure time skills of a creative nature. This demand leads to two curricular needs; first, a curriculum designed to develop specific skills which the individual can use immediately upon leaving school, and second, a general orientation of the curriculum away from viewing it solely as a means where the learner prepares himself only for productive *work*. Again, it must be emphasized that the curriculum should reflect the culture. If our culture is going to increasingly allow for leisure, then our schools must prepare individuals to use that time wisely. Some educators view this problem as solely the province of "adult" education; but this is a very limited viewpoint. Leisure is not confined to retirement (old age) or adult life (middle age) but is rightfully the property of all ages. In fact, one wonders what young people would do at present if more recreational skills were taught and more recreational opportunities were available.

It cannot be hoped that all of the above needs for curriculum reform will be met in a sweeping reform movement, nor would it be wise to do so even if it were possible. Much additional research is needed before educational progress can be effectively oriented toward meeting all of our needs.

Summary

In this chapter we looked at reasons why changes in the school curriculum occur. Often the stimulus for change comes from outside the schools. In other cases, the impetus clearly emerges within the school itself. In both cases the stimulus often arises suddenly, and there is little basis on which to predict the strength of an idea for change.

The curriculum worker who can identify problems and map plans to address these problems is probably doing about all that can be done. As simple as this declaration sounds, many proposals for change unfortunately do not specify the problems they are intended to solve. Defining problems is one of the major first steps in promoting change. After an appropriate problem has been identified the likelihood of promoting appropriate change improves. Change for the sake of change can be avoided if change for the sake of solving identifiable problems is a guiding principle.

The reader would profit by identifying trends, developments, conflicts, and major changes that are currently taking place, and then determining the consequences for the school curriculum in responding to these factors. As an activity in linking the society to schools it is worthwhile to base change on current developments because it promotes the kind of perceptive thinking required for curriculum developers and enhances the probability of success.

Chapter 15

The Induction of Curricular Change

"Just when we finally knock the new math into their heads, along comes the metric system!"

Phi Delta Kappan 56. 2 (October 1974): 130.

A simple approach to change is to recognize that (1) change occurs, (2) reasons for change can be identified, and (3) appropriate change can take place. But, within these three components there are complicating factors. The first two of these three have been presented in previous chapters. This chapter addresses the third issue—how appropriate change can be induced.

Disastisfaction with the current state of affairs and doing something about it creates a dynamic system that promotes continual activity. But how does change actually take place? What basis for change should be used and what criteria should our efforts follow? This chapter examines these questions about change.

Strategies for Large-Scale Curriculum Reform

Educational research is commonly criticized because results from studies with some samples of children showing marked improvement in achievement are not replicated when data about achievement are collected in new and more extensive settings. This criticism is reinforced by studies that apparently indicate schools have a relatively small effect on the learning of fundamental skills regardless of the curriculum patterns and practices followed. There are several possible explanations for this discrepancy. One explanation places the blame on the experimenters who fail to carry out research on a large scale successfully. The following passage by Alan

Gartner and Frank Riessman examines this discrepancy and presents a plan for effectively using small-scale research studies. In order for an experimental innovation to be successful on a larger scale the operating conditions under which its results are obtained must be established. If the innovation involves a new content or a new organization and method of presentation, these variables must be present in the large-scale setting. As you read the followng passage, about applying the research methods on a large scale see whether or not the same variables as those present in small-scale settings exist. Also consider critically each step in the model from the standpoint of what it is expected to accomplish.

☐

The charge is being made on many sides that schools are irrelevant—that the amount of money spent, the educational practice utilized, whether the schools are desegregated or not, the pupil-teacher ratio, etc., have no affect on the learning of children. The argument has had great impact in recent years, spearheaded by the ideological criticism of Ivan Illich and buttressed by the large-scale national studies of James Coleman, and more recently, Christopher Jencks.[1]

Yet, despite these data, there are numerous studies, experiments, and demonstrations which clearly indicate that a particular teaching practice, or a changed teacher-student ratio, or the use of new personnel such as paraprofessionals, or a new curriculum can have a decisive and measureable effect on children's learning. But these experiments have not been carried over into the educational system on a large scale. For example, Martin Deutsch has successfully demonstrated that stimulus enrichment for disadvantaged children in the early years has a striking effect on their cognitive development, later learning, and IQ even when they return to the standard school setting.[2] But in the nationwide Head Start program no such results were found.[3] Alan Gartner has cited a good number of studies where the utilization of paraprofessionals in schools has led to definite improvements in learning, reading scores, etc., on the part of children.[4]But there is no evidence that the large-scale use of paraprofessionals in the United States has had a similar effect on the learning of children. Kenneth Clark cites a number of studies, including even those of Bereiter and Englemann, that have decisively improved achievement scores of

Alan Gartner and Frank Riessman, "Strategies for Large-Scale Educational Reform" *Teachers College Record* 75, 3 (February 1974): 349–55. Reprinted by permission of the authors and publisher.

Footnotes have been renumbered consecutively throughout the chapter.

[1]See also the Organization for Economic Cooperative Development, 1969, unpublished report that summarizes the European experience and research indicating that expended funds and changed class ratio and educational policy do not affect educational outcomes.

[2]Marshall A. Smith and Joan S. Bissell, "Report Analysis: The Impact of Head Start," *Harvard Educational Review* 40, 1 (February 1970): 51–104.

[3]Smith and Bissell, "Report Analysis", pp. 51–104.

[4]Alan Gartner. *Paraprofessionals and Their Performance: A Survey of Education, Health and Social Service Programs* (New York: Praeger, 1971).

children.[5] And there are countless experiments showing that the IQ can be dramatically improved in a very short period of time, in some cases as little as three to five days, while again there is no evidence that any large-scale program has had similar effects.[6] Albert Shanker cites experiments which indicate clearly that if one lowers the pupil-teacher ratio below the typical cutting point of twenty-five definite improvements in the learning of children occur. But again, this has not been done on a nationwide basis, and thus the results are left isolated and do not show up in the findings reported by Jencks, Coleman, and others. . . .

The Role of Demonstration Experiments

The issue, of course, is how can these two sets of apparently contradictory data both be true. How can it be correct, as Coleman, Jencks, and others argue, that school factors, collectively and individually, have little effect upon children, while studies such as those cited above show marked and significant results? The big factor, or course, relates to the very character of the two assessments; namely, the Coleman, Jencks, and similar studies are surveys of large universes, using gross measures, able to detect only broad effects across a wide spectrum of subjects. On the other hand, the studies which have shown positive results look at specific projects, often limited in time, always circumscribed in a target population; in short, they are experiments or demonstrations of small order that typically have not been institutionalized. The need then is to analyze some of the reasons why the experimental and demonstration results have not been carried over into institutional change.

In some cases the results that are produced in a demonstration may be unique and not easily translatable on a national scale. The reasons for this may be that there was special powerful, charismatic leadership in the demonstration program; that it was so expensive utilizing such a tremendous overload of personnel and other resources that it would not be economical on a large scale; or that some special conditions, such as the selection of "creamed" populations or exceptionally trained and dedicated personnel, were involved.

There are, however, features of the demonstration that may have some interesting applicability at the large-scale level. For example, typically in a demonstration traditional rules are modified, or suspended, or used very flexibly, there is considerable commitment, a great deal of concentration and care, and keying on a particular result, and funding is sufficient.

Lest one believe, however, that there are only favorable aspects about new programs and demonstrations, it should be pointed out that many demonstrations essentially fail, and there are many factors working against success in any new venture. A new program charting unknown, unfamiliar paths evokes a natural resistance, since it is upsetting the tradition, the equilibrium, the stability, the routine. Because the demonstration or experiment is new, there are also likely to be a considerable number of negative serendipitious or unan-

[5]Kenneth B. Clark, *A Possible Reality* (New York: Emerson Hall, 1972).

[6]Ernest A. Haggard, "Social Status and Intelligence," *Genetic Psychology Monographs* 49 (1954): 141–86; also personal communication from Dr. Haggard.

ticipated consequences which, unless they are overcome, will lead to the essential failure of the deomonstration.

The point is that in the institutionalization of an idea that has been demonstrated there are often advantages which the demonstration itself did not have. The demonstration, if successful, has presumably debugged some of the difficulties; the territory is no longer new and uncharted; a body of practice has been developed through the demonstration which can be applied on a larger scale; the success of the demonstration indicates that it can be done and reduces some of the resistance to the new; finally, the demonstration, because of its relative success, may have won some advocates, some support, some desire for its expansion, and some trained cadre.

The transition from the demonstration to large-scale institutional change[7] raises a number of managerial issues which are typically ignored and to which the demonstration itself offers no solutions. . . .

From a managerial perspective two features must be considered at the outset. First, it must be recognized that the demonstration will not be equally applied everywhere. Special methods must be introduced to compensate for the watering down tendency—and, if possible, to reverse this tendency. Second, a strong effort should be made to improve upon the results found in the demonstration as new information is gathered and hopefully codified from a variety of new situations, and particularly from some model sites which can be established. Recognizing the limits of the demonstration, it should be possible to improve greatly on the demonstration findings if conscious attention is directed toward this objective and the necessary practices instituted. The approach implied in point two obviously can provide powerful medicine for compensating and even reversing the watering-down tendency that is inherent in instituting large-system change.

Proposed Methodology

Following are some of the steps and specific practices that might be useful in applying an effective practice on a large scale:

1. It is necessary to specify clearly the goals and objectives of the proposed change and to establish a *timetable* for achieving these goals. . . .

2. An aspect of point one is planned *phasing*—that is moving from the experimental demonstration in carefully planned steps to ever larger territory, rather than attempting to institute a new practice into the entire system at once. Phasing has a number of clear-cut advantages: It allows the idea to spread among those who are more receptive to it and perhaps more likely to institute it well; it develops experience beyond the demonstration relating to introducing the idea in relatively large systems, and

---

[7]Demonstrations essentially have two potential functions for systems: If they are kept isolated, narrow, and small, they can be used as showcases, enabling the system, whether it be education or other, to maintain its business as usual. In some cases, the demonstration may be relatively large and a parallel system constructed, still enabling the main system to maintain its stability. The other, more positive, function of the demonstration is to provide a mechanism whereby a system which is in trouble can be reformed by utilizing the findings and processes of the demonstration. It is to this agenda that this paper is directed.

produces a body of practical information that can be useful to ever larger systems; it enables the recruitment and development of a cadre that then can be useful to the further contagion of the idea; it is more manageable and allows for easier feedback and modification of the idea in practice —modification that may lead to the idea's enrichment; it leads to the development of a constituency supporting the practice. . . .

3. Model demonstration training sites should be established to develop the educational practice and to train personnel. These demonstration training bases should be well funded and equipped to evaluate the practice, develop it more fully, and disseminate its results rapidly throughout the system via conferences, newsletters, and most important, by training workers from other systems at the training base itself. . . .

4. An *ethos* should be built up around the practice . . . which emphasizes the importance and value of the practice even beyond its specific presumed efficiency. For example, Youth Tutoring Youth programs do more than improve the learning of children, they also increase cooperation and develop the power, resourcefulness, and creativity of children. These results give the program a much larger social meaning, which captures attention, wins a constituency even beyond the immediate users of the program, and may even gain legislative support and media attention. . . .

5. Depth training of cadre is an extremely important part of the implementation of a large-scale program. This training can be done at the model demonstration centers, at the work site itself, in special intensive conferences where specific work problems are simulated carefully and the cadre "overtrained" in ways of dealing with these problems and issues. It is extremely important to train school principals and administrators, as well as teachers and the specific program supervisors, along with members of community boards. . . .

There are a number of other points which should be mentioned briefly: Good administrative practice requires that there be someone clearly in charge of the program at the local level and in the large-scale effort who has no other conflicting responsibilities; expeditors, trouble shooters, or educational change agents should be dispatched quickly throughout the country to assess difficulties which can be corrected (to some extent this can be done through means of telephone conference calls and videotapes); a strong effort must be developed by the national leadership to fight the competitiveness and divisiveness and the role of small vested interests in hurting the program; as much as possible benefits must be found for a great variety of groups from the program; sufficient resources, particularly discretionary funds, must be provided; conferences and other strategies must be used to evoke powerful commitment and participation from all the participants whose ideas are fed in and considered; a major concentration of effort is crucial so that the program is not diffused by many different dimensions; small groups or teams of change agents should be introduced at every level to ensure a "critical mass" and to provide the necessary mutual reinforcement and monitoring. . . .

Conclusion

A successful transition to a large-scale program requires capturing and using some of the features that characterize the demonstration project: "esprit de corps"; flexible application of rules and procedures; zeroing in on the objectives of the program to the exclusion of all the various interferences or distractions that characterize school cultures; strong leadership and the designation of specific personnel to take charge of the program rather than assigning responsibility to people who have other responsibilities.

In addition to capturing the positive features of the demonstration, large-scale institutionalization of a reform requires a number of other managerial strategies to prevent the watering down of the practice: careful phasing, in-depth training of cadre, the use of model demonstration and training sites, the development of program ethos, and a managerial perspective that integrates the need to develop participation, involvement, autonomy, decentralization, flexibility, openness to the new, with the obligation to ascertain that the program is carried through efficiently, in a well-coordinated fashion, with quality control.

The moving of an idea or a program to large-scale application consists of much more than idea dissemination, for it involves organization change and system change. The change agents responsible for widespread institutionalization must have some understanding of organizational theory and particularly the managerial issues mentioned; otherwise, they may have the simplistic notion that merely disseminating the idea will lead to its institutionalization. Such a view will result in cynicism and despair very early in the game.

An Alternative to Systemic Change

Most constructions adhere to the logical sequence of planning followed by implementation. We view most of our activities in this format. Certainly the systems approach follows this pattern. However, there may be another approach to consider in school changes. It may be that careful planning in the early stages of promoting changes interferes with productive change as it emerges from activities. In the following article, David Shiman and Ann Lieberman raise this question and offer an alternative to "systematic" planning and implementation.

☐

Since the early 1960s a variety of educators, reformers, and critics have attacked American schools and argued for massive changes in our educational programs. . . .

David A. Shiman and Ann Lieberman, "A Non-Model for School Change," *The Educational Forum* 38, 4 (May 1974): 441–45. Reprinted by permission of the authors and publisher.

Proposals for change have come from many sources. They range from piecemeal curricular reforms to systematic overhauls of the entire educational process. The federal government has allocated millions of dollars for educational improvement. Passage of the Elementary and Secondary Education Act (Titles I, II, III, etc.), establishment of regional laboratories, partial implementation of the staff development or teacher center concept, flirtation with performance contracting, and the present infatuation with career education are but a few examples of the government's start-and-stop approach to educational change.

Professionals in universities and private corporations have also entered into the battle to save the schools and make them more relevant to the needs of our changing society. In the fields of mathematics and science, and more recently in social studies and English, they have provided new leadership in the creation of instructional materials and the promotion of new methodologies. . . .

Besides these reformers, who frequently merely add another irregularly shaped, ill-fitting piece to the patchwork quilt of educational change, there are those who criticize the inability to develop strategies for change that approach the problem of school improvement in a systematic way. They argue the need for clear models or designs that will assist schools in moving logically through the change process. They offer multi-stage models of the change process which might differ in terminology and orientation, but which suggest, if not prescribe, that the school is supposed to progress systematically from one step to the next.[8]

The implementation of a particular reform or the application of a specific change model, however, frequently results in disillusionment and frustration. Although the strategies might be neat, rational, and appear to have their own internal logic, such an approach to educational change often does not correspond to the reality of the school situation. Reform strategies tend to focus on what the change process *should* look like, or what changes *should* be made. This commitment to a program or idea too often results in the failure to take into consideration either the school as a culture[9] or the individual teacher and the values and demands of the job,[10] elements which we found to be overwhelmingly important. They do not take into account the realities of changes which occur sometimes fitfully, at times irrationally, and most assuredly not in any preordained order. They often neglect the nuances of day-to-day school life that must be considered when a school faculty seeks to make changes.

[8]Neal Gross, J. B. Giacquinta, and M. Bernstein, *Implementing Organizational Innovations; A Sociological Analysis of Planned Educational Change* (New York: Basic Books, 1971). Also see Louis M. Maguire, *Observations and Analysis of the Literature on Change* (Philadelphia: Research for Better Schools, Inc., 1970) for a discussion of various change strategies.

[9]Seymour Sarason, *The Culture of the School and the Problem of Change* (Boston: Allyn and Bacon, 1971).

[10]Howard S. Becker, "The Teacher in the Authority System," *Journal of Educational Sociology* 27 (1953): 128–41.

Our Findings

We were part of a five-year study of the process of change in eighteen schools in southern California.[11] We researchers, consultants, and the school faculties were part of the League of Cooperating Schools. Together we sought to get the schools to look at their problems and to explore the question: "How does a school faculty attempt to cope with change?" . . .

The process we observed in schools was comprised of five stages:

1. First, people talk about the possibility of bringing about some kind of change within the school. Some of the talk comes from teachers who are hoping to have changes legitimized from above. Some emerges from the stimulation of teachers and principals being together. Some ideas come from outside consultants. Expectations begin to rise. Big ideas are talked about (self-concept, student decision making, individual differences). There is a great deal of uneasiness as individual teachers begin to feel pressured to do something. The "tell us what to do" syndrome is rampant.[12] There is disequilibrium.

2. Activity ensues. Some teachers begin to do something. One or two teachers may decide to team. Others might try to individualize their reading program. It is rare that the whole school partcipates from the beginning (although we observed several instances of this). . . .

3. Out of such activity, teachers begin to ask questions. The broader implications of the activity come to the fore. "Why am I doing this?" "Am I now really meeting the needs of my children?" "Is this better than what I did before?" Discomfort is great at this time, for the activity has called upon both teacher and students to experiment with some new behaviors.

4. The whole program now begins to look shabby. Teachers who have individualized reading now find it difficult giving the same spelling test to thirty-six children. The stimulation of successful teaming in one subject area makes teaching the remainder of the day alone much less exciting.

5. The large philosophical questions get asked. Teachers begin to deal with goals for the *first* time. They start asking questions such as: "How can we ensure that our curriculum is relevant to our student population?" "How can we organize the school to meet individual differences?" "How can we make our staff a cohesive unit?" "How can I teach children to make decisions when I have been making all the decisions for them?"

---

[11]The project, called the Study of Educational Change and School Improvement began in 1966 and terminated in 1971. It was conducted by the Research Division of the Institute for Development of Education Activities, /I/D/E/A/, which is an affiliate of the Charles F. Kettering Foundation. For further information, see John J. Goodlad, *The Dynamics of Educational Change* (New York: McGraw-Hill, 1975), and M. M. Bentzen et al., *Changing Schools: The Magic Feather Principle* (New York: McGraw-Hill, 1974).

[12]Ann Lieberman, ed., *Tell Us What To Do, But Don't Tell Me What To Do* (Dayton, Ohio: Institute for Development of Educational Activities, 1971).

These questions open up others and the process begins again. Teachers talk, they move into activities, they question their activities, they examine the whole school program, they raise philosophical questions, and they struggle with goals.

Several social scientists have observed a pattern similar to the one we saw. For example, in talking about groups, Weick[13] discusses the pattern of an organization as one in which the organizing of the group comes first and the reason for organizing becomes apparent later. Actions *precede* goals. Lindblom's[14] discussion centers upon the day-to-day activities of public administrators. He describes two methods in regard to decision making, policy formulation, planning, etc. These are the "root" method and the "branch" method. The root method is essentially the rational step-by-step method referred to above, while the "branch" method is similar to that described by Weick. Lindblom notes that the "root" approach is most often written about but fails to describe adequately the complexity of what most public administrators actually do.

Our observations lead us to agree most strongly with Weick and Lindblom. Proposals for change often assume a simplistic model of the school. In fact, any curricular, organizational, or instructional change involves a complex array of factors. These include, among others: the culture and norms of the teacher group, the nature of the teacher's rather isolated life in the classroom, the principal's leadership style, and the community's orientation and values— all factors that can either facilitate or inhibit innovative behavior. Anyone working with schools must be conscious of and deal with these variables, as well as with the more generalized and sometimes undefined fears concerning change that many school teachers and administrators possess.

In addition to these, which might be called "entry characteristics," one must be cognizant of the internal dynamics of the school situation that are either already operative or likely to be set in motion by his actions. A change in any one of the variables mentioned earlier tends to disturb the equilibrium of the others. . . .

Conclusion

While most people involved in the business of effecting educational change would probably agree about the complexity of the school situation and the dynamics of the interactive process at work, they frequently fail to take these factors into consideration. Instead, they say, "First, we must define and clarify goals," or "First, we must determine priorities," or "First, we must develop the motivation to change," or "First, we must examine and evaluate what is being done." They want to start at *their* beginning and not take the school where it is.

The individual strengths of these educational innovators might lend them-

[13]Karl E. Weick, *The Social Psychology of Organizing* (Reading, Mass.: Addison-Wesley, 1969).

[14]Charles Lindblom, "The Science of Muddling Through," *Public Administration Review* 19 (1959): 79–88.

selves beautifully to promoting constructive change in schools. There are persons who are particularly adept at fostering creative disequilbrium, providing alternative instructional models, raising the larger philosophical questions, or helping in evaluation. Only if they are sensitive to the school's particular situation and knowledgeable about the process of change that is perhaps already underway, though, can they effectively relate their intervention to the school's needs. They must be able to understand, respond to, and work with the process rather than impose their own program, strategy, or idea. . . .

Converting Curriculum Thought into Action

When curriculum workers face the practical task of converting ideas into action they stop intellectualizing and start acting. Whose ideas will curriculum workers implement? What are the unique contributions and weaknesses of the team of people who supply information and make the effort to put new curricula into operation? The next article provides some recommendations about converting curriculum thought into curriculum action and what expectations we should have for different people.

☐

Scholars, as such, are incompetent to translate scholarly material into curriculum. They possess one body of discipline indispensable to the task. They lack four others, equally indispensable. As scholars, they not only lack these other four, but also, as individuals, they are prone at best to ignore and at worst to sneer at them. Possessors of the other four necessary disciplines have an equal handicap; they do not possess the discipline of the scholar; they do not know the bodies of knowledge which his discipline has produced; they are often overawed by him. Yet, all five disciplines are necessary, and the curriculum work their possessors do must be done in collaboration. They must learn something of the concerns, values, and operations which arise from each other's experience They must learn to honor these various groupings of concerns, values, and operations, and to adapt and diminish their own values enough to make room in their thinking for the others. They must bring these partially coalesced bodies of judgmental factors to bear on the body of scholarly materials.

These three operations—*discovery* of one another by collaborators, *coalescence* of what is discovered, *utilization* of the coalesced body of concerns as tools for generating new educational materials and purposes—take place, not serially, but simultaneously. The first two take place as the third is undertaken. The process is carried forward in a spiral movement toward a body of generated educational alternatives and choices among them—choices which satisfy entirely no one party to the collaboration but which do satisfy the collective

Joseph J. Schwab, "The Practical 3: Translation into Curriculum," *School Review* 81, 4 (August 1973): 501–22. Reprinted by permission of the author and publisher.

more than does any other constellation of educational means and purposes among those considered.

Agents of Translation

What are the five bodies of experience which must be represented in the group which undertakes the task of curriculum revision?

Subject matter   There must be someone familiar with the scholarly materials under treatment and with the discipline from which they come. . . .

Learners   There must be someone familiar with the children who are to be the beneficiaries of the curricular operation. This experience, too, must be manifold. It must include general knowledge of the age group under consideration: what it already knows, what it is ready to learn, what will come easy, what will be difficult, what aspirations and anxieties which may affect learning must be taken into account, what will appear to the child as contributing to an immediate desire or need. . . .

The milieus   References to community suggest a third body of experience which should be represented in the curriculum making group: experience of the milieus in which the child's learning will take place and in which its fruits will be brought to bear. The relevant milieus are manifold, nesting one within another like Chinese boxes.

These milieus include the school and classroom in which the learning and teaching are supposed to occur. . . .

Relevant milieus will also include the family, the community, the particular groupings of religious, class, or ethnic genus. . . .

Teachers   So far, three bodies of experience are to be represented in the curriculum group: experience of the scholarly subject matter and its discipline, of the child, and of the child's milieus. Another required body of experience is knowledge of the teachers. This should include knowledge of what these teachers are likely to know and how flexible and ready they are likely to be to learn new materials and new ways of teaching.

Curriculum making   The final required body of experience has to do with the curriculum making process itself. Each representative of a body of experience must discover the experience of the others and the relevance of these radically different experiences to curriculum making for a partial coalescence of these bodies of experience to occur. These are necessary, "concurrent preliminaries" to the actual process of making a defensible curriculum which has some likelihood of functioning effectively. . . .

Three Functions of the Curriculum Specialist

One vital task of the representative of the curriculum making process is to function as a countervailing force of these common tendencies. It is he who reminds all others of the importance of the experience of each representative to the (curriculum making) enterprise as a whole. It is he, as chairman, who monitors the proceedings, pointing out to the group what has happened in the course of their deliberations, what is currently taking place, what has not yet been considered, what subordinations and superordinations may have occurred which affect the process in which all are engaged. . . .

Embodiments   It is the curriculum specialist who knows the concrete embodiments, the material objects, which are the indispensable constituents of a curriculum. . . .

Curricular purposes, and reasons for them, must be communicated by language, by formulation. Such formulations will inevitably fall short of encompassing the full meanings and real intentions of the parties to the curricular deliberation. The meanings which matter are those which determine whether a given text, a given pattern of teaching, a given treatment of a topic, when examined and momentarily submitted to, is both felt and seen to be appropriate to the curriculum which has been envisaged. These meanings lie in the whole course of the deliberations which created them. The meanings lie as much in what was decided against as in what was decided for. . . .

The second function of the curriculum specialist is to instigate, administer, and chair this process of realization of the curriculum.

Values   There is another way in which terminal formulation fails to encompass and communicate the real intentions of a planning group. This second inadequacy stems from the deep psychology of intentions. Educational intentions are specified and projected *values* of the planning group, values possessed and understood in terms broader than education and much broader than any one concrete bit of educational curriculum. The breadth and generality of these values are so great that only in a rare instance can a merely rationally guided concrete specification of a stated educational intention be confidently identified (by merely rational means) as embodying or satisfying one or more of the broad values held by the planning group. . . .

The underlying value which gave rise to the stated intention has itself come closer to the surface and may be better understood. The value may even be so well illuminated that it becomes accessible to scrutiny, criticism, and change. At least, we may hope that, though the value may not be examined with an eye to changing it as a living value of the curriculum planner, it will be scrutinized with an eye to whether it should be imposed upon the student by way of the curriculum.

Instigation, encouragment, and monitoring of this process is a third function of the curriculum specialist.[15]

Size of a planning group   Although five bodies of experience must be brought together to effect translation of scholarly materials into defensible curriculum, it does not follow that five persons are required. The group may be smaller or

---

[15]For an illuminating statement of the role of the curriculum specialist, see Seymour Fox, "A Practical Image of the Practical," *Curriculum Theory Network* 10 (Fall 1972).

larger than five. It may be smaller to the extent that two or more of the required bodies of experience may be found in one person. . . .

There are also reasons why the group should be larger than five. Our knowledge of social milieus and of the development of children is knowledge produced out of the variform disciplines of the behavioral sciences. Different investigators in these sciences go about their inquiries in different ways, guided by differing conceptions of problem, method, and principle of investigation. More than one useful body of knowledge arises about an approximately common subject matter. Too often, the purveying possessor of such knowledge possesses only one of the several useful bodies of knowledge about the subject matter in question and needs to be complemented and corrected by another purveying specialist who knows another of the relevant bodies of knowledge.

The same pluralism holds for scholarly disciplines. . . .

Material to Be Translated

Defensible educational thought must take account of four commonplaces of *equal* rank: the learner, the teacher, the milieu, and the subject matter. None of these can be omitted without omitting a vital factor in educational thought and practice. . . .

Coordinating four commonplaces Coordination, not superordination-subordination is the proper relation of these four commonplaces. We can demonstrate this by considering the possible domination of one in the light of another. Imagine a child-centered planning which emphasizes above all else the present inclinations of students, the interests they bring with them or those which can be aroused by the shrewd placement of provocative objects and events in the educational space. In a curriculum so initiated and thoughtfully planned, the other three commonplaces will not be ignored. Indeed, they may be honored but in a subordinate role. The milieus will be honored as limiting conditions. They will be examined with an eye to predicting interests and facilitating planning of curricular activites. The milieus will also be honored as targets of education by emphases in which collaboration of children, establishment of "rules of the game," and the role of umpire made necessary by rules, constitute socializing aspects of the curriculum. Subject matters will be honored by being the source from which and by which selection is made of the provocative objects and events which serve as catalysts of curricular activity. The teacher will be honored as the person who willl most often serve in the role of umpire and serve more extensively as the more mature member of the learning community. . . .

Scholarship as Curriculum Potential

Let us consider two important attitudes which should be taken toward scholarly materials when they are translated into curriculum. First, they must be treated as *resources*. . . .

The use of scholarly material as a resource for curriculum can be perverted, and its perversion is as pernicious educationally as deprival of it is. Perversion consists of warping the scholarly materials out of their character in order to force them to serve a curricular purpose which fascinates the planners. Such perversions are exemplified by terminal formulations which begin, "How can we use science (or literature, or history, or moral dilemmas) to achieve *x, y,* or *z*?" where the *x, y,* or *z* originate the deliberation and the scholarly materials are dragged in by the heels. The perversion consists in degrading subject matter to the role of servant.

Three Faces of Scholarly Material

The second attitude to be taken toward scholarly material when it is translated into curriculum is that scholarly material possesses three faces, *is* three different things. It is, first, that which it conveys, its purport.

A piece of scholarly material is also that which produced it. . . .

Third, a piece of scholarly material is a compound object, a complex organization requiring certain access disciplines. . . .

Constant awareness of the existence of these three faces in every piece of scholarly material is crucial to the translator into curriculum because each face possesses and suggests its own richness of curricular possibility. The purport may have many curricular uses and this is the face to which most curricular efforts are addressed. But the other two faces have curricular potential as great or greater. Where the purport speaks to those curricular possibilities which can be summarized under "knowing that," the two disciplinary faces speak to the curricular possibilities summarized under "knowing how." . . .

Methods of Translation

The methods by which scholarly materials are translated into a defensible curriculum are not mere transformations of one kind or style of material into another. They are methods for assessing privations, perversities, errors, and misdevelopments in those who are to be recipients of the putative benefits of curriculum; then, methods for discovering in scholarly materials curricular potentials which serve the purposes which have been envisaged in the light of detected student needs; then, assessment of the probable advantages of one potential against others as a means toward educational benefits.

First Phase: Curriculum Effects

The method begins in two sources: (1) in knowledge of the young students and knowledge of their predecessors, now grown and exhibiting the good and bad effects of previous curriculums; (2) in a vision of the best student-grown (or several different "bests"), a vision deriving from the scrutinized values of the planning group. The method begins with an intertwining of two radically different strands: information and soul searching.

Each item of one strand must serve as an occasion for locating an item of the other. Each piece of information on the present condition of students or former students ought to be followed by voiced discoveries of how the planners feel about the condition in question: whether it is approved, and why; if disapproved, what alternate condition or conditions ought to replace it. . . . This initial stage of the deliberation serves two purposes. First, precisely because the group is commissioned to concern itself with scholarly materials, it begins by emphasis on other commonplaces, especially the student and his milieus. Second, it is the prime means by which each planner begins to discover himself—his values and their projections into educational intentions—begins to discover his colleagues, and begins to discover the loci at which each must begin to modify or contract himself to accommodate his colleagues' views and arrive at a collegiality which can function effectively in pursuing the task at hand. . . .

The Second Phase: Discovery of Curriculum Potential

The second phase of the deliberation is occasioned by introduction of a piece of scholarly material whose potential for the curriculum is to be determined. This phase has two subphases. There must be, first, the generation of alternatives. The piece of scholarly material is scrutinized in its three existences (its purport, its originating discipline, and its access disciplines) for its curriculum potentials. The basis for inventiveness in this regard consists of the other commonplaces, as these have come to be envisaged in the phase of self-discovery. One figuratively turns the piece of scholarly material from side to side, viewing it in different lights. . . .

The second subphase is entered when several pieces of scholarly material have been successfully treated in the first subphase. Now there are several potential curriculum bits competing for the time and energies of the students, for place in the curriculum. The second subphase is a process of choosing and deciding among the competing curricular bits, the intentions they seem to realize, the values they try to embody.

It is impossible to forecast the precise questions which ought to be asked of the alternatives under consideration. The appropriate questions are made appropriate by the character of each particular curricular bit, by the attitudes, values, and cognitive skills of the planners, by the community for which the planning is done, by the peculiarities of the children to whom the curriculum is to be submitted. . . .

The special obligation of the curriculum specialist chairman is to ensure that the group hunt out, recognize, and juxtapose the different considerations which are pertinent. Even when the arrogances of specialists have been mastered and collegiality established, there will still be a tendency to perseverate, to maintain attention on the one cluster of values which, for whatever reason, has intially interested the group at the start of one of its meetings. It is this perseveration which the chairman must interrupt. His task is to see that the deliberations of the group are appropriately saltatory. . . .

The generation and consideration of alternatives do not follow one another in strict seriality. There must be alternatives to consider, hence some must be generated before the second subphase can be entered. But the deliberations involved in the consideration of alternatives are themselves rich sources of new alternatives. The moments when such flashes of invention occur to a member of the group must be honored, however important the considerations under discussion may appear to be.

Neither generation nor consideration of alternatives conclude when the planning group has agreed on the curriculum bits it proposes to sponsor. The processes of invention and choice run on through the operations of evaluation earlier described and especially in that aspect of the evaluation which involves confrontation of the planning group with the untoward reponses of the children to the sponsored curriculum bit. The confrontation is one way in which the child can enter the curricular discussion and speak for himself. Other devices directed toward the same end—with reference to teacher and community as well as the child—should be sought.

The Curriculum Director's Role

The final selection in this chapter is a discussion of the curriculum director's role in curriculum change. Because of his position, experience, and knowledge the curriculum director has certain resources available. The quality of the curriculum often rests on his ability to use his authority, power, and influence appropriately. The techniques the curriculum director uses to introduce change makes a significant difference. When reading the next article consider the various techniques used and how effective they would be in promoting curriculum change.

☐

For the person responsible for generating the institutional response to the widespread demand for change—that is, the curriculum director—there is a most central question. That question, when posed in the first person, is: How can I successfully generate and guide the changes in curriculum and instruction in my own area of professional endeavor?

If we grant the curriculum director's expertise in matters of curriculum change and development . . . we can focus on the nature of the leadership he exerts as he discharges his professional responsibilities. Leadership in institutions can be said to involve three basic, interrelated, but distinguishable relationships which exist between the leader and those who are led. . . . The three notions are: (1) authority, (2) power, and (3) influence; and they are descriptive of particular kinds of relationships which leaders exercise when working with those they are responsible for leading.

The Exercise of Authority   Authority as used here, and the exercise of the authority relationships, is a sociological phenomena. For example, the highway patrolman has the authority to stop you on the highway if you are

James K. Duncan, "The Curriculum Director in Curriculum Change," *The Educational Forum* 38, 4 (November 1973): 51–77. Reprinted by permission of the author and publisher.

exceeding the speed limit. He may or may not have an authoritarian personality, and his personality characteristics may or may not intrude upon his exercise of the authority relationship he has with you. What, then, is an authority relationship? Let us define it in the following manner:

> An authority relationship is an interpersonal relationship in which one person is given the right to make selected decisions which affect another person's behavior.

Curriculum directors usually have authority over the staff members they supervise. In many instances the authority of the curriculum director's position is not clear either to himself, his superiors, or those he supervises. If you sense this to be the case in your own situation, you need to raise the following question for yourself as a curriculum worker. What is the nature of my authority? Over whom does my authority extend? How can I exercise my authority? . . .

The Exercise of Power You probably have heard an expression that runs something like this: "I don't want the authority and responsiblity unless you give me the power to back it up." Power and authority relationships are in some senses complementary relationships. They are, nonetheless, different and distinguishable from one another. There are situations in which authority is exercised without resorting to the use of power, and situations in which power is exercised without resorting to the use of authority.

> Power is defined as an interpersonal relationship in which one person has the capability of satisfying or not satisfying the needs of another person and as a result is capable of affecting the other person's behavior.

For example, if we can assume that you have a need to drive your car, it is an exercise of power if the state revokes your driver's license.

Curriculum directors sometimes have either direct or indirect control over staff pay raises. By granting pay raises they can satisfy the needs of selected members of their staff. By denying pay raises the curriculum director can selectively deny satisfaction to other members of the staff. . . .

The exercise of authority and the exercise of power are fundamental to the generation of change. . . . An unbridled exercise of authority and power leads to despotism. An *influence* relationship is necessary to temper the effects of the unlimited exercise of power and authority.

The Exercise of Influence The president of the United States probably has more power and authority vested in him than any other person in the United States.

The legislative branch and the judicial branch of the government continually serve to check the unbridled use of authority and power by the executive branch. But a much more fundamental check on the president's power and authority occurs in each presidential election year.

In a presidential election year, for example, the president of the United

States might go to the voters of the republic asking that the authority and power of the presidential office be placed again in his hands.

He does not have the authority to decide for whom you or I will vote. He does not have the power in his role as a candidate either to satisfy or not satisfy your needs or mine. His only hope is to *influence* us in such a way that we will vote for him.

> Influence is defined as an interpersonal relationship which is devoid of power and authority, and in which the behavior of one person affects the behavior of another.

... The example is not typical though. Curriculum directors for example, are not typically required to stand for reelection. A direct test of their influence with respect to their staff is not usually possible.

The evidence seems to suggest that if an influence relationship is to have real effects on the behavior of people, then the relationship must be *mutual* and *reciprocal* in nature. To put it more bluntly, I will be influenced only by those people with whom I have some influence, or I can influence only those people who can influence me.[16]

To this point, we have defined three interpersonal relationships, the exercise of which are fundamental to curriculum and instructional leadership for change. The three relationships are distinguishable both in the conceptual sense and in social and professional practice. They are, nonetheless, interdependent. ...

Distinguishing Among Authority, Power, and Influence Relationships

Authority, power, and influence relationships are deeply interrelated. With any given staff member, for example, the curriculum director maintains and exercises all three of these relationships. Futhermore, power and authority are usually lumped together. That is, the right to make decisions is usually accompanied by the power to force others to act according to the decision. And, as we have pointed out, the presence of significant amounts of influence makes the exercise of power and authority tolerable.

In general, the exercise of authority is the curriculum director's response to insitutional problems and concerns, while the exercise of power is a response to individual problems and concerns. This is an oversimplification, especially because power is so widely used in the preservation of institutions today. Power, nonetheless, has its primary impact on people, and its exercise has ramifications which may reach deeply into human affairs. Authority, on the other hand, has its primary impact on the functioning of the organization, and the exercise of authority has its ramifications in the order and structure provided for the achievement of institutional goals.

Influence When the curriculum director is *not* the curriculum director but is himself, he is capable of exercising influence. When he is interacting with

---

[16]I am speaking here of influence in face-to-face interaction. Athletes, movie and TV stars, etc., exert influence without being directly influenced in return.

a staff member on a person-to-person basis, he is capable of exercising influence. The hierarchical relationships of authority and power are not present in the influence relationship. The influence relationship is a subtle one. It is especially subtle for one accustomed to affecting people's behavior through the use of authority and power. . . .

Conceptualizing Curriculum and Instructional Change

In order for the curriculum director to utilize himself, his personal influence, and the power and authority of his position to effect intelligent curriculum change, the curriculum director must have a way of conceptualizing curriculum and curriculum change. . . .

Each curriculum event is composed of three essential and interrelated elements referred to as actors (people), artifacts (substantive materials), and operations (processes). Curriculum events are conceived as purposeful events, that is, curriculum experiences are directed toward certain ends. By using the terms actors, artifacts, and operations instead of people, substantive materials, or processes, we wish simply to evoke the sense of intents, purposes, and ends.

Our conceptual view of curriculum calls for seeing a curricular experience in its functional totality. Actors are involved, artifacts are involved, and operations are involved as are the relationships among these. They are nonetheless bounded considerations. The actors are those directly involved in curricular experiences. The artifacts are only those actually utilized by the actors. And the operations are those which modify either actors and/or artifacts or their relationships. The implicit demand in this conceptual view is that the intents and purposes inherent in the actors, artifacts, and operations be fully taken into account. We can turn now to a simple definition of the curriculum event and discuss beiefly what I call its preactive, active, and postactive nature.

A curriculum event is an event with the potential for reconstructing and reorganizing human experience.

. . . When the curriculum director views curriculum from the standpoint we have proposed, he focuses on the reality of actual happenings. He looks at any of the planned, implemented, and evaluated curriculum experiences in their totality and must account in his thinking for all of the essential elements of curricular events. Curriculum change, then, becomes a matter of changing the nature of curriculum events through changing their elements and their relationships or changing the events as entities.

Changing the Nature of Curriculum Events   You can change the nature of curriculum events by changing the actors, the artifacts, or the operations. You can change the nature of curriculum events by changing some combination of the elements or by changing their relationships.

By changing curriculum actors, substantial changes can be made in the nature of curriculum events. A practice of selective admission of students has been used extensively by colleges and universities over the years in their efforts to upgrade the quality of their programs. The selection and hiring of teaching personnel makes a direct impact on the nature and quality of the educational program. . . .

Each textbook change is a change in a curriculum artifact—although usually a minor change. Because the notion of artifacts represents all of those man-made things which the curriculum actors use or may use, the potential for change here is very great.The curriculum director who is concerned about change should make a careful study of the curriculum artifacts in use as well as a study of the artifacts that could be made available for use. . . .

The curriculum director can focus his efforts at curriculum change on two or more of the elements of curriculum events. He can provide a new set of artifacts, for example, and ask a group of staff members to work out potential program experiences using these curriculum artifacts. He can get teachers and materials producers together to develop curriculum materials. The curriculum director is concerned, in such cases, with at least two of the basic elements of curriculum experience. . . .

Goals, Objectives, and the Structure of Curriculum Events

In the conceptual view of curriculum that is provided here, I have implied and stated directly that curriculum events have a value dimension. The elements of actors, artifacts, and operations are so classifed because there is implicit in the terms the notion of purpose in each. Any careful examination of actual curriculum events will not only reveal this to be the case, but will also reveal that there are strong interactive effects among the values inherent in each of the curriculum elements. The implication of this is that the process of changing curriculum events is not simply a matter of changing the structure of the events or their process dimensions. It is also a matter of changing the inherent values imbedded in actors, artifacts, and operations. The goals and objectives of curriculum events are changed as *both* the events *and* the values inherent in them undergo change.

Attempts at curriculum change need to recognize this and be fully aware that such modification of values is probably the most difficult problem in curriculum change. . . .

The Role of the Curriculum Director in Curriculum and Instructional Change—Summary

The curriculum director has, by virtue of his position, two complementary working relationships which he can employ in working with his staff. In the *authority* relationship he is given the right to make *decisions* which affect the behavior of members of his staff. In the *power* relationship he has the capacity to *satisfy* or *not satisfy the needs* of members of his staff. Beyond these two working relationships, there is an important third relationship which the curriculum director can develop with staff members as he interacts with them over time. This is the *influence* relationship and is by definition devoid of the characteristics of the power and authority relationships. The influence relationship is *mutual* and *reciprocal* in nature and affects the behavior of the person being influenced. . . .

Summary

In the descriptions of how changes occur several principles seem apparent. One is that change is most likely to succeed when there is a specific, rather than a general, problem to be solved. Another is that resources—energy, personnel, financial—must support the effort.

What other guiding rules can you identify that generalize the change process? What do you regard to be the essential elements needed for change? How common and how idiosyncratic do you consider schools to be in regard to change? And finally, what is the relative strength of the arguments for systematic change that is carefully planned in contrast to spontaneous change that relies heavily on a dynamic and heuristic approach?

Part V

Evaluation of the Curriculum

This section contains three chapters on curriculum evaluation. Each chapter presents a separate concern: the characteristics of curriculum evaluation, the methods of curriculum evaluation, and the assessment of the school's effectiveness. Curriculum evaluation requires approaches different from those typically used to evaluate less complex areas.

Some evaluators insist that school objectives should be clearly stated and evaluated. Others claim that objectives cannot be stated precisely. They therefore take a dim view of evaluation aimed at behavioral objectives. Instead this group emphasizes the need to evaluate processes and affective outcomes. These opposing views typify the controversies that arise in curriculum development and instruction. They also underline basic issues about curriculum evaluation. These issues are presented in Chapter 16.

Depending on the evaluator's viewpoint, different aspects of the curriculum will come under scrutiny. Each component must be evaluated differently. Often evaluators differ about methods of evaluation, even when they agree upon the dimensions of the curriculum to be assessed. The methodology of curriculum evaluation is a separate issue that is treated in Chapter 17.

In Chapter 18 the results of evaluation are illustrated to show the form in which evaluative information is collected and analyzed. These three chapters provide the reader with the context and scope of curriculum assessment.

When reading these three chapters on evaluation try to review the kinds of curricula used, curriculum planning, diverse opinions about disciplines, how curriculum has developed and changed. Evaluations can be valuable only if all aspects of curriculum are taken into account. Only when the principles of evaluation are understood will more relevant and worthwhile curricula be included in school programs.

Those involved with producing knowledge must understand the role of evaluation: what to look for, what to ignore, what kinds of changes are meaningful, which changes produce positive changes in students, what measure to use other than or in addition to achievement (cognitive vs. affective).

Chapter **16**

Uniqueness of Curriculum Evaluation

"Well, it finally happened. Our evaluations show that 100% of the students interviewed couldn't care less about our new curriculum."

Phi Delta Kappan 56, 2 (October 1974): 119.

If schools were defined as machines, the definition would be complete by designating its parts, the relationship of parts to one another, and describing the machine's function. Some elements of the school can also be assembled according to a blueprint. Certainly the physical plant that houses pupils, teachers, and materials is built in much the same way as any other structure. School finance is somewhat more complex, but formulas can be followed for collecting and distributing funds that permit accurate descriptions of financial characteristics of any given school. When one attempts to predict and define the less concrete and more flexible aspects of the school according to formulas, descriptions become less precise. For example, professional staff characteristics are not simple to characterize. Teaching credentials and hiring criteria are two complex variables that are difficult to define and measure.

Orientation

It is important to know how well evaluation measures predict results. If a building contractor fails to comply with contractural specifications there is legal recourse based on solid evidence. If a school superintendent attempts to apply the same precision to personnel selection as he uses in constructing schools then difficulties arise. The errors that might lead to faulty construction can be easily pinpointed. The errors of choice that result in poor performance by personnel are difficult to determine except in the most extreme cases.

369

Who is at fault when a teacher fails to perform up to an expected standard? Is the hiring official at fault for making a poor choice? Is the teacher at fault? Are the standards at fault because they are unrealistic? Is the fault a combination of these factors? The lack of standards, rigor in their application, and accurate measurement of teaching performance lead to uncertainties and difficulties in determining the effectiveness of school personnel. These difficulties create questions about teachers' characteristics that should be taught and sought.

But is there any ideal model that distinguishes the outstanding teacher from the average and both of them from the incompetent? Might not one teacher who works poorly in one setting or grade level perform adequately or outstandingly in another? And how do those responsible for staffing the schools wrestle with these problems?

It should be apparent from the foregoing discussion that the elements that comprise the schools are not equally weighted. The clarity with which a school building can be described, planned, and constructed is not the same as the clarity with which selection and assignment of staff can be carried out. But what about the other aspects of the school? Specifically, what about the curriculum? Is it more like the construction of the school building or is it more like the problems of staffing the schools? Can curriculum be planned as an architect designs a building or must curriculum be established on the basis of less precise information. These and other similar questions are addressed in this chapter.

In reading this chapter, one must remember the difference between measurement and evaluation. Measurement means ordering objects by some characteristic or determining "how much" of a characteristic the object possesses. One might state that a metal object is 4' long and/or that it weighs 10 lbs. These figures describe "how much." Evaluation on the other hand requires judging the measurement. In the case of the metal piece, if it is to be used as a lever to move another object, a question of whether 4' is long enough to allow for proper placement on a fulcrum and sufficient mechanical advantage to move the object requires evaluation. The user's judgment, trial and error, or criteria to evaluate the object are required for this decision. Judgment must be added to measurement to evaluate the usefulness of the object. The use of measurement, judgment, and evaluation enters the study of concrete and abstract objects. A discussion of the differences in these two leads into the questions of curriculum study, its measurement and evaluation.

After recognizing differences between measuring physical and abstract properties, the question can be raised: Is the study of curriculum more like the study of physical objects or is it more like the study of abstractions? When curriculum is considered text materials, it is concrete and can be measured for accuracy, readability, sequence, etc. When curriculum is considered the attitudes or knowledge obtained by pupils, then curriculum is abstract and accurate measurement is more difficult. Inaccuracies arise partly because the instruments of measurement are inadequate and partly because the object of these studies is complex. Perfect accuracy of measurement does not exist in the physical world and is even less accurate in the world of abstractions. But more confidence can be placed in the measurement of physical objects before arriving at an evaluative decision through judgment. When measurement is more complex, less accurate, and cannot take into account all the critical variables in measuring abstractions, then judgment becomes a proportionally more significant part of evaluation. When measurement is functionally accurate, then the burden on judgment is reduced.

Much of curriculum study requires measurement and evaluation. As the object of curriculum study varies from the concrete to the abstract, the role of judgment increases and dependence on measurement alone decreases. If curriculum study merely required using existing instruments to obtain information and the application of best judgment to arrive at evaluation, then one could go about identifying instruments, refining those instruments, and utilizing judgment where measurement does not provide all of the information needed. However, the school's curriculum does not lend itself to this rather simplified approach.

Among the confounding factors in curriculum evaluation is the variance of opinion about purpose of the schools. The traditionalist may consider achievement as the major criterion for assessing the performance of the schools; the pragmatist may be primarily concerned with the utility of knowledge; the humanist may not be particularly concerned about the fundamentals or the utility of schooling but may wish to examine the social climate and acceptance of pupils by teachers and peers; the efficiency expert may study the costs and benefits of schools examining the expenditure of time and money; the didactic approach may be primarily concerned with teacher knowledge and performance; the inquiry-oriented curriculum worker may look at pupil activities and the ways pupils behave in schools.

Much educational evaluation conforms to straightforward measures of intended results and interpretations of data to determine the merit of certain courses, materials, or methods. Curriculum evaluation includes these concerns but also requires more than the traditional testing and assessment of the schools. For example, the follow-up of graduates and the unintended outcomes of schools are two additional topics to consider in curriculum evaluation. Both of these require a more comprehensive approach to evaluation than is the case, for instance, in the measurement of easily defined cognitive learning.

Perspectives on Curriculum Evaluation

Before engaging in curriculum evaluation, there are broad concerns and overall contexts that should be taken into account. There are also fundamental questions to be raised about the purpose of evaluation and its use in the curriculum. The next article by Lee Cronbach presents the reader with a viewpoint that raises some of these fundamental questions and suggests ways to approach curriculum evaluation that will include the wide range of direct and indirect consequences of schooling.

□

Programmatic Decisions

To draw attention to its full range of functions, we may define "evaluation" broadly as the collection and use of information to make decisions about an educational program.

Many types of decisions are to be made, and many varieties of information are useful. It becomes immediately apparent that evaluation is a diversified activity and that no one set of principles will suffice for all situations. But measurement specialists have so concentrated upon one process—the preparation of pencil-and-paper achievement tests for assigning scores to individual pupils—that the principles pertinent to that process have somehow become enshrined as *the* principles of evaluation. "Tests," we are told, "should fit the content of the curriculum." Also, "Only those evaluation procedures should be used that yield reliable scores." These and other hallowed principles are not entirely appropriate to evaluation for course improvement. . . .

We may separate three types of decisions for which evaluation is used:

1. Course improvement: deciding what instructional materials and methods are satisfactory and where change is needed.

2. Decisions about individuals: identifying the needs of the pupil for the sake of planning his instruction, judging pupil merit for purposes of selection and grouping, acquainting the pupil with his own progress and deficiencies.

3. Administrative regulation: judging how good the school system is, how good individual teachers are, etc.

Course improvement is set apart by its broad temporal and geographical reference; it involves the modification of recurrently used materials and methods. Developing a standard exercise to overcome a misunderstanding would be course improvement, but deciding whether a certain pupil should work through that exercise would be an individual decision. Administrative regulation likewise is local in effect, whereas an improvement in a course is likely to be pertinent wherever the course is offered.

It was for the sake of course improvement that systematic evaluation was first introduced. When that famous muckraker Joseph Rice gave the same spelling test in a number of American schools, and so gave the first impetus to the educational testing movement, he was interested in evaluating a curriculum. Crusading against the extended spelling drills that then loomed large in the school schedule—"the spelling grind"—Rice collected evidence of their worthlessness so as to provoke curriculum revision. As the testing movement developed, however, it took on a different function.

Lee J. Cronback, "Evaluation for Course Improvements," *The Teacher's College Record* 64, 8 (May 1963):672–83. Reprinted by permission of the author and publisher.

Footnotes have been renumbered consecutively throughout the chapter.

The Turning Tides

The greatest expansion of systematic achievement testing occurred in the 1920s. At that time, the content of any course was taken pretty much as established and beyond criticism save for small shifts of topical emphasis. At the administrator's direction, standard tests covering the curriculum were given to assess the efficiency of the teacher or the school system.

After 1930 or thereabouts, tests were given almost exclusively for judgments about individuals—to select students for advanced training, to assign marks within a class and to diagnose individual competencies and deficiencies. . . .

Although some instruments capable of measuring general outcomes were prepared during the 1930s, they were never very widely employed. The prevailing philosophy of the curriculum, particularly among "progressives," called for developing a program to fit local requirements, capitalizing on the capacities and experiences of local pupils. . . . Since each teacher or each class could choose different content and even different objectives, this philosophy left little place for standard testing.

Tests as Training

Many evaluation specialists came to see test development as a strategy for training the teacher in service, so that the process of test making came to be valued more than the test—or the test data—that resulted. The following remarks by Bloom[1] are representative of a whole school of thought.

> The criterion for determining the quality of a school and its educational functions would be the extent to which it achieves the objectives it has set for itself. . . . Our experiences suggest that unless the school has translated the objectives into specific and operational definitions, little is likely to be done about the objectives. They remain pious hopes and platitudes. . . . Participation of the teaching staff in selecting as well as constructing evaluation instruments has resulted in improved instruments on one hand and, on the other hand, it has resulted in clarifying the objectives of instruction and in making them real and meaningful to teachers. . . . When teachers have actively participated in defining objectives and in selecting or constructing evaluation instruments, they return to the learning problems with great vigor and remarkable creativity. . . . Teachers who have become committed to a set of educational objectives which they thoroughly understand respond by developing a variety of learning experiences which are as diverse and as complex as the situation requires.

Thus, "evaluation" becomes a local and beneficial teacher-training activity. The benefit is attributed to thinking about what data to collect. Little is said about the actual use of test results; one has the impression that when test making ends, the test itself is forgotten.

Bloom and Tyler describe both curriculum making and evaluation as integral parts of classroom instruction, which is necessarily decentralized. This outlook is far from that of "course improvement."

[1]B. S. Bloom, "Quality Control in Education," in *Tomorrow's Teaching* (Oklahoma City: Frontiers of Science Foundation, 1961), pp. 54–61.

When evaluation is carried out in the service of course improvement, the chief aim is to ascertain what effects the course has—that is, what changes it produces in pupils. This is not to inquire merely whether the course is effective or ineffective. Outcomes of instruction are multidimensional, and a satisfactory investigation will map out the effects of the course along these dimensions separately. To agglomerate many types of post-course performance into a single score is a mistake, because failure to achieve one objective is masked by success in another direction.

The greatest service evaluation can perform is to identify aspects of the course where revision is desirable. . . . But to call in the evaluator only upon the completion of course development, to confirm what has been done, is to offer him a menial role and to make meager use of his services. To be influential in course improvement, evidence must become available midway in curriculum development, not in the home stretch, when the developer is naturally reluctant to tear open a supposedly finished body of materials and techniques.

Hopefully, evaluation studies will go beyond reporting on this or that course and help us to understand educational learning. Such insight will, in the end, contribute to the development of all courses rather than just the course under test. In certain of the new curricula, there are data to suggest that aptitude measures correlate much less with end-of-course achievement than they do with achievement on early units.[2] This finding is not well confirmed, but it is highly significant if true. If it is true for the new curricula and only for them, it has one implication; if the same effect appears in traditional courses, it means something else. Either way, it provides food for thought for teachers, counselors, and theorists. Evaluation studies should generate knowledge about the nature of the abilities that constitute educational goals.

The aim to compare one course with another should not dominate plans for evaluation. To be sure, decision makers have to choose between courses, and any evaluation report will be interpreted in part comparatively. But formally designed experiments, pitting one course against another, are rarely definitive enough to justify their cost. . . .

Since group comparisons give equivocal results, I believe that a formal study should be designed primarily to determine the post-course performance of a well described group with respect to many important objectives and side effects. Ours is a problem like that of the engineer examining a new automobile. He can set himself the task of defining its performance characteristics and its dependability. It would be merely distracting to put his question in the form, "Is this car better or worse than the competing brand?" Moreover, in an experiment where the treatments compared differ in a dozen respects, no understanding is gained from the fact that the experiment shows a numerical advantage in favor of the new course. No one knows which of the ingredients is responsible for the advantage.

The three purposes—course improvement, decisions about individuals, and administrative regulation—call for measurement procedures having somewhat different qualities. When a test will be used to make an administrative judg-

2G. A. Ferguson, "On Learning and Human Ability," *Canadian Journal of Psychology* 8 (1954):95–112.

ment on the individual teacher, it is necessary to measure thoroughly and with conspicuous fairness; such testing, if it is to cover more than one outcome, becomes extremely time consuming. In judging a course, however, one can make satisfactory interpretations from data collected on a sampling basis, with no pretense of measuring thoroughly the accomplishments of any one class. . . .

One can accept the need for a pragmatic test of the curriculum and still employ opinions as a source of evidence. During the tryout stages of curriculum making, one relies heavily on the teachers' reports of pupil accomplishment—"Here they had trouble"; "This they found dull"; "Here they needed only half as many exercises as were provided," etc. This is behavior observation even though unsystematic, and it is of great value. . . .

Systematic observation is costly, and introduces some delay between the moment of teaching and the feedback of results. Hence, systematic observation will never be the curriculum developer's sole source of evidence. Systematic data collection becomes profitable in the intermediate stages of curriculum development, after the more obvious bugs in early drafts have been dealt with.

The approaches to evaluation include process studies, proficiency measures, attitude measures, and follow-up studies. A process study is concerned with events taking place in the classroom, proficiency and attitude measures with changes observed in pupils, and follow-up studies with the later careers of those who participated in the course.

The follow-up study comes closest to observing ultimate educational contributions, but the completion of such a study is so far removed in time from the initial instruction that it is of minor value in improving the course or explaining its effects. The follow-up study differs strikingly from the other types of evaluation study in one respect. I have already expressed the view that evaluation should be primarily concerned with the effects of the course under study rather than with comparisons of courses. That is to say, I would emphasize departures of attained results from the ideal, differences in apparent effectiveness of different parts of the course, and differences from item to item; all these suggest places where the course could be strengthened. But this view cannot be applied to the follow-up study, which appraises effects of the course as a whole and which has very little meaning unless outcomes can be compared with some sort of base rate. . . .

Attitudes can be measured in many ways; the choices revealed in follow-up studies, for example, are pertinent evidence. But measurement usually takes the form of direct or indirect questioning. Interviews, questionnaires, and the like are quite valuable when not trusted blindly. Certainly, we should take seriously any *un*desirable opinion expressed by a substantial proportion of the graduates of a course (e.g., the belief that the scientist speaks with peculiar authority on political and ethical questions, or the belief that mathematics is a finished subject rather than a field for current investigation).

Attitude questionnaires have been much criticized because they are subject to distortion, especially where the student hopes to gain by being less than frank. In group averages, many distortions balance out. But questionnaires insufficiently valid for individual testing can be used in evaluating curricula, both because the student has little motive to distort and because the evaluator is comparing averages rather than individuals.

Process and Proficiency

For measuring proficiency, techniques are likewise varied. Standardized tests are useful. But for course evaluation it makes sense to assign different questions to different students. Giving each student in a population of 500 the same test of fifty questions will provide far less information to the course developer than drawing for each student fifty questions from a pool of, say, 700. The latter plan determines the mean success of about seventy-five representative students on every one of the 700 items; the former reports on only fifty items.[3] Essay tests and open-ended questions, generally too expensive to use for routine evaluation, can profitably be employed to appraise certain abilities. One can go further and observe individuals or groups as they attack a research problem in the laboratory or work through some other complex problem. Since it is necessary to test only a representative sample of pupils, costs are not as serious a consideration as in routine testing.

Process measures have especial value in showing how a course can be improved because they examine what happens during instruction. In the development of programmed instructional materials, for example, records are collected showing how many pupils miss each item presented; any piling up of errors implies a need for better explanation or a more gradual approach to a difficult topic.

I have indicated that I consider item data to be more important than test scores. The total score may give confidence in a curriculum or give rise to discouragement, but it tells very little about how to produce further improvement. And, as Ferris[4] has noted, such *scores* are quite likely to be mis- or overinterpreted. The score on a single item, or on a problem that demands several responses in succession, is more likely than the test score to suggest how to alter the presentation. When we accept item scores as useful, we need no longer think of evaluation as a one-shot, end-of-year operation. Proficiency can be measured at any moment, with particular interest attaching to those items most related to the recent lessons.

In course evaluation, we need not be much concerned about making measuring instruments fit the curriculum. However startling this declaration may seem, and however contrary to the principles of evaluation for other purposes, this must be our position if we want to know what changes a course produces in the pupil. An ideal evaluation would include measures of all the types of proficiency that might reasonably be desired in the area in question, not just the selected outcomes to which this curriculum directs substantial attention. If you wish only to know how well a curriculum is achieving its objectives, you fit the test to the curriculum; but if you wish to know how well the curriculum is serving the national interest, you measure all outcomes that might be worth striving for. . . .

---

[3]F. L. Ferris, Jr., "Testing in the New Curriculums: Numerology, Tyranny, or Common Sense?" *School Review* 70 (1962):112–31.

[4]Ferris, "Testing in the New Curriculum."

Security, Content, Terms

The demand that tests be closely matched to the aims of a course reflects awareness that examinations of the usual sort "determine what is taught." If questions are known in advance, students give more attention to learning their answers than to learning other aspects of the course. This is not necessarily detrimental. Wherever it is critically important to master certain content, the knowledge that it will be tested produces a desirable concentration of effort. On the other hand, learning the answer to a set question is by no means the same as acquiring understanding of whatever topic that question represents. There is, therefore, a possible advantage in using "secure" tests for course evaluation. Security is achieved only at a price: One must prepare new tests each year and consequently cannot make before-and-after comparisons with the same items. One would hope that the use of different items with different students, and the fact that there is less incentive to coach when no judgment is to be passed on the pupils and the teachers, would make security a less critical problem.

The distinction between factual tests and tests of higher mental processes, as elaborated for example in the *Taxonomy of Educational Objectives,*[5] is of some value in planning tests, although classifying items as measures of knowledge, application, original problem solving, etc., is difficult and often impossible. Whether a given response represents rote recall or reasoning depends upon how the pupil has been taught, not solely upon the question asked. . . .

Too often, test questions are course-specific, stated in such a way that only the person who has been specifically taught to understand what is being asked for can answer the question. Such questions can usually be identified by their use of conventions. Some conventions are commonplace, and we can assume that all the pupils we test will know them. But a biology test that describes a metabolic process with the aid of the $>$ symbol presents difficulties for students who can think through the scientific question about equilibrium but are unfamiliar with the symbol.

Two Types of Transfer

The chief objective in many of the new curricula seems to be to develop aptitude for mastering new materials in the field. A biology course cannot cover all valuable biological content, but it may reasonably aspire to equip the pupil to understand descriptions of unfamiliar organisms, to comprehend a new theory and the reasoning behind it, and to plan an experiment to test a new hypothesis. This is transfer of learning. It has been insufficiently recognized that there are two types of transfer. But the more significant type of transfer may be the increased ability to learn in a particular field. There is very likely a considerable difference between the ability to draw conclusions from a neatly finished experiment, and the ability to tease insight out of the disor-

[5]B. S. Bloom, ed., *Taxonomy of Education Objectives* (New York: Longman, Green, 1965).

derly and inconsistent observations that come with continuous laboratory work on a problem.

Nearly all educational research on transfer has tested immediate performance on a partly new task. We teach pupils to solve equations in x, and include in the test equations stated in a or z. We teach the principles of ecological balance by referring to forests, and as a transfer test, ask what effect pollution will have on the population of a lake. We describe an experiment not presented in the text, and ask the student to discuss possible interpretations and needed controls. Any of these tests can be administered in a short time. But the more signficant type of transfer may be the increased ability to learn in a particular field. There is very likely a considerable difference between the ability to draw conclusions from a neatly finished experiment, and the ability to tease insight out of the disorderly and inconsistent observations that come with continuous laboratory work on a problem. The student who masters a good biology course may become better able to comprehend certain types of theory and data, so that he gains more from a subsequent year of study in ethnology; we do not measure this gain by testing his understanding of short passages in ethnology. There has rarely been an appraisal of ability to work through a problem situation or a complex body of knowledge over a period of days or months. Despite the practical difficulties that attend an attempt to measure the effect of a course on a person's subsequent learning, such "learning to learn" is so important that a serious effort should be made to understand how they may be fostered.

Toward Deeper Understanding

Old habits of thought and long established techniques are poor guides to the evaluation required for course improvement. Traditionally, educational measurement has been chiefly concerned with comparing score averages of competing courses. But course evaluation calls for description of outcomes. This description should be made on the broadest possible scale, even at the sacrifice of superficial fairness and precision.

Course evaluation should ascertain what changes a course produces and should identify aspects of the course that need revision. The outcomes observed should include general outcomes ranging far beyond the content of the curriculum itself—attitudes, career choices, general understandings and intellectual powers, and aptitude for further learning in the field. Analysis of performance on single items or types of problems is more informative than analysis of composite scores. It is not necessary or desirable to give the same test to all pupils; rather, as many questions as possible should be given, each to a different, moderate sized sample of pupils. Costly techniques, such as interviews and essay tests, can profitably be applied to samples of pupils, whereas testing everyone would be out of the question.

Asking the right questions about educational outcomes can do much to improve educational effectiveness. Even if the right data are collected, however, evaluation will have contributed too little if it only places a seal of approval on certain courses and casts others into disfavor. Evaluation is a fundamental part of curriculum development, not an appendage. Its job is to collect facts the course developer can and will use to do a better job, and facts from which a deeper understanding of the education process will emerge.

To Test or Not to Test

The article by Cronbach broadens the horizons of evaluation. It is important, according to Cronbach, to retain a multi-based approach to curriculum evaluation. Included in this multi-based approach are a number of possibilities, including testing pupil performance. The negative consequences of testing for student achievement loom so strongly that abolishing tests is sometimes proposed. A number of organizations including the NEA and those contending test bias limits opportunities for students, are calling for studying and possibly discontinuing achievement testing as it is traditionally administered. The next two articles list the pros and cons of achievement testing. The complex issues in this controversy cannot be adequately treated in two brief articles but the major arguments are raised. These two articles, one by Boyd Bosma and the other by Robert Ebel provide a basis for further discussion and analysis of the testing controversy.

☐

While the momentum has gathered for years, the furor over testing began to peak in the fall of 1971. National concern for equal educational opportunity, evidence of new testing and tracking programs in "desegregated" schools, use of the National Teacher Examination to eliminate black teachers in southern schools, increasing calls for "accountability," and the debates over the proposals of Jensen, Shockley, Hernnstein, and others brought a new awareness of the need for a national dialogue on testing. The Council on Human Relations of the National Education Association moved to convene its annual national conference on civil and human rights in education for 1972 on the topic "Violations of Human and Civil Rights: Tests and the Use of Tests."

This annual conference has served effectively since 1965 as a national forum in calling attention to and clarifying issues related to civil and human rights in education, and past conferences have dealt with such topics as teacher displacement in school desegregation, the treatment of minorities in textbooks, the myth of the melting pot, and cultural pluralism.

Response was immediate. More than 650 participants registered for the conference, set for February 18–20, 1972, including teachers, school administrators, state education officials, representatives of federal agencies and national organizations, students, and parents. Substantial numbers of test company employees and other representatives of the test industry arrived. . . .

By the final day of the conference most participants had become convinced

Boyd Bosma, "The NEA Testing Moratorium," *Journal of School Psychology* 11, 4 (1973): 304–6. Reprinted by permission of the author and publisher.

that significant and immediate action was called for in order to bring any level of resolution to the testing dilemma. Although differences of opinion remained, recommendations from the forums are instructive in understanding the mood of the conference participants.

Forum A (Bias in Testing) called for such actions as elimination of standardized or IQ scores in cumulative records, abolishing use of ᵗʰ ₋ NTE for certification or employment, and censure of the testing industry for not responding to the needs of culturally different children.

Forum B (Use of Tests: Educational Administration) concluded that tests cause psychological damage to all children, and especially minority children, and called for a three- to five-year moratorium on group and individual IQ testing; elimination of the NTE for purposes of hiring, promotion, dismissal, certification, retention, and demotion; and abolition of the term "IQ" along with group tests of mental ability.

Forum C (Use of Tests: Employment) asserted that no standardized tests free from bias had been developed and that serious question existed as to whether any could be developed. This group asked that the NTE be outlawed and that ETS be requested to withdraw the test from the market, additionally calling for organizations to demand from test publishers fair and equitable instruments, with a moratorium to be declared until this is achieved.

Forum D (Use of Tests: Self-Concept) also called for an immediate moratorium on testing, not to be lifted or abolished until "each of us as educators, state departments of education, national education associations, and state and local education associations" undertake appropriate activities.

Participants in the conference had heard the evidence and obviously had concluded that the crisis in testing was real and demanded direct action. Traditional solutions and attempts to improve the tests had not done the job. Passage of the resolution "That a moratorium on standardized tests, as recommended in this conference, be instituted immediately" was obtained by an overwhelming vote.

Such recommendations from a conference do not, as they should not, represent official policy of the nation's largest professional organization. NEA policy is established only by action of governing bodies, most usually the Representative Assembly; in the case of the testing moratorium, the resolution adopted by the delegates to the annual Representative Assembly seemed the most desirable avenue for testing members`ip attitudes about testing.

Spanish-speaking members of the NEA were deeply aware of the unfair uses of English-language tests on their children, and members of NEA's Chicano Caucus took the lead in developing a proposal for the moratorium, while additional resolutions were submitted from across the nation from NEA affiliates and from white, Indian, Asian-American, and black members alike. California teachers, concerned already about the bilingual issues, became additionally alarmed over the passage of the "Stull Bill," an accountability measure which threatened to jeopardize teachers' job security on the basis of student scores on standardized tests. Teachers in New Jersey and other states also were sensitive to political demands for "accountability" which threatened to make teachers scapegoats for all of the real and imagined failures of the system. Most commonly, however, support for action came from teachers in districts across the nation who felt tests and test information were being misused and that necessary moves toward educational reform were being impeded by continued administrative reliance on outdated, inappropriate testing programs.

More than 8,000 delegates were present at the Atlantic City Representative Assembly to adopt several items relating to test use and misuse, including continuing statements on the NTE and on national assessment. The key policy statement is found in Resolution 72–44, submitted by the Michigan delegation:

> The National Education Association strongly encourages the elimination of group standardized intelligence, aptitude, and achievement tests to assess student potential or achievement until completion of a critical appraisal, review, and revision of current testing programs.

New business items in the past have been used to call for specific actions to implement policy expressed in resolutions. New business item 28 was presented by members of NEA's Chicano Caucus:

> This Representative Assembly directs the National Education Association to immediately call a national moratorium on standardized testing and at the same time set up a task force on standardized testing to research and make its findings available to the 1975 Representative Assembly for further action.

New business item 51 had been recommended by the NEA Editing Committee and represented a compromise position:

> The NEA shall establish a task force to deal with the numerous and complex problems communicated to it under the general heading of testing. This task force shall report its findings and proposals for further action at the 1973 Representative Assembly.

With passage of the resolutions and new business items, the moratorium was on, with a task force to provide initial proposals and recommendations in 1973 and presumably again in 1975. While proposals for implementation of the moratorium were being developed, further action would depend on individual teachers and teacher associations at local and state levels and by school districts and other officials as word spread and recommendations could be adopted.

Is Achievement Testing All That Bad?

The moratorium on achievement testing can be argued effectively because the tests are imperfect. These imperfections can be identified and used as the basis for eliminating tests altogether. The argument against elimination suggests making the best of the tests in their present form but recognizing their strengths and weaknesses. The next article by Robert Ebel presents an analysis of some objections to the use of achievement tests.

☐

If the curriculum of a school encompasses all that the pupils are given the opportunity to learn while attending it, then the tests used to measure what the pupils have learned ought to be very closely related to that curriculum. In any reasonably good school the teachers see to it that the relationship is in fact about as close as it can be made to be, given the indefiniteness of many curricular objectives and the imperfections of many teacher-constructed tests. But when the school uses external tests of achievement, such as published standardized tests or statewide program tests, the relationship could be much less than ideal.

Curriculum specialists and educational administrators have not neglected to point out this possibility, and to express their concerns about it. These concerns involve beliefs that:

1. Teachers inevitably will "teach to" any test used to measure the achievements of their pupils.
2. This tendency effectively places control of the curriculum in the hands of the *test makers.*
3. Widespread use of the same test of achievement will tend to foster uniformity of curricula, regardless of unique local needs and opportunities, and discourage creative curricular innovations.
4. In their desperate efforts to equip their pupils to make a good showing on the external test, teachers will tend to use undesirable teaching methods, overemphasizing drill and rote memory.
5. Written tests are poorly suited to assessing any educational outcome other than cognitive competence. When great importance is attached to such tests, as is likely to happen as a result of external testing, other important social, behavioral, and affective outcomes probably will be neglected.

Let us examine each of these beliefs. What about "teaching to the tests?" If the teacher knows in advance precisely what questions will be asked on a test, and limits her instructional efforts to preparing pupils to answer only those questions, she is indeed "teaching to the test" in a way that is educationally undesirable and professionally reprehensible. But seldom does a teacher have that kind of advance information about the tests used in widescale testing programs. Seldom would a self-respecting teacher choose to misdirect her educational efforts so badly even if the information were available. And if she should choose to do so, seldom would her pupils, her supervisors, or her students' parents spare her from criticism for doing so.

On the other hand, if the teacher knows only in general what the test is likely to require, and if those requirements are closely related to what she ought to

Robert L. Ebel, "The Curriculum and Achievement Testing," *Educational Technology* 10, 5 (May 1970):22–23. Reprinted by permission of the author and publisher.

be teaching, then teaching to the test becomes a commendable and rewarding educational activity.

Good teachers have less to fear from external testing than poor teachers and hence are less likely to concentrate too much of their efforts on helping students to pass a particular test. Their pupils are likely to learn most of what they need to know to do reasonably well on a good external test in the course of the instruction they would normally get if no external testing were in prospect. Nor will the good teacher feel constrained to avoid useful content that may not be covered by the external test.

Does external testing give test makers control of the curriculum? Only to the extent that teachers are able and feel constrained to teach to the test. In many cases this extent is rather limited, as has been pointed out. Another fact that has reduced the apparent need for and the rewards to be expected from teaching to the test is the increasing use of tests of general educational development, rather than subject achievement, in widescale testing programs. But it cannot be denied that some teachers do attempt to teach to the external tests given in their schools. In the process they yield a measure of curricular control to the test makers.

But who are the test makers? In modern test construction practice test content is controlled not by specialists in testing, but by expert teachers. Such control as they exercise over the curricula of diverse local schools is probably far more beneficial than detrimental on the whole.

What of the effect of external testing on local curricular diversity and creative innovations? Let it be granted that dead level uniformity is a bad thing. But then so is undue curricular diversity, especially in a population as mobile as ours has become. Some degree of uniformity across schools in curricula is *not* a bad thing.

Let it also be granted that if external testing were to stifle creative innovations that too would be bad. But the recent decades have seen both the most rapid growth of external testing and the most radical programs of curricular innovation. In some cases the new curricula have called for different kinds of achievement tests, and these have been provided. In other cases the requirement of conventional tests of achievement has been waived, as it should be, when test requirements are not relevant to course objectives. When external tests are used, there is no necessity of using them either blindly or foolishly.

Do external tests force teachers to abandon creative teaching in favor of routine drill and rote memorization? Never, though inadequate teachers have often used external tests as an excuse for their inadequate teaching methods. The best way for students to prepare for any achievement test, even a factually oriented achievement test, is not to drill on disconnected items of factual information, in hope that they can be recalled when needed. A far better way is to relate the important facts to other facts, so that they can be understood; to build items of information presented into a structure of personal knowledge that makes sense. This is what good teachers try to do by the questions they ask, the implications they point out, and the tasks they set.

Are external tests limited largely to the assessment of cognitive competence? Indeed they are, but since the cultivation of cognitive competence is probably the school's major task, this is no serious limitation.

To summarize our assessment of the concerns that curriculum specialists have expressed over external testing of achievement, we have found them to a considerable extent unwarranted. It is possible to use tests so foolishly, or to respond to their use so foolishly, that considerable harm could result. But there is no real need for behaving foolishly, and most of those who make and have used external tests of achievement have not behaved foolishly. Curriculum specialists who choose to use tests wisely will find them strong allies in their well-considered efforts to improve education.

The Role of Achievement Tests in Curriculum Evaluation

One of the most common criticisms of curriculum development projects is that evaluations of the effectiveness of the new curricula have been inadequate. The implication is that if the curriculum developers had thought about it soon enough, or had attached proper importance to it, they could easily have gathered evidence to show whether or not the new curriculum was superior to the old. In this view, a controlled experiment, with the old curriculum serving as the reference point, could provide the evidence needed to determine unequivocally the merit or deficiency of the new curriculum. Unfortunately, the problem turns out to be a good deal more complicated than this.

For one thing, new curriculum developments often are based on *different educational objectives* than the old. Seldom are they offered simply as new means of attaining old ends. If the objectives of the new curriculum are different, tests that measure achievement validly are likely to be different too. The use of different tests in new and old curricula makes it difficult, if not impossible, to use test scores as a basis for evaluating relative merits.

A second problem arises as a consequence of the multitude of variables in addition to the curriculum that can affect the attainment of curricular objectives: variables like pupil ability and interest, teachers' skill and attitude, instructional resources, schedule differences, and competing innovations. Adequate control of all of these variables would be difficult to achieve in the most favorable experimental environment.

This points up the third problem. Most curricular developments occur in the ongoing educational process. The children being taught are not experimental subjects whose educational welfare can be regarded as less important than their contribution to the discovery of new educational knowledge. The experimenter must often compromise ideal experimental conditions to avoid unacceptable compromises in educational conditions.

As a consequence of these difficulties and limitations, attempts to evaluate alternative curricula in comparative experimental studies have seldom if ever yielded conclusive, unequivocal results. A higher mean achievement test score for pupils involved in Curriculum A than for those involved in Curriculum B can hardly ever be interpreted as strong evidence that Curriculum A is in fact superior to Curriculum B.

Thus, the role of achievement tests in curriculum evaluation is likely to be a rather limited one. Indeed, the role of educational research itself, in the stylized, formal, statistical sense is likely to be limited also. Research methods of proven effectiveness in scientific, agricultural or medical research tend to break down when applied to the more complex, more value-laden, more taboo-ridden problems of education. Despite the mountainous literature of educational research, preserved in tens of thousands of doctoral dissertations, evidence of the effectiveness of scientific research methods when applied to educational problems is hard to find.

Does this mean that curricular evaluation is a hopeless task? Not at all. It simply means that the evaluation is more likely to result from experience with the new curriculum, over the years and in a variety of circumstances, than from one or a few carefully designed evaluative experiments. A new curriculum must stand the tests of time and practical utility. Curricular aims, content, and procedures need to be examined critically and to be debated openly. Apparent successes and failures need to be reported and accounted for. But we should probably stop hoping that the educational scientist will ever be able to give us an easy, authoritative answer to the question, "Is this new curriculum better than the old?"

Call for Evaluation Relevant to Development

Edna Shapiro, in an article on the evaluation of the Bank Street-Sponsored Follow Through Program, provides an orientation to curriculum evaluation and the flaws that often exist. She presents a useful summary based on evaluation experiences with Follow Through. Her opening and summarizing statements illustrate the kinds of issues that arise in evaluation and the breadth of concerns that curriculum evaluators must take into account. Before reading this selection it would be helpful for you to state the purpose(s) of curriculum evaluation. When you finish the article compare your stated purposes with the views given in the selection.

☐

One way of knowing that educational evaluation has come into its own is that there has been, in the recent past, about as much writing about evaluation procedures and processes as there have been evaluation studies. We can now begin to sort out different ways of evaluating what evaluation is and what it should be. One of the first things to note is that evaluators are as different as the programs they assess. They differ in the kinds of research strategies they adopt, in the kinds of data they consider relevant and viable, in the statistical analysis they prefer, and in their opinion of the kind of impact evaluation has or should have on social policy. . . .

More and more programs are launched with the proviso that their effectiveness be assessed. The requests for proposals to undertake the assessment become more sophisticated, taking into account the inadequacies of previous

Edna Shapiro, "Education Evaluation: Rethinking the Criteria of Competence," *School Review* 81, 4 (August 1973):523–49. Reprinted by permission of the author and publisher.

studies, specifying precautions and controls, sampling strategies, scope of measurement, and niceties of statistical analysis, as well as timing and budget. The major national studies have a roster of high-powered consultants, and when the reports are published, the design is criticized, the data are reanalyzed, and the conclusions are reinterpreted by other, equally eminent experts. As Carol Weiss has noted, the "first line of attack is the study's methodology. Critics of every persuasion seem able to locate experts who find flaws in the sampling, design, choice of statistics, measurement procedures, time span, and analytic techniques—even though their real criticisms derive less from methodology than from ideology."[6]

Peter Rossi reminds us that initial programs to counteract some physical or social ill (swamp drainage to combat malaria, immunization against poliomyelitis, the introduction of compulsory schooling) may have dramatic impact, but that it is much more difficult to demonstrate the effects of subsequent efforts to refine and improve the treatments. He says: "The more we have done in the past . . . to provide social services, etc., the more difficult it is to add to the benefits derived from past programs by the addition of new ones."[7] Consequently, it becomes more difficult to demonstrate the differential impact of program refinements. This point of view leads to the expectation that studies of educational variations will yield very little that is new. . . .

There has been less consideration of certain basic questions which underlie any attempt to evaluate educational programs: What kinds of data are we getting in the first place? What are the measures that are being quantified and manipulated in such sophisticated ways? What are the conditions under which they are obtained? Discussions of evaluation research seldom pay much attention to the characteristics of the programs being compared or studied. Yet anyone who has ever spent any time in Head Start centers or elementary school classrooms knows that the first thing one can say about them is that they vary. The parameters of variation cannot be simply boxed off with notations of geography and ethnicity. Nevertheless, one finds few descriptive or analytic accounts of the educational transactions that take place in the schools or centers under study.[8] Finally, there is a notable dearth of what might be called developmental considerations. Measures for three-year olds are discussed and treated as though they were GRE scores. Age may appear on the abscissa to show cumulative learning or deficit, but developmental trends or stages are

[6]Carol H. Weiss, "The Politicization of Evaluation Research," *Journal of Social Issues* 26 (1970): 57–68; reprinted in *Evaluating Action Programs: Readings in Social Action and Education,* ed. Carol H. Weiss (Boston: Allyn and Bacon, 1972), p. 329.

[7]Peter H. Rossi, "Boobytraps and Pitfalls in the Evaluation of Social Action Programs," in *Evaluating Action Programs,* ed. Weiss, p. 226.

[8]In a recent review Rosenshine states that "data obtained from direct observation of classroom interaction are seldom collected and analyzed. For example, among hundreds of research and evaluation reports at the ERIC Clearing House on Early Childhood Education, Katz (1969) found only ten observational studies reported since 1960." Barak Rosenshine, "Evaluation of Classroom Instruction," *Review of Educational Research* 40 (1970): 279–300; Lillian G. Katz, "Teaching in Preschools: Roles and Goals," Document no. 70706-E-AO-U-26, mimeographed (Urbana: National Laboratory on Early Childhood Education, University of Illinois, 1969).

seldom explicitly taken into account in the design or interpretation of evaluation research.

I have become especially sensitive to such questions after conducting a pilot study designed to assess aspects of a Bank Street-Sponsored Follow Through Program. The plan for the implementation and evaluation of Project Follow Through has been considered to offer fewer perils and more possibilities for adequate assessment than had the plans for earlier programs, such as Head Start. Indeed, the core aspect of the Follow Through program is "planned variation" of sponsorship and program. There are more than a dozen different sponsors of Follow Through programs, each with its own definition of "improving the quality of education," its own methods, materials, and goals.[9]

The national evaluation of Follow Through is supposed to take this variation into account. The evaluators have therefore had to devise assessment techniques which cover the range of programs and their goals. . . .

Toward a Strategy for Evaluation

We conclude that psychological tests as presently conducted offer only a restricted evaluation of a young child's capabilities and that the degree of restriction or the discrepancy between competence and performance may be greatest for those children who are not part of the mainstream culture. Testing may continue to perpetuate a misevaluation and underestimation of the abilities of these children, especially in contrast to mainstream middle-class children. Does this mean that we should scrap efforts to evaluate programs? Or, as some have suggested, do we scrap schooling?

Programming that is national in scope—and that is the trend these days— offers rich possibilities for elegant sampling and analytic procedures. At the same time, its very size makes for chaotic implementation, lack of comparability, mismatching of program to population, and of measures to programs. There are different standards for staff selection, training, and performance, as well as loose control over the procedures and conditions of assessment and the competence of the testers. Marshaling the evidence of educational research over four decades, Stephens came to the dismaying conclusion that educational innovation makes little difference in children's achievement.[10] But can such a judgment be made when the educational researcher has sampled only an extremely narrow band of measurement within a constant and equally restrictive situation?

What is needed is a reexamination of the basic premises and uses of evaluation. Instead of attempting to justify programs and focusing on absolute measures of success and failure, evaluation should serve to inform teachers and program developers of children's progress and functioning, areas of compe-

---

[9]Communities have the opportunity to choose the sponsor and program that they prefer. This aspect has been criticized because it muddles the evaluation design: "The finest evaluation techniques, even if applied to each local program, will not yield very useful information as to which strategies tend to work best in which demographic situations" (Richard J. Light, "Report Analysis: National Advisory Commission on Civil Disorders," *Harvard Educational Review* 38 (1968): 756–67).

[10]John M. Stephens, *The Process of Schooling* (New York: Holt, Rinehart & Winston, 1967).

tence and confusion, attitudes and feelings which may be related to their ability to use what school has to offer. In order to begin to do that researchers have to be willing to look at what actually happens in different classrooms. Variables which are conventionally considered relevant—class size, homogeneous or heterogeneous grouping, participation in programs with unspecified characteristics, use of packaged curricula—remain *distal* variables—as remote as social class and ethnic background from specifying psychological processes.[11] Only by careful description and analysis of the transactions of the classroom can we begin to unravel the nexus of *proximal* stimulation.

Taking account of what happens in classrooms to provide more viable measures of children's competence and more valid assessments of programs is not a simple prescription. Here, too, we must reexamine what we have been doing and the kinds of data that have been gathered. For the most part, techniques for classroom observation have been subjected to the same constraints as those that have governed the use of standard tests. The quest for objective control over the multiplicity of interdependent events occurring in a classroom has led to a concentration on ever smaller units of behavior, divorced from context and sampled in rigorously scheduled time units. There has been little effort to deal empirically with variation in classrooms, to give psychological definition to antecedents in the search for consequences. We need to be able to describe classroom situations in a differentiated way. Such descriptions would necessarily include a systematic analysis of the rationale and objectives of the teacher's behavior as well as that of the children. Rochelle Mayer has analyzed differing preschool curriculum models, categorizing them in terms of their relative stress on different kinds of learning and experience. She suggests that the kinds of interactions most emphasized by a particular program (between child and teacher, child and materials, among peers) are those most consciously and extensively spelled out in that program. This reinforces the argument that research methodology must be suited to the particular characteristics of the situations under study, and that an omnibus strategy will not work.[12] Thus, different kinds of classrooms demand different kinds of observational techniques and skills and different research designs.

When the classroom becomes a place where individual children can engage in different activities at the same time, the task of the observer-coder has to be reformulated. It is then that the researcher sees more clearly what is also true but more muted in the conventional situation—that all children do not have the same experiences in the classroom. Those familiar with programs where children have the opportunity to select their own schedules and activi-

---

[11]Even when curriculum materials are carefully designed and their use is intricately spelled out, the implementation may bear little resemblance to the designer's intent. For example, analysis of the way more advanced inquiry-based science curricula were actually taught showed that the teachers had little understanding of the concepts they were supposed to be teaching. See Marshall D. Herron, "The Nature of Scientific Enquiry as Seen by Selected Philosophers, Science Teachers and Recent Curricular Materials" (Ph.D. thesis, University of Chicago, 1969); cited by Ian Westbury, "Curriculum Evaluation," *Review of Educational Research* 40 (1970): 239–60.

[12]Rochelle S. Mayer, "A Comparative Analysis of Preschool Curriculum Models," in *As the Twig Is Bent: Readings in Early Childhood Education*, ed. Robert H. Anderson and Harold G. Shane (Boston: Houghton Mifflin, 1971).

ties have long known that the program the teacher offers is not equivalently "received" by all children. The "curriculum" is an abstraction, even when concretely described: the children grew rock crystals; they worked out algebraic equations on the balance scales; they constructed a replica of the Acropolis; they discussed and analyzed the transportation needs of an urban center; and so on. But which children? How many actually participated in, contributed to, or understood what was happening in each case? It is necessary to distinguish between what is taught and what is learned; the distinction becomes more crucial as the program becomes more individualized.

The homogeneity and heterogeneity of the children's experience may be one of the critical points to consider in looking at classrooms. Individualized programs cannot be considered a treatment in the usual sense. Susan Stodolsky, reviewing some of the current evaluation data, concludes that "the structured and cognitively oriented programs look more effective . . . primarily because the measurements used are most closely articulated with the objectives of these programs and because the structured programs meet the important methodological criterion of being a treatment to be evaluated."[13] When the class group has had a pretty uniform experience, it can more legitimately be tested for group effects. Such programs have also, as I have argued earlier, prepared the children for test taking.

Stodolsky describes Karlson's recent doctoral study: he observed the activities that individual children chose in a Montessori preschool.[14] The amount of individual variation showed that even within the prepared and sequenced Montessori setting, each child devised his own curriculum. Karlson was able to relate the children's activity patterns to specific changes in WPSSI scores. A fine-grained and differentiated analysis of program, then, especially of programs where children can make choices, is a prerequisite for attempting to assess effects. Such analyses should also make it possible to take a further step: to delineate the characteristics of children who make different uses of particular classroom situations.

This kind of information would have value for teachers and program developers as well as for evaluators. It could even contribute to our understanding of psychological and educational processes, for it would enable us to describe and specify the social and psychological parameters of classroom situations. Then we can talk concretely about the similarities and differences, overlap and discontinuity, between situations; and we can fit together analytic units of different level and scope. We can begin to make statements about how particular kinds of educational situations lead to particular outcomes with particular kinds of children.

The outcome measures, however, have to be articulated with program goals and methods and must be developmentally appropriate as well as educationally significant. When and why do we want to know a child's IQ or his grade level

---

[13]Susan S. Stodolsky, "Defining Treatment and Outcome in Early Childhood Education," in *Rethinking Urban Education,* ed. Herbert J. Walberg and Andrew T. Kopan (San Francisco: Jossey-Bass, Inc., 1972), p. 90.

[14]A. L. Karlson, "A Naturalistic Method for Identifying Behavioral Aspects of Cognitive Acquisition in Young Children Participating in Preschool Programs" (Ph.D. thesis, University of Chicago, 1971); cited in Stodolsky.

equivalent score? (If it is to help the teacher, why do teachers usually not get that information until the end of the school year? Instead of keeping test results secret from the teachers, teachers should be one of the prime targets for this information.) How children perform should be used to help teachers and program developers improve the match between the content and style of teaching and what the children can do. The range of performance can help a teacher determine what kind of impact the program has on which children. Evaluation would then be closer to what Scriven has termed formative rather than summative or, in Zimiles's terms, operational rather than absolute.[15] Tests could be less rigidly psychometric than those designed to assess the worth of a program; there would be leeway for trying different kinds of measures, for using different kinds of situations (classroom, small group, and individual) in a flexible research design. The major value of program evaluation is, or should be, what it can contribute to program development, not its labeling of successes and failures.[16]

The assessment of the longer-term impact of a program, summative or absolute evaluation, should be deferred until children are older and there has been ample opportunity for the program to have an impact. With older children, who have experienced at least five or six years of a particular kind of schooling, there should be more of a basis for determining the influence of school experience. This would give less weight to the differential contribution of individual teachers with their different personal styles and ways of carrying out particular programs; it would allow for shifts and compensations in individual patterns of choice and preference. And it would take advantage of the fact that, as Stinchcombe puts it, "environments cumulate."[17] To determine the appropriate timing for the evaluation of impact, we must know when it is plausible and valid to expect children to be able to function readily and competently in a variety of situations, to switch from one form of communication to another, to be able to produce on demand. At what point and as a consequence of what kinds of experience does the restrictive influence of situational factors become less crucial?

Disproportionate effort is being expended on determining how rapidly children can learn to read and write and acquire simple numerical skills. "Learning to read, write or add are easy skills, well within the competence of all children who do not have serious brain damage. . . . Ninety out of every 100 children, black, yellow or white, are capable of adequate mastery of the intellectual requirements of our schools."[18] Yet pressure for early mastery of academic skills and the acquisition of knowledge that can be readily measured

[15]Michael Scriven, "The Methodology of Evaluation," in *Perspectives of Curriculum Evaluation,* by Ralph W. Tyler, Robert Gagne, and M. Scriven. AERA Monograph Series (Chicago: Rand McNally & Co., 1967); Zimiles (n. 24 above).

[16]Marshall S. Smith and Joan S. Bissell, "Report Analysis: The Impact of Head Start," *Harvard Educational Review* 40 (1970): 51–104.

[17]Arthur L. Stinchcombe, "Environment: The Cumulation of Events," *Harvard Educational Review* 39 (1969): 511–22.

[18]Jerome S. Kagan, "Inadequate Evidence and Illogical Conclusions," *Harvard Educational Review* 39 (1969): 274–77.

continues to shape the nature of both educational programming and educational evaluation.

Elkind and Rohrer, while arguing from different premises (Elkind from a Piagetian, Rohrer from an associative learning point of view), suggest that the timing of educational programs has been awry, that the focus on early academic instruction is psychologically unsound as well as uneconomic.[19] Their arguments, so different in all respects, point toward a more relaxed approach to the education of young children. A tremendous investment has already been made in determining how well children can perform according to the specifications of standard test situations, grade point averages, and achievement test scores. It would be far more useful to know how and in what situations individual children use their competencies, how extensive their repertoires are, how flexibly they can shift domains, in what kinds of situations they can function effectively, what their attitudes are about learning, what kinds of aspirations they have, and how relevant school is and will be to their out-of-school lives.

We can begin to answer such questions only when pychologists and educators begin to invent ways of promoting the development of facility in different domains, when the schoolroom itself provides opportunities for multiple kinds of communicative and cognitive competence. As we differentiate the criteria for competence, so also must we differentiate our expectations of how individual children acquire and demonstrate competence in different domains. Those who evaluate educational programs must begin to construct research strategies and measures that are developmentally relevant, that take account of individual variation, and are appropriate to differing kinds of educational situations.

Summary

Curriculum evaluation is a dynamic and never-ending activity that helps determine curriculum effectiveness and those who must make curriculum decisions. Precise measurement is not possible. But if the curriculum worker does not rely on the instruments that provide reliable information he must act on subjective opinions. When a curriculum decision is about to be made, questions about its effectiveness should be asked. If evidence as to its effectiveness is lacking, then an effort to obtain evidence should be made. Decisions about curriculum would be wiser and the quality of the curriculum will be improved if research and evaluation are properly used.

[19]David Elkind, "Piagetian and Psychometric Conceptions of Intelligence," *Harvard Educational Review* 39 (1969): 319–37 Rohrer (n. 7 above).

Chapter 17
Methods of Curriculum Evaluation

Instructor 83. 6 (April 1974): 132.

"It's another one of those curriculum development ideas that fizzled."

1. Orientation
2. An Objective Internal Procedure of Evaluations
3. Evaluation by Accrediting Procedures
4. An External Approach: National Assessment of Educational Progress
5. Developing Objectives and Exercises
6. What Do You Think?

There is a wide division of opinion about how the curriculum is to be evaluated. For a long time evaluating the curriculum has been done internally by the school system. Schools of various types of curriculum organization have used grade norms as a common denominator to judge their relative value. When this practice has not been followed, student achievement has been measured against specified behavioral objectives. The curriculum was judged as successful if the objectives were achieved. If the objectives were not achieved, the tests were criticized, and some claimed that the students still achieved certain intangibles even though they did not do well in cognitive objectives.

Orientation

Another internal approach to evaluating the curriculum has centered on using assessment criteria of accrediting agencies. This is simply a different version of the internal evaluation approach. While it is subjective it nevertheless involves school personnel in critically examining the school in an unbiased way.

Neither of these internal procedures give us information about how effective the curriculum is when judged in terms of societal benefits. Does the curriculum of the school prepare the student to be a good citizen, to be successful in a job. Are the countless things that an individual in a society is called upon to do (e.g., qualify for an automobile driver's license, read and grasp the significance of the contents of packaged foods, know how to buy insurance, or read and listen critically to various media) provided in the curriculum? To assess the curriculum from this standpoint is to engage in external evaluation. The information thereby gained tells us about the impact of the curriculum upon the out-of-school behavior of individuals.

It is the purpose of this chapter to provide information about these different approaches to curriculum evaluation.

An Objective Internal Procedure of Evaluation

The first article in this chapter, by Robert Gagné, presents a research-oriented approach to curriculum evaluation that determines school effectiveness by measuring the attainment of its goals. This approach requires statements of student behavior that exemplify the intended learnings of the school program. As you read the selection by Gagné, contrast the relationship between systematic development of objectives and their measurement with the complex and subtle outcomes that may be difficult or impossible to define. Before reading Gagné's article list a learner's outcome in the knowledge category of the cognitive domain and construct one test item that would assess the student's attainment of that objective. Next, name an objective that calls for synthesizing or evaluating, and also write one test item that would measure the student's attainment of the objective. After preparing these two test items, compare the difficulties in naming, defining, and evaluating the attainment of the two different objectives. To assist in completing this exercise refer to Bloom's taxonomy on the cognitive domain in Chapter 8 on Objectives in the Curriculum.

Discuss your reactions with other students who have also written two objectives and test items. Can you identify advantages and disadvantages to curriculum evaluation on the basis of testing student outcomes? Upon completing the article discuss your reactions to your own two-item "test" with your reactions to Gagné's position.

The questions I should like to address here are of the following sort: How can one test the principles used in curriculum design by empirical methods? What kinds of evidence can be sought to determine the extent to which a curriculum promotes the learning expected of it? Is it possible to use experimental methods to search for optimal "structure" and "sequence" in curriculum development? What dimensions of a curriculum may be varied in systematic experiments to determine their effects on students' learning?

Robert M. Gagné. "Curriculum Research and the Promotion of Learning," in *Perspectives of Curriculum Evaluation*. AERA Monograph Series on Curriculum Evaluation (Chicago: Rand McNally, 1967): 19–38. Reprinted by permission of the author and publisher.

Footnotes have been renumbered consecutively throughout the chapter.

Describing Content

As is usually the case, if one is interested in finding dependable answers to such questions, it is necessary first to define terms. The most important terms involved here are *content, curriculum,* and the items of which the latter is built, which may be called curricular *units.*

What is meant by content? Is it something that has its existence on a printed page of text, in chapter headings, in the oral instruction of a teacher, or in the student's head? Each of these possibilities has some obvious difficulties. If content is the pages of a textbook, the definition would seem to be incomplete in leaving out much that is imparted by the teacher, or by other sources. Similarly, what the teacher says would be an incomplete representation of content for the same reason. . . .

A more satisfactory conception of content is as related to the goals of instruction, rather than to its effects. . . . More specifically, content may be defined as *descriptions of the expected capabilities of students in specified domains of human activity.* It is important to note that such descriptions do not specify the expected behavior of the teacher, nor do they refer to the words in a textbook. They are descriptions of what the student is expected to be capable of doing, following some particular period of learning. . . .

Possibly the most fundamental reason for the central importance of defining educational objectives is that such definition makes possible the basic distinction between content and method. It is the defining of objectives that brings an essential clarity into the area of curriculum design and enables both educational planners and researchers to bring their practical knowledge to bear on the matter. . . .

What is a *unit* of content? First of all, it is a specific description of a single student capability. The difficulty in defining it derives from the fact that it is not a constant entity for all parts of a curriculum. In fact, the size of a unit has to vary with the particular content with which one is dealing, as this in turn is related to the capabilities of the student *prior* to his becoming involved with the objective being specified. Many examples could be given of this fact. For the six-year old, who must learn to write, the description "prints the letters E and F" may at one point constitute a unit of content. For a nine-year old, however, such a unit would normally be quite inappropriate, since he has already acquired a capability of "printing words," or "printing sentences." . . .

Thus, a unit of content may be defined as *a capability to be acquired under a single set of learning conditions,* among these conditions being certain specified prerequisite capabilities.

At this point it is possible to approach a definition of the word curriculum, which combines the idea of unit of content with the idea of prerequisites. *A curriculum is a sequence of content units arranged in such a way that the learning of each unit may be accomplished as a single act, provided the capabilities described by specified prior units (in the sequence) have already been mastered by the learner.* It is evident from this definition that a curriculum may be of any length, that is, it may contain any number of units. A curriculum is specified when (1) the terminal objectives are stated; (2) the sequence of prerequisite capabilities is described; and (3) the initial capabilities assumed to be possessed by the student are identified. . . .

Deriving Subordinate Capabilities

. . . In order to find the *prerequisites* of a given unit of content, one needs to identify those units of previously acquired capabilities which would permit the learning of the given unit under a single set of learning conditions.

Stated in another way, units of the curriculum subordinate to each major objective may be derived by subjecting this objective to analysis. It is a kind of *task analysis* (cf. Gagné, 1965b, 1965c), to give it a name developed in another context. The procedure is one which takes into account both (1) the components of a given objective and (2) the unity of the capabilities so defined, from the standpoint of learning conditions required to establish them. By progressively applying this analysis procedure beginning with the terminal objective and working backward, one can spell out an entire structure of knowledge which has its beginning in relatively simple capabilities that can be assumed to be known by the student.

I am sometimes asked whether this kind of analysis can be applied to many sorts of subject matter, or does it require a subject like mathematics? I believe it is widely applicable to just about any subject, although it seems to me that some are tougher than others to analyze. A key to ease of analysis, however, is good objective statements of human performance. With a terminal objective like "Understands the origins of the American Revolution," one scarcely knows how to begin. But should the statement, "States the sequences of events relating six major causes to the American Revolution," be acceptable, the process of analysis is considerably simplified.

Testing the Effectiveness of Curricula

. . . What one really wants to know about a given curriculum is whether it works. In more precise terms, one is interested in finding out whether learning is promoted by the presentation of particular content in a particular sequence.

A fairly straightforward method can be employed to test the appropriateness of a proposed curricular structure. This consists in designing and administering a test which has been specially constructed to yield pass-fail information on each knowledge unit within a total hierarchy. The data from such a test are then analyzed to reveal the sequential dependence of one unit on another. It may be noted that the test need not be given to students who have been instructed in accordance with a particular hierarchy—that is a later step in curriculum evaluation. But the test does need to be given to a group of students who have been exposed to instruction in the area identified by the hierarchy. That is to say, the instruction of the students to be tested should include the terminal objectives stated in the knowledge hierarchy under investigation.

In designing such a test, a couple of items are written to assess each unit of knowledge identified in the hierarchy. Two items are used for each, rather than one, in order to ensure accuracy of measurement—after all, it is easy to write a bad item, which doesn't measure what it's supposed to. Basically, though, each item is designed to test whether the student can or cannot exhibit the performance implied by each unit capability in the hierarchy. It may be noted that the concept of difficulty is not relevant to such items. They should be neither easy nor difficult, but simply designed to measure what the student can or cannot do in terms of what is stated as an objective. Variations in difficulty, under such assumptions, are simply an indication that the items are ambiguously worded, inaccurately stated, or incorrectly administered; in other words, they are bad items.

Having constructed a test to cover the entire knowledge hierarchy along these lines, the investigator then gives the test to a group of students who are supposed to have recently learned the domain of knowledge that the hierarchy identifies. The test should also be given to a group of students who have *not* had such instruction, in order that units can be identified which are *already learned*. In the description that follows, I shall assume that this initial step has already been taken, so that when a high percentage of students attains a unit correctly, it may be inferred that they have recently learned this unit, not that they already had it in their repertoire before the instruction was given. The data from such an administration may be analyzed to reveal the dependence of one unit of the curriculum on another. Figure 17–1 indicates some of the reasoning that enters into such an analysis.

First, one may look at the kinds of comparisons of adjacent knowledge units required by the analysis. Assume that one unit has been placed higher than another unit, so that, by hypothesis, the learning of the higher unit depends upon mastery of the lower unit. Did all, or nearly all, of those students who passed the higher unit also pass the lower? And did all, or nearly all, of those students who passed the lower unit pass the higher? These first two comparisons are indicated in the first four rows of Figure 17–1. Notice that the implication is that there *may* be a correct sequence here. However, it must be noted that these two units, called "higher" and "lower," may actually have a coordinate relation to each other; they both may depend upon a third unit in the same way. Therefore, an additional step in the analysis must be taken, to see how each behaves with respect to the *next lower* unit in the sequence. This additional analysis makes possible a determination of whether they are dependent one on another, or whether they both depend upon a third and lower unit.

The next row in the figure indicates a pretty clear determination. For the group of students who passed the lower unit, we find only a few who passed the upper unit. The meaning is quite obvious. These students were unable to progress to the higher unit from their knowledge of the lower unit. As for the proposed curriculum hierarchy, this means that one or more additional units must be inserted between the higher and lower unit.

The final row presents another situation having a clear implication. In this case, of the group that were able to complete the unit tested as "higher," only a few were able to pass the unit called "lower." Clearly, the ability to pass the higher unit did not, according to this result, depend upon the possession of what was hypothesized as the "lower" capability. Therefore, these units are incorrectly arranged in sequence.

These, then, are the kinds of analysis that appear to be needed to determine whether a *feasible sequence* of curriculum units has been planned. . . .

Figure 17-1. Hypothetical test results from groups of students on a higher and a lower knowledge unit in a curriculum sequence.

Group	Comparison	0 Per Cent Passing 100	Implication
Passed Lower	Higher unit Lower unit		Possible correct sequence: additional
Passed Higher	Higher unit Lower unit		analysis required
Passed Lower	Higher unit Lower unit		Additional unit needed
Passed Higher	Higher unit Lower unit		Incorrect sequence

One additional point should be made concerning the use of this method to provide information about the sequence of a curriculum. It should be particularly noted that such a method does not provide an *evaluation* of a curriculum. It tells us merely whether a given hypothesized sequence is pedagogically reasonable, or feasible. It does *not* tell us how good the curriculum is. For the latter purpose, there is of course no shortcut method. One must actually put the curriculum into use, and then measure the results in terms of student achievement or of some other specified criterion.

Implications for Research

The general implications of these techniques and the findings they have yielded to date seem to be pretty clear. Let me state those that seem to me to have the broadest import.

1. The design of a curriculum, by which is meant the appropriate sequencing of units of content, can be based upon empirical evidence. It doesn't have to be a matter of speculation about what students are capable of learning, on the one hand, nor a matter of elegance of logical derivation, on the other.

2. A second kind of implication of these techniques concerns the subject of learning. Most learning studies, even when they are designed around material highly relevant to a school program, have been concerned with determining the effectiveness of learning conditions for *single units* of a curriculum, or at the most, of a very few units. Obviously, the larger problem must be oriented toward the learning, not of a single task, but of an entire sequence of curriculum units. . . .

There are many learning questions to be examined in connection with longer units of instruction. One thinks immediately of investigations of problem-solving strategies, of the timing and frequency of occasions for review, of the processes of knowledge generalization, and many others. It is of importance to note, however, that such studies must solve the problem of specification of the content of curriculum, if they are to yield results of lasting value. One cannot draw valid conclusions about differing *methods* of instruction unless there is an experimental way of controlling *content*. The design of curriculum hierarchies, and the sequences of instruction based upon them, offers one way of solving this difficult methodological problem. . . .

3. But there are additional implications of these techniques for the study of the process of extended-sequence learning. Presumably, more than one hierarchical sequence may end with the same terminal objective. . . . There is also the whole question of the generalizable effects of a curriculum sequence, in the sense of transfer of learning. . . . Are some units more generalizable than others? Do some sequences lead to greater amounts of transfer of learning than others? Again, it is my belief that the method of curriculum development described provides a basic means of studying these questions in a systematic sense, irrespective of the particular content.

It seems possible that the method of curriculum development I have described provides some new opportunities for studies designed to relate individual differences to learning variables. Again, it is primarily the possibility of *control* provided by the method which seems of greatest potential significance.

4. A related area of research suggested by this method of analysis is that of individual differences or, more specifically, the relation of individual differences to learning.

The basic rationale for research on individual differences in learning, under specified conditions of mastery of curriculum units, seems fairly clear. Yet I need to emphasize the warning that in order to study the matter in this way, certain concepts traditional to the field of psychological measurement must be voluntarily abandoned, at least for the purposes of these investigations. The basic measurement to be obtained, and one which provides the means of control, is whether the student *has* or *has not* acquired the specific unitary capability being measured. One cannot admit *degrees* of mastery into this kind of measurement, and one cannot deal with the concept of difficulty.

The potentialities of this method for getting a new purchase on the problem of individual differences in learning therefore seem quite good. When the learned prerequisites of a task can be specified and controlled within an entire group of learners, fairly precise questions can be formulated about the kinds of differences that may account for such things as rate of learning, permanence of learning effects, or generalizability of learning. . . .

Evaluation by Accrediting Procedures

Gagné relies heavily on student performance to determine the viability and proper sequence of the curriculum. These are reasonable emphases in curriculum evaluation but quite another basis for assessing the curriculum is found in the approach used in the accreditation of secondary schools.

The next section provides excerpts from the accrediting criteria and discussion of this approach.

In the accrediting approach the school faculty is asked to write the philosophy and objectives which they subscribe to. They are also expected to characterize the community served by the school. Next the curriculum is described and rated according to how well the school program matches the school's philosophy and community characteristics. A series of rating scales, criteria for making ratings, checklists, and open-ended questions are provided for the accreditation procedure.

We present selections from the Evaluative Criteria in which the questions and information about the school's curriculum are provided. Notice how heavily this evaluation depends on the experience of the staff and the opinions about the effectiveness of the curriculum and its development.

The general accrediting procedure requires the secondary school to complete a self-study by using the Evaluative Criteria as a guide. After the self-study has been completed, a visiting committee examines the written self-study and verifies or refutes the accuracy of the report during a brief but thorough site visit.

Study the information from the Evaluative Criteria and contrast this approach with the recommendations made in the previous selection by Gagné.

☐

Guiding Principles

These principles are offered for your acceptance, rejection, or modification. Please feel free to make changes.

Although the term "curriculum" may be interpreted to include all constructive learning experiences provided under the direction of the school, it is used here to designate those activities, both formal and informal, carried on in relation to planned courses of instruction. It functions through learning experiences and instructional materials from various fields of knowledge. Attempts are made to provide learning experiences that meet not only the general needs but also the specialized needs related to the unique abilities, interests, and expectations of each individual.

Instructional activities are planned to develop knowledge, understanding, attitudes, ideals, habits, and skills that are appropriate to a full life in American society. Sound teaching techniques are developed in relation to established theories of learning, new media, and recent research. *It is imperative that all teachers make provisions for individual differences among students.* Students are encouraged to assume as much responsibility for advancing their own learning as their maturity permits.

Continuous evaluation of the curriculum is needed to determine the degree to which the instructional objectives are being achieved, as well as the appropriateness of the curriculum design. The procedures for developing improve-

National Study of Secondary School Evaluation. *Evaluative Criteria,* 4th ed. (Washington: National Study of Secondary School Evaluation, 1969), pp. 33–44. Reprinted by permission of the author and publisher.

ments in the curriculum should be flexible and should encourage change and innovation where appropriate. Professional leadership, widespread faculty involvement, and adequate material resources assure a commitment to continuous evaluation and improvement of the curriculum.

General   Members of school staffs making self-evaluations should understand that a regular part of the evaluation process consists of modifying the statements of guiding principles and of checklist and evaluation items. The purpose of the modifications is to make the statements consistent with the characteristics of the school and community and with the objectives of the school. Unless it is obvious, the school should explain the reason for the change and its relation to the philosophy and objectives and to the needs of the students.

The two pivotal points of this evaluation are (1) the characteristics of the school and community, and (2) the school's philosophy and objectives. Therefore, Section 2, "School and Community," and Section 3, "Philosophy and Objectives," should be kept in mind when the various features of this section are being checked and evaluated. Persons making evaluations should ask: "How well do the practices in this school meet the needs of the school and community?" and "How well do the practices conform to the philosophy and objectives of the school?" When evaluations are made, factors such as size, type, location of school, financial support available, and state requirements should not be permitted to justify failure to provide a program and facilities appropriate to the needs of the school and community and to the philosophy and objectives of the school. Also, the twofold nature of the work—evaluation and stimulation to improvement—should be kept in mind. Careful, discriminating judgment is essential if these purposes are to be served satisfactorily.

Checklists and Evaluations   The checklists and evaluations should be evaluated on the following four-point scale:

4 Excellent
3 Good
2 Fair
1 Poor or missing
na Not applicable

Questions will frequently arise about the basis for comparison of points on the scale. The answer is extremely difficult to give. In any entity as complex as a school, it is not easy to describe in detail what *excellent* or *poor* really means in the hundreds of items for which evaluations are required. The best answer seems to be that the evaluator should draw upon his total experience in schools and make the best judgment he can on the basis of that experience. It should be kept in mind that 4 does not mean ideal or perfect. There is reason to believe that some schools are underrated in the self-evaluation because an impression is held that 4 should be reserved for an unattainably high condition.

Each person who makes an evaluation should try to be as accurate as possible. *If a slight change in the wording of an evaluation item would make it more appropriate to the school being evaluated, such a change should be made. If important elements of the school's program are omitted, the subcommittee members should consider themselves free to add checklist or evaluation items that will make the description more complete.*

On this scale, if you wish to indicate the most desirable condition possible, circle the number 4. One the other hand, if you wish to indicate the least favorable response or indicate a condition that is missing, circle the 1. If you wish to show an evaluation that is good but less than excellent, circle the number 3. Likewise, to show a trait that is less than good, but better than poor, circle the number 2.

Let us consider an example that will help in understanding these directions. Examine the statement "Classroooms are equipped with demonstration facilities." If, in your judgment, the classrooms are equipped with demonstration facilities that are exemplary, excellent, or some of the best that you have ever seen, you will then circle the number 4. One the other hand, if you decide that the demonstration facilities in the classroom are good but not the best, you will circle the number 3. If the demonstration facilities are missing or are totally inadequate, you will circle the 1. If, however, the facilities are not good, but are not poor enough to deserve a 1, you will circle the number 2.

Comments   The space under the heading "Comments" at the end of each subsection should be used to provide additional information needed to give a complete report of that area and to describe any condition that is not adequately covered elsewhere in the subsection. The space can also be used to clarify or amplify items in the checklists or evaluations. Subcommittees are encouraged to use this space every time that its use will aid in describing the area or in explaining a judgment or rating.

Supplementary Data and Additional Areas   Some facets of programs may not be described by the checklist and evaluation statements. For this reason, additional information items are sometimes requested under Supplementary Data. If portions of a program—or additional subject areas—cannot be adequately covered by amplifying Supplementary Data and Comments, it is suggested that the following outline (which is also that employed in most of the sections) be used:

  I. Organization
 II. Nature of Offerings
III. Physical Facilties
IV. Direction of Learning
 V. Outcomes
VI. Special Characteristics
VII. General Evaluation

I. OFFERINGS

A. ORGANIZATION AND EXTENT OF OFFERINGS

NOTE: In column 1, enter under the appropriate field the titles of courses offered. In column 2, indicate by *Yes* or *No* whether the course is required. In column 3, enter the grade or grades in which the course is offered; if it is ungraded, record *U*. Attach a copy of the Program of Studies.

1 FIELD AND COURSE	2 REQ.	3 GRADE(S)	1 FIELD AND COURSE	2 REQ.	3 GRADE(S)	1 FIELD AND COURSE	2 REQ.	3 GRADE(S)
Example: AGRICULTURE Voc. Agric. 1	No	9, 10						

Continued on next page

Ability Groupings

Courses Where Grouping Occurs	Grade at Which Grouping Is Carried On	Number of Levels Used	Factors Used in Grouping
Example: English 1	9	4	Reading, grades, IQ, teachers

Evaluations

a) *How adequate and appropriate are offerings for the youth of the community?*   no 1 2 3 4

b) *How well do offerings contribute to attainment of the stated objectives of the school?*   no 1 2 3 4

c) *How well balanced are offerings in relation to the needs of students and the community?*   no 1 2 3 4

B. ORGANIZATION OF OFFERINGS

Checklist

The pattern of course offerings and special arrangements:

1. Implements the principles and objectives of the school.   no 1 2 3 4
2. Has been developed out of an analysis of the educational needs of youth.   no 1 2 3 4
3. Provides organized sequences of courses.   no 1 2 3 4
4. Provides for students at different ability levels and with differing needs.   no 1 2 3 4

5. Provides a flexibility in time allotments.   no 1 2 3 4
6. Implements a balanced and appropriate program.   no 1 2 3 4
7. Provides for special interests and talents of students.   no 1 2 3 4
8. Is assessed periodically to determine needed changes.   no 1 2 3 4
9.   no 1 2 3 4

Supplementary Data

1. Describe briefly all types of team teaching arrangements.

2. Describe briefly any flexible scheduling practices.

Continued on next page

Supplementary Data—Continued

3. List the fields of study or courses for which the following are available:

a) Ability-grouped *sequences*

_____

_____

_____

_____

_____

b) Remedial programs

_____

_____

_____

c) Programs for the academically talented
   (1) Advanced placement

_____

_____

_____

_____

   (2) Honors courses

_____

_____

_____

_____

   (3) Advanced seminars

_____

_____

_____

d) Ungraded classes

_____

_____

e) Summer school

_____

_____

_____

_____

f) Television

_____

_____

_____

_____

_____

g) Programed materials

_____

_____

_____

_____

h) Teacher aides

_____

_____

_____

i) Departmental learning laboratories

_____

_____

_____

_____

_____

j) Correspondence study

_____

_____

_____

_____

k) Team teaching

_____

_____

_____

_____

l) Large-group arrangement

_____

_____

_____

_____

B. ORGANIZATION OF OFFERINGS—Continued

m) Small-group arrangement   *n*) Independent study   *o*) Other.

_____   _____   _____

_____   _____   _____

_____   _____   _____

_____   _____   _____

_____   _____   _____

Evaluations

a) *How well does the curricular pattern serve the common needs of all students?*   na 1 2 3 4

b) *How well do offerings serve different ability levels and needs?*   na 1 2 3 4

c) *How well does the pattern of offerings provide for sequential study?*   na 1 2 3 4

d) *How well is the program of offerings organized so that each student has opportunity, under guidance, to plan a balanced educational program?*   na 1 2 3 4

e) *How responsive is the program to change?*   na 1 2 3 4

Comments

II. CLASSROOM PROCEDURES

This section summarizes general characteristics of instructional activities in all areas of the program of studies. Instructional activities related to specific fields of study are considered in the subsections related to the respective fields.

Checklist

1. Instruction is planned to contribute to the school's objectives.   no 1 2 3 4
2. Instruction in each course is directed toward clearly formulated, comprehensive objectives that have been cooperatively developed and adopted by the appropriate authority.   no 1 2 3 4
3. There is evidence of careful planning and preparation by the teachers for motivation of the students.   no 1 2 3 4
4. Student purposes are served through the identification of their needs and interests and the use of their experiences in the planning and direction of instructional activities.   no 1 2 3 4
5. Extensive use of varied educational media, through the library and other sources, characterizes the school's instructional activities.   no 1 2 3 4
6. Instruction is individualized through such techniques as grouping of students with particular needs, differentiated assignments, and single-student instruction.   no 1 2 3 4

7. Community resources are used to enrich the instructional program.   no 1 2 3 4
8. Teachers work cooperatively, under responsible leadership, in coordinating instruction.   no 1 2 3 4
9. There is indication that the teaching of content material is looked upon as a means to education, rather than as an end in itself.   no 1 2 3 4
10. Most of the activities in the representative classroom are student centered, with wide student involvement.   no 1 2 3 4
11. In its furnishings, equipment, and arrangements, the classroom has the attributes of a laboratory for learning.   no 1 2 3 4
12.   no 1 2 3 4

Evaluations

a) *How adequate is the planning and preparation for instruction?*   no 1 2 3 4

b) *How adequate is instruction in its general characteristics to meet the particular needs of individual students in the school?*   no 1 2 3 4

c) *How adequate is instruction in its general characteristics to meet the common needs of all students in the school?*   no 1 2 3 4

d) *To what extent is a variety of instructional materials used?*   no 1 2 3 4

e) *To what extent are community resources used?*   no 1 2 3 4

f) *To what extent is instruction related to course objectives?*   no 1 2 3 4

g) *How good is the quality of instructional activities throughout the school?*   no 1 2 3 4

h) *How satisfactorily is factual knowledge treated as the means to, rather than the end of, education?*   no 1 2 3 4

i) *To what extent do classroom procedures permit students to share in the planning, the implementation, and the evaluation of their learning experiences?*   no 1 2 3 4

Comments

III. CURRICULUM DEVELOPMENT PROCEDURES

Curriculum development activities include both those conducted within the school and those of larger educational units, such as city, district, county, and state agencies, when these contribute to the development of the school's curriculum. All of these activities should be considered in the checklists and evaluations of this division.

Checklist

1. Curriculum development procedures include analysis of student needs, community needs, and the relationship of these to needs of the total society.   no 1 2 3 4
2. The local staff members make use of national, regional, and state resources for curriculum development.   no 1 2 3 4
3. All staff members have the opportunity to participate in curriculum development processes that include consideration both of sequential progression within specific disciplines and of the total curriculum of the school.   no 1 2 3 4
4. Curriculum development procedures provide for the development of new content.   no 1 2 3 4
5. Teachers are relieved of other assignments to assist in curriculum development.   no 1 2 3 4
6. Funds are provided for curriculum planning and development.   no 1 2 3 4
7. Parents and other community lay leaders are involved in curriculum development activities.   no 1 2 3 4
8. Suggestions of students are considered in curriculum development.   no 1 2 3 4
9. Professional consultants are used in curriculum development procedures.   no 1 2 3 4
10. Curriculum development within the school is coordinated with that of the district or other larger units.   no 1 2 3 4
11. Curriculum development procedures provide for the evaluation of student growth.   no 1 2 3 4

12. Provision is made for interdisciplinary communication leading to coordination, integration, and articulation of subject areas.   no 1 2 3 4
13. Curriculum development provides for the incorporation of new knowledge of learning procedures.   no 1 2 3 4
14. Curriculum development procedures include the use of (place a check in front of those used):   no 1 2 3 4
    ____ Follow-up studies of all students who have left school.
    ____ Analysis of reasons for student failures.
    ____ Study of curricular materials used in other schools.
    ____ Study of reports of research.
    ____ Continuous evaluation of the educational program.
    ____ Studies of the community served by the school.
    ____ Experimentation with new materials and procedures.
    ____ Publications of state departments of education and of state, regional, and national organizations and agencies.
    ____ _____

15.   no 1 2 3 4

Supplementary Data

1. Indicate your organizational pattern and procedures for curriculum development.

Evaluations

a) *To what extent has the staff participated in curriculum development?* . . . . no 1 2 3 4
b) *To what extent are resources such as materials and specialists* available *for use in curriculum study?* no 1 2 3 4
c) *To what extent are resources such as materials and specialists used in curriculum study?* . . . . no 1 2 3 4
d) *To what extent do curriculum development procedures recognize the needs of students and the community served?* . . . . no 1 2 3 4

Comments

IV. EVALUATIVE PROCEDURES

In this section, the methods of evaluating the curriculum are to be summarized.

1. What procedures does the school use to evaluate the total curriculum in light of the objectives stated in Section 3, "Philosophy and Objectives"?

2. How well are stated objectives being met as determined from observed student behavior?

3. How and to what extent does the staff acquire knowledge of the characteristics of individual students (e.g., through the results of standardized tests; studies of interests, attitudes, peer group relations, family background, and future plans)? How does the staff use such information?

4. Describe the achievement testing program of the school and how it is used to evaluate and improve the curriculum.

5. *a*) What follow-up studies of former students (graduates and dropouts) are currently being conducted?

b) Attach outlines of recently completed follow-up studies and summarize briefly significant findings as they relate to the curriculum.

c) Outline projected follow-up studies.

6. How do organizational devices such as the master schedule, individual student schedules, and course outlines reflect staff efforts to implement objectives of the school's curriculum?

7. *a*) How do students participate in evaluative procedures?

b) How are the students and parents kept aware of student progress?

8. *a*) How and to what extent are all teachers involved in evaluating the broad objectives and design of the school's curriculum?

b) How do teachers evaluate the effectiveness of their own teaching?

c) What methods other than the above are used to evaluate teacher effectiveness?

Continued on next page

9. *a*) How do laymen participate in an organized and constructive effort to cooperate with the professional staff in evaluating the curriculum?

b) List some constructive suggestions from laymen in the community that have resulted in changes in the curriculum within the past four or five years.

10. *a*) To what extent is professional research and experimentation being used to evaluate the school's curriculum?

b) What are some specific changes made in the school's curriculum in recent years that have been based on professional research and experimentation?

V. GENERAL EVALUATIONS

Evaluations

a) *To what extent does the curriculum meet the needs of students as indicated in Section 2, "School and Community"?*   no 1 2 3 4

b) *To what extent is the curriculum consistent with the philosophy and objectives as developed in Section 3, "Philosophy and Objectives"?*   no 1 2 3 4

c) *To what extent is the school identifying problems in the curriculum and seeking their solution?*   no 1 2 3 4

An External Approach: National Assessment of Educational Progress

The National Assessment of Educational Progress (NAEP) has developed an external approach to evaluation. NAEP has capitalized on previous testing experiences and combined this past knowledge with the society's expectations to create an index of educational achievement. The procedures employed by NAEP follow.

☐

History and Purpose of National Assessment

By the early 1960s many billions of dollars were being invested annually in the formal education of our young people. The only available measures of educational quality resulting from this investment had been based upon *inputs* into the educational system such as teacher-student ratios, number of classrooms, and number of dollars spent per student. The tenuous assumption had been that the quality of educational *outcomes*—what students actually learn—was directly related to the quality of the inputs into the educational system. No significant direct assessment of educational outcomes had been made. The typical state-administered or school-administered achievement tests, which provided scores whereby one student could be compared with others, were useful for categorizing students; but they provided very little information about what students were actually learning.

This insufficiency of information became the concern of Francis Keppel, United States Commissioner of Education (1962–1965), who initiated a series of conferences to find ways in which it might be overcome. In 1964, as a result of these conferences, John W. Gardner, president of the Carnegie Corporation, asked a distinguished group of educators and lay persons to form the Exploratory Committee on Assessing the Progress of Education (ECAPE). This committee, chaired by Dr. Ralph W. Tyler, was to examine the possibility of conducting an assessment of educational attainments on a national basis.

After much study, ECAPE deemed that it was feasible to inaugurate an assessment project to fill the information gap regarding the quality of educational outcomes by periodically assessing the knowledges, understandings, skills, and attitudes in ten subject areas[1] at four age levels (nine, thirteen, seventeen, and adult—age twenty-six to thirty-five). The project began its first assessment of the subject areas of science, citizenship, and writing in the spring of 1969. Later that same year, the project came under the auspices of the Education Commission of the States and was named the National Assessment of Educational Progress (NAEP). . . .

The Philosophy of Assessment

The typical achievement test measures *people.* Individuals respond to a number of questions or tasks (items), and a score is determined for each individual. On the basis of many such individual scores, one individual can be compared with any other or with the mean (average) score for the entire group. Little attention is paid to the specific knowledges or skills possessed either by the individual or by the entire group.

National Assessment measures *knowledges, understandings, skills,* and *atti-*

National Assessment of Educational Progress, *General Information Yearbook* (Denver: NAEP, May 1972), pp. 1–11. Reprinted by permission of the publisher.

[1]Art, career and occupational development, citizenship, literature, mathematics, music, reading, science, social studies, and writing.

tudes. We do not obtain scores on individuals. Rather, we obtain the percentages of individuals (at the four age levels mentioned above) in the nation as a whole and certain groups who are able to respond acceptably to exercises which reflect specific knowledges, understandings, skills, or attitudes.

National Assessment respondents respond to a set of questions or tasks much the same as they would on a typical achievement test. Since we do not obtain individual scores for these sets of questions or tasks, we call the sets "packages" rather than tests. We also call the qeustions or tasks "exercises" since they allow the respondent to demonstrate whether or not he possesses the knowledge, understanding, skill, or attitude to respond acceptably to the exercise.

All standardized achievement test *items* ideally are of medium difficulty to assure maximal discrimination. Assessment *exercises* are equally represented by easy, medium, and hard difficulty levels, i.e., we expect certain knowledges, understandings, skills, and attitudes to be possessed by a larger percentage of individuals than others.

Developing Objectives and Exercises

Criteria for Developing Objectives and Exercises

One of the most important features of National Assessment's developmental work is the formulation of educational objectives which govern the direction of the assessment in any given subject area. These objectives define a set of goals which are agreed upon by both laymen and educators as desirable directions in the education of young people. For National Assessment, these educational objectives must be acceptable to three major groups of people. First, the objectives must be considered important by scholars in the discipline of a given subject area. Second, objectives should be acceptable to most educators and be considered important teaching goals in most schools. Finally, and most uniquely, lay citizens interested in education must agree that the objectives are important for young people to attain and that these objectives are of value in modern life.

People from each of these three groups, representing different geographical sections of the country as well as different viewpoints, are brought together to help formulate and review National Assessment objectives. This does not mean that National Assessment objectives are the only ones with which all educators and lay people agree, but rather that the final set of objectives for any area is a summarization of the feelings of a cross section of the scholars, educators, students and lay citizens in this country. In addition, the final set of objectives for any area includes objectives which express minority viewpoints as well as those objectives which a majority of the people in these three groups consider important. To keep the objectives current and have them meet increasing demands for information pertinent to the evaluation of American education, these objectives are reviewed and revised when a new assessment cycle begins.

Once these educational objectives are identified, exercises are developed that will be used to measure the extent to which young people are achieving them. . . . The results of assessment are reported in terms of individual exercises; for example, "90 percent of all 17-year olds know the name of their states, but only 20 percent know the name of their representative in Congress." In addition to providing information on the achievement of 9-, 12-, and 17-year olds and adults, age 26 to 35, for the nation as a whole, National Assessment also provides results by regions of the country, size and type of community, sex, parental education, and color.

Because of the uniqueness of the National Assessment approach to information gathering, the following criteria have been identified as guidelines for the development of National Assessment exercises.

Content Validity Every exercise must be a direct measure of some important knowledge, understanding, skill, or attitude that reflects one or more objectives in a subject area. An exercise must be meaningful, and directly related to the objective that it is intended to fulfill. . . . The chief criterion for determining content validity is that an exercise pass extensive reviews by subject matter and lay groups. . . . But to further ensure that its exercises are meaningful and relevant. National Assessment involves young people at the ages being assessed in both the formation and review of its exercises.

Clarity Every exercise must be easy to understand so that the respondent knows what he is being asked to do. This means that the directions and formats which go with the exercises must be simple enough for anyone to understand and the vocabulary, phraseology, and length of sentences must not be confusing.

Type of Exercises and Formats National Assessment instructs developers of its exercises to use that format which provides the best and most direct measure of the objective being assessed, and to create exercises which obtain actual samples of a young person's skills. In doing this, they are also encouraged to use, whenever possible, individual interviews, group discussions, or observations of group tasks to supplement the usual paper and pencil exercises. NAEP asks its exercise writers to experiment with unconventional stimulus materials such as pictures, tapes, films, or practical everyday items in order to heighten interest and bring greater variety to the format. Most importantly, NAEP emphasizes the necessity for developing a pool of exercises which will reflect the cultural pluralism that exists in America and which will have meaning for all groups in our society.

Difficulty Level Since National Assessment does not intend to rank people in order, it is not appropriate that its exercises be of medium difficulty as usually they are in standarized tests. The intent of National Assessment is instead to be able to describe the knowledges, understandings, skills, and attitudes of the *most* and *least able* young people as well as those of the *average* young person. Therefore, it develops easy, medium, and difficult exercises which are aimed at each of these three groups.

Overlap Between Ages   In National Assessment an exercise which "overlaps" is one that is appropriate for more than one age level. An exercise generally overlaps between two adjacent age levels, but may overlap three or even all four age levels. The development of these overlapping exercises has been encouraged because of the interesting comparisons that can be made by giving the same exercise to two or more age levels.

Instructions for Scoring   Particularly those for open-ended types of exercises, determine what information is finally reported. Because of this, National Assessment requires its exercise writers to submit a detailed explanation of how to score and report each exercise. . . .

Procedures for Developing Objectives and Exercises

During the first years of the project most of the development of objectives and exercises was handled exclusively by large contracting organizations such as Educational Testing Service, Science Research Associates, and American Institutes for Research. . . . However, since 1970, there has been a considerable increase in the size of the National Assessment staff, and newly created interdepartmental teams have brought about a greater coordination of developmental activities. In some areas, subject matter specialists have assisted the assessment in the preparation of objectives and exercises. The developmental process currently in use incoroporates previous developmental experiences, and provides for closer monitoring by National Assessment staff of its contractors (individual specialists as well as large testing organizations). This development process is divided into five major phases:

Phase A.	Development (or revision) and Review of Objectives and Prototype Exercises
Phase B.	Preparation of Exercises and Exercise Development Tryouts
Phase C.	Review and Revisions of Exercises
Phase D.	Field Testing and Review of Tryout Results
Phase E.	Final Reviews and Selection

Following is a description of each of these five phases.

Phase A. *Development (or revision) and Review of Objectives and Prototype Exercises*
    This phase allows for reconsideration and possible revision of objectives in a previously assessed area for the development of objectives in a new area. . . . The developer of material reviews the literature in the field and collects appropriate information from universities, state departments of education, school districts, and objectives exchanges around the country in order to determine the latest ideas in objectives development. Subject matter or objectives specialists formulate new objectives or revise the existing ones. These specialists, representing a broad cross section from around the country, are selected from

elementary and secondary schools (public, private, and parochial) as well as from colleges, universities, and other professional organizations. . . .

The next step is to hold a review by a separate group of subject matter specialists to critique the new or reformulated objectives. Again, as in the case of the specialists who helped formulate the objectives, there is broad professional representation. The specialists evaluate the objectives for content validity, appropriateness, relevance, and reportability. If three reviewers think it necessary, the objectives may be further revised and refined.

In the process described above, both subject matter specialists and educators participate. The next step is to seek the reactions of lay citizens. Lay people from around the country are invited to attend a review of the objectives at which numerous panels are convened with each panel having representation from different occupations, socioeconomic backgrounds, and areas of the country. Comments from these panels are used as the basis for further refinement of the objectives.

While the objectives approach their final form, exercise writers develop prototype exercises. A prototype exercise is one which serves as a model for the development of other exercises; it must be a measure of an objective, it must be clearly stated and include a rationale, directions to administrators, scoring instructions, a key or sample of acceptable and unacceptable responses, and a scheme for reporting of results. The ideas for prototype exercises originate with subject matter specialists representing different specialties within the field and people experienced at different levels of performance. When they are collected, they are placed in an exercise format and given a small scale tryout. The results from the tryouts and the prototype exercises themselves are then reviewed by an Exercise Development Advisory Group consisting of leading education and measurement specialists. This group either recommends that the prototypes be further refined or that the production of exercises should begin, with the prototype exercises guiding the contractor in the types of exercises that should be produced.

Phase B. *Preparation of Exercises and Exercise Development Tryouts*
The number of exercises produced depends upon the number of total minutes that can be administered in the assessment for a particular area and the number of exercise minutes that already exist (unreleased exercises from a previous assessment or exercises in a previous pool). The development contractor uses as varied a range of writers as feasible, including some of the writers who helped develop the prototype exercises. Once he has a pool of new exercises, the contractor conducts a limited tryout to obtain some samples of actual responses. Ideally, this tryout should be conducted by the exercise writers so that they can obtain some data on the clarity of the task, scoring categories, and administrative feasibility. Another purpose of the tryout is to provide information for lay and subject matter reviewers about the results the exercises will yield and the possible problems that will have to be investigated before the actual assessment.

Phase C. *Review and Revisions of Exercises*
National Assessment submits the exercises to both subject matter specialists and lay people for their review and criticism. . . . The subject matter specialists

in their review of the exercises are primarily concerned with content validity, relevance, administrative feasibility, completeness of scoring and reporting instructions; the lay reviewers are primarily concerned with appropriateness and relevance.

Phase D. *Field Testing and Revision of Exercises*

After the exercise pool has been revised according to suggestions made by the reviewers there is a full scale tryout involving representatives of the community, socioeconomic, racial, sex, and regional groups that are found in the actual assessment. The purpose of the tryout is to give some indication of how each exercise will probably function in an assessment, and to provide information that can be used to improve administrative and scoring instructions.

Following the tryout, subject matter specialists review the results to make sure that the scoring guides reflect actual responses and will provide important and desirable information.

Phase E. *Final Reviews and Selection*

At this point all the exercises have been through thorough reviews by both subject matter specialists and lay citizens, and are candidates for the assessment. However, the number of exercises developed always exceeds the number that can actually be used in an assessment. Specialists in the area rate each exercise according to its importance and quality, and these ratings are then reviewed by a committee consisting of subject matter and measurement specialists plus National Assessment and contractor staff members who have been involved in the development of the area. This committee designates the exercises to be administered in the actual assessment on the basis of the quality ratings and reporting needs (coverage of objectives). The selected exercises are then forwarded to the United States Office of Education to be checked for any infringement of privacy on the part of respondents or possible offensiveness. . . .

What Do You Think?

The three basic methods of curriculum evaluation are (1) inschool analysis based on pupil performance, (2) inschool programs based on professional opinion and information, and (3) national assessment of pupil attainment of society-based objectives. These methods illustrate three variations on methods of curriculum evaluation. What are the major strengths of each? What weaknesses occur to you as you examine each approach? Can you devise another method? What strengths and weaknesses of your method can you identify? You should find that the answers to these questions provide a way for you to extend the topic of curriculum evaluation beyond the ideas presented here.

Chapter **18**

How Effective Is the Curriculum?

Hoppes

Instructor 84, 8 (April 1975):136.

"I wish *we* had a successful-looking system like this instead of the constant bickering and confusion our educational system on Mars presents."

When is the curriculum deficient? What should be measured to determine if the curriculum contains weaknesses? What standards or comparisons should be the basis for arriving at conclusions about the effectiveness of the curriculum? This chapter introduces these questions and supplies readings that address them.

Orientation

Curriculum's effectiveness is not easy to determine because the curriculum is complex, evaluators have different viewpoints, and the curriculum is intertwined with other elements of the school. Questions about curriculum's effectiveness are further complicated by time. A student who expresses satisfaction with the curriculum during adolescence may find, upon retrospect as an adult, that the school program was deficient. The reverse may also happen. The student who is discontent in school may discover that his adult achievements were enhanced considerably by the schooling he received.

The best way to make sense out of answers about curriculum effectiveness is to identify the kind of evidence required to decide its effectiveness. When this evidence is known, effectiveness can be judged according to whether the curriculum appears to meet the established criteria. A few examples can clarify this point.

One might regard pupils' achievement to be a primary factor in determining curriculum effectiveness. This approach would call for selection of those areas in which achievement should occur, the selection and application of instruments to measure that achievement, and the standards to be applied. On the basis of comprehensive testing in various subject areas and grade levels, it would be possible to draw conclusions about the curriculum's effectiveness with this approach. After obtaining this information a second task remains; namely, to differentiate among the variables that contribute to the pupil's achievement: learning conditions, teaching performance, content studied, and other significant factors. If the content is different from that of the achievement tests employed, then student achievement will be lower than if contents matched. If classroom content matched test content but is poorly taught, scores may also be low. The distinction between these two results is critical if the effectiveness of the curriculum in contrast to the effectiveness of other components of the school are to be differentiated. In an effort to separate the variables that effect school effectiveness, the Rand Corporation analyzed research findings on school effectiveness on the basis of pupil learning. The summary of the Rand report is the first selection in this chapter; it reveals the difficulty and danger of trying to draw hard and fast conclusions about curriculum effectiveness.

Oftentimes, as noted in the preceding chapter, the evaluation of school programs is based on internal criteria. This means that if pupils learn sufficiently at one grade level to succeed at the next grade level, the school is adequately serving these pupils. Usually the faculty determine whether or not the school is serving the pupils effectively. However, internal criteria alone may have little to do with the effectiveness of the curriculum in helping students cope with the larger society. The basis on which curriculum content is established initially depends on the role assigned to schools by society. But unless there is an examination of the success of students according to society's expectation, the schools will not know how well they are functioning. When the schools chief concern is to instruct pupils to continue to do well in school, then cognitive, affective, or skill learnings can be selected according to in-school criteria. But, another approach taken to evaluate curriculum is to specify the out-of-school demands on pupils that the schools are trying to teach. Then pupils are assessed according to their performance on simulated or actual tasks, drawn from expectations outside of the school. (See Chapter 17 for a more detailed description.)

A third assessment approach is to use comparisons, perhaps between different schools throughout the country, between contemporary schools and schools in the past, or between schools among countries. Each of these approaches has its own difficulties. The problem contrasting the variables that operate in different schools makes such comparisons difficult and potentially damaging. For example, the accomplishments in different schools in the same country should be based on their projected potential rather than some inappropriate or arbitrary standard. Local variables can contaminate such comparisons to the point of uselessness. If comparisons are made between the schools of today and the schools of a previous era, perhaps twenty-five or fifty years ago, this comparison might prove interesting but would tell little about the effectiveness of today's schools. Society has also changed dramatically during the same time period. Comparing schools in this country to schools in other countries must be done on a macro level. Thus, characteristics of individual schools would not be well represented. However, comparing U.S. schools to non-U.S. schools has the advantage of comparing schools within the same time frame, and also avoiding the risky comparisons that come from contrasting individual schools or districts with one another. The merit of this procedure is illustrated in a third selection describing international comparisons.

Thus the question of curricular effectiveness is addressed through three approaches. One approach identifies pupil achievement as the determinant, but also discusses the difficulties of sorting out the variance that contributes to this achievement. These variants operate in all comparisons whether they are made within schools, with other schools, with society's standards, or with other nations. A second approach assesses pupil abilities to perform day-to-day tasks required by society. This approach has the advantage of linking schools to society. A third approach compares the relative effectiveness of the schools in the United States to school effectiveness in other parts of the world. This comparison allows one to examine the differences and similarities among schools as well as provides evidence on the relative success of schools in different settings with different orientations and resources.

Whether the schools succeed or fail according to internal standards, out of school utility, or international comparison, public opinion remains critical because support for schools is heavily dependent on the public's confidence. Conceivably, the actual success or failure of schools could be less important than the public view about the schools. Of course a public relations program to "sell" inadequate schools will not likely succeed over a long period of time; good schools and good attitudes about schools should be highly correlated. Polling the public about schools has been an annual event since 1969. A summary of the first five years of these polls reveals the public view about schools, and raises fundamental issues about the relationship between school effectiveness and the public. A final selection in this chapter presents the findings of these polls and a more detailed report of the 1975 survey.

Does the Curriculum Make a Difference?

The following selection from a study sponsored by the President's Commission on School Finance, asks the question "How Effective is Schooling?" A review of research, a summary of their findings, and a discussion of methods employed in the study are provided. The reader should remember that the basis for determining school effectiveness is pupil achievement. Those who conducted the study admitted that noncognitive outcomes and social outcomes are of major importance. However, when they selected research evidence on which to base their judgments it became necessary for them to consider "educational outcome" as the student's cognitive ability as measured by standardized achievement tests. Therefore, their report should be read with the full understanding that achievement testing became a major criterion in the selection of research that was used in compiling the study.

□

Objectives and Method

The objective of our study was to assess the current state of knowledge regarding the determinants of educational effectiveness. To this end, we conducted a critical survey of educational research. The word "critical" emphasizes the most important aspect of our efforts. We have attempted throughout our analysis to examine the validity and credibility of research results. In the case of each research effort that we reviewed, we tried to discover whether the researcher pursued proper methods for the questions asked (internal validity), and, if so, were the results credible in the light of accumulated knowledge (interstudy consistency)? Our study, then, is not a classical survey of research listing findings without much evaluation of the results; rather, it is our answer to the question, "What does the research tell us about educational effectiveness?"

Five Research Approaches

The body of research on educational effectiveness is very large. We found it useful to organize our analysis according to basic research approaches used by researchers—that is, according to the aspect of education being studied, the question being asked, and the methods deemed appropriate to answer that question. We identified five basic approaches used in educational research: input-output, process, organizational, evaluation, and experiential.

The *input-output* approach assumes that students' educational outcomes are determined by the quantities and qualities of the educational resources they receive. The *Equality of Educational Opportunity* survey—known as the Coleman Report after its principal author, James Coleman—is the best-known example of this, the educational economist's, approach to educational research.

The *process* approach includes most of the work done by educational psychologists, as well as certain studies by sociologists and clinical and experimental psychologists. These studies attempt to examine the processes and methods by which resources are applied to students.

The *organizational* approach consists of case studies of school systems that assume what is done in the school is not the result of a rational search for effective inputs or processes, but is a reflection of history, social demands, and organizational change and rigidity. These studies are typically done by politi-

Harvey A. Averch et al., *How Effective is Schooling? A Critical Review and Synthesis of Research Findings* (Santa Monica: The Rand Corporation, 1972), pp. v–x, 148–58. Reprinted by permission of publisher.

Footnotes have been renumbered consecutively throughout the chapter.

cal scientists or sociologists and focus on the ways in which the factors that influence or impinge on the various decision makers in the school system affect the behavior of the system.

Studies of relatively large-scale interventions in school systems are included in the *evaluation* approach. Examples include the evaluations of compensatory education programs for the disadvantaged, funded by Title I of the Elementary and Secondary Education Act (1965), and the evaluations of Head Start programs. The central issue in these studies is whether broad-based interventions affect students' outcomes.

Finally, we include in the *experiential* approach the so-called "reform" literature. These are books and articles, typically written by teachers or advocates of educational reform, that describe how the school system works and what it does to those on the inside, particularly students. They share the view that what happens to the student in school is an end in itself, rather than a means toward some further end, such as the acquisition of specific skills. . . .

Procedure

The formal procedure we used in our analysis is outlined in Figure 18–1. We examined individual studies in each approach and attempted to determine whether they were internally valid. . . .

The next step was to bring together the results of the individual studies and of the previous reviews. We attempted to derive general conclusions as to what were the overall results of the many research efforts. Our primary criterion was interstudy consistency. . . .

Finally, we combined these five sets of results to derive overall conclusions as to what is now known about educational effectiveness. It was from these conclusions that we drew our policy implications.

Limitations of Available Research

Before presenting our conclusions, we must emphasize that in assessing the results of research on educational effectiveness, we discovered that the research done thus far is subject to many limitations. . . .

First, the data used by researchers are, at best, crude measures of what is really happening. Education is an extremely complex and subtle phenomenon. Researchers in education are plagued by the virtual impossibility of measuring those aspects of education they wish to study. For example, a student's cognitive achievement is typically measured by his score on a standardized achievement test, despite the many serious problems involved in interpreting such scores.

Second, educational outcomes are almost exclusively measured by cognitive achievement. Although no one would deny that students' noncognitive outcomes and social outcomes beyond the individual student level are of major importance, research efforts that focus on these outcomes are sparse and largely inconclusive and offer little guidance with respect to what is effective. In general, then, whenever we refer to "educational outcome" throughout the

Figure 18-1. Formal procedure used in analysis.

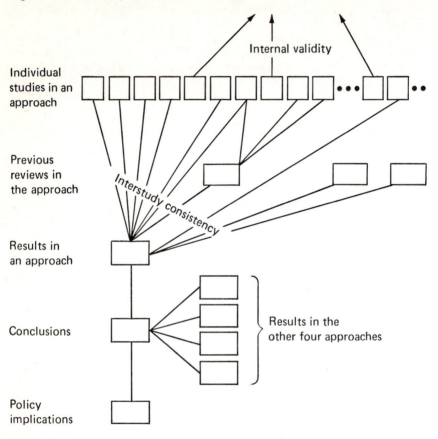

discussion, we mean the student's cognitive ability as measured by standardized achievement tests.

Third, there is virtually no examination of the cost implications of research results. This makes it very difficult to translate research results into policy-relevant statements.

Finally, few studies maintain adequate controls over what actually goes on in the classroom as it relates to achievement. Thus, researchers' data may well be affected by circumstances unrecognized in their analyses. For example, it is not unusual to find a researcher comparing the relative effectiveness of instructional methods A and B. He might train one group of teachers in the use of method A and another in the use of method B, and at some later point, he would measure and compare the cognitive skills of the students who were taught by teachers in the two groups. The validity of the results generated in such a study would depend, among other things, upon whether the teachers did in fact use method A or method B in their classrooms.

Where We Are Now

With the limitations of research clearly in mind, we return to the basic issue of educational effectiveness. The current status of research in this area can be described by the following propositions:

Proposition 1: Research has not identified a variant of the existing system that is consistently related to students' educational outcomes.

Proposition 2: Research suggests that the larger the school system, the less likely it is to display innovation, responsiveness, and adaptation, and the more likely it is to depend upon exogenous shocks to the system.

Proposition 3: Research tentatively suggests that improvement in student outcomes, cognitive and noncognitive, *may* require sweeping changes in the organization, structure, and conduct of educational experience.

In Proposition 1, the phrase "a variant of the existing system" is used to describe a broad range of alternative interventions in the existing system. We include changes in school resources, processes, organization, and aggregate levels of funding.

We must emphasize that we are not suggesting that nothing makes a difference, or that nothing "works." Rather, we are saying that research has found nothing that consistently and unambiguously makes a difference in student outcomes. . . .

Summary and Discussion of Findings

The Input-Output Approach   This approach focuses on the relationship between the amounts of various resources that are provided to students and their educational outcomes (defined as cognitive achievement). Overall, the input-output studies provide very little evidence that school resources, in general, have a powerful impact upon student outcomes. When we examine the results across studies we find that school resources are not consistently important. The particular resources that seem to be significant in one study do not prove to be significant in other studies that include the same resources in the analysis.

Background factors, on the other hand, are always important. In study after study a student's background has a strong influence on his educational outcomes. Furthermore, the results are consistent across studies. The socioeconomic status of a student's family—his parents' income, education, and occupation—invariably prove to be significant predictors of his educational outcome.

The role of peer-group influences is more complex. There is good reason to believe that these variables are, in reality, measures of a student's background or of his school district's selection and assignment policies. On balance, there is little evidence that a student's classmates exercise a strong, independent influence on his educational outcomes.

The results from the input-output approach do not mean that school resources fail, actually or potentially, to affect student outcomes. We simply observe that so far these studies have failed to show that school resources *do* affect student outcomes. In particular, the studies do not show what would happen if the educational system received a massive increase or decrease in resources.

The Process Approach . . . We have divided the results into two parts: those derived from studies of operating classrooms and those derived from the laboratory. For each set of results, we indicate the focus, the questions being asked, and the answers to the questions.

Looking first at the classroom studies, we find the following:

1. The research on teaching approaches, teacher differences, class size, and the like shows no consistent effect on student achievement, as measured by standardized cognitive tests.
2. Work on instructional methods suggests no difference among methods; none currently appear better than conventional methods. That is, in terms of differences in achievement, conventional methods appear as effective as, say, teaching by television, although the latter enables one to reach far greater numbers of students.

We consider the following results from the laboratory studies to be particularly interesting and important:

1. Work on the presentation of material suggests that it is not so much the medium of instruction that is important as its sequencing and organization. There seem to be interaction effects; individual methods of presentation appear superior for some tasks and some students, but it is still hard to match student characteristics, tasks, and type of instruction.
2. The work on concept attainment, retention, and learning rewards provides a number of positive findings, but the tasks in the laboratory are so unlike classroom learning that there is a difficult problem of translation. For example, the more meaningful the material, the faster it is learned and the more it is retained. But the definition of "meaningful" is a laboratory one, relating, say, to the difference between nonsense sentences or syllables and those that make sense.
3. What are termed interaction effects seem to exist among various types of personality, methods of reward, ability to grasp meaningful material, and so on; but these interactions have not yet been studied in detail. . . .

The Organizational Approach . . . Most of the work in this approach consists of case studies, and the rules for internal and external validity are weak at best. Furthermore, there have been few attempts to extract important organizational propositions from the literature. The case studies provide some evidence for the following:

1. There is a positive correlation between system size and centralization.

2. The larger the educational bureaucracy and the more centralization, the less innovation and adaptation there is likely to be.
3. Rigidities in the schools can be overcome partly by choice of teachers and principals. However, teacher qualities that are purchased—say, experience—have little to do with innovative teaching.
4. Real innovation depends on the leverage that can be exerted from outside the system—by the federal government or by citizens.

The Evaluation Approach . . . Virtually without exception, all the surveys of large, national compensatory education programs have shown no beneficial results on average. However, the evaluations on which the surveys report are often based upon suspect research designs.

Two or three smaller surveys show modest positive effects of compensatory education programs in the short run. And a number of quite carefully designed interventions display gains in pupil cognitive performance—again, in the short run. In particular, pupils from disadvantaged socioeconomic backgrounds tend to show greater progress in more highly structured programs. However, there is considerable evidence that many of the short-run gains from educational interventions fade away after two or three years if they are not reinforced. Also, this "fade-out" is much greater for the more highly structured programs, which are most unlike regular public school practice.

The Experiential Approach . . . Because this literature is one of social reform, it is not subject to the same tests of internal consistency as the approaches discussed above. In effect there are two elements in this literature, description and prescription. The description of the schools as constituted at the present time almost invariably emphasizes a set of common themes:

1. Schools are authoritarian toward students.
2. Schools make little or no allowance for individual differences in learning styles and needs.
3. Schools focus on methods that stress rightness and wrongness in learning, thereby destroying independence and creativity, as well as equipping children poorly for the complexities and ambiguities of the real world.
4. Schools impose a certain set of social, cultural, and ethical views on their students, thereby imposing feelings of inadequacy and resentment on those who share neither those views nor the traditions they imply.
5. Schools as institutions are mindless in the sense that they fail, in any operationally useful way, to question either the assumption upon which they operate or the relevance of their approach to children's needs.

The prescriptions are far more varied than the descriptive research. They range from recommendations for moderate reform within the system (Silberman) to abolition of the schools (Illich). In some cases the value systems leading to the prescriptions are made explicit, in others, not. In general, however, the experiential literature agrees on the merits of educational systems that are less rigid, more responsive to individual diversity, and more decentralized than the current system. . . .

Conclusions and Policy Implications

With the limitations of research clearly in mind, we return to the issue of educational effectiveness. The first major implication of the research is:

Research has not identified a variant of the existing system that is consistently related to students' educational outcomes.

The term "a variant of the existing system" is used to describe the broad range of alternative educational practices that have been reviewed above. We specifically include changes in school resources, processes, organizations, and aggregate levels of funding.

We must emphasize that we are not suggesting that nothing makes a difference, or that nothing "works." Rather, we are saying that research has found nothing that *consistently* and *unambiguously* makes a difference in students' outcomes. . . .

We must also emphasize that we are not saying that school does not affect student outcomes. We have little knowledge of what student outcomes would be were students not to attend school at all. Educational research focuses on variants of the existing system and tells us nothing about where we might be without the system at all.

Furthermore, nothing we have found in the educational research literature proves that our current educational system *cannot* be substantially improved. But the research results we review above provide little reason to be sanguine. Our general conclusion, so far, is that there are few consistent, positive, policy-relevant findings. . . .

Finally, the educational practices for which school systems have traditionally been willing to pay a premium do not appear to make a major difference in student outcomes. Teachers' experience and teachers' advanced degrees, the two basic factors that determine salary, are not clearly related to student achievement. Reduction in class size, a favorite high-priority reform in the eyes of many school systems, seems not to be related to student outcomes. In general, the second major implication of the research (and the most important one for school finance) is:

Increasing expenditures on traditional educational practices is not likely to improve educational outcomes substantially.

The third major policy implication of the research is:

There seem to be opportunities for significant reduction or redirection of educational expenditures without deterioration in educational outcomes. . . .

Educational research consists almost entirely of effectiveness studies. There are very few cost-effectiveness studies. The tremendous volume of "negative" results—negative according to the peculiar bias of educational research, which seeks only improvement on the effectiveness side—must surely contain many "positive" results in the sense of indicating less costly methods of accomplishing as much as is currently attained.

The research contains some evidence supporting a fourth major implication:

Innovation, responsiveness, and adaptation in school systems decrease with size and depend upon exogenous shocks to the system. . . .

The implication of this tentative conclusion is clear. There is currently a good deal of interest in federal leverage and in the question of whether federal aid to the schools should be tied or untied. *The literature that we have examined suggests that federal influence is important in getting innovation into urban school systems,* although the hypothesis has not really been tested rigorously.

Our review of educational research supports a fifth major implication:

Educational research is seriously deficient in terms of the size, scope, and focus of research efforts and in the integration of research results.

Beyond these specific limitations, educational research has tended to be small in scale, narrow in scope, diffuse, maldistributed, and lacking in focus. By comparison with other major sectors, the amount of research activity devoted to educational problems is surprisingly small. . . .

The body of educational research now available leaves much to be desired, at least by comparison with the level of understanding that has been achieved in numerous other fields. This does not reflect the quality of the contemporary educational researcher but rather the nature of the research community and its history. The typical education study is not founded on a wealth of previous knowledge and understanding nor is it directed toward the needs of the educational policy maker. There are virtually no research-based, problem-solving units in the typical operating agency. In 1968 there were only 1,300 person-years devoted to research, development, or innovation in the almost 20,000 state and local education agencies; most of that was devoted to testing and to gathering statistics (Levien, 1971).

Finally, the sixth major implication of our work is:

Research tentatively suggests that improvement in student outcomes, both cognitive and noncognitive, may require sweeping changes in the organization, structure, and conduct of educational experiences.

This inference follows from the first four conclusions cited above, as well as from the testimony of the experiential approach. Even the fifth conclusion, which cites the paucity of educational research, tends to reinforce this point because it implies that marginal changes in research will be inadequate to indicate clearly the directions educational improvement should take.

International Comparison: What Is Learned About the Curriculum?

In contrast to the general statements made previously in the Rand Corporation report, the statements in the following excerpt provide specific recommendations about curriculum and instruction. These recommendations are presented by Benjamin Bloom and are based on the work of the International Association for the Evaluation of Education Achievement. At first glance, it may seem fallacious to draw firm conclusions from a study as broadly based as an international study. However, the reader should examine the procedures, findings, and conclusions and then judge the appropriateness of an international approach to curriculum analysis.

☐

The International Association for the Evaluation of Education Achievement (IEA) is an organization of twenty-two national research centers which are engaged in the study of education.[1] Organized in 1959, this group published a pilot study in 1962[2] and a study of mathematics achievement in 1967.[3] It has just published studies of achievement in science,[4] reading comprehension,[5] and literature[6] and will in the near future publish studies of achievement in French as a foreign language,[7] English as a foreign language,[8] and in civic education.[9] . . .

A major feature of IEA is that its evaluation instruments and data collection procedures have been developed especially for the purpose of international comparison and study. In previous cross-national studies test items and styles of test construction tended to be specific to the country in which the instru-

Benjamin S. Bloom, "Implications of the IEA Studies for Curriculum and Instruction," *School Review* 82, 3 (May 1974):413–35. Reprinted by permission of the author and publisher.

[1]The centers are located in Australia, Belgium, Chile, England, Federal Republic of Germany, Finland, France, Hungary, India, Iran, Ireland, Israel, Italy, Japan, Netherlands, New Zealand, Poland, Rumania, Scotland, Sweden, Thailand, and the United States.

[2]A. W. Foshay, ed., *Educational Achievements of 13-Year-Olds in Twelve Countries* (Hamburg: UNESCO Institute for Education, 1962).

[3]Torsten Husén, ed., *International Study of Achievement in Mathematics: A Comparison of Twelve Countries*, vols. 1, 2 (New York: John Wiley & Sons; Stockholm: Almqvist & Wiksell, 1967).

[4]L. C. Comber and John P. Keeves, *Science Education in Nineteen Countries: International Studies in Evaluation. I* (New York: Wiley; Stockholm: Almqvist & Wiksell, 1973).

[5]Robert L. Thorndike, *Reading Comprehension Education in Fifteen Countries: International Studies in Evaluation. III* (New York: Wiley; Stockholm: Almqvist & Wiksell, 1973).

[6]Alan C. Purves, *Literature Education in Ten Countries: International Studies in Evaluation. II* (New York: Wiley; Stockholm: Almqvist & Wiksell, 1973).

[7]John B. Carroll, *The Teaching of French as a Foreign Language in Eight Countries: International Studies in Evaluation. V* (New York: Halsted Press, 1975).

[8]E. Glyn Lewis, *The Teaching of English as a Foreign Language in Ten Countries: International Studies in Evaluation. IV* (New York: Halsted Press, 1975).

[9]Judith V. Torney et al., *Civic Education in Ten Countries: International Studies in Evaluation. VI* (New York: Halsted Press, 1976).

ments were constructed. The evaluation instruments developed in one country typically showed that country to be superior to the other countries included in the study.

International Evaluation Instruments   This concern with internationally validated evaluation instruments impelled IEA to create international as well as national committees in each subject. Both types of committees studied national curricula and examinations and attempted to identify subject matter content and educational objectives of major significance in the different countries which participated. . . .

The IEA surveys provide baseline data for each country against which future changes in education may be appraised. The IEA instruments and the increased sophistication about evaluation in each of the countries provide methods and procedures for the systematic evaluation of the effectiveness of new approaches to education.

Perhaps the most dramatic findings of all the IEA studies during the past decade and a half have to do with differences among countries. For highly developed countries there is a difference of about one standard deviation between the means of the highest scoring and lowest scoring of these countries. But there are approximately two standard deviations between the means of the highest of the developed nations and the average of the developing nations.

One can translate these statistics in a number of ways.

If the mean of the highest scoring nation is used as the criterion of what it is possible for students to learn, about 85 percent of the students in the lowest scoring of the developed nations would be below this mean while about 98 percent of the students in the developing nations would be below this point.

If school marks were assigned in the various nations on the basis of the highest nation's standards (where perhaps the lowest fifth might be regarded as failing), then almost 50 percent of the students in the lowest scoring of the developed nations would fail but about 85 percent of the students in the average developing nation would fail.

These results may also be considered in terms of grade norms. If judged by test results in the highest scoring nation, the average student in the lowest scoring of the developed nations would be at about the eighth grade norm after twelve years of schooling, while the average student in the developing nations would be at about the sixth grade norm after twelve years of schooling. This would be true even when selectivity at the secondary level is held constant. Although one may have misgivings about such attempts to put schooling in terms of age or grade norms in the highest scoring nation, it is evident that the attainment obtained in one year of schooling in the highest nation requires one and one-half or two years of schooling in less favored nations. To put it in terms of time and human resources spent, it may cost twice as much for a particular level of learning in one place as it does in another. . . .

Perhaps the most important variable in accounting for the differences between national systems—even where they are equally selective—is the opportunity to learn as judged by teachers. Teachers were asked to evaluate each item in the IEA test as to the proportion of their students who had an opportunity to learn the idea or process underlying that item. When the results for particular groups of teachers and students across a nation are correlated, the IEA studies show a very high relation between these teachers' judgments and the overall performances of the students. . . .

There is evidence that the competence of teachers in both subject matter and methods of teaching varies greatly between nations. In one developing country a sample of science teachers took the IEA science test and scored below the average secondary school student on the international norms. It is unlikely that students can learn much from teachers who do not thoroughly understand the subject they are teaching.

If Beeby is correct about the levels of teaching that can be provided by teachers with different levels of postsecondary education,[10] some developing countries must either wait decades before they can provide adequately trained teachers at all levels of schooling or they must find a way in which a small number of well-trained teachers can provide the bulk of instruction through the use of mass media in the classroom. . . .

The IEA studies typically consist of separate samples of students participating in each subject study. But a selected sample of students did participate simultaneously in the studies of literature, science, and reading. The median intercorrelations for these subjects in fifteen countries are shown in Table 18–1. Several generalizations can be drawn from these correlations.

1. Learning in both science and literature is highly related to reading comprehension. This is true to such a degree that there is almost no residual relation between science and literature when the level of reading comprehension is held constant.

2. Reading comprehension is more highly related to literature than to science.

3. The relation between reading comprehension and science or literature declines with age or grade of school—probably because the schools drop the students less able in reading comprehension.

Table 18–1: Median intercorrelations for literature, science, and reading

| | Students | | |
	Age 10	Age 14	Final year secondary education
Science vs. reading comprehension	.68	.60	.44
Literature vs. reading comprehension	. . .	.68	.54
Science vs. literature	. . .	.41	.28
Science vs. literature (holding reading comprehension constant)	. . .	.00	.05

[10]C. E. Beeby, *The Quality of Education in Developing Countries* (Cambridge: Harvard University Press, 1966).

While the relation between subject matter competence and word knowledge is somewhat lower, the same generalizations tend to hold. These generalizations are true, almost without exception in each of the nations included in this portion of the IEA studies.

If we view reading comprehension and world knowledge as two facets of what British psychologists term "verbal education," it is apparent that this type of learning tends to dominate and in large part determine what students learn in the schools in all the countries included in the IEA studies.

These two aspects of verbal learning are important because most teacher instruction and most of the learning materials in the schools are verbal. Unless the student can understand the teacher's explanations and instructions, he has difficulty in learning. Verbal skills enable students to learn from the instructional materials even when the teaching is less than adequate. The early development of verbal ability (vocabulary and reading comprehension) appears to be necessary if the child is to learn well—or even to survive—in school. . . .

Throughout the world there appears to be a curriculum and instruction in the home as well as a curriculum and instruction in the school. The effects of the home curriculum and instruction for reading comprehension and word knowledge appear to be so powerful that schools are not able to compensate adequately for the differences already present when children enter school. Differences in verbal ability developed at home before age 6 are exaggerated by the schools in the period between ages 6 and 10 and the school period between ages 10 and 14. By age 18, the schools' selective policies have weeded out all except the most able students in verbal ability.

Societies which wish to improve children's school learning have only two realistic policies to follow: increase the effectiveness of the early education of children and/or increase the effectiveness of verbal education in the schools, especially during the ages of 6 to 10.

Many countries are exploring the possibility of providing early childhood education (ages 3–6) for children—especially for children who are likely to be deprived because of inadequacies in the home curriculum and instruction. Mass media appear to be quite effective for some kinds of instruction at this age level.

Research in the United States indicates that it is possible to find ways of helping parents to improve some of the learning conditions in the home.[11] When this is done, the results in verbal learning, attitude toward school, and ability to learn in school are likely to be as good as or better than the results obtained through the use of nursery schools alone. Even better results are obtained when parents and nursery schools collaborate in the effort to help the children. . . .

When one looks at the emphasis in the curriculum as indicated by syllabi and curriculum experts, or when one looks at the "opportunity to learn" as judged by teachers, it is evident that the pattern of decreasing scores from lower to higher mental processes reflects these emphases. Schools, teachers,

---

[11]E. Kuno Beller, "Research on Organized Programs of Early Education," in *Second Handbook of Research on Teaching*, ed. Robert M. W. Travers (Chicago: Rand McNally, 1973).

and textbooks throughout the world are apparently largely directed toward filling a presumably "empty head" with things to be remembered. Although teachers, curriculum makers, and testers profess more complex objectives for education, the actual emphasis in the classroom is still largely on the learning of specific information. . . .

The real problem in every country is how to provide preservice and inservice education for teachers in inquiry skills, problem solving, and higher mental processes. Little progress in developing these higher processes in the schools can be expected until teachers develop the necessary capabilities and are helped to find ways of teaching higher intellectual processes to the students in their classes.

In the IEA studies, there was an attempt to secure evidence on such affective objectives as interest in the subject and attitudes toward the subject, school, and school learning. In each country there is a significant correlation between measures of the affective and cognitive objectives. . . .

The evidence collected in the IEA studies and other research summaries[12] suggests that the affective objectives are largely being developed as a by-product of the cognitive objectives. That is, students who master the cognitive objectives well develop positive interests and attitudes in the subject. Students who believe they are succeeding in school come to like school.

Patterns of Objectives—Cognitive and Affective

The IEA tests have been developed to sample the content and objectives in each subject. In the final data processing, scores and other types of indices have been reported for each of the cognitive and affective objectives in each subject.

Cognitive Objectives . . . In each subject, in almost every country, students perform best on the lower mental processes involving knowledge, perform less well on items involving some interpretation or comprehension, and perform least well on test problems requiring applications, higher mental processes, and complex inferences. . . .

If only the developed nations in the IEA are considered it will be found that on most of the subject tests, the top 5 percent of students across the world are roughly equal in their achievement at age 14 and at the final year of secondary education. This will generally be true whether one is considering the upper 5 percent of the entire age group sampled—such as the 14-year level where typically 90 percent or more of the students are still in school—or the approximations to the top 5 percent of the age group at the final year of secondary education where the countries differ widely in the percent of the age group still in school (from 9 percent in one country to 75 percent in another country).

Thus, in spite of differences in curriculum, instructional procedures, and many other differences among countries, it appears that the upper 5 percent of students in these countries are roughly comparable in their achievement as measured by these tests. . . .

[12]S. B. Kahn and Joel Weiss, "The Teaching of Affective Responses," in *Second Handbook of Research on Teaching*, ed. Robert M. W. Travers (Chicago: Rand McNally, 1973), p 759–804.

Countries differ in their treatment of students below the top 5 or 10 percent of the group. In most countries in the IEA studies a high proportion of the remaining 90 percent are dropped from school somewhere between ages 14 and 18. In spite of differences in retention of students in school there is considerable evidence that very few countries do an "adequate" educational job for the majority of this age group—and especially for the lower 50 percent of students.

What are the implications for the schools if nations are to more adequately serve the entire population of youth rather than only the top students who survive relatively well because of or in spite of the schools as they are now? If we sketch a picture based on the bottom half of students, several suggestions may be made.

Characteristically these students are drawn from the part of the population with the least favorable conditions for education in their homes.

These are students with the lowest verbal ability and least adequate reading comprehension. They spend less time in reading on their own. They do not have positive attitudes toward school, and their interests in particular academic subjects are not high. They receive few favorable rewards and reinforcements in school from their learning, from their teachers, or even from their peers.

With this group of students, the school is largely on its own and must provide for instruction without counting on the home to provide supplementary instruction or to aid the student when he is having difficulty in school.

These students are in special need of verbal education in the preschool years or in the primary period of schooling if they are to survive in schools as now organized. Schools must also provide the models of learning and incentives for education and learning—without counting on the home to do this. Some strategies have already been experimented with in a number of countries and characteristically have enabled about four-fifths of students to do as well as the upper one-fifth of students under more conventional approaches to instruction.[13] These instructional strategies make use of the existing curriculum but provide frequent feedback to students on their learning development or learning problems and follow the feedback with changes in instructional procedures and with help and correctives as needed. . . .

Curriculum makers have rarely had this group of students in mind as they attempted to formulate the specifications for the curriculum or the learning materials to be used in instruction. One might hope that in the future curriculum makers in each country would attempt to deal more directly with the learning of this group of students. National curriculum centers could profit greatly from an exchange of experiences and approaches with other nations on this problem.

IEA and the Future for Curriculum and Instruction

The IEA studies provide a glimpse of education in a large number of countries. While the emphasis is on the evaluation of student learning in each subject, the variety of data on the countries, the schools, the teachers, the students, and

[13] James H. Block, ed., *Mastery Learning: Theory and Practice* (New York: Holt, Rinehart & Winston, 1971).

the students' home background provides the richest store of information on education that has ever been assembled.

Hopefully, scholars will become acquainted with the IEA data banks and the many possibilities for further investigation which they offer. . . .

We have learned from the IEA data as well as from other research throughout the world that the curriculum and instruction provided by the home are in many ways related to the curriculum and instruction provided by the school. The largest problem each country faces is to understand how these two educational forces may best relate to each other if the education of each child is to be in his best interests as well as in the society's best interests. The problem is even more complex in that it involves the school as one subsystem of a society. No longer can we think of the system of schooling as relatively insulated from other parts of the society. In the future, the schools of most nations will be under pressure to relate more clearly to the other parts of the social system. We will increasingly try to determine what can best be learned in the schools, what can best be learned elsewhere, and what can be learned only through an effective interrelation of different parts of the social system. This is the grand vision of the Edgar Faure UNESCO report.[14] Its implementation will involve all of us in education for many years to come.

What The Pollsters Tell Us About the Schools

The public's opinion of schools is critical if their support is to continue. Information about schools is transmitted from the usual sources: newspapers, television, newsletters, and children's comments. Schools get information from the public in parent conferences, at school board meetings, through letters to the editor, and at the polls.

Compilation of views is a vital element in determining the school's effectiveness. In 1969 the pollsters began asking the American public about its schools. Since that time an annual survey has been conducted to determine the confidence, or lack of it, that the public has in its schools. The next selection reports a summary of the polls taken during the first five years. Following this summary of the early polls, excerpts from the poll for 1975 are provided.

The *raison d'etre* of these annual surveys sponsored by CFK Ltd. is to help guide the decisions of educators. Progress is only possible when the people are properly informed and when they are ready, through their tax dollars, to bear the costs of progress. For these reasons, these surveys are directed chiefly

[14]Edgar Faure et al., *Learning to Be* (Paris: UNESCO; London: Harrap, 1972).

Stanley Elam, ed., *The Gallup Polls of Attitudes Toward Education, 1969–1973* (Bloomington, Ind.: Phi Delta Kappa, 1973), pp. 1–7. Reprinted by permission of the author and publisher.

toward appraising the state of public knowledge and ascertaining public attitudes toward present practices, readiness to accept new programs, and ideas for meeting educational costs. In the performance of this work, we, too, sincerely hope that we are making a contribution to the field of education.

The public schools have passed through a trying period during the five years covered by the surveys reported in this book (1969–1973). The dominant mood of the nation during this period has been one of disillusionment brought about by the war in Vietnam, students protests, racial strife, and Watergate. Nevertheless, respect for and confidence in the public schools, this peculiarly American institution, remain at a high level.

Education in the United States is still widely regarded as the royal road to success.... At the same time, a few clouds are appearing on the horizon; unless those who are interested in the continued strength and well-being of the public schools heed these portents, public education in the nation could face a worrisome future.

Perhaps the best measure of the strength of these adverse forces is to be found in the failure of school bond issues to win majority acceptance in many school districts. Views of the public on matters relating to the financial needs of the public schools have been gauged from year to year in these CFK Ltd. surveys. During the five-year period there has been little change in the public's attitudes, with a majority taking a negative view about meeting the full financial requests of their local school boards.

The Public's Chief Concerns

The public harbors many concerns about the public schools. Chief among these is the lack of discipline. In all but one of the last five years, the nation's adults sampled in these surveys have named discipline as the number one problem of the schools in their own communities.

Court rulings defending student rights have not helped the discipline situation, although they have almost ended the *in loco parentis* principle, at least at the college level.

Another factor in the discipline situation is the state laws which compel young people to remain in school until the age of 17 or 18, even though some students are wholly uninterested in academic work and become troublemakers in the classroom. Since the public is reluctant to change these age requirements, it remains for school administrators and teachers to find better ways to motivate the uninterested students, or, failing this, to devise disciplinary measures that will be more effective than those presently utilized.

The obvious way to reach students who are not interested in academic subjects is to expand and give greater emphasis to career education programs. The public strongly supports this idea, as has been found in these surveys.

In fact, the public has responded favorably to proposals that students be permitted to spend their school time outside the school, learning what they can from local business or industry and fitting themselves for jobs in the community following high school graduation. Such plans have the double merit of removing malcontents from the classroom and placing them in training situations that offer an opportunity to become productive members of the community at an early age.

The importance of providing a different kind of education for those students who are most responsible for the discipline problems of the school cannot be underestimated. The many good things which the schools are achieving in every community seldom come to light in the local press. Student fights, vandalism, and turbulence in the classroom, on the other hand, are nearly always front page news.

The unfavorable publicity which this discord generates is likely to have two consequences: It increases the difficulties of getting bond issues passed and, in many districts, leads to a flight from the public schools to the independent schools by children from the more affluent homes. It needs hardly to be added that parents who pay substantial sums for tuition in private schools are not likely to carry the flag to get school bonds passed, nor are those citizens who are distressed by the turmoil in the schools likely to go to the polls to cast a "yes" vote.

In short, while discipline is properly a responsibility of the home, the schools must perforce be more effective in mitigating this problem, or they will continue to suffer the consequences. . . .

The adverse factors in the public's thinking about the public schools need to be balanced against the favorable. Important among the latter is the public's receptiveness to new ideas and to change. In every community a few rock-ribbed individuals will fight any attempt to institute reforms or new programs, but the majority—too often inarticulate—generally approves any proposal for improving the educational program if the proposal sounds reasonable.

Some of the proposals that the public has supported in this series of surveys include:

1. Sex education in the schools
2. Performance contracts
3. Management experts to advice on costs/educational goals
4. Year-around schools
5. Nongraded schools
6. Alternative schools

The questionable success of some innovations that have enjoyed the enthusiastic support of educators and later have failed to live up to expectations —some reading and math programs, to cite two examples—will almost certainly provide those who oppose change with poweful arguments against any type of reform. Their arguments must be met with objective proof that has been lacking in the case of too many innovations in the past.

Racial integration must be considered one of the positive changes that has occurred in the schools in recent years. In many communities integration has been a disruptive issue, and one of the most sensitive with which schools have had to deal. Survey findings offer some useful insights into public attitudes on this divisive question. Most important, perhaps, is the fact that where integration has taken place there is general acceptance of the situation and approval of the step. What has confused many writers and commentators is the distinction which the public makes between integration, the goal, and busing, a means to this end. Busing is widely disapproved, but this disapproval does not carry over to integration itself.

The flight by whites from the inner cities to the suburbs, we learned this year, is not primarily due to the desire of parents to take their children out of schools that are largely attended by blacks, but is for virtually the same reasons that people without school age children wish to escape from the congestion and attendant ills of the big cities. At least this is what respondents told us.

A successful resolution of the discipline problem would almost certainly bring a change in the attitudes of those parents who are moving to the suburbs chiefly to remove their children from inner-city schools.

Correcting Misapprehensions About the Schools

The schools of the nation have had a "poor press" during the last five years. But since a properly organized information program can overcome the bad publicity which too often colors the public's thinking, there is the very real possibility that this situation can be changed.

Any survey that seeks to reveal the public's understanding of what the public schools are doing, or trying to do, will uncover a shocking lack of information, especially in the case of those individuals who do not have children presently attending the public schools And since most of the opposition to bond issues comes from this sector of the public, it is imperative that the public schools give far more attention than they have to informing the general public.

The press is set up to report events, and the more traumatic are more likely to reach the front page. Usually the "good" news will go neglected unless school administrators themselves take the trouble to find it and see that it is dealt with in an interesting and informative manner. In fact, most newspapers welcome this kind of help, since few of them can afford to hire educational experts for their news staff and since few reporters spend the time it takes to dig up interesting articles. The costs to the school of providing this kind of information are entirely justifiable. Taxpayers have every right to know what they are getting for their money, especially in a time when educational costs are constantly increasing, and this cannot be achieved by neglecting to tell the positive side of what the schools are doing.

Making Parents Part of the Program

It seems obvious to me that the educational program of the nation must take into account more fully than it has in the past the home environment of the student. Any scientific assessment of student success is certain to reveal the important part played by the home in educational achievement. Historically, the schools have avoided making parents part of the teacher team, under the mistaken notion that teachers should not meddle in outside matters. Partly, this reluctance arises out of fear of parental criticism. Consequently, a wall has been built between the two, and contacts of a constructive order have been few and unavailing.

This situation must change if the school is to meet its full responsibility for the education of youth. . . . Parents must become an integral part of any educational program, and their instructional effort in the home must be seen as essential to the success of the child in school. Programs must be launched in every school district to educate parents and to see that they live up to their responsibilities. This step will not be as difficult to take as one may think. An earlier study, which we conducted under the aegis of the Charles F. Kettering Foundation, brought to light the noteworthy fact that most parents, even those with college educations, want help and guidance. Most parents are eager to learn what they can do in the home to help their children in school. After all, every parent wants his children to be successful in life. Obviously, not all parents can be expected to give up one evening a week or a month to learn what they should do at home to aid their children's progress in school, but the vast majority say they are willing to do so. If the programs for accomplishing this are really helpful, and if there is objective evidence to prove they are, then the educational system in the nation can, and should be, broadened to include the home as well as the school.

A properly conceived plan of helping parents do a more effective job of motivating their school age children, organizing their home life to enable them to do the best work in the classroom, and instructing them in the many areas not included in formal education offers, in my opinion, the greatest opportunity to reach higher educational standards and at the lowest cost.

What the Public Thinks of the School and Its Curriculum.

The next article presents details of Gallup's public opinion polling efforts. The support of and broad-based interest in conducting each survey suggests that public opinion is important. Analyze the excerpts provided from the poll in terms of its design and findings. Can you find significant trends by contrasting the summary of the first five years with the findings in 1975? What interpretation can you give to the poll as it applies to the school's curriculum?

☐

Research Procedure

The Sample.   This year the sample—described as a modified probability sample—included 1,558 adults (18 years and older). All interviewing was done by

George H. Gallup, "Seventh Annual Gallup Poll of Public Attitudes Toward Education," *Phi Delta Kappan* 57, 4 (December 1975): 227–40. Reprinted by permission of the author and publisher.

a trained staff of interviewers, maintained by the Gallup organization, who conducted personal, in home interviews in all areas of the country and in all types of local communities. . . .

Major Problems Confronting the Public Schools in 1975

. . .The major problems which the public names this year, 1975, are substantially the same as those mentioned in the 1974 survey, with one exception. This year, for the first time, the number of respondents mentioning "crime" (vandalism, stealing, etc.) is great enough to place this problem among the top ten. Actually, in number of mentions, it ranks in eighth place. And this year, for the first time, "drinking" (use of alcohol) is mentioned by enough respondents to establish a new category, although it is not one of the top ten.

Comparing this year's findings with those of 1969, the first survey, brings to light a significant drop in the number who say that "lack of proper facilities" is a major problem in their local schools.

Below, in order of mentions, is the list of the top ten problems of the public schools, as viewed by the public, in the year 1975:

1. Lack of discipline
2. Integration/segregation/busing
3. Lack of proper financial support
4. Difficulty of getting "good" teachers
5. Size of school/classes
6. Use of drugs
7. Poor curriculum
8. Crime/vandalism/stealing
9. Lack of proper facilities
10. Pupils' lack of interest.

Rating of the Public Schools

. . .Students are often given the grades A, B, C, D, and FAIL to denote the quality of their work. Suppose the *public* schools themselves, in this community, were graded in the same way. What grade would you give the public schools here — A, B, C, D, or FAIL?

During the year, a significant drop has been registered in the number of persons giving the schools a grade of A. The change is from 18 percent last year to 13 percent this year.

The lowest ratings of the public schools come, understandably, from parents whose children are now attending independent/parochial schools. In this group, only 5 percent give the public schools an A rating; 34 percent give them a rating of either D or FAIL.

The public's rating of the schools may be influenced by the general loss of confidence in and respect for all American institutions. Education and the church, it should be pointed out, still have much higher confidence ratings than Congress, the Supreme Court, organized labor, or big business. A Gallup Poll released in July 1975 shows that the public gives a high confidence rating of 67 percent to the schools as opposed to a 40 percent confidence rating for Congress, a 38 percent confidence rating for organized labor, and a 34 percent rating for big business. . . .

Ratings given to the public schools in 1974 and those given in 1975 indicate these changes during this period:

Ratings given the public schools	National totals	
	1974 %	1975 %
A rating	18	13
B rating	30	30
C rating	21	28
D rating	6	9
Fail	5	7
Don't know/ no answer	20	13

Parents with children in the public schools—the group in the best position to judge the quality of education in the schools—give the schools a higher rating than do those who have no children in the public schools.

	National totals %	No children in schools %	Public school parents %	Parochial school parents %
A rating	13	11	17	5
B rating	30	26	36	25
C rating	28	27	29	24
D rating	9	9	8	16
Fail	7	7	7	18
Don't know/ no answer	13	20	3	12

When the results are analyzed by the socioeconomic groups in the population, a fact important to the educational profession comes to light. The two bellwether groups—the college educated and the young adults—give the public schools the lowest ratings. Clearly, this should be regarded as a warning signal.

	A %	B %	C %	D %	Fail %	Don't know/ no answer %
National Totals	13	30	28	9	7	13
Sex						
Men	11	30	28	10	8	13
Women	14	30	28	8	7	13
Race						
White	13	31	28	9	7	12
Nonwhite	14	23	28	11	10	14
Age						
18 to 29 years	6	26	37	12	7	12
30 to 49 years	13	33	29	11	8	6
50 years and over	18	29	19	5	7	22
Education						
Elementary grades	21	25	17	7	9	21
High school	12	29	30	9	8	12
College	9	34	31	10	6	10
Community size						
1 million and over	11	29	23	9	9	19
500,000 to 999,999	14	27	27	11	8	13
50,000 to 499,999	10	28	30	12	7	13
2,500 to 49,999	17	30	30	5	5	13
Under 2,500	13	32	28	9	8	10
Region						
East	14	32	24	7	7	16
Midwest	14	30	29	8	8	11
South	12	30	29	9	7	13
West	10	26	29	15	8	12

In 1974, 40 percent of the 18–29 age group gave the public schools an A or B rating. This year only 32 percent of this age group gave the schools an A or B rating. Last year, 51 percent of those who had attended college gave the schools an A or B rating. In 1975 this proportion has dropped to 43 percent. In the present survey, 41 percent of those who attended college gave the schools a C or D rating, compared to 29 percent who gave the schools a C or D last year. . . .

Schools with More Strict Behavior Standards

The growing reaction against low standards of behavior in the public schools is reflected in the responses to a question asking where respondents would like to send their children to school. The option offered was a special public school that had strict discipline, a strict dress code, and placed emphasis on the three Rs.

The special school with more strict behavior standards appeals to all groups, even the group composed of parents of children now attending public school. . . .

	National totals %	No children in schools %	Public school parents %	Parochial school parents %
Yes, would send children to special school	57	56	56	70
No, would not	33	32	36	22
Don't know/ no answer	10	12	8	8

When respondents were asked why they chose the special school, they gave as their reason the fact that children need discipline, strict rules, and respect for others. The next reason, in number of mentions, is the superiority of this type of education to the present public schools in their community. And third is the need for a more strict dress code. . . .

More Work for Students

Further evidence of the public's negative attitude toward what they regard as the too great permissiveness of the public schools comes from answers to another question. This one asked respondents if children in the elementary schools of their communities and in the high schools were required to work too hard, or not hard enough. . . .

The first question: *In general, do you think elementary school children in the public schools here are made to work too hard in school and on homework, or not hard enough?*

	National totals %	No children in schools %	Public school parents %	Parochial school parents %
Elementary School Students				
Too hard	5	5	5	6
Not hard enough	49	46	53	53
About right amount	28	25	35	23
Don't know/no answer	18	24	7	18
High School Students				
Too hard	3	4	2	3
Not hard enough	54	53	54	66
About right amount	22	21	24	13
Don't know/no answer	21	22	20	18

The second question: *What about students in the public high schools here—in general, are they required to work too hard or not hard enough?*

Minimum Requirements for Graduation

Educators and laypersons interested in the nation's educational system have sought, in many recent studies, to define the goals of education for the present generation of students. . . .

Findings from this survey approach reveal what earlier survey results have shown about the pragmatic philosophy of the American people. The priorities they set reflect their attitudes about the chief purpose of the school system—to prepare students to get jobs and to advance in the business and professional world.

The question was asked:

What requirements, if any, would you set for graduation from high school for those students who do not plan to go on to college but who plan to take a job or job training following graduation? I'll read off a number of requirements, and then you tell me how important each one is as a requirement for graduation for these students. We would like to know whether you think it is very important, fairly important, or not important.

The results show the percentage of the public who describe each of the nine requirements as being "very important," "fairly important," etc. Percentages are shown in descending order.

Close agreement is found in the views of all major groups regarding these minimum requirements. Those who do not have children now attending school agree almost exactly with those who do. . . .

Reading requirements	Very important %	Fairly important %	Not important %	Don't know/ no answer %
How important is it that these students be able to read well enough to follow an instruction manual?	96	3	–	1
. . . be able to write a letter of application using correct grammar and correct spelling?	92	6	1	1
. . . know enough arithmetic to be able to figure out such a problem as the total square feet in a room?	87	10	2	1
. . . have a salable skill, such as typing, auto mechanics, nurse's aide, business machines?	85	12	2	1

Reading requirements	Very important %	Fairly important %	Not important %	Don't know/ no answer %
. . . know something about the U.S. government, the political parties, voting procedures?	75	21	3	1
. . . know something about the history of the United States, such as the Constitution, Bill of Rights, and the like?	68	27	4	1
. . . know something about the major nations of the world today, their kind of government, and their way of life?	49	40	10	1
. . . know something about the history of humanity, the great leaders in art, literature?	33	44	21	2
. . . know a foreign language?	18	28	51	3

Training Programs Planned by the Public Schools

In most of the seven annual surveys in this series, questions have been asked about training programs for students who are not interested in the usual curricular subjects and who stay on in school only because they are required to by law.

The public has favored by large majorities all the proposals for dealing with these young people—all except the plan to let them quit school and go it alone without supervision.

While the public has recognized the problem presented by students who are wholly uninterested in academic work, still no program has emerged or been put into effect on a national scale. . . .

The question:

It has been suggested that the public schools be given the responsibility to set up special job training programs for young people, age 15 to 18, who are out of work and out of school. Would you favor or oppose such a plan?

	National totals %	No children in schools %	Public school parents %	Parochial school parents %
Favor giving schools this responsibility	86	87	85	84
Oppose	11	9	12	15
Don't know/no answer	3	4	3	1

The Nongraded School

The nongraded school concept has wide appeal. In fact, all major groups of the public favor the idea by margins of more than two to one. The high percentage favoring nongraded schools indicates that the public is ready to accept innovations in a period when many persons are inclined to blame new methods and new viewpoints in the educational world for an apparent decline in student performance. . . .
    The question:

Should a student be able to progress through the school system at his own speed and without regard to the usual grade levels? This would mean that he might study seventh-grade math, but only fifth-grade English. Would you favor or oppose such a plan in the local schools?

	National totals %	No children in schools %	Public school parents %	Parochial school parents %
Favor	64	62	66	73
Oppose	28	28	28	25
No opinion	8	10	6	2

Instruction in Morals and Moral Behavior

Presumably, the home and the church are the proper places to give children instruction in morals and moral behavior. But in the absence of such instruction in many homes, the responsibility shifts, unfairly perhaps, to the schools. At least to meet the present need, an overwhelming majority of all major groups in the population would like to see such instruction provided by the schools. And, significantly, one of the groups most in favor is that composed of parents of children now attending public schools. . . .
    The question:

Would you favor or oppose instruction in the schools that would deal with morals and moral behavior?

	National totals %	No children in schools %	Public school parents %	Parochial school parents %
Favor instruction in morals/moral behavior	79	76	84	85
Oppose	15	17	12	13
Don't know/no answer	6	7	4	2

Textbook Censorship

The weight that should be attached to parental objections to books that students are assigned to read has become a controversial issue in some states.

To shed light on the public's viewpoint on this matter, the following question was asked:

When parents object to books or material in textbooks on grounds of religion, politics, race or sex discrimination, how much consideration should be given to the parents' views in deciding whether to keep these books in the school—a great deal, some, little, or none? ...

	National totals %	No children in schools %	Public school parents %	Parochial school parents %
A great deal	33	31	37	38
Some	43	44	42	36
Little	12	11	13	14
None	7	7	6	9
Don't know/no answer	5	7	2	3

Awareness and Attitudes with Respect to Open Education

The open concept of education, which came originally from England and which has been adopted in many schools throughout the United States in recent years, is still relatively unknown to a majority of Americans and even to parents whose children now attend the public schools. ...

These questions were asked:

Do you happen to know what is meant by the "open" school concept or idea?

If yes:

In your own words, how would you describe an "open" school?

How do you feel about "open" schools? Do you approve or disapprove of them?

	National totals %	No children in schools %	Public school parents %	Parochial school parents %
Awareness of open education				
Said they knew what is meant by open schools	27	24	30	33
Didn't know	60	63	56	54
Weren't sure	13	13	14	13
*Attitudes toward open education**				
Approve of open schools	13	12	14	18
Disapprove	10	8	12	11
Don't know/no answer	4	4	4	4
	27	24	30	33

*Percentages of those who said they knew what is meant by open education.

448

The Decline in National Test Scores

Educators have cited many reasons for declining national test scores reported in recent years, particularly in the case of the SAT tests given to high school seniors who are interested in going on to college.

Do parents and the general public hold the same opinions as educators? To find out, an "open" question dealing with this problem was included in the survey.

Analysis of the public's verbatim responses shows that the reason offered most often for declining test scores is lack of student interest and motivation. The public offers one explanation seldom stressed by professional educators. In earlier years, competition to find places in college proved to be a powerful incentive to work hard and to get good grades. Now students know that, even if they do poorly in school, they can still find some college that will admit them. Moreover, a college education is not deemed as important as it once was in finding a job. Many respondents point out that college graduates are having a hard time getting jobs. The net effect of this has been to remove some of the drive to work hard and to excel. . . .

Many other causes for the declining scores of students were offered, among them the idea that television occupies too much of young peoples' time and that outside activities draw too much of their interest. Respondents also cited overcrowding, drugs, and such other reasons as "the complete breakdown of the public school system" and "the disintegration of the family." The question:

The national tests that have been given to students throughout the nation indicate that students today do not have as high scores as they had a few years ago in many subject areas. What do you think is the reason for this?

	Percent
Students' lack of interest/motivation	29
Lack of discipline in the home and school	28
Poor curriculum (too easy, not enough emphasis on basics)	22
Inadequate teachers, uninterested teachers	21
Too many outside interests, including TV	8
Miscellaneous, including integration, overcrowding, drugs, etc.	13
No opinion	13

(Figures add to more than 100 percent because of multiple answers.)

Further Breakdowns

Detailed and different breakdowns of some of the responses to the 1975 poll questions are provided in this section as a supplement to tables already presented.

The Major Problems

What do you think are the biggest problems with which public schools in this community must deal?

. . .

	National totals %	No children in schools %	Public school parents %	Parochial school parents %
Lack of discipline	23	23	23	21
Integration/segregation/ busing	15	17	11	16
Lack of proper financial support	14	13	15	13
Difficulty of getting "good" teachers	11	11	12	12
Size of school/classes	10	7	13	5
Use of drugs	9	10	9	10
Poor curriculum	5	4	7	5
Crime/vandalism/ stealing	4	5	4	–
Lack of proper facilities	3	2	3	4
Pupils' lack of interest	3	4	2	2
Parents' lack of interest	2	2	3	3
School board policies	1	1	1	2
There are no problems	5	4	6	5
Miscellaneous	12	11	13	24
Don't know/no answer	10	13	6	5

Note: Totals add to more than 100 percent because of multiple answers.

Suspension from School

A U.S. Supreme Court decision requires school principals to give written notice to a student and his parents and hold a hearing when the student is suspended from school. Have you heard or read about this ruling?

. . .

	Have heard or read %	Have not heard or read %	Don't know/ no answer %
National Totals	41	55	4
Sex			
Men	41	55	4
Women	42	55	3
Race			
White	42	55	3
Nonwhite	40	53	7
Age			
18 to 29 years	40	57	3
30 to 49 years	44	53	3
50 years and over	39	56	5
Education			
Elementary grades	39	55	6
High school	39	58	3
College	49	49	2
Community size			
1 million and over	36	59	5
500,000 to 999,999	44	54	2
50,000 to 499,999	44	53	3
2,500 to 49,999	39	59	2
Under 2,500	43	52	5
Region			
East	40	57	3
Midwest	40	56	4
South	40	55	5
West	47	51	2

Do Students Work Hard Enough in School?

In general, do you think elementary school children in the public schools here are made to work too hard in school and on homework, or not hard enough?
. . .

	Too hard %	Not hard enough %	About right amount %	Don't know/ no answer %
National Totals	3	54	22	21
Sex				
Men	3	54	20	23
Women	3	54	23	20
Race				
White	3	53	22	22
Nonwhite	5	62	16	17
Age				
18 to 29 years	3	54	22	21
30 to 49 years	3	56	22	19
50 years and over	4	51	22	23
Education				
Elementary grades	7	49	21	23
High school	2	53	24	21
College	3	58	18	21
Community size				
1 million and over	2	57	20	21
500,000 to 999,999	4	56	15	25
50,000 to 499,999	3	53	21	23
2,500 to 49,999	4	50	28	18
Under 2,500	3	53	24	20
Region				
East	2	53	23	22
Midwest	4	54	23	19
South	3	50	25	22
West	3	61	14	22

What about students in the public high schools here—in general, are they required to work too hard or not hard enough?

. . .

	Too hard %	Not hard enough %	About right amount %	Don't know/ no answer %
National Totals	5	49	28	18
Sex				
Men	4	51	27	18
Women	6	47	30	17
Race				
White	5	47	30	18
Nonwhite	4	65	19	12
Age				
18 to 29 years	6	46	29	19
30 to 49 years	6	52	32	10
50 years and over	5	47	23	25
Education				
Elementary grades	7	49	24	20
High school	5	48	30	17
College	4	51	28	17
Community size				
1 million and over	4	52	20	24
500,000 to 999,999	3	54	20	23
50,000 to 499,999	5	47	31	17
2,500 to 49,999	6	44	33	17
Under 2,500	6	48	34	12

Job Training

It has been suggested that the public schools be given the responsibility to set up special job training programs for young people, age 15 to 18, who are out of work and out of school. Would you favor or oppose such a plan?

. . .

	Favor %	Oppose %	Don't know/ no answer %
National Totals	86	11	3
Sex			
Men	84	13	3
Women	88	8	4
Race			
White	85	11	4
Nonwhite	93	5	2
Age			
18 to 29 years	89	9	2
30 to 49 years	83	13	4
50 years and over	87	9	4
Education			
Elementary grades	88	7	5
High school	86	10	4
College	84	14	2
Community size			
1 million and over	84	10	6
500,000 to 999,999	87	10	3
50,000 to 499,999	89	9	2
2,500 to 49,999	88	10	2
Under 2,500	82	13	5
Region			
East	86	10	4
Midwest	83	15	2
South	90	6	4
West	84	11	5

Instruction in Morals

Would you favor or oppose instruction in the schools that would deal with morals and moral behavior?

. . .

	Favor %	Oppose %	Don't know/ no answer %
National Totals	79	15	6
Sex			
Men	77	16	7
Women	82	13	5
Race			
White	79	16	5
Nonwhite	84	9	7
Age			
18 to 29 years	68	26	6
30 to 49 years	84	12	4
50 years and over	83	10	7
Education			
Elementary grades	82	10	8
High school	81	14	5
College	73	21	6
Community size			
1 million and over	78	17	5
500,000 to 999,999	84	11	5
50,000 to 499,999	79	16	5
2,500 to 49,999	75	17	8
Under 2,500	81	13	6
Region			
East	74	19	7
Midwest	81	15	4
South	84	10	6
West	78	15	7

Composition of the Sample

	Percent
No children in schools	57
Public school parents	39*
Parochial school parents	7*

*Totals exceed 43% because some parents have children attending more than one kind of school.

Sex	Percent	Income (cont.)	Percent
Men	48	$3,000 to $4,999	11
Women	52	Under $2,999	7
	100	Undesignated	2
Race	Percent		100
White	88	Political affiliation	Percent
Nonwhite	12	Republican	22
	100	Democrat	42
Religion	Percent	Independent	34
Protestant	62	Other	2
Roman Catholic	26		100
Jewish	2	Region	Percent
Others	10	East	27
	100	Midwest	28
Age	Percent	South	27
18 to 24 years	16	West	18
25 to 29 years	10		100
30 to 49 years	40	Community size	Percent
50 years and over	34	1 million and over	18
	100	500,000 to 999,999	13
Occupation	Percent	50,000 to 499,999	25
Business & professional	22	2,500 to 49,999	17
Clerical & sales	11	Under 2,500	27
Farm	3		100
Skilled labor	18	Education	Percent
Unskilled labor	24	Elementary grades	19
Non-labor force	18	High school incomplete	16
Undesignated	4	High school complete	34
	100	Technical, trade, or	
Income	Percent	business school	5
$20,000 and over	17	College incomplete	14
$15,000 to $19,999	15	College graduate	12
$10,000 to $14,999	26	Undesignated	*
$7,000 to $9,999	12		100
$5,000 to $6,999	10		

*Less than 1%.

Summary

What better way to end a book on curriculum development than to examine the school's "report card" according to the public it serves. Our country's unique approach to creating a public school system with lay control, professional workers, schooling for all, and broad-based tax support is measured by its effectiveness. This final chapter concentrated on effectiveness and the form in which it is reported. Achievement measurement, educational attainment, comparisons with other countries, and public opinion comprise the bases on which the schools can be judged.

Given the evidence provided in this final chapter, how do you think the schools measure up? What school characteristics do you want to retain? What are the weaknesses you would attack? And, most importantly, how do you assess your role as an educator involved in curriculum development?

Author Index

Combs, Arthur W., 63
Commager, Henry, 294n
Commoner, Barry, 140
Cox, C. B., 210n
Crawford, Jack, 308
Cremin, Lawrence A., 5, 8n
Cronbach, Lee J., 12n, 372

Davies, I.K., 108, 152
Dewey, John, 7n, 11–12, 12n, 69n
Doll, Ronald C., 323
Donovan, Frank, 309
Duncan, James K., 358
Dworkin, Martin, 6n

Ebel, Robert L., 157, 382
Eisner, Elliot W., 160n, 161, 164
Elam, Stanley, 436
Elkind, David, 391n
Emmet, E. R., 100n
English, Raymond, 67

Faure, Edgar, 436n
Ferguson, C. A., 374n
Ferris, F. L., Jr., 376n
Florino, A. John, 330
Foshay, A. W., 271, 430n
Fox, Seymour, 354

Gagné, Robert M., 257, 394
Gallup, George H., 440
Gartner, Alan, 344
Gertler, Diane B., 187
Giacquinta, J. B., 349n
Goodlad, John J., 296, 350n
Gordon, William J., 77
Grinker, Roy R., 179n
Gross, Neal, 349n

Hack, Walter, 145n
Haggard, Ernest A., 345n
Hammack, David Conrad, 6n
Hardy, Clifford, 46
Harris, William T., 6, 7n, 11
Hempel, Carl G., 211n
Hencley, Stephen P., 145n
Herron, Marshall D., 388n
Holbrook, David, 72n
Homans, George C., 212n, 213n
Husen, Torsten, 430n

Jones, Richard M., 71n

Kagan, Jerome S., 390n
Kahn, S. B., 434n
Karlson, A.L., 389n
Katz, Lillian G., 386n
Katz, Michael, 6n
Kaufman, Draper L., 145n
Keeves, John P., 430n
Kelley, Earl C., 62
Key, V. O., 238n
Kilpatrick, William Heard, 248
Kirst, Michael W., 49
Kohl, Herbert, 71n
Krathwohl, David R., 157n

Lewis, E. Glyn, 430n
Lieberman, Ann, 348, 350n
Lindblom, Charles, 351n
Lindvall, C. M., 158n
Little, W. W., 213n
Lundgren, Ulf P., 31
Lynd, Staughton, 72n
Lyon, Harold C., 71n

Mager, Robert R., 157n
Marklund, A. M., 429n
Marksberry, Mary Lee, 276
Marshall, J., 48
Maslow, Abraham H., 62–63
Massialas, Byron G., 210n
Mayer, Rochelle S., 388n
Moore, Edgar W., 213n
Morris, Charles, 234n

Nagel, Ernest, 214n
Nelson, J., 47

Oliver, G. L., 282
Oppenheim, A. M., 429n
Orlosky, Donald E., 231, 241, 302

Paddock, Paul, 140
Paddock, William, 140
Pareto, Vilfredo, 235n
Phenix, Phillip H., 83
Popham, W. James, 13–17, 147
Posner, George J., 262
Pressey, S. L., 158n
Psacharopoulos, George, 232n, 234n, 237n, 242n

Subject Index

Gallup polls, 402, 436–56
Goals of teaching, 262–63
Grading systems
    abolition of, 124, 129–45
Graduation
    minimum requirements, 445–46

High school curriculum
    distribution of enrollment, 187–90
    trends, 190
Humanism
    for learners, 71
    in classrooms, 71
    in subject matter, 71, 76
    structure for, 73–78
Hylenergetics, 177

Innovations
    origin, 303–308
    persistence of, 303–308
    studies of, 331–34
    target of change, 303–308
Input-output studies, 422, 425–26
Instructive knowledge
    analytic simplification, 85–87
    dynamism, 87–88
    synthetic coordination, 87
Integrative knowledge, 184
Internal evaluation
    defined, 394
    evidence sought, 394–99
    research implications, 398
International Association for the
        Evaluation of Education
        Achievement, 430
International evaluation
    cognitive achievement, 434
    curriculum and instruction,
        435–36
    instruments, 431–34

Knowledge
    advanced vs. elementary, 93
    explosion, 41–46
    general, 99, 101
    instructive criterion, 84
    logical order, 92
    problem solving, 102
    structure, 44
    structure of curriculum, 94
    transfer of training, 93

Law-like
    generalizations, 209–213
    in discourse, 215–17
    principles, 195
    statements, 209
    statistics, 210
Lifelong learning, 43

Macro-reform vs. micro, 344
Macro sequencing
    intellectual development, 252–56
    relating knowledge to
        development, 251
Measurement
    of abstractions, 371
    of concrete objects, 370–71
    of curriculum, 374–76
    procedures, 376–77
Metric education
    establishment of, 308–313
    history, 309
    problems in teaching, 311
    teacher training, 311–12
Micro-reform
    effects of, 344
Microsequencing
    prerequisite knowledge, 256
Model of curriculum design, 264–65

National Assessment of Educational
        Progress, 412–17
    development of exercises,
        413–17
    history, 412
    philosophy, 412–13

Objectives
    behavioral, 156
    difficulties in, 159–60
    expressive, 164–68
    instructional, 152, 164
    justification, 157
    limitations, 160
    origin, 157
    related to learning, 163
    taxonomy of, 152–56
Organizational studies, 422, 426–27

Parent role in schools, 439–40
Persistent problems in reform, 128–29

30 / 104